AF814315

All in One®

Computer Applications

CBSE Class 10

Focused Theory | Practice Exercise | Sample Papers & Board Papers

Recommended by Teachers
Trusted by Toppers

All in One®

Computer Applications

CBSE Class 10

Focused Theory | Practice Exercise | Sample Papers & Board Papers

Author
Neetu Gaikwad
(B.Tech, MBA)

arihant
SUCCESS AND NOTHING LESS

arihant
SUCCESS AND NOTHING LESS

ARIHANT PRAKASHAN
(School Division Series)

卐 ADMINISTRATIVE & PRODUCTION OFFICES

Regd. Office

'Ramchhaya' 4577/15, Agarwal Road, Darya Ganj, New Delhi -110002
Tele: 011- 47630600, 43518550; Fax: 011- 23280316

卐 *Head Office*

Kalindi, TP Nagar, Meerut (UP) - 250002, Tel: 0121-7156203, 7156204

卐 SALES & SUPPORT OFFICES

Agra, Ahmedabad, Bengaluru, Bareilly, Chennai, Delhi, Guwahati, Hyderabad, Jaipur, Jhansi, Kolkata, Lucknow, Nagpur & Pune.

PO No : TXT-XX-XXXXXXX-X-XX

Published By Arihant Publications (India) Ltd.

For further information about the books published by Arihant, log on to www.arihantbooks.com or e-mail at info@arihantbooks.com

Follow us on

卐 PRICE ₹ 300.00

PRODUCTION TEAM

Publishing Managers	Cover Designer	Inner Designer
Mahendra Singh Rawat & Keshav Mohan	Rakesh Rawat	Ankit Tyagi
Project Head	**Page Layouting**	**Proof Reader**
Shruti Aggarwal	Ravinder Kumar	Sumit

Index *cum* Study Planner

UNIT I Networking

UNIT II HTML

One Book- Endless Features
to Help you Succeed

Chapter Checklist

At the start of each chapter, all the topics of the chapter have been listed , so that students may know what they are going to study.

CHAPTER **01** Unit I

Internet Basics

Chapter Checklist

- History of Internet
- Working of Internet
- Uses of Internet
- Connecting to the Internet
- World Wide Web (WWW)
- Web Page

The Internet has gained popularity and emerged as an important and efficient means of communication. The term Internet is derived from the words 'interconnection' and 'networks'. A network is a collection of two or more computers, which are connected together to share information and resources. The Internet is a worldwide system of computer networks, i.e. **network of networks**. Through Internet, computers become able to exchange information with each other and find diverse perspective on issues from a global audience. Most of the people uses Internet for sending and receiving E-mail and net surfing for retrieving information.

Simplified Theory

Each chapter contains the necessary study material well supported by Definitions, Facts, Figures, Flow Charts, etc.

Uses of Internet

Internet has been the most useful technology of the modern time, which helps us not only in our daily lives, but also in our personal and professional lives developments.

Thus, some uses of Internet are as follows:

- E-Commerce (auction, buying and selling products etc.)
- Research (online journals, magazines, information etc.)
- Education (E-learning, distance learning etc.)
- E-Governance (online filling of application, Income Tax, Sales Tax etc.)

- **Interactive** WWW provides interactivity using hyperlinks and input boxes (i.e. textboxes and checkboxes).
- **Frames** WWW supports frames that allow users to display more than one independent section on a single Web page.

HyperText and Hyperlinks

HyperText is the text that appears on the page, on which we can click and reach to another page with which it is linked. HyperText is also a combination of hyperlinks and multimedia. Hyperlink or dynamic link simply called a **link**, may be an icon, graphic or text in a document that links to another document.

Boxed Matter

Information in the boxes is given to focus important points related to the concept.

GIGO

Random and Important Facts that enhance the knowledge about particular topic.

Gigo

- **A modem** changes the digital data into analog data and *vice-versa* at source computer in a format that can be carried by telephone lines. Modem stands for Modulator and Demodulator.
- **Bandwidth** is the amount of data that a circuit or a signal can carry.
- **TCP/IP** was designed in 1973, which in 1983 became the standard for communicating between computers over the Internet.
- **ISDN** (Integrated Services Digital Network) establishes the connection using the phone lines which carry digital signals instead of analog signals.
- **ISP** (Internet Service Provider) refers to the companies that provide Internet connections to the users.Some popular ISPs of India are:
  - Data Communication Ltd.

One Book- Endless Features

to Help you Succeed

Illustrative Figures

To make the concepts completely visible, illustrative diagrams have been given at various place.

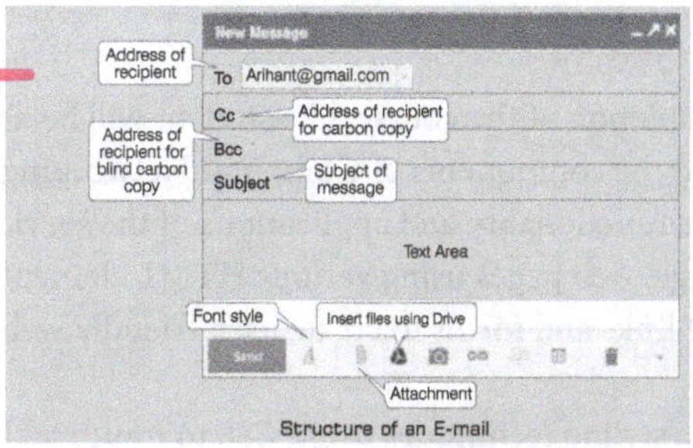

Structure of an E-mail

Exam Practice

To make students completely prepared for examination, this Exercise contains Exam Pattern Questions. This exercise covers all types of questions, like; MCQs, Fill in the blanks, True or False, VSA, SA, LA Type & Application Oriented Questions.

Chapter Summary

Summary of chapter given at the end of each chapter helps to revise the chapter quickly at the time of examination or routine school tests.

SUMMARY

- An Internet is the network of networks spread all over the world.
- Internet started with interconnection of ARPANET, NSFnet and other small and private networks.
- Internet is not governed by any particular organisation. It is coordinated by many volunteer organisations like IAB, IETF, IRTF, W3C etc.
- Any organisation that provides access to the Internet is called ISP (Internet Service Provider).
- Internet provides three ways of connection as:
  1. Dial-up connection 2. Broadband connection 3. Wireless connection
- WWW is a set of rules/protocols by which, we can retrieve information on Internet.
- Web page is a file/document on Internet that contains text, graphics and links.
- Website is a collection of Web pages that are linked together with the help of hyperlinks.
- Web browser goes to a Web page using a Web address. Also, it downloads the HTML files stored at that address and than reads and translates the HTML file.
- A web client is an application that communicates with a Web server, using HTTP.
- Web server is a program that helps the browser to retrieve information.
- Web address or URL is a method of addressing documents on Web.
- E-mail address is a name that identifies an electronic post office box on network where E-mail can be sent.
- A blog is a Website or a Web page belonging to an individual to describe his/her view.

Exam Practice

Multiple Choice Questions

1 What can you do with the Internet? **CBSE 2011**
(a) Exchange information with friends and colleagues
(b) Access pictures, sounds, video clips and other media elements
(c) Find diverse perspective on issues from a global audience
(d) Exchange information, access pictures, find diverse perspective on issue from a global audience.

Ans. (d) Internet exchange information, access pictures, find diverse perspective on issues from a global audience.

2 The first network was
(a) ARPANET (b) Internet (c) NSFnet (d) NET

Ans. (a) The Advanced Research Projects Agency NETwork (ARPANET) was the world's first operational packet switching network.

3 Which communication protocol is used by Internet?
(a) TCP/IP (b) WWW (c) HTML (d) W3C

Ans. (a) TCP/IP is a communication protocol used by Internet which manages the transmission of data/file document on the Internet.

7 To joint the Internet, the computer has to be connected to a
(a) Internet architecture board
(b) Internet society
(c) Internet service provider
(d) None of the above

Ans. (c) Internet service provider is used to joint the Internet.

8 An organisation responsibles for providing Internet services to customer is commonly known as
(a) government (b) ISP
(c) TCP/IP (d) HTTP

Ans. (b) ISP are the companies that register themselves under the government domain according to the copyright law.

9 Which of these services will not be provided by a typical Internet Service Provider (ISP)?
(a) An E-mail address
(b) Modem
(c) A connection to the Internet
(d) Technical help

SAMPLE QUESTION PAPER 1

A Sample Question Paper for CBSE Class 10th

Computer Applications

Instructions

Please read the instructions carefully.

1. This question paper has 5 Sections A, B, C, D, E.
2. All questions are compulsory. However, internal choices have been provided in some of the questions.
3. Section A has 12 questions carrying 1 mark each.
4. Section B has 7 Very Short Answer (VSA) type questions carrying 2 marks each.
5. Section C has 4 Short Answer (SA) type questions carrying 3 marks each.
6. Section D has 1 Long Answer (LA) type question carrying 4 marks.
7. Section E has 2 Source-based/Case-based/Passage-based questions carrying 4 marks each.

Time : 2 hours *Max. Marks : 50*

Section A

(12 × 1 = 12)

1. Netiquette is short for
(a) Etiquette (b) Internet etiquette (c) Social etiquette (d) None of these

2. A search engine is a program to search ....
(a) for information (b) Web pages
(c) Web pages for specified index terms (d) Web pages for information using specified search terms.

3. When you copy a Web page or a file from a server to your local computer, this process is called
(a) conferencing (b) downloading (c) uploading (d) None of these

4. E-reservation is a process of making reservations of
(a) tickets (b) hotel rooms (c) tourists packages (d) All of these

5. Identify the software that helps you in sending and receiving an E-mail.
(a) MS-Office (b) Internet Explorer (c) Gmail (d) None of these

Sample Question Papers

To make students practice of examination in real sense, there are 3 Sample Question Papers at the end. All these Sample Questions Papers are exactly prepared on the latest syllabus & pattern of examination.

Latest Course *Structure*

Learning Outcomes

After the completion of the course, like student will be able to:

1. Understand the components of Computer Networking including web servers and network protocols.
2. Explore the functionality and applications of the services available on the Internet.
3. Create simple web pages using various HTML elements
4. Implement links and forms to create user-friendly web pages that facilitate navigation and data collection.
5. Apply basic styling techniques using CSS to improve the visual appearance and layout of web content.
6. Understand the importance of netiquettes, intellectual property rights, and responsible online behaviour

Distribution of Marks and Periods

Unit No.	Unit Name	Marks
1.	Networking	15
2.	HTML	25
3.	Cyber Ethics	10
4.	Practical	50
	Total	**100**

UNIT I Networking

- **Internet** World Wide Web, web servers, web clients, web sites, web pages, web browsers, blogs, news groups, HTML, web address, e-mail address, downloading and uploading files from a remote site. Internet protocols: TCP/IP, SMTP, POP3, HTTP, HTTPS. Remote login and file transfer protocols: SSH, SFTP, FTP, SCP, TELNET, SMTP, TCP/IP.
- **Services available on the internet:** information retrieval, locating sites using search engines and finding people on the net;
- **Web services:** chat, email, video conferencing, e-Learning, e-Banking, e-Shopping, e-Reservation, e-Governance, e-Groups, social networking.
- **Mobile technologies:** SMS, MMS, 3G, 4G.

UNIT II HTML

- **Introduction to web page designing using HTML:** create and save an HTML document, access a web page using a web browser.
- **HTML tags:** html, head, title, body, (attributes: text, background, bgcolor, link, vlink, alink), br (break), hr(horizontal rule), inserting comments, h1..h6 (heading), p (paragraph), b (bold), i (italics), u (underline), ul (unordered list), ol (ordered list), and li (list item). Description lists: dl, dt and dd. Attributes of ol (start, type), ul (type).
- **Font tags (attributes:** face, size, color).
- **Insert images:** img (attributes: src, width, height, alt), sup (super script), sub (subscript).

- **HTML Forms:** Textbox, radio buttons, checkbox, password, list, combobox.
- Embed audio and video in a HTML page.
- **Create a table using the tags:** table, tr, th, td, rowspan, colspan
- **Links:** significance of linking, anchor element (attributes: href, mailto), targets.
- **Cascading style sheets:** colour, background-colour, border-style, margin, height, width, outline, font (family, style, size), align, float.

UNIT III Cyber Ethics

- Netiquettes.
- Software licenses and the open source software movement.
- Intellectual property rights, plagiarism and digital property rights.
- Freedom of information and the digital divide.
- E-commerce: Privacy, fraud, secure data transmission.

Lab Exercises

- Create static web pages.
- Use style sheets to enforce a format in an HTML page (CSS).
- Embed pictures, audio and videos in an HTML page.
- Add tables and frames in an HTML page.
- Decorate web pages using graphical elements.
- Create a website using several webpages. Students may use any open source or proprietary tool.
- Work with HTML forms: text box, radio buttons, checkbox, password, list, combo box.
- Write a blog using HTML pages discussing viruses, malware, spam and antiviruses.
- Create a web page discussing plagiarism. List some reported cases of plagiarism and the consequent punishment meted out. Explain the nature of the punishment in different countries as per their IP laws.

Breakup of marks for the practicals:

S.No.	Unit Name	Marks
1.	**Lab Test (20 Marks)**	
	HTML (design One Web Page Based on a Diagram)	20
2.	**Report File + viva** (20 Marks)	
	Report File: At least 10 HTML pages.	15
	Viva Voce (based on the report file)	5
3.	Project (That Uses Most of the Concepts that Have Been Learnt)	10
	Total	50

CHAPTER

01

Unit I

Internet Basics

Chapter Checklist

- History of Internet
- Working of Internet
- Uses of Internet
- Connecting to the Internet
- World Wide Web (WWW)
- Web Page
- Website
- Web Browser
- Web Client
- Web Server
- Web Address/URL
- Domain Name
- E-mail Address
- Blogs
- Newsgroup
- HyperText Markup Language (HTML)
- Internet Protocols
- Remote Login and File Transfer Protocols

The Internet has gained popularity and emerged as an important and efficient means of communication. The term Internet is derived from the words 'interconnection' and 'networks'. A network is a collection of two or more computers, which are connected together to share information and resources. The Internet is a worldwide system of computer networks, i.e. **network of networks**. Through Internet, computers become able to exchange information with each other and find diverse perspective on issues from a global audience. Most of the people uses Internet for sending and receiving E-mail and net surfing for retrieving information.

Network of networks

History of Internet

In 1969, the University of California at Los Angeles and the University of Utah were connected with the beginning of the **ARPANET** (Advanced Research Projects Agency NETwork) using 56 kbit/s circuits, which is sponsored by U.S. (United States) Department of Defense (DoD). The goal of this project was to connect computers at different Universities and U.S. defense.

In mid 80's another federal agency, the National Science Foundation (NSF) created a new high capacity network called **NSFnet** (National Science Foundation Network), which was more capable than ARPANET. The only drawback of NSFnet was that it allowed only academic research on its network and not any kind of private business on it.

Now, several private organisations and people started working to build their own networks, named **private networks**, which were later (in 1990's) connected with ARPANET and NSFnet to form the **Internet**. The Internet really became popular in 1990's after the development of World Wide Web (WWW).

Working of Internet

The computers on the Internet are connected to each other through small networks. These networks are connected through the gateways to the Internet backbone.

All computers on the Internet, communicate with one another using TCP/IP, which is a basic protocol of the Internet. TCP/IP (Transmission Control Protocol/Internet Protocol) manages the transmission of data/file/document on the Internet by breaking the data/file/document into small pieces or parts called **packets** or **datagrams.**

Each packet contains actual data and address part, i.e. addresses of destination and source upto 1500 characters.

Functioning of TCP and IP are as follows:

- **TCP** It breaks message into smaller packets that are transmitted over the Internet and also reassembles these smaller packets into the original message that are received from the Internet.
- **IP** It handles the address part of each packet, so that the data is sent to the correct address. Each gateway on the network check this address to see where to forward the message.

Uses of Internet

Internet has been the most useful technology of the modern time, which helps us not only in our daily lives, but also in our personal and professional lives developments. Thus, some uses of Internet are as follows:

- E-Commerce (auction, buying and selling products etc.)
- Research (online journals, magazines, information etc.)
- Education (E-learning, distance learning etc.)
- E-Governance (online filling of application, Income Tax, Sales Tax etc.)
- E-Reservation (online reservation, online ticket booking etc.)
- Online Payments (credit and debit card payments etc.)
- Video Conferencing
- Exchange of Views (files, music, folders etc.)
- Social Networking Sites (facebook, twitter etc.)
- Entertainment (play music, videos, games etc.)

Advantages of Internet

(*i*) Greater access to information reduces research time.

(*ii*) Allows you to easily communicate with other people.

(*iii*) Global reach enables one to connect everyone on the Internet.

(*iv*) Publishing documents on the Internet saves paper.

(*v*) A valuable resource for companies to advertise and conduct business.

Disadvantages of Internet

(*i*) Cyber frauds may take place involving credit/debit card numbers and details.

(*ii*) Unsuitable and undesirable material is available that sometimes can be used by notorious people such as terrorists.

(*iii*) It is a major source of computer viruses.

(*iv*) Messages sent across the Internet can be easily intercepted and are open to abuse by others.

(*v*) It is difficult to check the accuracy of information available on the Internet.

Who Governs the Internet?

Internet is not governed by any single organisation. Some volunteer groups had been formed to help, coordinate and wrist with the development of the Internet.

These organisations are as follows:

- **Internet Architecture Board** (IAB) It is a technical advisory group of the Internet society and is chartered to provide oversight of the architecture of the Internet, its protocols and resources.
- **Internet Engineering Task Force** (IETF) It develops and maintains the Internet's communication protocols.
- **Internet Research Task Force** (IRTF) It looks into long-term research problems that could be critical in five or ten years.
- **Internet Network Information Center** (InterNIC) It provides various registry services needed for the Internet to operate effectively.
- **World Wide Web Consortium** (W3C) It develops standards for the evolution of the Web.
- **Internet Society** (ISOC) It concerns with the growth and evolution of the Internet and the way in which the Internet can be used.

Connecting to the Internet

There are mainly three ways of connecting to the Internet, which are as follows:

1. Dial-up Connection

It is a temporary connection, set-up between your computer and ISP server.

Dial-up connection uses the telephone line (Public Switched Telephone Network-PSTN) and modem to connect to the Internet. The modem connects the computer through the standard phone lines, which serves as the data transfer medium. When a user initiates a dial-up connection, user needs to enter the password and specify a username and modem dials a phone number of an Internet Service Provider (ISP) that is designated to receive dial-up calls.

The ISP then establishes the connection, which usually takes about 10 sec and is accompanied by several beeping and buzzing sounds.

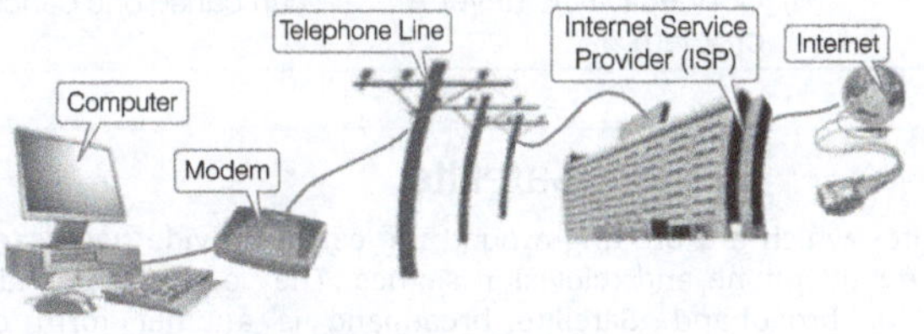

Dial-up connection

2. Broadband Connection

The term broadband commonly refers to high speed Internet access that is always ON and faster than the traditional dial-up access. It is the short form of broadband width, that uses a telephone line to connect to the Internet. Speed of broadband connection is measured in Mbps (Megabits per second).

Broadband access allows users to connect to the Internet at greater speed than a standard 256 Kbps (Kilobits per second) modem or dial-up access. Broadband access requires the use of a broadband modem. Broadband includes several high speed transmission technologies, which are as follows:

Digital Subscriber Line (DSL)

It is a popular broadband connection which provides Internet access by transmitting digital data over the wires of a local telephone network. It uses the existing copper telephone lines for Internet access.

A special modem is necessary in order to be able to use a DSL service over a standard phone line.

Following are the several versions of DSL technique available today:

- High Data rate DSL (HDSL)
- Very High Data rate DSL (VHDSL or VDSL)
- Asymmetrical DSL (ADSL)
- Symmetrical DSL (SDSL)
- Rate adaptive DSL (RDSL)
- ISDN DSL (IDSL)

Cable Modem

This service enables cable operators to provide broadband using the same co-axial cables, that deliver pictures and sound to your TV set. A cable modem can be added to or integrated with a set-top box that provides your TV set for Internet access. They provide transmission speed of 1.5 Mbps or more.

Broadband over Power Line (BPL)

It is the delivery of broadband over the existing low and medium voltage electric power distribution network. Its speed is generally comparable to DSL and cable modem speeds. BPL can be provided to homes using existing electrical connections and outlets. It is also known as **power-band**.

BPL is good for those areas where there are no broadband connections, but power infrastructure exists. e.g. in rural areas.

- **A modem** changes the digital data into analog data and *vice-versa* at source computer in a format that can be carried by telephone lines. Modem stands for Modulator and Demodulator.
- **Bandwidth** is the amount of data that a circuit or a signal can carry.
- **TCP/IP** was designed in 1973, which in 1983 became the standard for communicating between computers over the Internet.
- **ISDN** (Integrated Services Digital Network) establishes the connection using the phone lines which carry digital signals instead of analog signals.
- **ISP** (Internet Service Provider) refers to the companies that provide Internet connections to the users.Some popular ISPs of India are:
  - Data Communication Ltd.
  - Mahanagar Telephone Nigam Ltd. (MTNL)
  - Airtel
  - Reliance

3. Wireless Connection

Wireless broadband connects a home or business to the Internet using a radio link between the customer's location and the service provider's facility. Wireless broadband can be mobile or fixed. Unlike DSL and cable, wireless broadband requires neither a modem nor cables.

The distance between the devices connected to each other through a wireless Internet connection does not affect the rate of data transfer between them.

Some ways to connect the Internet wirelessly are as follows:

Wireless Fidelity (Wi-Fi)

It is a universal wireless networking technology that utilises radio frequencies to transfer data. Wi-Fi allows high speed Internet connections without the use of cables or wires. Wi-Fi networks can be designed for private access within a home or business. It can be used for public Internet access at 'hot spots' that offers Wi-Fi access such as restaurants, coffee shops, hotels, airports, convention centres and city parks.

Wi-Fi network

Worldwide Interoperability for Microwave Access (WiMAX)

Today, it is one of the hottest broadband wireless technology. These systems are expected to deliver Broadband Wireless Access (BWA) services upto 31 miles (45 km) for fixed stations and 3-10 miles (5-15 km) for mobile stations. WiMAX would operate similar to Wi-Fi but at higher speed, over greater distances and for a greater number of users. It has the ability to provide services even in areas that are difficult for wired infrastructure to reach. Also, it has the ability to overcome the physical limitations of traditional wired infrastructure.

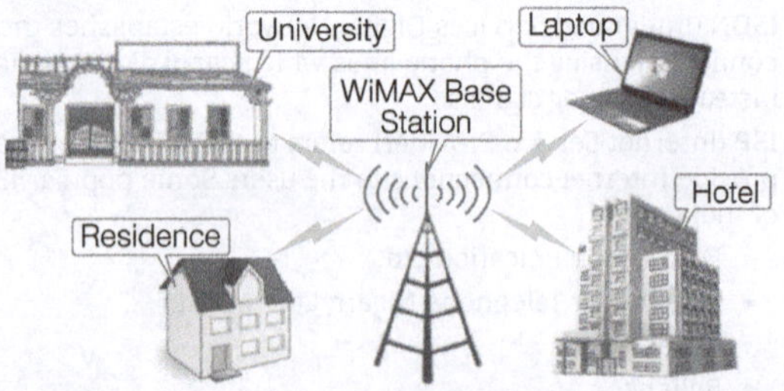

WiMAX network

Long Term Evolution (LTE)

It is a high-speed wireless broadband technology designed to support roaming Internet access by cell phones and handheld devices. LTE is designed to allow upto 300 Mbps download and upto 75 Mbps upload with latency as low as 5 ms. LTE works on multiple frequency bands often varying by country.

Some advantages and disadvantages of different types of connections are as follows:

Connection types	Advantages	Disadvantages
Dial-up	(a) Easily available. (b) Available at low cost. (c) Can be used through fixed or cellular phone.	(a) Slower than broadband. (b) Needs expensive set-up. (c) Phone remains busy.
Broadband	(a) Telephone can be used with Internet connection. (b) Faster than a dial-up connection. (c) Always on; no wait to connect	(a) Expensive than dial-up. (b) Not available in all areas.
Wireless	(a) No phone line required. (b) Easy and inexpensive to set-up. (c) No limitation of location. (d) Connectivity is never a problem.	(a) Vulnerable (b) Limited security mechanisms. (c) Medical disadvantage can cause one cancer.

Satellite

Satellites which are orbiting around the earth, provide necessary links for telephone and television service. They can also provide links for broadband. Satellite broadband is another form of wireless broadband and is also useful for serving remote or sparsely populated areas.

Check Point 01

1 The ARPANET was released in
(a) 1969 (b) 1995
(c) 1981 (d) 1990

2 Name the organisations that govern the Internet.

3 Internet provides three ways of connection, name them.

World Wide Web (WWW)

WWW was introduced on 13th March, 1989 by Tim Berners-Lee. It is a system of Internet servers that supports hypertext and multimedia to access several Internet protocols on a single interface. It is often abbreviated as the Web or WWW or W3. It is a way of exchanging information between computers on the Internet, trying to tie them together into a vast collection of interactive multimedia resources. It is only a portion of what makes up the Internet, but it is the fastest growing part of the Internet.

The Web lets people, organisations and companies publish information for other people to see. This makes the Web a very useful tool for finding information about any topic.

WWW Attributes

WWW provides various attributes, which are as follows:

- **User-friendly** The WWW resource works smoothly with most Web browsers, such as Internet Explorer, Firefox etc.
- **Multimedia documents** WWW allows users to create and display Web pages that contains various graphics, audio, video, animation and text.
- **Interactive** WWW provides interactivity using hyperlinks and input boxes (i.e. textboxes and checkboxes).
- **Frames** WWW supports frames that allow users to display more than one independent section on a single Web page.

HyperText and Hyperlinks

HyperText is the text that appears on the page, on which we can click and reach to another page with which it is linked. HyperText is also a combination of hyperlinks and multimedia. Hyperlink or dynamic link simply called a **link**, may be an icon, graphic or text in a document that links to another document.

Web Page

The backbone of the World Wide Web is made up of files or documents called **pages** or **Web pages**, that contain information and links to resources both *text* and *multimedia*. It is created using HTML. The Web is a collection of large number of computer documents and Web pages that stored on computers around the world which are connected to one another using hyperlinks.

CBSE Web page

Website

A group of related Web pages that follow the same theme and are connected together with hyperlinks is called a *Website*. In other terms, "A Website is a collection of digital documents, primarily HTML files, that are linked together and that exist on the Web under the same domain".

A Website displays related information on a specific topic. Each Website is accessed by its own address known as **URL** (Uniform Resource Locator).

e.g. http://www.carwale.com is a Website, while http://www.carwale.com/new/ is a Web page.

Two terms that are associated with a Website are as follows:

Home Page

The main or first page of a Website is known as *home page*.

Advantages of Home Page

(*i*) It helps viewers to find out what they can find on that particular site.

(*ii*) It helps in the publicity of an individual or a community.

(*iii*) It makes the visitors more comfortable with the Website.

Web Portal

It is a specially designed Website that often serves as the single point of access for information. It also has hyperlinks to many other Websites.

Advantages of Web Portal

(*i*) Easy for users to customize personal places.

(*ii*) It provides communication between portals (i.e. different applications).

(*iii*) It provides flexible content and layout.

Web Browser

It is a software application that is used to locate, retrieve and display some content on the WWW, including Web pages. These are programs used to explore the Internet. It is an interface that helps a computer user to gain access over all the content on the Internet. We can install more than one Web browsers on a single computer. The user can navigate files, folders and Websites with the help of a browser.

There are two types of Web browsers, which as follows:

Text Web Browser

A Web browser that displays only text-based information is known as *text Web browser*. e.g. Lynx.

Graphical Web Browser

A Web browser that supports both text and graphic information is known as *graphical Web browser*.

The first graphical web browser was NCSA Masaic.

e.g. Internet Explorer, Firefox, Netscape, Safari, Google Chrome, Opera.

Some Popular Graphical Web Browsers

NETSCAPE It was introduced in 1994. Netscape comprises the major portion of the browser's market.

INTERNET EXPLORER (IE) It is a product of Microsoft. This is the most commonly used browser in the world. This was introduced in 1995 alongwith Windows 95 launch and it has passed Netscape popularity in 1998.

FIREFOX It is a new browser derived from Mozilla. It was initially released in 2002 and has grown to be the second most popular browser on the Internet.

SAFARI It is a Web browser developed by Apple Incorporation and included in Mac OS X. It was first released as a public beta in January 2003. Safari provides good support for latest technologies like XHTML, CSS2 etc.

GOOGLE CHROME This Web browser was developed by Google. Its beta and commercial versions was released in September 2008 for Microsoft Windows.

OPERA It is smaller and faster than most other browsers, yet it is fully featured. It is the most popular mobile Web browser.

Gigo

- **Intranet** is a collection of private computer networks within an organisation. It is also known as **corporate portal** or **private business network**.
- **Extranet** refers to network within an organisation, using Internet to connect to the outsiders in controlled manner.

Web Client

Web client is a computing term which describes a special program designed as a user interface, through which messages are sent to a 'web server'. Web clients usually operate within a web browser window, although some are installed to a mobile or computer as downloadable software.

A web client contains two parts: dynamic Web pages and the Web browser. Dynamic Web pages are produced by components that run in the Web tier, and a Web browser delivers Web pages received from the server.

Web client is also known as a *thin client* because it does not execute heavy-duty operations such as querying databases, performing complex business tasks or connecting legacy applications.

Web Server

It is a computer program that serves requested HTML pages or files from the Web client. Every Web server that is connected to the Internet is associated with a unique address, i.e. IP address.

Web server software generally requires a fairly robust operating system like Unix, Windows NT. Every Website need to be stored on a computer called the Web server from which it can be accessed.

Currently, there are five major Web servers commonly used for hosting Websites as follows:

Apache HTTP Server

It was developed by Apache Software Foundation. The Apache HTTP server is the most popular Web hosting server in the world. This software can be installed virtually on all operating systems including Windows, Linux, Mac OS X, UNIX etc. At present, 60% of server machines run on the Apache Web server.

Internet Information Server (IIS)

It is a product of Microsoft and is considered to be a very high performance Web hosting server. It is easily administrable and integrated with the Windows platforms.

Lighttpd

This is a free Web hosting server distributed under the BSD license. It is considered fast, reliable, secure and power efficient CPU. Lighttpd, Web servers are compatible with Windows, Linux, Mac OS X, Unix and Solaris operating systems.

Sun Java System Web Server

It is developed by Sun Microsystems. It is not an open source server. It supports Windows, Linux and Unix operating systems.

Sun Java also supports many different technologies, scripts and languages including PHP, PERL, ASP, ColdFusion, Python etc.

Jigsaw Server

This is a free open source server for Website hosting that comes straight from the W3C. The Jigsaw Web hosting server is written in Java and supports both PHP (Personal Home Page) programs and CGI (Common Gateway Interface) scripts. It supports different platforms like Linux, Mac OS X, Windows, Unix, FreeBSD etc.

Check Point 02

1 Which software runs on a user's computer and is used to make a request for and display information in the form of a Web page?
(a) Internet (b) Web browser
(c) HTTP (d) Web server

2 Name the first graphical Web browser.

3 Which Web server was developed by Sun Microsystems?

Web Address/URL

Web is a collection of documents (Web pages) stored on computers around the world. Each Web page has an address describing where it can be found. This address is known as **Web address** or **URL (Uniform Resource Locator).** A Web address identifies the location of a specific Web page on the Internet, such as

```
http://www.learnyoga.com
```

Every computer connected to the Internet has its unique Web address, without which it cannot be reached by other computers.

Parts of URL

The URL contains three parts, which are as follows:

(*i*) The name of the protocol to be used to access the file resource.

(*ii*) A domain name that identifies a specific computer on the Internet.

(*iii*) A path name with hierarchical description that specifies the location of a file in that computer. e.g.

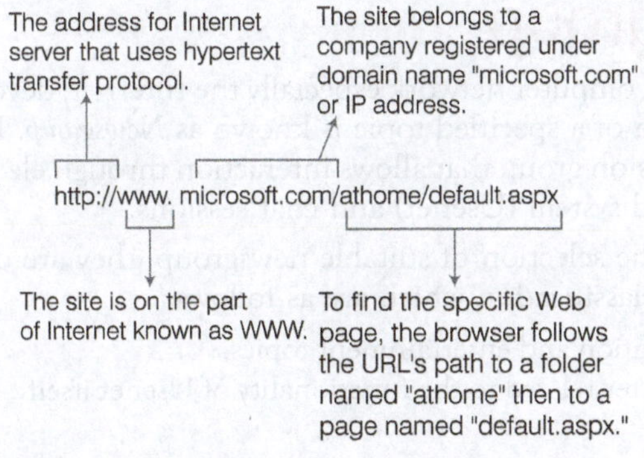

Types of URL

URLs vary depending on the location of the document to which user will link. Basically, URLs fall into two categories:

- **Absolute URL** It specifies the exact location of a file/directory on the Internet. Absolute URL identifies that each URL is unique, which means that if two URLs are identical then they point to the same file. It uses the following format:

```
scheme://server/path/resource
```

- **Relative URL** It points to a file/directory in relation to the present file/directory. It locates a resource using an absolute URL as a starting point. It typically consists of the path and optionally, the resource but no scheme or no server.

Domain Name

It is the text name corresponding to the numeric IP address of a computer on the Internet. Internet users access your Website using your domain name. It is a way to identify and locate computers connected to the Internet. It must be unique. Domain name always have two or more parts, separated by periods (dots).

e.g.

```
google.com, yahoo.com etc
```

Domain Abbreviation

Domain are organised by the type of organisation and by the country. A three letter abbreviation indicating the organisation and usually two letter abbreviation indicating the country name. Most common domain abbreviations for organisation are as follows:

info	Informational organisation
com	Commercial
gov	Government
edu	Education
mil	Military
net	Network resources
org	Usually non-profit organisation

Some domain abbreviations for country are as follows:

in	India
au	Australia
fr	France
nz	New Zealand
uk	United Kingdom

Domain Name System (DNS)

It translates domain names (computers host names) into IP addresses. It also stores and associates many types of information with domain names. It provides world wide keyword based redirection service.

DNS can be quickly updated and specifies the technical functionality of database service. The naming scheme by which servers are identified is known as the *domain name system*. e.g. the domain name www.example.com might translate to 198.105.232.4.

Numeric Computer IP Address

IP addresses are in aaa.aaa.aaa.aaa format, where each aaa is a number from 0 to 255. The length of IP address is 4 bytes. IP addresses identify the host computers, so that packets of information reached to the correct computer.

e.g. 162.192.1.89

The IP address has the following characteristics:

- IP addresses are unique.
- No two machines can have the same IP address.
- IP addresses are also global and standardised.
- All machines connected to the Internet agree to use the same scheme for establishing an address.

E-mail Address

E-mail stands for 'Electronic Mail'. It is a paperless method of sending messages, notes, pictures and even sound files from one place to another using the Internet as a medium.

It is an individual name, which is used to send and receive E-mail on the Internet. It is used to specify the source or destination of an E-mail message.

The format of an E-mail address is user@domain. Where,

- user identifies a unique user name.
- "@" separates the user from the domain. domain identifies the mail server.

e.g.

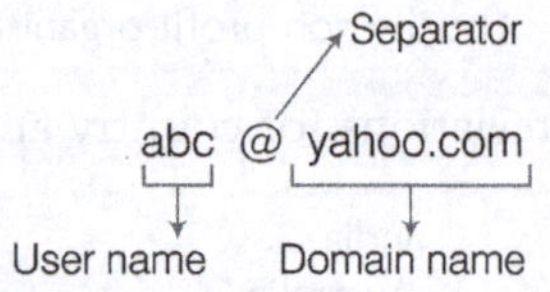

Some sites which provide the E-mail services are Gmail, Yahoo! mail, Rediffmail etc.

Blogs

A blog is a Website or a Web page, in which an individual records opinion links to other sites on regular basis. A blog content is written frequently and added in a chronological order. It is written online and visible to everyone.

A typical blog combines text, images and links to other blogs, Web pages and other media related to its topic. In education, blogs can be used as instructional resources. These blogs are referred to as **edublogs**. The entries of blog are also known as **posts**.

A person who writes a blog or a Weblog is known as **blogger**. *Blogging is the act of posting content on a blog.*

Blogs are fall into various categories: Personal blog, News and views, Company blogs and Micro-blogs.

Advantages of Blogs

(*i*) You can work at any time of the day and work with your ease.

(*ii*) Blogger does not require more efforts to write articles for his/her blog.

(*iii*) Easy and quick to update or add new posts.

(*iv*) People can leave comments on your blog.

(*v*) It increases blog revenue.

(*vi*) Blogs can be set-up quickly.

(*vii*) It is all about being social. You (blogger) need to answer to peoples' queries and for that, reading should be a part of day-to-day tasks.

Disadvantages of Blogs

(*i*) The common problem of full time blogger is isolation from society.

(*ii*) Mostly people love blogging but they don't have a fix source of income. Some choose freelance writing job for earning money and few chooses to depend on their parents to fulfil the need of money.

(*iii*) If the blogger get ill, then they don't get time to update their blog and it ultimately results in loss of blog income and traffic.

Newsgroup

An area on a computer network especially the Internet, devoted to the discussion of a specified topic is known as *Newsgroup*. It is an online discussion group that allows interaction through electronic bulletin board system (Usenet) and chat sessions.

To simplify the selection of suitable newsgroup, they are divided into subject classification which are as follows:

- ***rec***–Recreation and entertainment topics.
- ***news***–Matter related to the functionality of Usenet itself.

- *sci*–Science related topics.
- *soc*–Discussion related to society and social subcultures.
- *comp*–Computer related topics.

A newsgroup is a world wide platform for exchanging its content, ideas and information by common minded people. Newsgroup and contents are stored on special servers called **Network News Transfer Protocol** (NNTP) servers. The groups can be either "moderated", where a person or group decides which postings will become part of the discussion or "unmoderated", where everything posted is included in the discussion.

e.g. alt.tennis, alt.astrology, comp.lang.C++ etc.

Advantages of Newsgroup

(*i*) Newsgroup is similar in some ways to mailing lists, but it has a better structure.

(*ii*) It is also easier to access a newsgroup.

(*iii*) Usually, you will be able to find a FAQ (Frequently Asked Questions) section on a newsgroup, which is always helpful for those who are not sure of certain things.

(*iv*) Free to subscribe and post.

Disadvantages of Newsgroup

(*i*) A newsgroup is not as quick as an E-mail or even a mailing list.

(*ii*) The information on newsgroup is submitted by people who may have no real idea of what they are talking about.

(*iii*) It is not user friendly and the risk of viruses is high.

HyperText Markup Language (HTML)

It is a markup language used for designing Web pages. A markup language is a set of markup (angular bracket, < >) tags, which tell the Web browser, how to display a Web page's words and images for the user. Each individual markup code is referred to as an **element** or a **tag.** The text placed between a pair of angular brackets (< >) defines an HTML element.

HTML elements have two basic properties, i.e. attributes and content. **Attributes** are used to apply the desired style on the text and **content** refers to the text that you want to display on the browser. When a Web page is opened in a Web browser, then the formatted content is displayed.

Internet Protocols

Protocol refers to the set of rules applicable for a network. Many different types of network protocols and standards are required to ensure that your computer (no matter which operating system and network card or application, you are using) can communicate with another computer located on the next desk or half-way around the world.

The protocol defines standardised format for the data packet to be transmitted through the network.

In a computer network, a protocol allows the setting up of a valid connection, communication and data transferring between two computing end points or computer system. Some of the commonly used protocols are as follows:

HTTP (HyperText Transfer Protocol)

HTTP is an application level protocol. This protocol is used by the world wide web. HTTP defines how messages are formatted and transmitted and what actions web servers and browsers should take in response to various commands. It is a stateless protocol because each command is executed independently without any knowledge of the commands that came before it. e.g. when you enter a URL in your browser, this actually sends a HTTP command to the web server directly, to fetch and transmit the requested web page. It is generic, stateless and object oriented protocol.

TCP/IP (Transmission Control Protocol/Internet Protocol)

TCP/IP is the communication protocol for the Internet. It defines the rules, computers must follow to communicate with each other over the Internet. The TCP/IP is a protocol used with E-mail transmission. Infact, it is a set of protocol, i.e. TCP and IP.

The TCP/IP is a protocol which is responsible for finding path for the destination. It also splits the message into several datagrams, if it does not fit in one datagram. Therefore, these datagrams are sent through different alternate paths towards the destination. The TCP makes sure that the datagram arrives at the destination correctly.

IP (Internet Protocol) used by the Internet for transferring messages from one machine to another. The messages are sent in the form of packets. IP defines the packet structures that encapsulate the data to be delivered. It also defines addressing methods that are used to label the datagram with source and destination format.

SMTP (Simple Mail Transfer Protocol)

SMTP is the standard protocol for E-mail services on a TCP/IP network. SMTP provides the ability to send and receive E-mail messages.

SMTP is an application-layer protocol that enables the transmission and delivery of E-mail over the Internet.

The SMTP standard defines the conversation between the sender of an E-mail and the SMTP mail server that delivers the mail. In a SMTP conversation, the sender issues a certain sequence of commands to the receiving SMTP server. Generally, if the sender issues valid commands and the intended recipients of the E-mail are valid accounts on the receiving server, the receiving server will accept the message and attempt to deliver it.

POP3 (Post Office Protocol Version 3)

It is a standard mail protocol used to receive E-mails from a remote server to a local email client. POP3 allows you to download E-mail messages on your local computer and read them even when you are offline. When you use POP3 to connect to your E-mail account, messages are downloaded locally and removed from the E-mail server. This means that if you access your account from multiple locations, that may not be the best option for you. On the other hand, if you use POP3, your messages are stored on your local computer, which reduced the space of your E-mail account uses on your web server.

HTTPS

HTTPS is a secure version of HyperText Transfer Protocol. It is the primary protocol used to send data between a web browser and a website. HTTPS is encrypted in order to increase security of data transfer.

The use of HTTPS protects against eavesdropping and man-in-the-middle attacks. This is particularly important when users transmit sensitive data, such as by logging into a bank account, E-mail service or health insurance provider.

HTTP vs HTTPS

HTTP	*HTTPS*
It is used for unsecured communication over Internet.	HTTPS is used for secured communication over computer network used as Internet.
Do not use any security protocols.	It uses security protocols at transport layer SSL/TSL and also at layer-2 and layer-3.

Remote Login and File Transfer Protocols

A remote login is a technique to create connection with a remote computer. Remote file transfer is the process of transferring or sending a file to a device or network node external to the local network. Some protocols are used for this purpose which as follows

FTP (File Transfer Protocol)

It is a standard network protocol used to transfer files from one host to another host over a TCP-based network, such as the Internet.

FTP is based on client/server principle. It establishes two connections between the hosts. One connection is used for data transfer, which is opened and closed for each file transfer and the other for control information, which remains connected during the entire interactive FTP session.

Remote Login (Telnet)

Telnet is a protocol used for creating a connection with a remote computer. Once your telnet client establishes a connection to the remote host, telnet client becomes a virtual terminal, allowing you to communicate with the remote host from your computer. It establishes a connection either with command line client or with a programmatic interface. Telnet provides an error free connection, which is always faster than the latest conventional modems.

SSH (Secure Shell)

The SSH protocol is a method for secure remote login from one computer to another. It provides several alternative options for strong authentication and it protects the communications security and integrity with strong encryption. It is a secure alternative to the non-protected login protocols (such as telnet) and insecure File Transfer Methods (such as FTP).

SFTP (Secure File Transfer Protocol)

SFTP also called SSH File Transfer Protocol, is a network protocol for accessing, transferring and managing files on remote systems. It allows businesses to securely transfer billing data, funds and data recovery files. SFTP uses SSH to transfer files and requires that the client be authenticated by the server.

SCP (Secure Copy)

It is a file transfer protocol, which helps in transferring computer files securely from a local host to a remote host. It works on the Secure Shell (SSH) protocol technique.

The term secure copy refers to either the SCP protocol or the SCP program. The SCP protocol is a file transfer network protocol, which supports encryption and authentication features.

Check Point 03

1. How many parts of URL can be divided?
2. State whether statement is Ture or False. The first part of E-mail address is domain name.
3. Which protocol is known as stateless protocol?
4. What is the name of protocol used for creating a connection with a remote computer?

SUMMARY

- An Internet is the network of networks spread all over the world.
- Internet started with interconnection of ARPANET, NSFnet and other small and private networks.
- Internet is not governed by any particular organisation. It is coordinated by many volunteer organisations like IAB, IETF, IRTF, W3C etc.
- Any organisation that provides access to the Internet is called ISP (Internet Service Provider).
- Internet provides three ways of connection as:
  1. Dial-up connection 2. Broadband connection 3. Wireless connection
- WWW is a set of rules/protocols by which, we can retrieve information on Internet.
- Web page is a file/document on Internet that contains text, graphics and links.
- Website is a collection of Web pages that are linked together with the help of hyperlinks.
- Web browser goes to a Web page using a Web address. Also, it downloads the HTML files stored at that address and then reads and translates the HTML file.
- A web client is an application that communicates with a Web server, using HTTP.
- Web server is a program that helps the browser to retrieve information.
- Web address or URL is a method of addressing documents on Web.
- E-mail address is a name that identifies an electronic post office box on network where E-mail can be sent.
- A blog is a Website or a Web page belonging to an individual to describe his/her view.
- Newsgroup is an open discussion forums by people from all over the world.
- HTML elements form the building blocks of all Websites. It allows images and objects to be embedded and can be used to create interactive forms.
- Protocol refers to a set of rules that coordinates the exchange of information.
- HTTP is an access method used on Internet to access hypertext file.
- TCP/IP is a protocol which is responsible for finding path for the destination.
- SMTP distributes E-mail messages and attached files to one or more electronic mail boxes.
- FTP transfers files between a server and a computer.
- Secure Shell (SSH) protocol is a method for secure remote login from one computer to another.

Exam Practice

Multiple Choice Questions

1 What can you do with the Internet? **CBSE 2011**

(a) Exchange information with friends and colleagues

(b) Access pictures, sounds, video clips and other media elements

(c) Find diverse perspective on issues from a global audience

(d) Exchange information, access pictures, find diverse perspective on issue from a global audience.

Ans. (*d*) Internet exchange information, access pictures, find diverse perspective on issues from a global audience.

2 The first network was

(a) ARPANET (b) Internet (c) NSFnet (d) NET

Ans. (*a*) The Advanced Research Projects Agency NETwork (ARPANET) was the world's first operational packet switching network.

3 Which communication protocol is used by Internet?

(a) TCP/IP (b) WWW (c) HTML (d) W3C

Ans. (*a*) TCP/IP is a communication protocol used by Internet which manages the transmission of data/file document on the Internet.

4 Which part of TCP/IP is responsible for dividing a file or message into very small parts, at the source computer?

(a) TCP (b) IP
(c) Both (a) and (b) (d) None of these

Ans. (*a*) TCP part breaks the message into smaller packets that are transmitted over the Internet.

5 In Internet Protocol (IP), data is organised in the form of

(a) bundles (b) packets
(c) switches (d) parts

Ans. (*b*) IP has the task of delivering packets from the source host to the destination host.

6 Digital information is converted into analog information by the modem at **CBSE 2011**

(a) destination computer
(b) source computer
(c) Both (a) and (b)
(d) Neither (a) nor (b)

Ans. (*b*) Digital information is converted into analog information by modem at source computer.

7 To joint the Internet, the computer has to be connected to a

(a) Internet architecture board
(b) Internet society
(c) Internet service provider
(d) None of the above

Ans. (*c*) Internet service provider is used to joint the Internet.

8 An organisation responsibles for providing Internet services to customer is commonly known as

(a) government (b) ISP
(c) TCP/IP (d) HTTP

Ans. (*b*) ISP are the companies that register themselves under the government domain according to the copyright law.

9 Which of these services will not be provided by a typical Internet Service Provider (ISP)?

(a) An E-mail address
(b) Modem
(c) A connection to the Internet
(d) Technical help

Ans. (*a*) ISP refers to a company that provides Internet services, modem, connection and technical help. It does not provide an E-mail address.

10 Nick connects to the Internet at home using a laptop computer with a wireless connection. Nick is going to change to a desktop computer using a 1 Gbps ethernet cable connection.

Which of these should be the result of making the changes?

(a) Increased portability and decreased speed.
(b) Decreased portability and increased speed.
(c) Increased portability and increased speed.
(d) Decreased portability and decreased speed.

Ans. (*b*) Decreased portability and increased speed will be the result.

11 Combination of multimedia and hyperlink is called

(a) hypermedia (b) E-mail
(c) hypertext (d) None of these

Ans. (*c*) Hypertext refers to the combination of text, graphic images, audio and video tracks and hyperlinks.

12 On Internet, to go to other Web page through button, the user should use **CBSE 2012**

(a) Search tools (b) Find and replace
(c) Search engine (d) hyperlink

Ans. (*d*) On Internet, to go to other Web page available through button, the user should use hyperlinks.

13 A collection of Web pages linked together in a random order is **CBSE 2014**

(a) a Website (b) a Web server
(c) a search engine (d) a Web browser

Ans. (*a*) A Website is a collection of Web pages linked together in a random order and displays related information on a specific topic.

14 Home page helps viewers to find out what they can find on the particular site. Home page is the

(a) first page of a Website (b) index page
(c) about page (d) None of these

Ans. (*a*) Home page refers to the initial or main or first Web page of a Website, sometimes called the front page.

15 Which of the following is/are a popular Web browser? **CBSE 2019**

(a) Firefox (b) Safari
(c) Navigator (d) All of these

Ans. (*d*) Firefox, Safari, Navigator all are popular Web browser.

16 .... is an example of text-based browser, which provides access to the Internet in the text-only mode.

(a) Mozilla Firefox (b) Lynx
(c) Internet Explorer (d) All of these

Ans. (*b*) Lynx is a highly configurable text-based Web browser.

17 Google Chrome is an example of

(a) Web browser (b) Web server
(c) HTTP (d) WWW

Ans. (*a*) Web browser is the program that is used to explore the Internet. Thus, Google Chrome is an example of Web browser.

18 A Web page is located using a

(a) Universal Record Linking
(b) Uniform Resource Locator
(c) Universal Record Locator
(d) Uniformly Reachable Links

Ans. (*b*) URL (Uniform Resource Locator) specifies the location of a specific Web page on the Internet.

19 In URL, http://www.arihant.com/index.htm, which component identifies the path of a Web page?

(a) http (b) www.arihant.com
(c) /index.htm (d) All of these

Ans. (*c*) /index.htm, because path name identifies the path of a Web page.

20 In URL, http://www.arihant.com/index.htm, which component identifies the Website?

(a) http (b) www.arihant.com
(c) /index.htm (d) All of these

Ans. (*b*) www.arihant.com, because domain name identifies the Website.

21 Kirti, a student, has written some points about Web pages and URL. **CBSE 2015**

(*i*) Which of the following statements are true about Web pages?
(a) You cannot E-mail a link of Web page.
(b) You cannot create a Web page.
(c) Web pages are written in HTML.
(d) Web pages are viewed through browser.

(*ii*) Which of the following statements are true about URL?
(a) URL means Uniform Resource Locator.
(b) You can enter URL into address bar.
(c) An example of URL is we@fg.com.
(d) It is not necessary for URL to be unique.

Ans. (*i*) (c) and (d) (*ii*) (a) and (b)

22 Domain names always have two or more parts, separated by

(a) commas (b) periods (called dots)
(c) semicolon (d) None of these

Ans. (*b*) A domain name is a hierarchical series of character strings representing different levels of domains separated by dot/period.

23 A domain name ending with .org belongs to

(a) an educational institution
(b) an organisation
(c) a site that is highly organised
(d) a commercial Website

Ans. (*b*) On the Internet, all Websites owned and operated by an organisation are part of the .org domain.

24 In all computers on the Internet, owned and operated by education institution form part of the

(a) .com domain (b) .edu domain
(c) .mil domain (d) .org domain

Ans. (*b*) The domain name edu provides domain registration at no cost to educational institutions.

25 Each computer connected to the Internet must

(a) be a pentium machine
(b) have a unique IP address
(c) have a Web browser
(d) have a modem connection

Ans. (*b*) Each computer connected to the Internet must have a unique IP address.

26 An IP address is a string of .... numbers separated by periods. **CBSE 2011**

(a) 3 (b) 4 (c) 2 (d) 5

Ans. (*b*) An IP address consists of 4 numbers separated by periods.

27 IP addresses are converted into **CBSE 2013**

(a) a binary string
(b) alphanumeric string
(c) a hierarchy of domain names
(d) a hexadecimal string

Ans. (*c*) DNS translates domain names into their IP addresses and *vice-versa*.

28 A blog consists of

(a) images (b) text
(c) links (d) All of these

Ans. (*d*) A blog consists of images, text and links.

29 Online discussion through posts about various topics is called

(a) E-Discussion
(b) Newsgroup
(c) E-mail
(d) Chat

Ans. (*b*) Newsgroup helps for online discussion.

30 HTML is a markup language for describing Web document. HTML uses

(a) pre-specified tags
(b) user defined tags
(c) tags only for linking
(d) fixed tags defined by the language

Ans. (*d*) HTML uses fixed tags defined by the language.

31 A set of rules that governs data communication is

(a) protocol (b) information
(c) HTML (d) E-mail

Ans. (*a*) A protocol is a set of rules that governs the communication between computers on a network.

32 Which of the following would you use to transfer files over the Internet?

(a) FTP (b) E-mail
(c) HTTP (d) Browser

Ans. (*a*) FTP is used to transfer files between computers on a network.

33 Full form of FTP is **CBSE 2018**

(a) Force Transfer Protocol
(b) File Transport Protocol
(c) File Transmission Protocol
(d) File Transfer Protocol

Ans. (*d*) FTP is a protocol through which Internet users can upload files from their computer to a website. In which, FTP stands for File Transfer Protocol.

Fill in the Blanks

1 Internet is a network of .... **CBSE 2011**

Ans. networks

2 A .... is a temporary connection that uses the Public Switched Telephone Network (PSTN) to connect to the Internet.

Ans. dial-up connection

3 .... refers to the amount of data that a signal or a circuit can carry. **CBSE 2013**

Ans. Bandwidth

4 Web pages on a site are linked together through a system of ....

Ans. hyperlinks

5 Safari is a Web browser developed by ....

Ans. Apple

6 In WWW, a client is called .... and a server is called ....

Ans. Web client, Web server

7 .... is a computer program that provides services to other computer programs.

Ans. Server

8 The address of location of the document on WWW is called ....

Ans. URL

9 The character based naming system by which server are identified is known as .... **CBSE 2013**

Ans. domain name system

10 abc@mnc.co.in represents an ....

Ans. E-mail address

11 Blogging is the act of posting content on a .... .

Ans. blog

12 The bulletin board which produces news over Internet is known as ....

Ans. Newsgroup

EXAM PRACTICE

13 In Internet, ……….. is responsible for handling the address of destination computer.

Ans. Internet protocol

14 ……… protocol defines how messages are formatted and transmitted.

Ans. HTTP

True or False

1 TCP helps in converting the digital signal to analog signal and *vice-versa*.

Ans. **False** The process of converting digital signal into analog signal is called modulation and is done by a modem.

2 WWW is an Internet service.

Ans. **True** The World Wide Web (WWW) is a set of programs, standards and protocols that allows the multimedia and hypertext files to be created, displayed and linked on the Internet.

3 Web pages and Websites are same.

Ans. **False** Website is the collection of Web pages .

4 Website can be accessed by URL.

Ans. **True** Each Website is accessed by its own address known as URL.

5 Home page is the server page of a Website.

Ans. **False** Home page is the first Web page of a Website. When a Website is opened, its home page is displayed.

6 Firefox is a Web server.

Ans. **False** Firefox is a Web browser.

7 URL is an Internet machine.

Ans. **False** URL is the Web address for a Website or a Web page.

8 Domain name .mil describes military address.

Ans. **True** .mil is a top level domain that describes military address.

9 .edu is an education domain.

Ans. **True** .edu is a top level domain for education.

10 IP address is given to every computer for its unique identification.

Ans. **True** An IP address serves two principle functions:

(*i*) Host or network interface identification

(*ii*) Location addressing

11 HTML is used to create Web pages.

Ans. **True** HTML is a markup language which is used to create Web pages.

Very Short Answer (VSA) Type Questions

1 Why is Internet so popular? **CBSE 2004**

Ans. Due to its extensible use and sharing of data, Internet becomes so popular.

2 Mention any two major uses of Internet.

Ans. The two major uses of Internet are as follows: **CBSE 2003**

(*i*) For the students and educational purposes, Internet is widely used to gather information so as to do the research.

(*ii*) We can send/receive the mail all over the world.

3 Write two advantages of using Internet. **CBSE 2006**

Ans. Advantages of using Internet are as follows:

(*i*) It is used for communication, entertainment, searching information and for providing many types of services.

(*ii*) It provides the facility of E-mail.

4 Name any five DSL broadband service providers in India.

Ans. BSNL, Airtel, Reliance, MTNL and Tata Indicom.

5 Write the name of any two Internet Service Providers (ISPs) in India. **CBSE 2004, 02**

Ans. MTNL and Airtel.

6 Name any two ways of wireless connections of Internet.

Ans. Wi-Fi and WiMax.

7 What is WWW? **CBSE 2018**

Ans. WWW (World Wide Web) is a system of Internet servers that supports hypertext and multimedia to access several Internet protocols on a single interface.

8 What can a user do with WWW?

Ans. Using WWW, a user can download files, listen to music view video files and jump to other documents or Websites by using hypertext links.

9 Name any two major services provided by Internet.

Ans. E-mail and WWW.

10 Mr. Lal owns a factory which manufactures automobile spare parts. Suggest him the advantages of having a Web page for his factory.

Ans. The Web page provides the information to the clients about his factory of spare parts. Moreover, he can receive the order on the Internet from the clients using the Web page.

11 Name any two popular Web browsers.

Ans. Internet Explorer and Mozilla Firefox.

12 Write the relationship between a Website and a Web server.

Ans. Web server is a computer on which a Website is hosted.

13 What is the full form of URL? **CBSE 2019**

Or What is URL?

Ans. URL means Uniform Resource Locator. It is a full unique address of a Web page on the Internet. It specifies the Internet address of a file stored on a host computer connected to the Internet.

14 Can we use URL to access a Web page? How?

Ans. Yes, as a location on a Web server, which is called a Website and each Website has a unique address known as URL. So, URL can be used to access a Web page.

15 Write the Web extensions (top level domain names) given to a Websites of the following types of organisations. **CBSE 2008**

(*i*) educational

(*ii*) government

Ans. (*i*) .edu (*ii*) .gov

16 Write Web extensions given to sites of the following types of organisations. **CBSE 2007**

(*i*) network organisation (*ii*) government agencies

Ans. (*i*) .net (*ii*) .gov

17 Expand the following Web extensions using with Web addresses.

(*i*) .org (*ii*) .in

Ans. (*i*) Organisation (*ii*) India

18 Write any two Web extensions used with Web addresses.

Ans. .org and .com

19 Identify Web addresses and E-mail addresses from the following **CBSE 2009**

(*i*) www.scrapbook.com

(*ii*) aba@scrapbook.com

(*iii*) www.countrywide.co.in

(*iv*) 123@hotshot.co.in

Ans. (*i*) and (*ii*) and (*iii*) are Web address while (ii) and (*iv*) are E-mail address

20 Identify Web addresses and E-mail addresses from the following **CBSE 2009**

(*i*) www.kool.com

(*ii*) raga100@rediffmail.com

(*iii*) www.hotspider.co.in

(*iv*) 123hotshot@elixir.co.in

Ans. (*i*) and (*iii*) Web address (*ii*) and (*iv*) E-mail address

21 Which language is helpful to create Web pages?

Ans. HTML is used for designing or creating Web pages.

22 Name any two Internet protocols used by Web.

Ans. HTTP and FTP.

23 Name the protocol, which helps you to communicate between a Web server and a Web browser.

Ans. HTTP

24 Briefly discuss the role of a Web browser in Internet surfing. **CBSE 2019**

Ans. A Web browser is a software program that allows a user to locate and display Web pages, acts as Internet surfing.

25 Distinguish between FTP and Telnet.

Ans. FTP (File Transfer Protocol) facilitates the transfer of files from one point to another while Telnet is a connection protocol that allows a user to connect to a remote server.

26 What do you understand by telnet?

Ans. Telnet is a protocol that facilitates remote login on a computer.

27 What do you understand by remote login?

Ans. Remote login or remote access is the ability to get access to a computer or a network from a different computer.

Short Answer (SA) Type Questions

1 How did the Internet begin?

Ans. Refer to text on Page No. 1-2.

2 How do Internet help us?

Ans. Internet can be useful for us in following ways:

(*i*) Allows organisations to advertise their products.

(*ii*) Provides information.

(*iii*) Easily communicate with other people.

(*iv*) Save paper as we can publish documents on the Internet.

3 Write three disadvantages of using Internet.

Ans. The three disadvantages of using Internet are as follows:

(*i*) Cyber frauds (*ii*) Information misuse

(*iii*) Computer virus circulation

4 What is MODEM? **CBSE 2006**

Ans. MODEM stands for MOdulator/DEModulator. It is a hardware device that enables a computer to send and receive information over telephone lines by converting the digital data used by your computer into an analog signal used on telephone lines and then converting back once received on the other end.

5 Define home page. Give two advantages of home page.

Ans. A home page is the first page of a Website.

The two advantages of home page are as follows:

(*i*) It helps viewers to find out what they can find on that site.

(*ii*) Publicity of an individual or a community.

6 How do you differentiate between a Web address and an E-mail address? **CBSE 2018**

Ans. The basic differences between a Web address and an E-mail address are as follows:

(*i*) E-mail address is a network address whereas Web address is the Internet address.

(*ii*) An E-mail address always contains the 'at the rate' sign (@) whereas, a Web address never does.

7 Discuss the role of web servers and web clients briefly. **CBSE 2019**

Ans. **Web server** is a computer program that serves requested HTML pages or files from the web client. Every web server that is connected to the Internet is associated with a unique address, i.e. IP address.

Web client is a computing term which describes special program designed as a user interface, through which messages are sent to a web server.

8 What do you understand by the term URL? How is it different from an email address?

Or What do you understand by a newsgroup? How is it different from a blog?

CBSE SQP Term-II

Ans. **Uniform Resource Locator** (URL) refers to the address or the location of a web page or the website on the Internet. Each website on the Internet has a unique address. For example, http://www.google.com is a URL.

The difference between URL and email address are

URL	Email Address
URL is the address of the website.	An email address is an account on a mail server.
A URL never had an '@' sign in it.	An email address contains an '@' sign.
URL starts with www.	An email address does not start with www.

Or **Newsgroups** enable remotely connected users to share, discuss and learn about their topic of interest by exchanging text messages, images, videos and other forms of digital content. These are discussion forums on the Internet. There are various categories within newsgroups.

Within each category, the discussion gets more and more specific.

The difference between newsgroup and blog are

Newsgroup	Blog
In a newsgroup, anyone can share opinions as per their interest.	Blogs consist opinion of the author.
In a newsgroup, anyone can post and comment also.	In blogs, persons can just comment on posts they cannot post anything.
On the newsgroup, we can share information.	On blogs, we can share our stories and poetry.
Newsgroup mainly focused to spread knowledge.	Blogs mainly focused to entertain people.

9 "A web browser is different from a web server". Explain any two differences in web browser and web server with suitable example of each. **CBSE SQP Term-II**

Ans. A web server is a computer capable of storing a large number of web pages. It makes the web pages available

EXAM PRACTICE

on the web, on request by the user. Web servers are computers that deliver web pages. Every web server has an IP address and a domain name.

Some examples of good web servers are as follows

- Apache https://httpd.apache.org/
- Nginx https://www.nginx.com/
- Lighttpd https://www.lighttpd.net/

The browser acts as the application interface between the computer user and the Internet on the computer. The task of a browser is to read the page from its site and render it on the browser window. Some of the web browsers available are

Microsoft Edge, Internet Explorer, Mozilla Firefox, Google Chrome, Opera and Netscape

Navigator are some notable examples of browsers.

Long Answer (LA) Type Questions

1 Why is Internet called 'Network of Networks'?

Ans. Internet is called 'Network of Networks' because it is global network of computers that are linked together by cables and telephone lines making communication possible among them. It can be defined as a global network over a million of smaller heterogeneous computer networks. The network which consists of thousands of networks spanning the entire globe is known as Internet. The Internet is a world wide collection of networked computers, which are able to exchange information with each other very quickly.

Mostly people use the Internet in two ways, E-mail and World Wide Web. In Internet, most computers are not connected directly, they are connected to smaller networks, which in turn are connected through gateways to the Internet backbone. A gateway is a device that connects dissimilar networks. A backbone is central interconnecting structure that connects one or more networks.

2 What is DNS and also explain its functions? **CBSE 2013**

Ans. DNS stands for Domain Name System. It is a hierarchical distributed naming system for computers, services or any resources connected to the Internet or a private network. It associates various information with domain names assigned to each of the participating entities.

The different functions of DNS are as follows:

(*i*) It translates meaningful domain names into the numerical IP addresses, which is needed for the purpose of locating computer services and devices world wide.

(*ii*) It serves as the phone book for the Internet by translating human friendly computer host names into IP addresses.

(*iii*) The DNS can be quickly updated, allowing a service's location on the network to change without affecting the end users.

(*iv*) It distributes the responsibility of assigning domain names and mapping those names to IP addresses by designating authoritative names servers for each domain.

(*v*) It also specifies the technical functionality of database service. It defines the DNS protocol, a detailed specification of the data structure and data communication exchanges used in DNS, as part of the Internet Protocol Suite (IPS)..

Application Oriented Questions

1 *Read the following paragraph. Find six network and communication related abbreviations and give their expanded form alongwith a single-line definition of each of them.* **CBSE 2011**

The RBI is planning to expand its connectivity with all major banks of India. The plan includes providing TCP connectivity through HTTP for easy access points and seeks help from some ISPs to join hands in this venture.

Also, there is a plan to set-up IIS and SMTP servers. Some banks will go for ADSL line while others will use leased line connectivity to access these services.

The RBI is also taking help of IIT professors in this venture.

Ans. Six network and communication related abbreviations are as follows:

(*i*) TCP (Transmission Control Protocol) A protocol developed for the Internet to get information from one network device to another.

(*ii*) HTTP (HyperText Transfer Protocol) A protocol that transmits hypertext over networks. This is the protocol of the Web.

(*iii*) ISP (Internet Service Provider) An organisation that provides access to the Internet through various connectivity methods.

(*iv*) **IIS** (Internet Information Server) It is a Microsoft proprietary Web server software.

(*v*) **SMTP** (Simple Mail Transfer Protocol) It distributes E-mail messages and attached files to one or more electronic mail boxes.

(*vi*) **ADSL** (Asymmetrical Digital Subscriber Line) A data communication technology that enables faster data transmission over copper telephone lines than a conventional voice band modem can provide.

2 *The following sentences describe the term Web browser.*

Web browsers are programs used to explore the (i)………….. . A Web browser is an interface that helps a computer user gain access to all the content that is on the Internet and the hard disk of the computer.

It can view (ii)…………, text documents, audio and video files, games etc. More than one (iii)…………. can also be installed on a single computer. The user can navigate through files, folders and (iv)……….. with the help of a browser. When the browser is used for browsing (v)………., the pages may contain certain links which can be opened in a new browser. Multiple tabs and windows of the same browser can also be opened. An example of Web browser is (vi)…………… .

Fill in the blanks with words from the list given below:

Internet	TCP
Images	Web browser
Photos	Websites
SMTP	Web pages
Google Chrome	

Ans. (*i*) Internet (*ii*) Images
(*iii*) Web browser (*iv*) Websites
(*v*) Web pages (*vi*) Google Chrome

CHAPTER

02

Internet Services and Mobile Technologies

Chapter Checklist

- Information Retrieval
- Search Engine
- Downloading and Uploading Files from/to Remote Sites
- Web Services
  - Chat
  - E-mail
  - Video Conferencing
  - E-Learning
  - E-Banking
  - E-Shopping
  - E-Reservation
  - E-Governance
  - E-Groups
  - Social Networking
- Mobile Technologies

The diversity of the services available on the Internet, makes it very popular. Out of these services, Web services have expanded to become more popular. A Web service is a method of communication between two electronic devices over a network.

With its help, you can retrieve or search the desired information, E-mail your friends, do video conferencing, store or retrieve files, participate in a discussion forum etc. Providers of Web services are generally known as **application service providers**.

Information Retrieval

It is the process of accessing information that is stored on the Internet. The process of exploring and retrieving the information from the Internet is known as **net surfing**. When your PC is connected to the Internet, you are ready to retrieve information from it. You need a particular software called **Web browser** to retrieve information.

When you type the URL of a particular Website in the address bar of the Web browser and press Enter key, the browser retrieves the Web page from the Internet and stores its content.

Some useful sites to visit are as follows:

- **http://www.netscape.com** It contains useful information including the latest versions of Web browser Netscape Navigator, list of Internet directories etc.
- **http://www.funbrain.com** It contains many educational games, math problems etc., for children. It also provides helpful stuff for teachers and parents.
- **http://www.britannica.com** It refers to the world famous encyclopedia that is now available online.
- **http://www.enwikipedia.org** It refers to free encyclopedia using wiki software.
- **http://www.crayola.com** It contains creativity tips for students, parents and educators.

Connecting your PC to Internet

To set-up an Internet connection, do the following steps:

Step 1 Connect the necessary hardware like modem, ethernet cable etc and run necessary softwares such as LAN driver.

Step 2 Make a preliminary connection using ethernet cable or a wireless connection.

Step 3 Go to the router's default IP address. e.g. 192.168.0.1.

Step 4 Set-up the Internet connection using login name and password, which is provided by the ISP.

Step 5 Save your settings.

Search Engine

It is a Website that provides the required data on specific topics. It turns the Web into a powerful tool for finding information on any topic. Search engine allows users to enter keywords (queries or terms) related to particular topics and retrieve information about the Websites containing these keywords. It is a program designed to search for information on the Web through a database of Web pages queries or keywords.

When search query is submitted in the search engine by user, the software used for search algorithm scans the index to find Web pages over the Internet.

Some of the most popular search engines are as follows:

Google	http://www.google.com
AltaVista	http://www.altavista.com
Yahoo	http://www.yahoo.com
Hotbot	http://www.hotbot.com
Lycos	http://www.lycos.com
Excite	http://www.excite.com
Web Crawler	http://www.webcrawler.com
Bing	http://www.bing.com

Working of a Search Engine

Search engine works with three elements, which are as follows :

1. **Web Crawler** It is a software that browses the Internet in a systematic manner. It retrieves the information, which follows every link on the site that are stored by Web search engines. It is also known as **spider, ant, automatic indexer** or **Web scutter.**
2. **Indexing Software** It is a software that receives the list of Web documents and addresses collected by Web crawler. Some search engines provide proximity search which allows users to define the distance keywords.
3. **Search Algorithm** It is a concept based searching, where the research involves using statistical analysis on pages containing the words or phrases you are searching for.

Locating Sites using Search Engines

A search engine is also an information retrieval system designed to find information stored on the WWW.

For searching any particular information, following steps are to be taken:

Step 1 Go to the **home page** of the search engine.

Step 2 On the home page, a textbox will appear somewhere.

Step 3 In that textbox, type a **keyword** that you want to search.

Step 4 After that, there will be a button that looks like an image and has the word (such as Google Search, Web Search etc.) search written on it. Clicking on that button, search will start and will bring up a new Web page with a list of Websites related to that topic.

Step 5 Clicking on one of the links in the list will access that Website.

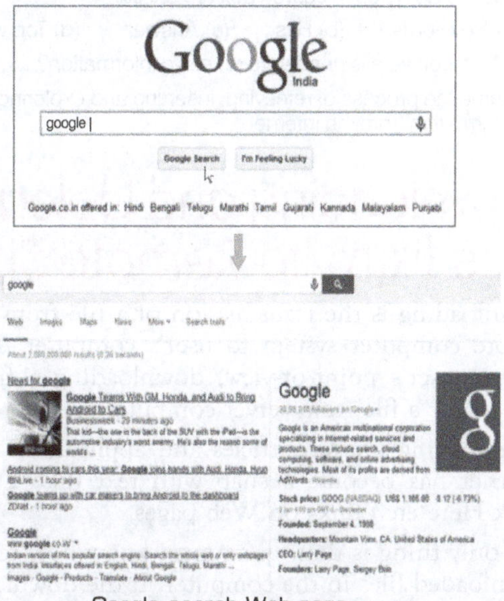

Google search Web page

Many search engines also have directories or lists of topics that are organised into categories. A list of Websites that contains the information are known as **hits.** The words typed in search box are called **keywords.** Browsing these directories is also a very efficient way to find information on a given topic. To effectively search for desired information, you must learn the art of framing search queries.

The following table provides a number of operators for doing advanced searches on most search engines:

Operator	*What it does*	*Example*
" "	Indicates a series of words that must appear next to each other.	"Good day sunshine" returns pages with this exact phrase.
+	Indicates that all the words must appear in the Web page.	Computer + architecture will return pages that include both words computer and architecture.
–	Searches for pages that include first term but not the second.	Computer-architecture will return pages with word computer but not with an architecture.
*	Use the wildcard (*) to search for plurals or variations of words.	sing* will return pages that include a string starting with sing such as singing, sings etc.
AND, OR and NOT	Can be used in some search engines to specify your search.	Sports AND hockey, baseball OR basketball.

Check Point 01

1 The words typed in search box are called
(a) Keywords (b) Hits (c) Answer (d) Top words

2 Which software is needed to retreieve information?

3 Name the process of retrieving, inserting and exploring the information from the Internet.

Downloading and Uploading Files from/to Remote Sites

Downloading is the transmission of a file from server or remote computer system to user's computer. From the Internet-user's point-of-view, downloading a file means request for a file from server computer and to receive it.

Downloading images, articles and applications from the Internet has become a snap with text (like Download, Click Here etc.) links on Web pages.

The only thing is that, users must know how to find the downloaded files in the computer. If the downloaded file is an application, it must be installed, which can be an automatic operation or require the user to take one more step for running the installed program.

Uploading is the transmission of a file from local system to a server or remote computer. From an Internet-user's point-of-view, uploading is sending a file to a computer that is set-up to receive it. The most common type of uploading is when a user uploads a digital image to an Internet site. The uploaded files are stored on the Website's servers and can be seen by anyone who has the Internet connection and it is necessary to use the right software for viewing it.

Web Services

Web service is a standardized medium to propagate communication between the client and server applications on the world wide web.

Some of web services are as follows

Chat

It is the online textual or multimedia conversation. It is a real-time communication between two users *via* computer. It is widely interactive text-based communication process that takes place over the Internet.

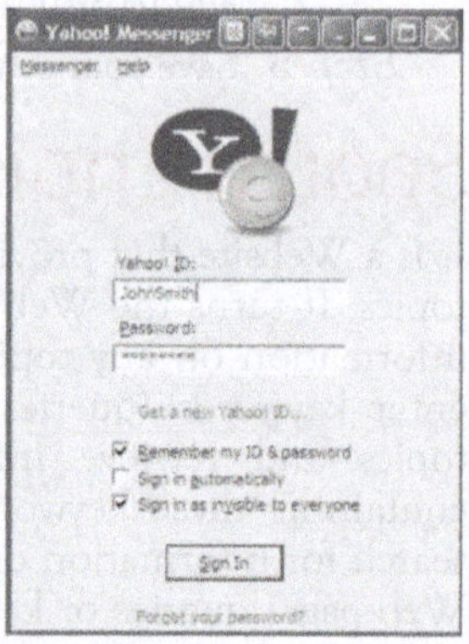

Yahoo Messenger window

Chatting is a virtual means of communication that involves the sending and receiving of messages, share audios and videos between users located in any part of the world.

In chatting, you type a message in your chat box, which is immediately received by the recipient, then the recipient types a message in response to your message, which is instantly received by you.

> Some popular chat applications are as follows :
> - WhatsApp
> - WeChat
> - Hike
> - Facebook Messenger
> - Tango

In addition, there are many browser based services that do not require downloaded chat program.

e.g. Facebook has a built-in chat feature and gmail allows you to chat with your contacts whenever you are logged into your gmail account. There are two basic modes for chatting on the Internet as follows:

1. **Text-based chat** Enables communication through sending and receiving text messages.
2. **Multimedia chat** Enables communication through audio and video transmission.

A *chat room* is the hub of Internet chatting. Chat rooms (virtual rooms) are actually chat servers that allow several users to login to them simultaneously. After joining a room, you can read the messages of other users and send your own messages to them or to anyone else.

Advantages of Chat

(*i*) Photos can be sent using an instant messaging.
(*ii*) Emotions can be expressed easily when communicating with a person.
(*iii*) It is almost same as talking to someone face-to-face.
(*iv*) You can also chat in a group.
(*v*) It makes it possible for user to keep in contact and chat to each other even if, they are in different countries.

Disadvantages of Chat

(*i*) Viruses can be easily spread *via* texting.
(*ii*) Children tend to spend more time in chatting with friends instead of bonding with their family and studies.

E-mail (Electronic Mail)

It is an electronic version of sending and receiving letters. The E-mail is transmitted between computer systems, which exchange messages or pass them onto other sites according to certain Internet protocols or rules for exchanging E-mail. You can send E-mail from your computer at anytime to any address around the world and your electronic letter or E-mail will arrive at its destination in seconds after you send it, even if the receiver is not online.

For sending and receiving an E-mail, you must have an E-mail account, which is either a Web based online E-mail account or an E-mail account on your ISP server.

Web based online E-mail account can be created through many sites like Gmail, Yahoo mail, Rediffmail etc.

Elements of E-mail Account

Some important elements or folders that are used to organise your E-mail messages are as follows:

Inbox It contains all incoming messages.

Outbox The message is stored in the outbox until, it is successfully sent to the recipient.

Sent mail It contains all sent messages.

Draft It contains the messages, which are ready to be sent.

Trash It contains deleted messages.

Spam It contains junk E-mails.

Formats of an E-mail Message

There are two formats of an E-mail message, which are as follows :

1. **Plain text** (txt) **E-mail** It can be read by anyone type of E-mail application. It does not support text formatting options such as bold, italic, colored fonts etc. It can have attached pictures or graphics, but they cannot be inserted.
2. **Rich text** (rtf) **E-mail** It cannot be read by any type of E-mail application. It supports text formatting options such as bold, italic, colored fonts etc. Pictures or graphics can also be inserted.

Structure of an E-mail Message

The general structure of an E-mail message has the following components:

Components	*Description*
To	This field contains the E-mail address of recipient.
Cc	Cc stands for Carbon Copy. This contains the address of recipients to whom you want to send a copy of an E-mail message.
Bcc	Bcc stands for Blind Carbon Copy. This field also contains the list of recipients. Bcc recipients can see the To and Cc addresses but Bcc recipients name is not visible to others.
Subject	This field contains the title of a message.
Body	It includes text of an E-mail message.
Attachments	You can attach any document with E-mail message.
Formatting	Using the formatting tab, you can format the message.
Other options	Other options like emoticons, bold, italic, hyperlinks etc, are used to make messages more interactive.
Send button	You have to click the Send button to send the mail.

An example of the structure of an E-mail is given below:

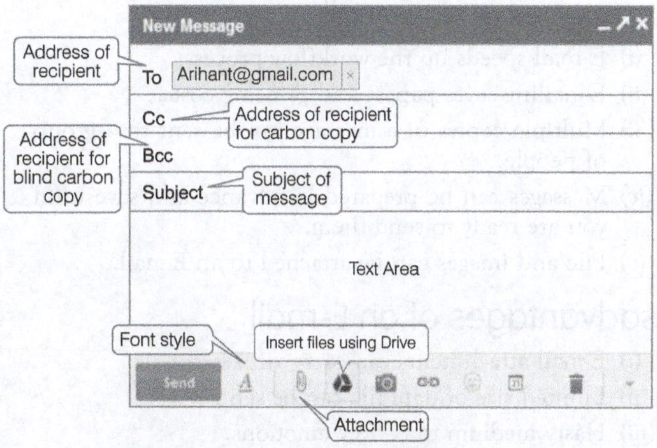

Structure of an E-mail

Emoticons

Emoticons or smileys are elements that help you to express your emotions or feelings in your E-mails and text messages. They provide a direct and funny way to express yourself in addition to the words in your messages.

Some commonly used smileys are as follows:

Emoticon symbol	*Meaning*	*Emoticon symbol*	*Meaning*
:)	Smile	:D	Bigsmile
:O	Surprise	:P	Razz
;)	Wink	:(	Sad
:-O	Shouting		
:~(	Crying	: I	Indifferent
:$	Embarrassed	:@	Angry
<:o)	Party!	*-)	Confused
		8-)	Roll Eyes

Acronyms

Apart from emoticons and symbols, you can also use acronyms and abbreviations for most frequently used words.

Some of the most widely used acronyms are as follows:

Acronym	*Meaning*
AAMOF	as a matter of fact
BBL	be back later
BRB	be right back
BTW	by the way
CU	see you
CUL	see you later
FAQ	frequently asked questions
FTF	face-to-face
FYI	for your information
L8R	later
WB	welcome back
W8	wait

Advantages of an E-mail

(*i*) E-mail speeds up the workflow process.
(*ii*) E-mailing saves papers and printing costs.
(*iii*) Multiple copies of a message can be sent to a group of people.
(*iv*) Messages can be prepared in advance and save until you are ready to send them.
(*v*) File and images can be attached to an E-mail.

Disadvantages of an E-mail

(*i*) E-mail attachments can carry viruses.
(*ii*) Limited size of data file can be sent.
(*iii*) Hasty medium to convey emotions.
(*iv*) No guarantee that the mail will be read until the user logs on and check E-mail.

Video Conferencing

Video conferencing

It is a communication technology that integrates videos and audios to connect users anywhere in the world, as if they are in the same room. This term usually refers two way communication between two or more users who are in atleast two different locations, rather than one-to-one communication and it often includes multiple people at each location.

Each user or group of users who are participating in a video conference typically must have a computer, a camera, a microphone, a video screen and a sound system.

Basically, this is a system that allows you to conduct meetings or trainings in different places simultaneously. So, this technology is most popular in the field of business because it allows meetings or conferences to be held without the need for all the participants to travel to a single location and thus, it saves time and money. Many people can hear and see each other, share whiteboard and other applications through video conferencing.

Some popular video conferencing applications are as follows:
- Skype
- Tango
- Hangouts
- Viber
- IMO

Advantages of Video Conferencing

(*i*) It reduces your travel costs by working remotely and also increases productivity through collaborative working.
(*ii*) Many people can share their videos with each other at the same time.
(*iii*) PowerPoint and other visual displays can be shared with everyone attending the conference at the same time.
(*iv*) Virtual whiteboard allows people from different locations to add their own thoughts or ideas into one collaborative space.
(*v*) With more advanced services, a document can be changed and typed directly from other computers connected to the conference.

Disadvantages of Video Conferencing

(*i*) In the middle of an important meeting, you may be disconnected at any time and have to wait to be reconnected.

(*ii*) There is no substitute for a face-to-face meeting in getting to know someone.

(*iii*) For a long time, video conferencing equipments have been expensive and out of the reach of smaller businesses.

(*iv*) Senders and receivers must be online at the same time.

Check Point 02

1 Copying a file from a host system to your computer is known as what?

2 State whether the statement is True or False.
Two modes for chatting on the Internet are available.

3 What are meant by emoticons : D and : P?

E-Learning (Electronic Learning)

It refers to an electronic mode of delivering learning, training or educational programs to users.

E-learning is the mode of acquiring knowledge by means of Internet and computer based training programs. E-learning can be done anywhere and at anytime.

E-learning

The modules of E-learning are designed to provide not only adequate and relevant information but also make learning highly engaging and interactive using multimedia.

Broadly, E-learning is synonymous with Computer Based Instruction (CBI), Computer Based Training (CBT), Internet Based Training (IBT), Web Based Training (WBT) and online education. E-learning applications and processes include Web based learning, computer based learning, virtual classrooms and digital collaboration.

E-learning can be divided into the following categories:

- **Synchronous** It means "at the same time," interaction of participants with an instructor *via* the Web in a real-time.
- **Asynchronous** It means "not at the same time." It allows the participants to complete the Web based training at their own place, without live interaction with an instructor.

Advantages of an E-Learning

(*i*) Class work can be scheduled around office and family.

(*ii*) Reduces travel time and travel costs for off-campus students.

(*iii*) Self-paced learning modules allow students to work at their own pace.

(*iv*) Learning can accommodate different learning styles and facilitate learning through a variety of activities.

(*v*) Develops knowledge of an Internet and computer skills that will help learners throughout their lives and careers.

(*vi*) Successfully completed online or computer based courses build self-knowledge and self-confidence and encourages students to take responsibility for their learning.

Disadvantages of an E-Learning

(*i*) Without the routine structures of a traditional class, students may get lost or confused about course activities and deadlines.

(*ii*) Students may feel isolated from an instructor and classmates.

(*iii*) Instructor may not always be available when students are studying or need help.

(*iv*) Slow Internet connections or older computers may make accessing course materials frustrating.

(*v*) Hands-on or lab work is difficult to simulate in a virtual classroom.

E-Banking (Electronic Banking)

It is defined as the automated delivery of new and traditional banking products and services directly to the customers through an electronic and interactive communication channels. E-banking is also known as **Internet Banking**, **Online Banking** or **PC Banking**.

In Internet banking system, the bank has a centralised database, i.e. Web enabled. All the services that the bank has permitted on the Internet are displayed in menu. Any service can be selected and further interaction is dictated by the nature of service. It allows customers to access account specific information and possibly conduct transactions from a remote location such as at home or at workplace.

Customers can access E-banking services using an intelligent electronic devices, such as a Personal Computer (PC), Personal Digital Assistant (PDA), Automated Teller Machine (ATM) etc.

E-banking can be broadly classified into the two categories, which are as follows:

1. **Transactional** It involves performing financial transactions. Transactional activities are as follows:
   - Electronic fund transfer
   - Bill payments
   - Loan application and repayments
   - Buying investment products
2. **Non-Transactional** It involves viewing bank statements. Non-transactional activities are as follows:
   - Account balance viewing
   - Bank statement downloading
   - Cheque book ordering
   - Provision of account/bank statement

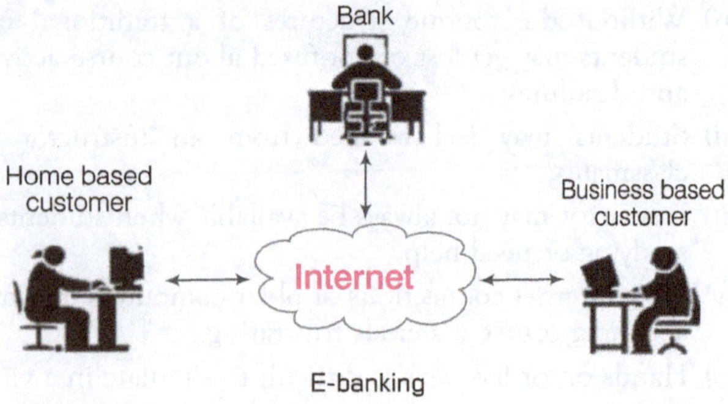

Advantages of an E-Banking

(i) There are no geographical barriers and the services that can be offered at a minimum cost.

(ii) Through Internet banking, you can check your transactions at any time and as many times as you want to.

(iii) If the fund transfer has to be made outstation, where the bank does not have a branch, the bank would demand outstation charges, whereas with the help of online banking, it will be absolutely free for you.

(iv) Internet banking deploys the Internet as a medium for financial transaction.

Disadvantages of an E-Banking

(i) Understanding the usage of Internet banking might be difficult for a beginner at the first time.

(ii) You cannot have access to Internet banking, if you don't have an Internet connection.

(iii) Security of transactions is a big issue. Your account information might get hacked by unauthorised people over the Internet.

> **Mobile Banking**
>
> It is a way for the customer to perform E-banking actions on his/her cell phones or other mobile devices. It is a quite popular method of banking. It might also be referred to as **M-banking** or **SMS banking**.
>
> Services of M-banking are as follows:
> - Account information
> - Transaction
> - Investments
> - SMS service

E-Shopping (Electronic Shopping)

E-shopping or Online Shopping is the process of buying goods and services from merchants who sell their products on Internet. Consumers buy a variety of items from online stores. In fact, people can purchase just about anything from companies that provide their products online.

Books, clothing, household appliances, toys, hardware, software and health insurance are just some of the hundreds of products, consumers can buy from an online store.

The main components of E-shopping are as follows:
- Selling place
- Product
- Accessibility to people
- Placement of orders
- Mode of payment
- Delivery mechanism

Some E-shopping sites are Naaptol, Flipkart, Yebhi, HomeShop18, Amazon.com (Prefer for buy books) etc.

Advantages of E-Shopping

(i) Finding a product online is much more easier than looking for it in the local store.

(ii) Now-a-days online shopping is very reliable.

(iii) Most of the stores provide money back guarantee.

(iv) You have infinite options to choose a product.

(v) If you do not find any product within your country then you can shop online from an international store.

Disadvantages of E-Shopping

(i) The customer might be worried as to the similarity of the product being ordered and the product being received.

(ii) You have to wait for delivery.

(iii) You may be a victim of online fraud.

(iv) You may have to pay for shipping, while returning.

(v) You cannot really see/feel the items, you purchase.

E-Reservation (Electronic Reservation)

It means making a reservation for a service *via* Internet. You need not personally go to an office or a counter to book/reserve railways, airways tickets, hotel rooms, tourist packages etc.

Examples of E-reservation sites are as follows:

- www.irctc.com
- www.makemytrip.com
- www.yatra.com
- www.bookingsite.com

Advantages of an E-Reservation

(*i*) Real-time process (if you book a seat, it will automatically be updated so, no one else can take that seat. If you used an agent that did not use computers, they would need to call other agents saying 'Seat X had been taken').

(*ii*) Can access more information and find other details online about your reservation.

(*iii*) Websites can compare different flight prices and details.

Disadvantages of an E-Reservation

(*i*) Need an Internet and PC experience.

(*ii*) Might need a credit card or some other form of payment.

(*iii*) Viruses/Torjans may steal your information.

(*iv*) If the Website is not working properly then, due to some server issue, reservation can't be done.

E-Governance (Electronic Governance)

It is the integration of Information and Communication Technology (ICT) in all the processes, with the aim of enhancing government ability to address the needs of the general public. The basic purpose of e-governance is to simplify processes for all, i.e. government, citizens, business etc at National, State and local levels. Through e-governance, the government plans to raise the coverage and quality of information and services provided to the general public, by the use of ICT in an easy, economical and effective manner.

Types of Interactions in E-Governance

1. G2G (Government to Government)
2. G2C (Government to Citizen)
3. G2B (Government to Business)
4. G2E (Government to Employees)

Advantages of E-Governance

(*i*) Cost effective

(*ii*) Speed, efficiency and convenient

(*iii*) Minimum use of hard copy

(*iv*) Increase interest of citizens

(*v*) Easily accessible

Disadvantages of E-Governance

(*i*) Poor IT literacy.

(*ii*) Lack of electricity in rural areas.

(*iii*) Privacy problems.

(*iv*) Lack of communication between different departments.

E-Groups (Electronic Groups)

An E-group or online clubbing is a group of persons or individuals who come together over the Internet for a specific or common purpose using the best Internet communication tools to share ideas, different opinions, experiences and to learn from each other. E-groups are Internet based discussion groups. A message posted in discussion is known as **post.** All the posts are visible to all the group members.

Advantages of an E-Groups

(*i*) It helps to create and maintain social relationship.

(*ii*) It facilitates communication among members.

(*iii*) It facilitates research as members assist one another.

(*iv*) It facilitates learning.

(*v*) Less time and cost is used.

(*vi*) It keeps members abreast with new development and knowledge.

Disadvantages of an E-Groups

(*i*) There is no privacy, if intimate issues are discussed.

(*ii*) Every wrong information has a negative impact on each other.

(*iii*) It is hard to follow the logical sequence of discussion.

Social Networking

It is the grouping of individuals into specific groups, like small rural communities or a neighbourhood sub-division. This service is an online service, platform or site that focuses on facilitating the building of social networks or social relations among people e.g. who share interests, activities, backgrounds or real life connections.

When it comes to online networking, social networking Websites are commonly used. These Websites are known as *social networking sites.*

Finding People on the Net

There are numerous sites on an Internet and search engines that can be used to help for finding people on Internet.

- Search on social networking sites such as Facebook, MySpace, BlackPlanet etc. for the person.
- Perform an online search for the person by name. Sites such as Bing, Yahoo search etc.

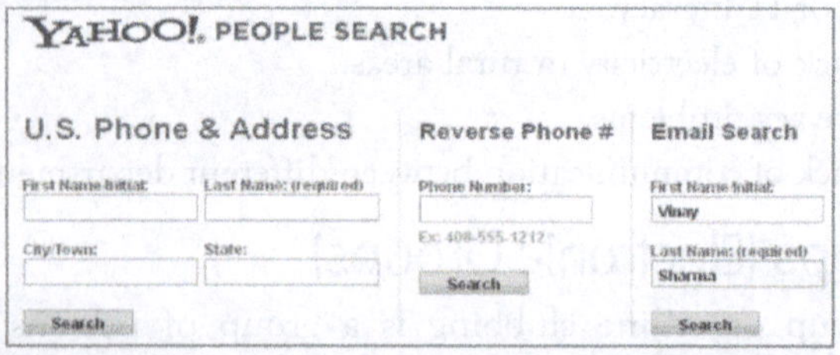

Search online directories such as WhitePages, SuperPages for the person. The directories sometimes include directory information for a person, who is not listed in your local phone book.

Some of the different sites with their description of locating someone online are as follows:

Name of Social Networking Sites	Website with their Description
Facebook	http://www.facebook.com/ Today, Facebook is one of the largest online social networks with over 500 million people.
WhitePages	http://www.whitepages.com/ It is used for finding basic information about people in the United States.
SuperPages	http://www.superpages.com/ SuperPages is a online directory to find the information about people.
MySpace	http://www.myspace.com/ MySpace is a social networking service, where people come to discover, share and connect with videos, music, images etc.
BlackPlanet	http://www.blackplanet.com/ It is the world's largest free African, American online community where Black women and Black men meet to chat and discuss the matters.

These Websites provide simple tools to create a custom profile with text and pictures. Advanced profiles may include videos, photo albums, online applications (in Facebook) or custom layouts (in MySpace). After creating a profile, users can add friends, send messages to other users and leave comments directly on friends profiles. These features provide the building blocks for creating online communities.

Advantages of Social Networking

(*i*) Social networking sites help us to find our long-lost and childhood friends and relatives.

(*ii*) No software or setting changes necessary to PC/phone.

(*iii*) It is an easy and cost effective way to reach your consumers and people in your network.

(*iv*) For business purposes, connecting with your customers on a personal and professional level will make them loyal to your company and brand.

(*v*) It helps in building credibility amongst the customers.

Disadvantages of Social Networking

(*i*) Lack of anonymity.

(*ii*) Social networking usually requires you to input your name, location, age, gender and many other types of personal information.

(*iii*) Scams and harassment.

(*iv*) Being online you are at risk of facing cases of cyber stalking and theft identity.

(*v*) Time consuming.

(*vi*) If you are new to social networking, learning process can be time consuming.

- Internet service was launched in India on 15 August, 1995 by Videsh Sanchar Limited.

Check Point 03

1. What are the categories in which E-banking is divided?
2. IBT, CBT services are provided by ....
3. What is refer to the electronic mode of delivering learning, training or educational programs to user?
4. List any two social networking Websites.

Mobile Technologies

Mobile technologies is a form of technology that is mostly used in cellular communication and other related aspects. It uses a form of platform where by many transmitters have the ability to send data at the same time on a single channel. This platform is called Code Division Multiple Access.

The mobile technology has improved from a simple device used for phone call and messaging into a multitasking device used for GPS navigation, Internet browsing, gaming, instant messaging tool, etc.

Some terms related to mobile technologies are as follows:

3G (Third Generation)

3G is short for Third Generation of mobile telecommunications technology also called Tri-Band 3G.

3G telecommunication networks support services that provide the information transfer rate of atleast 200 Kbps. It adds multimedia facilities that allow video, audio and graphics applications. However, many services advertised as 3G provides higher speed than the minimum technical requirements for a 3G service. Recent 3G releases, often denoted 3.5G and 3.75G, also provide mobile broadband access of several Mbps to smartphones and mobile modems in laptop computers. 3G finds application in wireless voice telephony, mobile Internet access, fixed wireless Internet access, video calls and mobile TV.

4G (Fourth Generation)

In telecommunications, 4G is the Fourth Generation of mobile phone communication standards. It is a successor of the Third Generation (3G) standard. A 4G system provides mobile ultra-broadband Internet access. It will be based on packet switching only and these systems are projected to provide speeds up to 100 Mbps while moving and 1 Gbps while stationary.

e.g. laptops with USB wireless modems, smart-phones and other mobile devices. Conceivable applications include amended mobile web access, IP telephony, gaming services, high-definition mobile TV, video conferencing, 3D television and cloud computing.

Two 4G candidate systems are commercially deployed the mobile WiMAX standard (at first in South Korea in 2006) and the first release Long Term Evolution (LTE) standard (in Oslo, Norway since 2009).

SMS (Short Message Service)

SMS, commonly referred to as text messaging, is a service for sending short messages of up to 160 characters to mobile devices, including cellular phones, smartphones and PDAs.

SMS are transmitted within the same cell or to anyone with roaming service capability.

MMS (Multimedia Messaging Service)

MMS is mobile phone service that allows users to send multimedia messages to each other. This includes images, videos and sound files. MMS is an extension of SMS, which is used to send and receive text messages.

MMS support is typically integrated into the text messaging interface and activates automatically when needed. e.g. if you type a text message only, it will be sent using SMS. If you add a graphic or video, the multimedia portion will be transmitted *via* MMS.

Check Point 04

1 Third generation of mobile telecommunications technology also called

(a) Tri Band 3G

(b) USB

(c) 3.5 G

(d) None of the above

2 What is the successor of the third generation standard?

3 Which does include images, videos and sound files?

SUMMARY

- The activity of looking at different sites on Internet, especially when you are looking for any topic is known as net surfing.
- Search engine refers to the software used to search information from the Internet according to a specified criteria.
- Downloading is copying a file from a host system to your computer.
- Uploading means sending files from your computer to your home directory on the host system.
- Chat is online textual conversation wherein the message typed by the sender is instantly made available to the recipient and *vice-versa*.
- Sending and receiving message electronically is called an E-mail.
- An emoticon is a short sequence of keyboard letters and symbols, usually copying a facial expression that complements a text message.
- Video conferencing is the audio-visual communication between user sitting at two different computers.
- E-learning can be divided into two categories:
  1. Synchronous
  2. Asynchronous
- E-banking can be classified into two categories:
  1. Transactional
  2. Non - Transactional
- E-shopping is a facility available on Internet wherein one can do shopping online, as well as can sell any product online.
- E-reservation is the most convenient facility for online real-time reservation.
- E-governance is the application of ICT to the processes of government functioning to bring about Smart, Moral, Accountable, Responsive and Transparent Governance.
- E-group helps in becoming a member of a group with common interests.
- Social networking sites are Web based services that allow individuals to create a public profile. Some popular social networking sites are Facebook, Twitter, LinkedIn etc.
- Mobile technologies is a form of technology that is mostly used in cellular communication.
- SMS (Short Message Service) is commonly referred to as text messaging.
- MMS (Multimedia Messaging Service) is mobile phone service that allows users to send multimedia messages to each other.

Exam Practice

Multiple Choice Questions

1 A search engine is a program to search
(a) for information
(b) Web pages
(c) Web pages for specified index terms
(d) Web pages for information using specified search terms.

Ans. (*d*) A search engine is a software system that is designed to search for information on the Web pages.

2 Which of the following statements about search engine is true? **CBSE 2011**
(a) Search engines discriminate between good and bad sites.
(b) Search engines have fixed hours, when we can use them.
(c) Search engines are waste of time as they do not provide relevant information.
(d) Search engine is a program designed to search for information on the Web using keywords.

Ans. (*d*) Search engine is a program designed to search for information on the Web using keywords.

3 A software that searches through a database of Web pages for particular information is known as
(a) domain (b) E-mail client
(c) modem (d) search engine

Ans. (*d*) Search engine searches a software through a database of Web pages for particular information.

4 Which software browse the Internet in a systematic manner? **CBSE 2013**
(a) Web crawler
(b) Web browser
(c) Indexing software
(d) Search algorithm

Ans. (*a*) Web search engine works by storing information about many Web pages, retrieved by a Web crawler.

5 Shri wants to search about computer vendor in Meerut excluding Dell category. Which of the following search query best suits his requirements?
(a) Computer vendor Meerut Dell
(b) Computer vendor Meerut not Dell
(c) Computer vendor + Meerut – Dell
(d) Computer vendor + Meerut + Dell

Ans. (*c*) Computer vendor + Meerut – Dell

6 When you copy a Web page or a file from a server to your local computer, this process is called
(a) conferencing (b) downloading
(c) uploading (d) None of these

Ans. (*b*) Because we store information from a server computer to a user computer.

7 Image files uploaded and downloaded over the Internet can be processed with a compression application. Why are image files compressed before transmitted over Internet?
(a) to increase security
(b) to make them easier to open
(c) to reduce transmission time
(d) to improve the quality of images.

Ans (*c*) Image files are compressed before transmitted over Internet to reduce transmission time.

8 Identify the software that helps you in sending and receiving an E-mail:
(a) MS-Office (b) Internet Explorer
(c) Gmail (d) None of these

Ans. (*c*) Gmail is preferred E-mail client which is used for sending or receiving an E-mail.

9 Bcc field contains the list of recipients. Bcc stands for **CBSE 2014**
(a) Basic carbon copy (b) Blind carbon copy
(c) Blind client copy (d) Basic client copy

Ans. (*b*) Bcc denotes the Blind carbon copy.

10 A two way video conversation among multiple participants is called
(a) video chatting (b) video talking
(c) video conferencing (d) video watching

Ans. (*c*) Two or more people hear and see each other, share white board and other applications through video conferencing.

11 ……… services typically include reviewing account activity and balance, sending electronic payments and transferring funds between accounts electronically.
(a) E-banking (b) E-reservation
(c) E-posting (d) E-mail

Ans. (*a*) E-banking provides all transactional and non-transactional activities.

12 Which of the following sites, would you prefer to buy books? **CBSE 2011**

(a) www.yahoomail.com
(b) www.sun.com
(c) www.msn.com
(d) www.amazon.com

Ans. (*d*) www.amazon.com is the world's largest online retailer and a best site for buying books.

13 E-reservation is a process of making reservations of

(a) tickets (b) hotel rooms
(c) tourists packages (d) All of these

Ans. (*d*) E-reservation is a process of making reservation of tickets, hotel rooms, tourists package etc.

14 Which mobile technology system provides mobile ultra-broadband Internet access?

(a) 3G (b) 4G
(c) SMS (d) MMS

Ans. (*b*) 4G stands for Fourth Generation. It provides mobile ultra broadband Internet access.

Fill in the Blanks

1 Information is retrieved through Internet using ....

Ans. search engine

2 .... is a real-time communication between two or more users *via* computer. **CBSE 2013**

Ans. Chat

3 E-mail is the process of sending and receiving messages ....

Ans. electronically

4 .... elements help to express emotions or feelings in E-mail or text messages.

Ans. Emoticon

5 ..... helps us to learn anywhere using Internet.

Ans. E-learning

6 Computer Based Training (CBT) is a type of ....

Ans. E-learning

7 .... allows customers to conduct financial transactions on a secure Website.

Ans. E-banking **CBSE 2011**

8 Internet can be used to get reservation of trains and air planes through .... service.

Ans. E-reservation

9 .... helps to create and maintain social relationship.

Ans. Social networking

10 LinkedIn is an example of .... Website.

Ans. social networking

11 .... is the online directory to find the information about people.

Ans. SuperPages

12 .... is an extension of .... which is used to send and receive text messages.

Ans. MMS, SMS

True or False

1 AltaVista is used for searching of available Internet connection.

Ans. **False** AltaVista is a search engine, which is used for searching information on a particular topic.

2 Downloading of files means transferring files from host computer to the Internet. **CBSE 2011**

Ans. **False** Downloading of files means transferring of files from an Internet to your host computer.

3 Chat rooms are actual rooms, where chat session can take place. **CBSE 2011**

Ans. **False** Chat rooms are actually chat servers that allow several users to login them simultaneously.

4 Plain text (txt) E-mail messages can be read by any type of E-mail application.

Ans. **True** Plain text E-mail contains text without any formatting options such as bold, italic, colored fonts etc., so these can be read by any type of E-mail application.

5 Video conferencing enables two or more people to only see one another.

Ans. **False** People can also communicate with the help of video conferencing. It often includes multiple people at each location.

6 E-learning only supports text materials.

Ans. **False** E-learning includes numerous types of media that deliver text, audio, images, animation and streaming videos.

7 We can make groups of our friends and family members on a social networking site. **CBSE 2011**

Ans. **True** Social networking provides various sites like Facebook and Orkut for making groups of our friends and family members.

Very Short Answer (VSA) Type Questions

1 Write the purpose of search engine. **CBSE 2005**

Ans. The main purpose of search engine is to help people to find more information on any topic, which user wants.

2 Give any two examples of popular search engines. **CBSE 2018**

Ans. (i) Google (ii) Yahoo

3 What do you understand by uploading a file on Internet? Name software used for it.

Ans. To transfer a file from your computer to a server is called uploading a file on Internet. FileZilla is the software which is used for it.

4 What do you understand by downloading files from Internet?

Ans. Downloading is transferring files from a server to a client's computer.

5 Give the name of any two Websites which are used to send E-mail.

Ans. www.gmail.com and www.rediffmail.com

6 How can a Word document be sent alongwith an E-mail?

Ans. By attaching the Word file with an E-mail.

7 How multiple E-mail addresses are defined in To, Cc, Bcc field?

Ans. By using comma between E-mail addresses.

8 Write one advantage and one limitation of E-mail over traditional mail.

or Why is E-mail so popular over conventional mail?

or Mention any two advantages of E-mail over conventional mail. **CBSE 2010, 08, 04, 03**

Ans. Advantages

- E-mail is extremely cost effective.
- E-mail takes lesser time for transmitting data than conventional mail.

Disadvantage

- Need of Internet connection to send/receive mail.

9 How is newsgroup different from E-mail messages?

Ans. Unlike E-mail messages, which are visible only to the sender and specified recipients, newsgroup messages can be read by anyone, who view the group that they are posted in.

10 Write down one main advantage of E-Shopping. **CBSE 2018**

Ans. One main advantage of E-Shopping is wide variety/range of products are available and convenience of shopping at home.

11 State one advantage of video conferencing over personal face-to-face business meetings.

Ans. Video conferencing allows you to interact with many people face-to-face without being at same place.

12 How many forms can E-learning occur?

Ans. E-learning can be CD-ROM based, network based, Intranet or Internet based.

13 What are e-groups? **CBSE 2018**

Ans. An e-groups is a group of persons who come together over the Internet for a specific or common purpose using the best Internet communication tools to share ideas, different opinions, experiences and to learn from each other.

14 Give the name of five Websites for locating someone online.

Ans. Facebook, WhitePages, SuperPages, MySpace and BlackPlanet.

15 What is the mean by SMS?

Ans. SMS (Short Message Service) commonly referred to as text messaging, is a service for sending short messages up to 160 characters to mobile devices.

Short Answer (SA) Type Questions

1 What is search engine? What is its usage? Give example.

or

What is a search engine? Give one example of search engine. **CBSE 2006, 02**

Ans. A search engine is a Website that lets you search the Internet for Websites on specific topics. Search engines turn the Web into a powerful tool for finding information on any topic. There are several benefits of using search engine like,

- Search engines do have the ability to provide refined or more precise results.
- Search engine provides a wealth of information for professional and personal use.
  e.g. Google

2 When using a search engine, what does a minus sign used with keywords in the search box mean?

Ans. Search engine is a Website that provides the required data on specific content. It also allows users to enter keywords related to particular topics and retrieve information. The minus sign in front of a word or phrase means that it includes first term but not the second term.

3 Why uploading and downloading a file is required? Explain with example.

or

What is the need of uploading and downloading files?

Ans. When we need a file which is located at the server end, we have to download the file that means transmission of file from server to user's computer. Similarly, if we want to share something like file, picture etc., we have to upload that file or picture on the Internet that means transmission of file from user computer to server.

4 What is chatting? Is it necessary to be online while chatting?

Ans. Chatting is the textual or multimedia conversation over the Internet. It is a real-time communication between two users *via* computer. It is widely interactive text based communication process that takes places over the Internet. Yes, it is necessary to be online, while chatting.

5 What is an E-mail? Write two advantages of an E-mail. **CBSE 2012, 10**

Ans. E-mail (Electronic mail) is a popular Internet service, which is used for sending or receiving messages electronically over a computer network.
The advantages are as follows:

- E-mail is a cost effective medium of communication.
- Ease of use.

6 Mention some disadvantages of an E-mail.

Ans. Refer to text on Page No. 24.

7 Match Web services/URL given in column 'A' with corresponding Web services/URL given in column 'B': **CBSE 2018**

Column A	*Column B*
Social Networking Site	https://www.amazon.in
https://web.skype.com/	E-Banking
E-Shopping	Video Conferencing
https://www.onlinesbi.in/	https://www.facebook.com/

Ans. Match the following

Social Networking site → https://www.facebook.com/
https://web.skype.com/ → video conferencing
E-shopping → https://www.amazon.in
https://www.onlinesbi.in/ → E-banking

8 Briefly explain the significance of video conferencing. **CBSE 2019**

Ans. (*i*) Video conferencing reduces your travel costs by working remotely and also increases productivity through collaborative working.

(*ii*) Many people can share their videos with each other at the same time.

9 List some benefits of E-learning.

Ans. Some benefits of E-learning are as follows:

(*i*) It is self paced.
(*ii*) It can work on any location and anytime.
(*iii*) Online computer based courses are available.
(*iv*) Reduces travel time and travel cost.

10 Mention the services which are provided by transactional category of an E-banking.

Ans. Refer to text on Page No. 26. **CBSE 2014**

11 What do you mean by E-shopping? Give three advantages of it. **CBSE 2015**

Ans. Refer to text on Page No. 26.

12 What are the differences between MMS and SMS?

Ans. Differences between MMS and SMS are as follows :

MMS	*SMS*
MMS stands for Multimedia Messaging Service.	SMS stands for Short Message Service.
MMS are used to send multimedia files attaching with a message such as pictures, music, audio and video.	SMS is used for sending text based messages including symbols and emoji.

EXAM PRACTICE

13 What is E-learning? Explain any two merits of E-learning. **CBSE SQP Term-II**

Ans. Refer to test on page no. 25.

14 Explain any two differences between 3G and 4G mobile technologies. **CBSE SQP Term-II**

Ans. Refer to text on page no. 29.

Long Answer (LA) Type Questions

1 When using a search engine to search, then would you use quotation marks around search terms? **CBSE 2007**

Ans. Quotation marks should be used around a phrase or search terms. Surrounding terms with quotation marks limit the search results to only those Web pages that contain the exact phrase, we have specified.

Doing this ensures that, the concept will be searched for as a whole and not picked apart by the search engine or we can say, without the quotation marks, the results will include any page that contains the words we have used regardless of what order those words are in.

2 Transferring files through E-mail is restricted due to file size. Justify.

Ans Over the Internet, a message will often pass through several mail transfer agents to reach the recipients. Each of these has to store the message before forwarding it on and many therefore, need to impose size limits.

The result is that while large attachments may internally send within an organisation, they are unreliable when sending across Internet.

e.g. In general, 10 MB is considered safe for the maximum size of an E-mail but, Google's gmail service increased its limit to 25 MB.

3 Discuss the structure of an E-mail message.

Ans. In an E-mail message, you will see the following fields which are as follows:

(*i*) **To** Mail-id of recipient.

(*ii*) **Cc** (Carbon copy) It allows you to send the same mail message to multiple recipients at the same time.

(*iii*) **Bcc** (Blind carbon copy) It allows the sender to send same mail message to multiple recipients without letting them (To and Cc) know that some other person has also received the same message.

(*iv*) **Subject** It is the title of the mail message.

(*v*) **Body** It contains the text of a message.

(*vi*) **Attachment** It allows you to attach one or more files or documents like Word document, image, video, Web page etc.

(*vii*) **Other options** Other options like emoticons, bold, italics, hyperlink etc., are used to make message more interactive.

(*viii*) **Formatting** Using the formatting tab, you can format the message.

(*ix*) **Send button** Once you complete the E-mail message, click at Send button to send the E-mail message.

4 List some advantages and disadvantages of an E-mail.

Ans. Advantages of E-mail are as follows:

(*i*) **Low cost** We can send the E-mail to other person at a very low cost. It requires only Internet connection cost to send the E-mail.

(*ii*) **Speed** E-mail can be sent at a very high speed.

(*iii*) **Waste reduction** E-mail goes a long way towards reducing the cluster of papers in the modern office, not to mention saving many trees.

(*iv*) **Ease of use** It is easy to send an E-mail as compared to traditional letter.

Disadvantages of E-mail are as follows:

(*i*) **Hardware requirement** You need a computer to read or print E-mail.

(*ii*) **Impermanent** Your sent mail messages can be altered in all the ways.

(*iii*) **A hasty medium** It is a limitation because E-mail is so easy to use, it is also easy to send a message that you later regret.

(*iv*) **Hard to convey emotions** Without the extra clues of voice, posture and expression, it is difficult to understand what someone really means in a message.

5 Write short notes on the following terms: **CBSE 2014**

(*i*) Information retrieval (*ii*) E-banking
(*iii*) Online shopping (*iv*) E-reservation
(*v*) E-groups

Ans. (*i*) **Information retrieval** It refers to the process of accessing the information that is stored on the Internet.

(*ii*) **E-banking** It refers to the automated delivery of new and traditional banking products and services directly to customers over the Internet.

(*iii*) **Online shopping** It refers to the activity of purchasing items from different Websites on Internet.

(*iv*) **E-reservation** It refers to the process that helps users to reserve movie, train and airline tickets as well as hotel rooms through Internet.

(*v*) **E-groups** It refers to an online environment where users sharing common views and ideas that come together to meet and discuss topics of their interest.

6 Give the benefits of social networking.

Ans. Benefits of social networking are as follows:

(*i*) People sharing views can connect and form a group.
(*ii*) Individuals from all around the world can connect and thereby know about new cultures and languages etc.
(*iii*) It is an easy and cost effective way to reach your consumers and people in your network.
(*iv*) It helps in building credibility amongst the customer.
(*v*) For business purposes, connecting with your customers on a personal and professional level will make them loyal to your company and brand.
(*vi*) Connecting with people in your friend's networks or your work networks will benefit you in the long run. It will help you to gain connections which may be useful in the future.

7 What are the dangers associated with social networking? **CBSE 2013**

Ans. Dangers associated with social networking are as follows:

(*i*) **Lack of anonymity** Social networking usually requires you to input your name, location, age, gender and many other types of personal information.
(*ii*) **Scams and harassment** Being online you are at risk of facing cases of harassment, cyber stalking, online scams and theft identity.
(*iii*) **Time consuming** If you are new to social networking, learning the process can be very time consuming.
(*iv*) **The illusion of security** The Internet is definitely not secured as social or human hackers can hack one's personal account.
(*v*) **Isolation** Social networking sites do not provide isolation. As, once information is posted to a social networking site, it is no longer private.

Application Oriented Questions

1 Somya wants to collect some information regarding the history of India.

(*i*) What is the fastest and easiest way of doing this that saves her efforts as well?
(*ii*) Write down the following steps in the correct order to show, how Somya could find information.
(a) Type keywords.
(b) Look at the list of Websites starting at the top.
(c) Load a Search engine.
(d) Click the Search button.
(e) Open the Web browser.

Ans. (*i*) Online search using search engine.
(*ii*) (e) Open the Web browser
(c) Load a search engine
(a) Type keywords
(d) Click the Search button
(b) Look at the list of Websites starting at the top.

2 Anila works in a Multinational Company (MNC) and needs to work online from home also. She requires fast Internet connection. Which type of Internet connection in your view would be best suited for her? Apart from browsing on the Internet she will require uploading/downloading of files to/from remote sites. Which protocol will help her to perform this activity?

Ans. She should prefer broadband connection. FTP (File Transfer Protocol) protocol will help her in uploading and downloading of files.

3 Now-a-days people can communicate to each other with the help of E-mail facility. It is gradually replacing other communication means such as telephone, post.

(*i*) What is meant by the term E-mail?
(*ii*) Which one of the following is an advantage of using E-mail compared to using post?
(a) Same delivery time anywhere in the world.
(b) The E-mail can contain pictures.
(c) You can send it anywhere.

Ans. (*i*) E-mail means Electronic Mail. It is a basic Internet service for sending or receiving messages electronically over the Internet.
(*ii*) (a) Same delivery time anywhere in the world.

4 Mary has a prepaid Internet plan. She has a data limit of 14 GB. The average size of an E-mail with an attachment that Mary downloads is 1.4 MB. Approximately, how many E-mails can Mary download without exceeding her data limit?

(a) 1.4 (b) 14 (c) 1000 (d) 10000

Ans. (*d*) 10000

5 Gargi set-up the following Auto Delete options on her Web-based E-mail account.

Inbox	Never
Sent	Never
Draft	Never
Personal	Never
User created	Never

EXAM PRACTICE

Trash	Older than 1 month
Filtered spam	Submit

What is the most likely reason, she has set the Trash folder to delete 'Older than 1 month'?

Gargi wants

(a) all E-mails to have a delete date.

(b) all sent E-mails to be deleted after 1 month.

(c) all deleted E-mails to only remain in the Trash folder for 1 month.

(d) all E-mails in her inbox to be moved to the Trash folder after 1 month.

Ans (*c*) all deleted E-mails to only remain in the Trash folder for 1 month.

6 Ram wants to attach a CD-ROM to an E-mail. Can it be possible? Also, give some items that can be attached to an E-mail.

Ans. No, it is not possible.

You can attach following items to an E-mail:

- A Word document
- A digital photograph
- A program
- A slide show
- Audio file
- Video file
- Web page

7 Sharvan Joshi is a student of Political Science and is a keen researcher of political issues related to various countries and states. He wants to share his research and his own opinions on these issues on day-to-day basis with everyone on World Wide Web (WWW).

He is also interested in collecting views of others to enhance his research and knowledge related to his area of interest. He belongs to a middle class family and cannot afford his own Website. Also being a non-technical person he cannot create a dynamic Website to deal with day-to-day inputs.

(*i*) Suggest an easy way for Sharvan to achieve the same.

(*ii*) Also, name two popularly used free services that can help Sharvan in this regard.

Ans. (*i*) Sharvan should develop a blog.

(*ii*) Twitter and Facebook.

8 As life gets busy, it becomes difficult for everyone to keep track with school and college friends, old colleagues, old neighbours and favourite teachers. It is important to keep in touch with all your near and dear ones. At times, people sitting miles away doing similar kind of activity or solving similar kind of problems can help you to achieve goals faster by sharing their experience.

Similarly, people belonging to different socio-economic background can change your perspective and can enhance your understanding of various cultures. **CBSE 2011**

(*i*) Suggest any two real-time tools that are suitable for the above mentioned activities.

(*ii*) What is the generic name used for such tools?

Ans. (*i*) Twitter and Facebook.

(*ii*) Social networking.

9 *Read the case study given below and attempt any 4 sub-questions (out of 5). Each sub-question carries 1 mark.*

Mr. Harish, an accountant, works in an IT firm and due to the pandemic, has been asked to work from home. He has set up his online office at his home. He has purchased a laptop, web camera and other accessories. Now, he has started working from home and performs his various duties online.

(i) Mr. Harish wants to hold an online meeting with the company's client such that he can interact as well as see them. Which web service should he avail?

(ii) Mr. Pritish sends an email to Harish requesting him to prepare the balance sheet. Which network protocol is involved during this email communication?

(iii) The company's financial head needs to send some high security documents to Mr. Harish. He uses an application which supports the ____________ protocol.

(iv) In order to gather some information on latest accounting trends, Mr. Harish has to do some research. He can do this by locating sites online using a ________ .

(v) Joseph, the company secretary sends a link to Mr. Harish which contains important company files. What should he do in order to access the files? **CBSE SQP Term-II**

Ans. (i) Mr. Harish can use video conferencing service with the help of which he can interact as well as see them. Video conferencing can be possible through application like Skype, Zoom, etc.

(ii) SMTP(Simple Mail Transfer Protocol) and POP(Post Office Protocol) are involved during an email communication.

(iii) SSH(Secure Shell) protocol is a set of standards and an associated network protocol that allows establishing a secure channel between a local and a remote computer.

(iv) Mr.Harish can locate file using a search engine/web browser.

(v) Mr.Harish should download the files from the link.

Unit Test 1

Multiple Choice Questions

1 How can you send E-mail to more than one recipient at the same time?
(a) By sending an E-mail with a notice to be forwarded to the rest of the recipients.
(b) This is not possible at this time.
(c) By adding a second recipient in the "Cc" field.
(d) By adding all recipient's E-mail address in the "To" field separated by semicolons.

2 The ARPANET project was sponsored by
(a) The US department of Internet
(b) The US department of defense
(c) The US telecom department
(d) The US military department

3 Which one of the following is a search engine?
(a) Google (b) Rediffmail
(c) India times (d) Yahoo mail

Fill in the Blanks

4 The Internet is most often used for the exchange of ...... and ....

5 ...... is an interactive text based communication process that takes place over the Internet.

6 Chrome and Opera are the examples of ....

True or False

7 IP address is given to every computer for its unique identification.

8 A Web browser is an application that resides on the client's computer.

9 FTP is used for uploading and downloading files.

Very Short Answer Type Questions

10 What is E-reservation?

11 Can any computer facilitate you with E-mailing?

12 Write any two Web servers, which are commonly used for hosting Websites.

Short Answer Type Questions

13 Define the following.
(i) HTTP
(ii) ARPANET
(iii) Intranet

14 Due to lack of time Mr. Amit cannot continue his studies in college, so please suggest him the easiest way to keep his studies continue and how?

15 What are benefits of using wireless Internet connections?

Long Answer Type Questions

16 What is the role of TCP/IP in working of Internet?

17 What does it mean, when we say that Lynx is a text-based Web browser? Name some graphical Web browsers.

18 Briefly describe the three elements used by a search engine. Also, list out some popular search engine.

Application Oriented Questions

19 Read the following paragraph and find any two Internet services used. Also define each of them in one line.
When Neeru visited her facebook account, she saw an update about a job opportunity. She sent her resume on the given E-mail address. When she went back home, she saw her mother talking to Vishwas on laptop, who live in US. They were discussing about blog written by him. She received a prepaid package from myntra.com, for which she has placed on order. Neeru lives to login in Yahoo! messenger to talk to her friends and is a member of various groups over Internet.

20 Saurabh creates a Website to advertise his business. He choose an ISP to host his Website.
(i) State what Saurabh should have on home page to help users navigate his Website?
(ii) State what ISP means?

Unit Test 2

Multiple Choice Questions

1 ...... is the protocol suite for current Internet.
(a) WWW (b) TCP/IP
(c) SMTP (d) All of these

2 Symbols used to express emotions in an E-mail are known as
(a) emoticons (b) cartoons
(c) E-symbols (d) None of these

3 Service of M-banking is
(a) Shopping (b) Learning
(c) SMS service (d) Reservation

Fill in the Blanks

4 A .... room or online forum allows user to communicate through typed messages, which are displayed almost instantly.

5 A two way video phone conversation among multiple participants is called ....

6 The .... are documents that use HTTP.

True or False

7 A domain name must be registered, so that one domain name does not represent more than one server.

8 Google Chrome is the most popular search engine.

9 The words typed in search box are called keywords.

Very Short Answer Type Questions

10 What is the use of 4G mobile technology?

11 Mention the FTP based communication channels.

12 Sometimes you find the Web pages load very slowly in your home PC. Why?

Short Answer Type Questions

13 What do you understand by Web portal? Also write its advantages.

14 Search engines are programs that search documents. It works with various elements. Define any one out of them.

15 Name the different volunteer organisations that are responsible for governing and administering the Internet.

Long Answer Type Questions

16 Expand and explain the following terms
(i) HTML (ii) WWW
(iii) WiMax (iv) LTE

17 What do you understand by e-governance? Mention some advantages and disadvantages of e-governance.

18 Write the steps to search the following queries:
(i) Information about the book 'Discovery of India'.
(ii) Information about colleges in India offering bachelor course in 'Economics'.

Application Oriented Questions

19 Emoticons and acronyms are frequently used in E-mail messages and chatting.
(i) Why are emoticons and acronyms included in E-mail messages and chatting?
(ii) Briefly describe any five emoticons.
(iii) Briefly describe any five acronyms.

20 Aamir likes to remain always up-to-date in emerging technologies. Due to his studies and sports activities, he does not get sufficient time to either read the newspaper or magazine on a daily basis. What should he do to pursue his interest?

Unit Test 3

Multiple Choice Questions

1 The WWW uses the .... protocol.

(a) FTP (b) HTTP

(c) Web (d) SMTP

2 A Website is a collection of

(a) audio and video files

(b) HTML pages

(c) graphics

(d) All of the above

3 Which of the following is not a feature/service of the Web?

(a) E-mail (b) Telnet

(c) CPU (d) Chat

Fill in the Blanks

4 .... is a electronic message sent from one computer to another through the Internet.

5 The unique address of a Web page is called ....

6 A ...... engine is a software program used by a search site to retrieve information.

True or False

7 Mozilla Firefox is a text based Web browser.

8 An online talk using text messages is called video conferencing.

9 Amazon is a popular website for online shopping.

Very Short Answer Type Questions

10 Write any two advantages of Web portal.

11 How many types of URL are there? Name them.

12 Describe the role of search engine.

Short Answer Type Questions

13 How downloading is different from uploading?

14 Expand the following domain name extensions used with Web address.

(i) .com (ii) .gov

15 Explain the elements of E-mail account.

Long Answer Type Questions

16 Explain mobile technologies with its various types.

17 Briefly explain the following terms

(i) E-learning

(ii) FTP

(iii) Social networking

18 What are the advantages and disadvantages of online shopping over traditional shopping?

Application Oriented Questions

19 Mawana Sugar Private Limited has a head office in Mawana and a large number of branches nationwise. The head office used video conferencing to communicate with the branch managers.

(i) Identify the requirements to be filled by each branch for video conferencing.

(ii) Give some advantages of using video conferencing.

20 Rani is researching history of computers on the Internet. She uses a search engine.

(i) The computer sometimes takes a long time to respond when Rani enters a question into the search engine. Give a reason why this might happen?

(ii) The search engine returned a large number of links when she entered computers. What should Rani do to reduce the number of links?

CHAPTER

03

Unit II

Introduction to HTML

Chapter Checklist

- HTML Elements or Tags
- HTML Structure
- Creating and Saving a HTML Document
- Viewing HTML Document in a Browser
- Basic HTML Tags
  - <HTML> Tag
  - <HEAD> Tag
  - <TITLE> Tag
  - <BODY> Tag
  - <FONT> Tag
  - <BASEFONT> Tag
  - <CENTER> Tag
  - Comment Tag
  - Heading Tags
  - Paragraph Tag
  - Line Break Tag
  - Horizontal Rule Tag
- Style Tags
- HTML Lists

HTML is a markup language, which is used to define the layout and attribute of a World Wide Web (WWW) document as well as to create links between Web pages.

HTML is the underlying foundation of Website design. It is a subset of SGML (Standard Generalised Markup Language) and a high-level markup language.

It was developed by Tim Berners Lee in 1990.

HTML is a short form of **HyperText Markup Language**, which means

(*i*) **HyperText** is simply a piece of text that has some extra features like formatting, images, multimedia and links to another document.

(*ii*) **Markup Language** is a way of writing layout information within documents.

HTML is a page layout and hyperlink specification language. It allows images and other objects to be embedded that can be used to create interactive forms. HTML documents are described through HTML elements or tags.

HTML Elements or Tags

HTML is written in the form of tags. A tag or element refers to a string enclosed within angular brackets (< and >). HTML elements represent semantics or meaning.

- HTML tags are predefined and are not case-sensitive.
- The opening tags are written within the less than (<) and greater than (>) signs. e.g. `<HTML>`
- The closing tags are written within the < and > signs with a forward slash (/) appended before the name of the tag.

  e.g. `</HTML>`
- The attributes are always specified in the opening tags, which provide additional information about that tag. It comes in name/value pairs like name = "value".

  e.g. `<FONT size ="5">`

There are two kinds of elements, i.e. container elements and empty elements.

Container Elements

These types of HTML elements always wrap around the text or graphics which come in a set with an opening as well as a closing tag.

In other words, HTML tags that include both On and Off tags are known as *container tags*.

e.g.

<HTML>...</HTML>

Empty Elements

On the other hand, the empty elements are standalone tags, i.e. empty tags do not have to be wrapped around text or graphics and do not require a closing tag.

In other words, HTML tags that include only On tag and there is no Off tag then, these tags are known as *empty tags*.

e.g.

<HR> inserts a horizontal line

 adds a line break

The Needed Apps/Software to make HTML Files

Firstly, HTML is written in plain text. That means, you do not need any fancy software programs to create your HTML files. You need a simple text-editor, i.e. already on your system.

For MACs, that would be Simple Text and for Windows, Notepad or WordPad.

Secondly, you need a browser. The most common browser is Microsoft Internet Explorer.

But, other browsers such as Opera, Google Chrome and Mozilla Firefox can also be used.

HTML Structure

HTML document is a combination of various tags, which define the structure and appearance of the Web page.

Following four basic elements are always present in every HTML document:

(*i*) The <HTML> tag tells the browser that this is an HTML document. You must begin your html files with this tag and must end your HTML file with matching closing tag.

(*ii*) The <HEAD> tag is used for text and tags that do not appear directly on the Web page. It acts as a header of file and contains some information like setting the title of the Web page.

(*iii*) The <TITLE> tag contains the document title. This tag lies between <HEAD> and </HEAD> tags. The title specified inside this tag appears on the browser's title bar.

(*iv*) The <BODY> tag is used for text and tags that appears directly on the Web page. It helps us to create a look and feel of the Web page. It holds all your content words, pictures and other stuff.

The most basic structure needed for creation of any Web page are as follows:

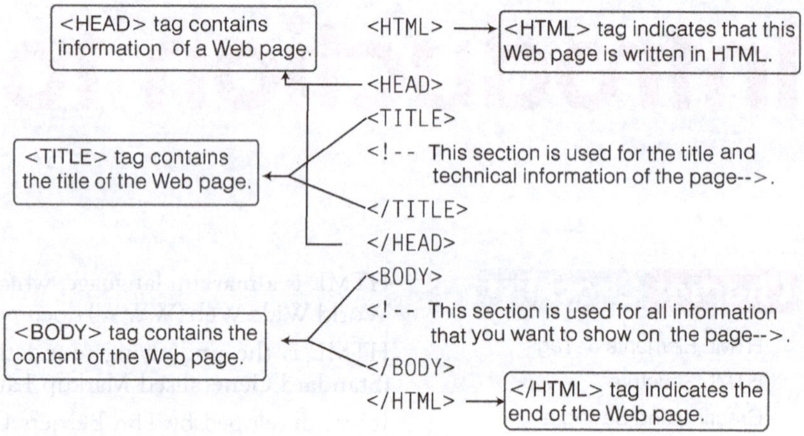

Creating and Saving a HTML Document

Since, HTML documents are just text files, they can be written in any simple text editor like Notepad, FrontPage, Dreamweaver, WordPad etc.

If you are using a Notepad to create a HTML document, the steps are as follows:

Step 1 Open Notepad by clicking at **Start → All Programs → Accessories → Notepad.**

Step 2 Type the HTML document code in Notepad as shown in the following figure:

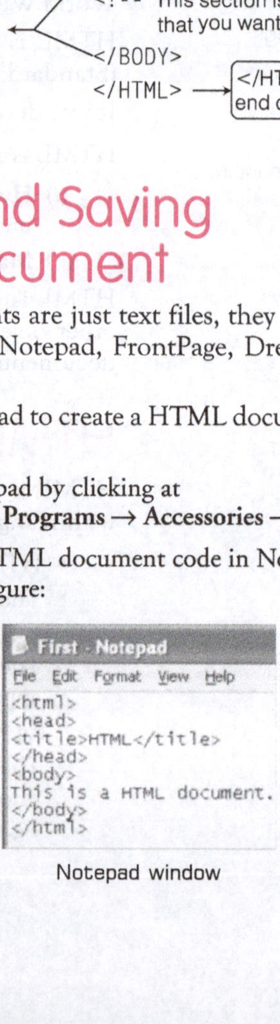

Notepad window

Step 3 To save the document, click at **File** menu → **Save As** command.

Step 4 The **Save As** dialog box will appear as shown in the following figure:

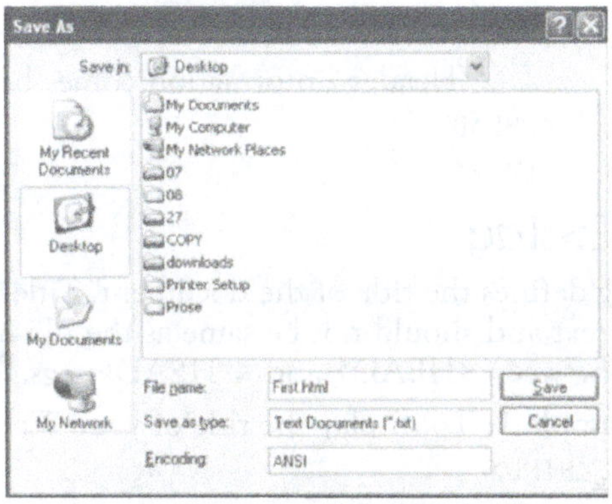

Save As dialog box

Step 5 In **Save As** dialog box, after selecting the desired folder, give the desired file name along with the extension **.htm** or **.html** in the **File name:** box and then, click **Save** button. In the above figure, we have saved out HTML document under name **First.html.**

Viewing HTML Document in a Browser

You can view HTML document in any Web browser such as Internet Explorer, Mozilla Firefox, Opera, Apple Safari, Netscape Navigator, Google Chrome etc. Here, we are using Internet Explorer Web browser to view the HTML document.

To view an HTML document, the steps are as follows:

Step 1 Open Internet Explorer, by clicking at **Start → All Programs → Internet Explorer.**

Step 2 To open the document First.html, select **File** menu → **Open.**

Step 3 The **Open** dialog box will appear as in the following figure:

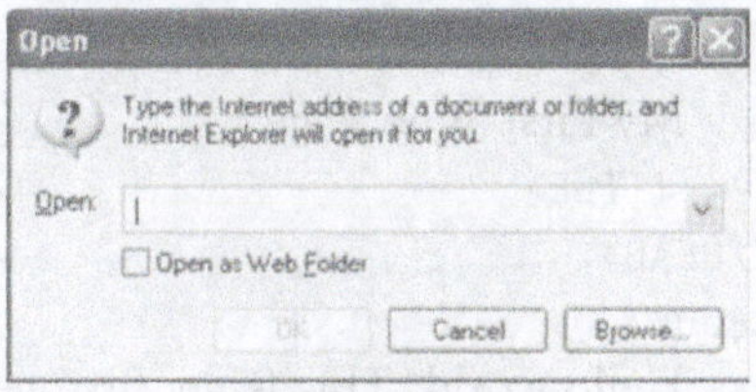

Open dialog box

Step 4 Click the **Browse...** button, the **Microsoft Internet Explorer** dialog box will appear and select the file **First** as shown in the following figure:

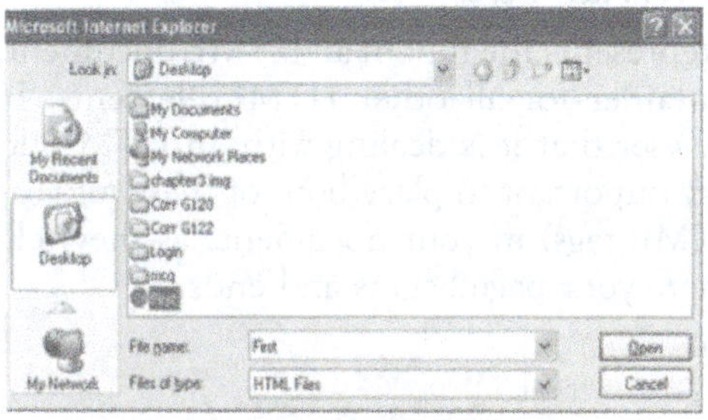

Microsoft Internet Explorer dialog box

Step 5 Click **Open** button, and then click **OK** button.

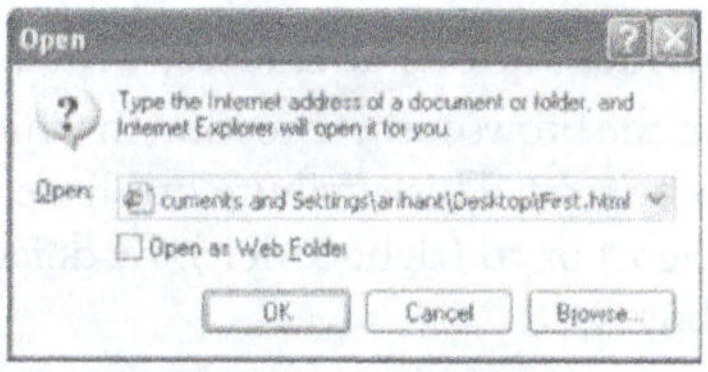

Open dialog box with path

Step 6 Now, you will be viewing your desired page as shown in the following figure:

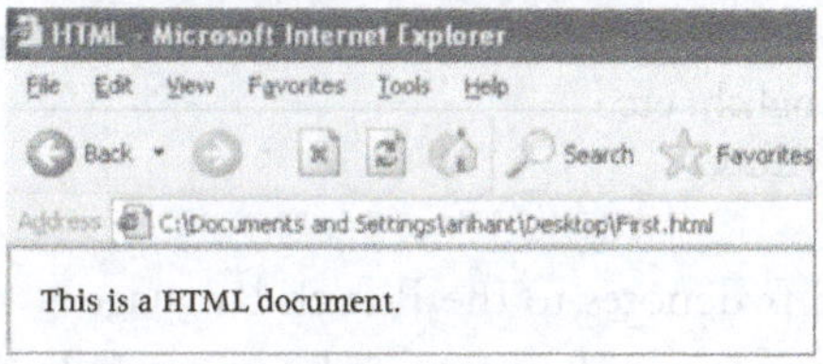

- To view the source code (coding of the Web page) of the current page in a Web browser, Right click on the Web page → Select View Source from context menu.
- The order in which opening and ending tags appear, follow an important rule. If a tag is opened within another, then that tag must close before the other tag is closed.

Check Point 01

1. Which extension is used to save HTML code?
2. Which of the following elements contains an opening as well as a closing tag?
   (a) Empty (b) NULL
   (c) Container (d) Containing
3. Write the names of four basic HTML structure tags.

Basic HTML Tags

HTML provides some basic tags which are required for HTML code:

<HTML>Tag

It represents the root of an HTML document, so it acts as a container for all other HTML elements. It informs the browser that it is dealing with an HTML document. It is very important to place both of these tags (open and close HTML tags) in your documents as they tell the browser, where your page begins and ends.

e.g.

```
<HTML>
:
</HTML>
```

Attributes of <HTML> Tag

This tag provides various attributes, which are as follows:

- **dir** It tells the browser the direction in which the displayed text is to be read. This attribute can have values either ltr (left-to-right) or rtl (right-to-left). By default, the value of dir attribute is ltr.

  Syntax

  ```
  <HTML dir="ltr"/"rtl">
  ```

- **lang** It specifies the language of an element content and attribute values. Now-a-days, Web pages are designed in many languages. e.g. German, Hindi, Greek, Spanish, English, etc.

  Syntax

  ```
  <HTML lang="fr">
  ```

Here, fr denotes to the French language.

Some common language codes are as follows:

Code	Language	Code	Language
en	English	hi	Hindi
fr	French	es	Spanish
de	German	ar	Arabic
it	Italian	ru	Russian
nl	Dutch	zh	Chinese
el	Greek	ja	Japanese

<HEAD> Tag

This element is a container for all the header elements. The <HEAD> tag must include a title for the document that can include scripts, styles, meta information and many more. The second line of your HTML document should be <HEAD>.

The content contained in the head section of your document provides information to the browsers and search engines but, it is not displayed directly on the Web page. The end of the head tag is indicated by </HEAD>.

e.g.

```
<HTML>
  <HEAD>
     //Header information comes here
  </HEAD>
</HTML>
```

<TITLE> Tag

This tag defines the title of the document. Title must be a simple text and should not be same as the file name. It is placed between <HEAD> and </HEAD> tags.

Example 1. To display the title of your Web page.

```
<HTML>
  <HEAD>
    <TITLE>
      This is the title of my page.
    </TITLE>
  </HEAD>
</HTML>
```

Output

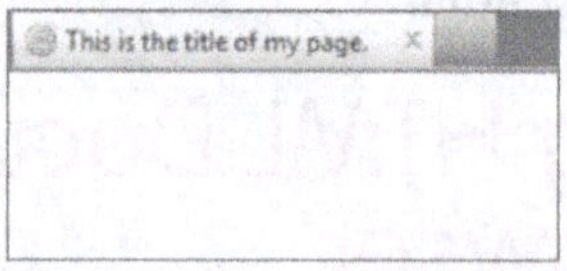

<BODY> Tag

This tag defines the document's body. It is used to set the basic page characteristics. It contains all the necessary contents of a HTML document, such as text, hyperlinks, images, tables, lists etc. The content of your Web page is placed in between the opening <BODY> and closing </BODY> tags.

The <BODY> tag is opened just after the head section is closed. It is closed just before closing the <HTML> tag.

Example 2. To display document's body.

```
<HTML>
  <HEAD>
    <TITLE>
      My First Web Page
    </TITLE>
  </HEAD>
  <BODY>
      Hello world. This is my first web page.
  </BODY>
</HTML>
```

Output

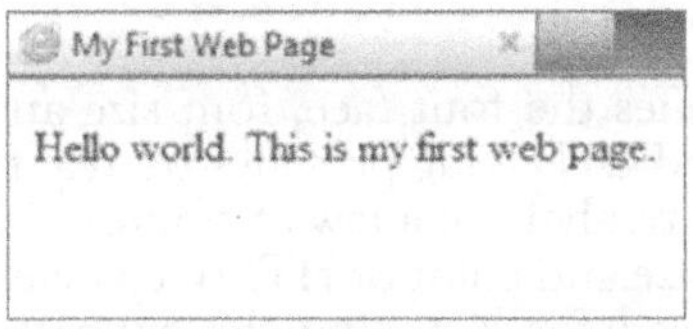

Note The titles can be maximum upto 64 characters long and the length of an attribute value is limited to 1024 characters.

Attributes of <BODY> Tag

This tag provides various attributes, which are as follows:

background

This attribute specifies a background image for a document. HTML supports various graphics format such as .gif, .jpg etc.

Syntax

```
<BODY background="URL">
```

Where, URL may be an image name or a path of an image.

Example 3. To display background image in a Web page using background attribute.

```
<HTML>
  <HEAD>
   <TITLE>
     Background Image
   </TITLE>
  </HEAD>
  <BODY background ="image.jpg">
  </BODY>
</HTML>
```

Output

text

This attribute specifies the color of the text in a document.

Syntax

```
<BODY text="color_name|hex_number|rgb_number">
```

Attribute Values

Value	Description
color_name	Specifies the text-color with a color name (like "red").
hex_number	Specifies the text-color with a hexadecimal code (like "#FF0000") where, # stands for the color number.
rgb_number	Specifies the text-color with a rgb (red, green, blue) code (like "rgb(255,0,0)").

e.g.

```
<HTML>
  <BODY text="red">
     Arihant Publication
  </BODY>
</HTML>
```

bgcolor

This attribute specifies the background color of a document.

Syntax

```
<BODY bgcolor="color_name|hex_number|rgb_number">
```

e.g.

```
<HTML>
  <BODY bgcolor="red">
  </BODY>
</HTML>
```

link

This attribute specifies the color of an unvisited link in a document. The default color of link attribute is blue (#0000FF).

Syntax

```
<BODY link="color_name|hex_number|rgb_number">
```

e.g.

```
<HTML>
  <BODY link="red">
  </BODY>
</HTML>
```

alink

This attribute specifies the color of an active link in a document (a link get activated when it is clicked). The default color of an alink attribute is red (#FF0000).

Syntax

```
<BODY alink="color_name|hex_number|rgb_number">
```

e.g.

```
<HTML>
  <BODY alink="blue">
  </BODY>
</HTML>
```

vlink

This attribute specifies the color of a visited link in a document. The default color of vlink attribute is purple (#800080).

Syntax

```
<BODY vlink="color_name|hex_number|rgb_number">
```

e.g.

```
<HTML>
  <BODY vlink="blue">
  </BODY>
</HTML>
```

topmargin

Sets a topmargin (distance between the top of the document and the top of the browser window) of your body element.

Syntax

```
<BODY topmargin="value">
```

Example 4. To set a topmargin.

```
<HTML>
  <HEAD>
    <TITLE>Topmargin</TITLE>
  </HEAD>
  <BODY topmargin="65">
    Arihant Publications is one such reputed
    name in the field of books which has the
    best available books in the market.
  </BODY>
</HTML>
```

Output

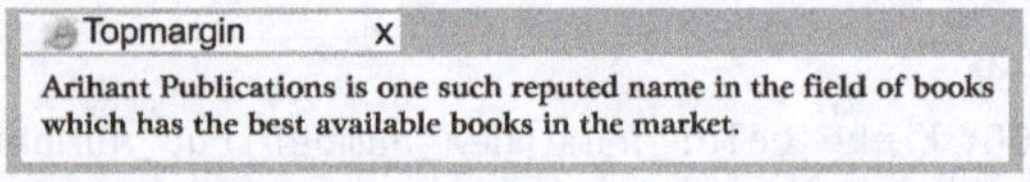

leftmargin

Sets a left hand margin (distance between the left side of the document and the left edge of the browser window) of your body element.

Syntax

```
<BODY leftmargin="value">
```

Example 5. To set a leftmargin

```
<HTML>
  <HEAD>
    <TITLE> Leftmargin </TITLE>
  </HEAD>
  <BODY leftmargin="65">
    Arihant Publications is one such reputed
    name in the field of books which has the best
    available books in the market.
  </BODY>
</HTML>
```

Output

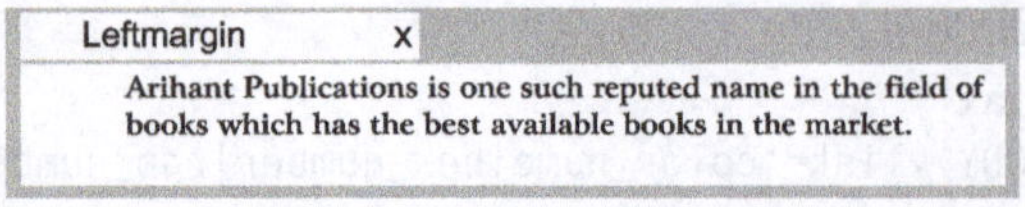

<FONT> Tag

This tag specifies the font face, font size and font color of the text. The <FONT> tag provides no real functionality by itself but with the help of a few attributes, this tag is used to change style, size and color of HTML text elements. This tag is generally used for changing the appearance of a short segment of text. It can be set for a character, sentence or entire document.

Attributes of <FONT> Tag

Following are the attributes of <FONT> tag:

size

This attribute specifies the size of the text inside a <FONT> tag. The range of accepted values goes from 1 (the smallest) to 7 (the largest). We can also set the relative size to the current size using (+) ve or (–) ve sign.
e.g. size = +2

Syntax `<FONT size="number">`

Attribute Value

Value	*Description*
number	A number from 1 to 7, that defines the size of the text. Default number of value is 3.

Example 6. To display a paragraph in size 3.

```
<HTML>
  <HEAD>
    <TITLE>
      Font Size
    </TITLE>
  </HEAD>
  <BODY>
    <FONT size="3">
      This is the default size.
    </FONT>
  </BODY>
</HTML>
```

Output

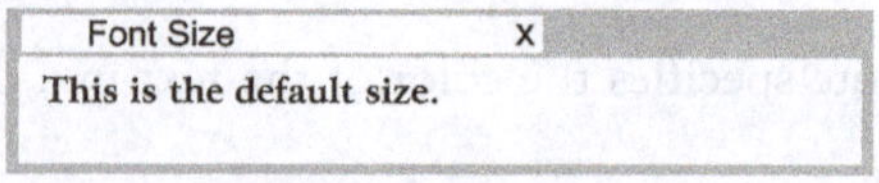

face

This attribute specifies the font name or type face of the text inside a <FONT> tag.

Syntax `<FONT face="font_family">`

Attribute Value

Value	*Description*
font_family	The font name of the text specifies a prioritised list of several fonts, separate the names with a comma (like <FONT face="verdana, arial, sans-serif">.

Example 7. To display a text in verdana font.

```
<HTML>
  <HEAD>
    <TITLE>
      Font Face
    </TITLE>
  </HEAD>
  <BODY>
    <FONT face="verdana">
      This is some text!
    </FONT>
  </BODY>
</HTML>
```

Output

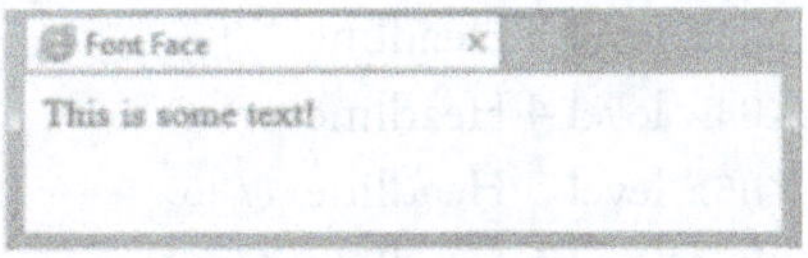

color

This attribute specifies the color of the text inside a <FONT> tag.

Syntax

```
<FONT color="color_name|hex_number|rgb_number">
```

e.g.

```
<HTML>
  <BODY>
    <FONT color="red">
      This is some text!
    </FONT>
  </BODY>
</HTML>
```

Some examples of using <FONT> tag are as follows:

- <FONT size="3" color="orange">
  This is an example!</FONT>
- <FONT face="arial" color="green">
  This is a table!</FONT>
- <FONT size =+"2"> ABC </FONT>

<BASEFONT> Tag

This tag specifies a default font color, font size or font family for all the text in a document that follows it, which is only supported by Internet Explorer Web browser.

Ending tag (</BASEFONT>) of basefont is optional. This tag can also have face, size and color attributes, which can be used exactly in the same way as face, size and color attributes of <FONT> tag.

Attributes of <BASEFONT> Tag

Following are the attributes of <BASEFONT> tag:

color

This attribute specifies the color of the text inside a <BASEFONT> tag.

Syntax

```
<BASEFONT color="color_name|hex_number|rgb_number">
```

face

This attribute specifies the face type of the text inside a <BASEFONT> tag.

Syntax

```
<BASEFONT face="font_family">
```

size

This attribute specifies the size of the text inside a <BASEFONT> tag.

Syntax

```
<BASEFONT size="number">
```

Differences between <FONT> Tag and <BASEFONT> Tag

<FONT> tag	***<BASEFONT> tag***
The <FONT> tag has "ending" tag.	The <BASEFONT> tag has optional "ending" tag.
The <FONT> tag affects all text that lies between its starting and ending tags.	The <BASEFONT> tag affects all text in a document that follows it.

<CENTER> Tag

This tag is used to centralise a segment of text to be displayed on browser's window. With the <CENTER> tag, closing tag </CENTER> is always used. Anything between these two tags will be centered including text, images or tables.

Syntax

```
<CENTER> ... </CENTER>
```

Example 8. To centralise a text.

```
<HTML>
   <HEAD>
      <TITLE> Center </TITLE>
   </HEAD>
   <BODY>
      <CENTER>
        This text will be center-aligned.
      </CENTER>
   </BODY>
</HTML>
```

Output

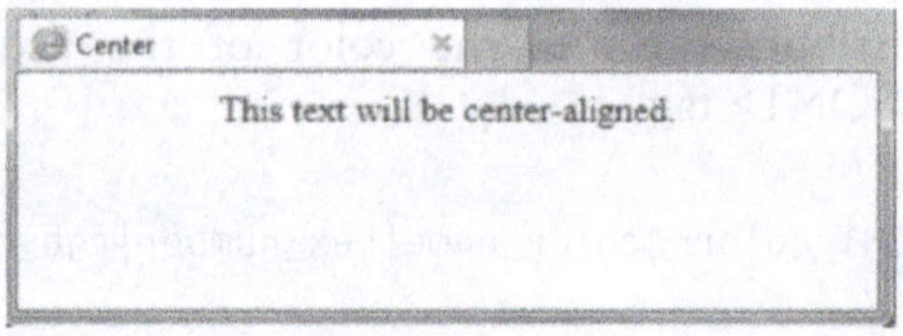

Comment <!- -... - -> Tag

This tag is used to insert comments in the source code of the Web page. Comments are not displayed in the browser's window.

All the text inserted inside this tag (`<!- - ...- - >`) will be ignored by the browser that made invisible for the user. You can use comment to explain your code, it can help you, when you edit the source code later. This is especially useful, when you have a lot of codes.

Syntax

```
<! - - ... - ->
```

Example 9. To illustrate the use of comment tag.

```
<HTML>
   <HEAD>
      <TITLE> Comment </TITLE>
   </HEAD>
   <BODY>
      <!- - This is a comment.  - ->
      This is body.
   </BODY>
</HTML>
```

Output

Heading Tags

In HTML, heading tags are used to display the text as a heading. It can also be used to give section headings.

There are six levels of headings, ranging from <H1>...</H1> to <H6>...</H6>. <H1> defines the most important largest heading level and <H6> defines the smallest heading level.

Syntax

```
<Hn> - - - -</Hn>
```

Where, *n* may be any number from 1 to 6.

Example 10. To display multiple headings using H1... H6 tags.

```
<HTML>
   <HEAD>
      <TITLE> Heading Level </TITLE>
   </HEAD>
   <BODY>
      <H1> level 1 Headline </H1>
      <H2> level 2 Headline </H2>
      <H3> level 3 Headline </H3>
      <H4> level 4 Headline </H4>
      <H5> level 5 Headline </H5>
      <H6> level 6 Headline </H6>
   </BODY>
</HTML>
```

Output

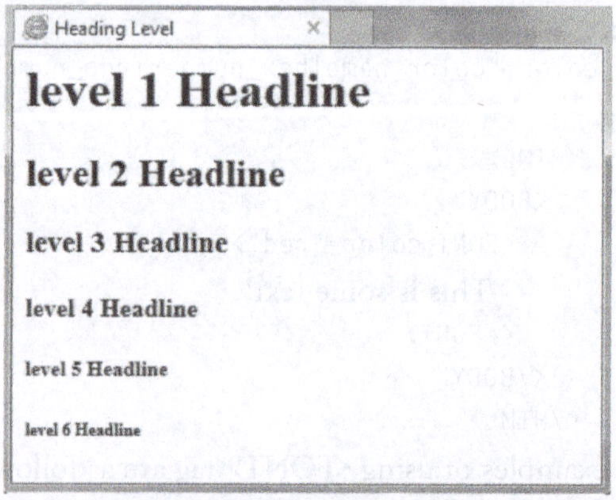

Attribute of Heading Tags

Following is the attribute of Heading tag:

align

This attribute specifies the alignment of the text as heading. By default, alignment is left.

Syntax

```
<Hn align="center|left|right|justify">…</Hn>
```

Where, *n*=1 to 6

Example 11. To display multiple headings with different alignment using H1…H6 tags with align attribute.

```
<HTML>
   <HEAD>
     <TITLE> Heading in HTML </TITLE>
   </HEAD>
  <BODY>
   <H1 align = "center"> level 1 Headline</H1>
   <H2> level 2 Headline </H2>
   <H3 align = "right"> level 3 Headline</H3>
   <H4> level 4 Headline </H4>
   <H5 align = "center"> level 5 Headline</H5>
   <H6> level 6 Headline </H6>
  </BODY>
</HTML>
```

Output

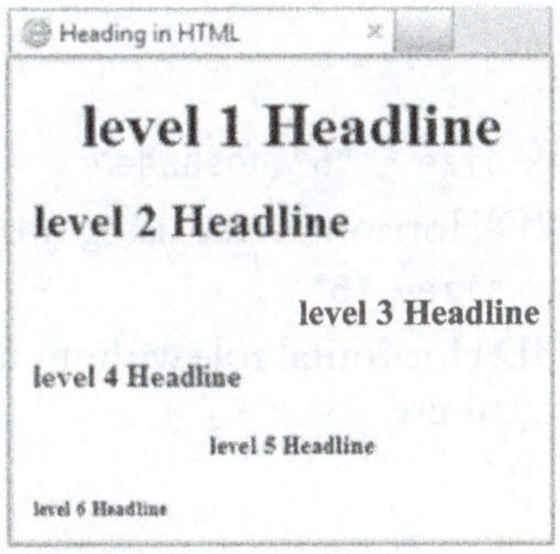

Paragraph <P> Tag

This tag is used to mark a block of text as a paragraph. It is used to insert a line break with extra space in the beginning. This is a container tag.

Syntax `<P> ....... </P>`

Example 12. To display text in paragraph form.

```
<HTML>
  <HEAD>
    <TITLE> Paragraph </TITLE>
  </HEAD>
  <BODY>
    <P>This is some text in a paragraph.</P>
  </BODY>
</HTML>
```

Output

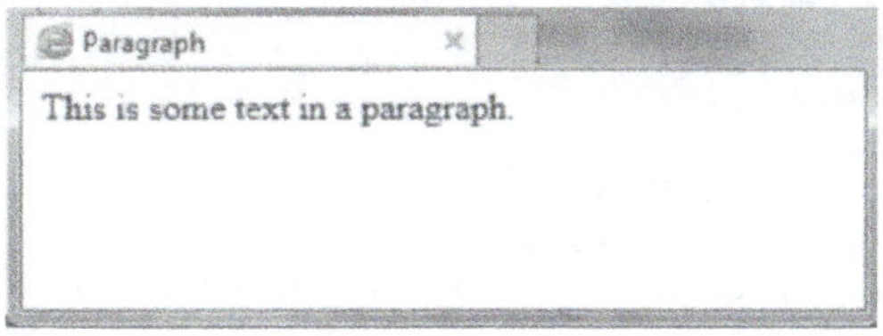

Attribute of <P> Tag

Following is the attribute of <P> tag:

align

This attribute specifies the alignment of the text within a paragraph. By default, alignment is left.

Syntax

```
<P align="left|right|center|justify">
```

Example 13. To illustrate the use of align attribute in <P> tag.

```
<HTML>
  <HEAD>
    <TITLE>
      P tag with align attribute
    </TITLE>
  </HEAD>
  <BODY>
    <P align="right">
      This is some text in a paragraph.
    </P>
  </BODY>
</HTML>
```

Output

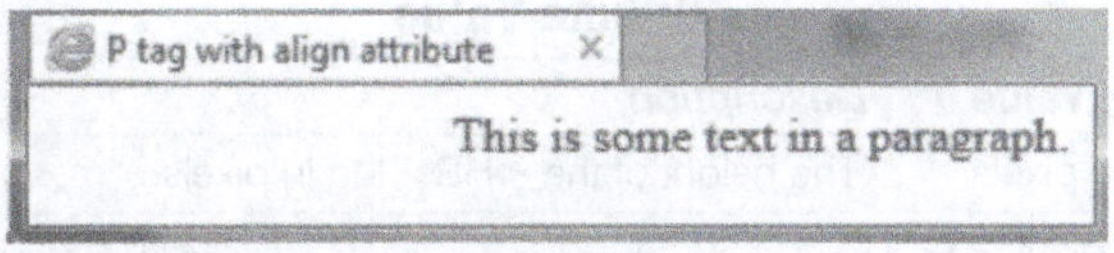

Line Break
 Tag

This tag is used to insert a line break which means the text/image following the tag will be moved to the next line when displayed in the browser. To add a single line of space, you can use a line break <BR> tag.

This is an empty tag, i.e. no need of closing tag. You can also use the <BR> tag to insert one or more blank lines.

Example 14. To display text with line break.

```
<HTML>
  <HEAD>
    <TITLE>
      Line Break
    </TITLE>
  </HEAD>
  <BODY>
      This text contains <BR> a line break.
  </BODY>
</HTML>
```

Output

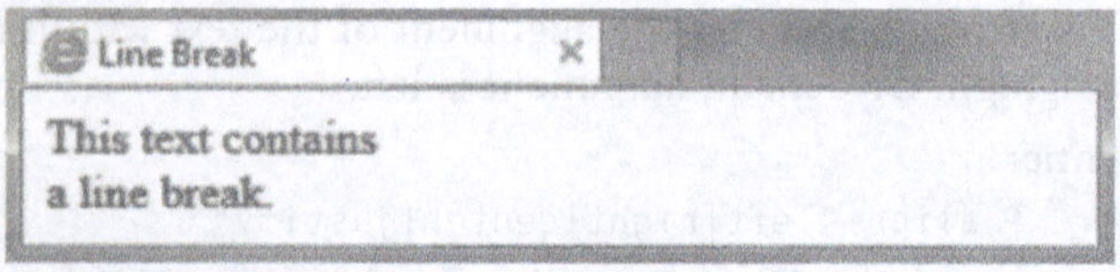

Horizontal Rule <HR> Tag

To create a horizontal line on your Web page, you have to use the empty tag <HR>. This horizontal line can be used to divide information into sections.

Attributes of <HR> Tag

Following are the attributes of <HR> tag:

size

This attribute specifies the height of the rule in pixels. *A* ***pixel*** *is a tiny dot that makes up the display of your computer.* Its default value depends directly on the browser. Generally, the default size of a rule is 3 pixels.

Syntax

```
<HR size="pixels">
```

Attribute Value

Value	*Description*
pixels	The height of the <HR> tag in pixels.

Example 15. To display horizontal rule of size 7.

```
<HTML>
  <HEAD>
    <TITLE>
      HR tag with size attribute
    </TITLE>
  </HEAD>
  <BODY>
  <HR size="7">
      This is a line.
  </BODY>
</HTML>
```

Output

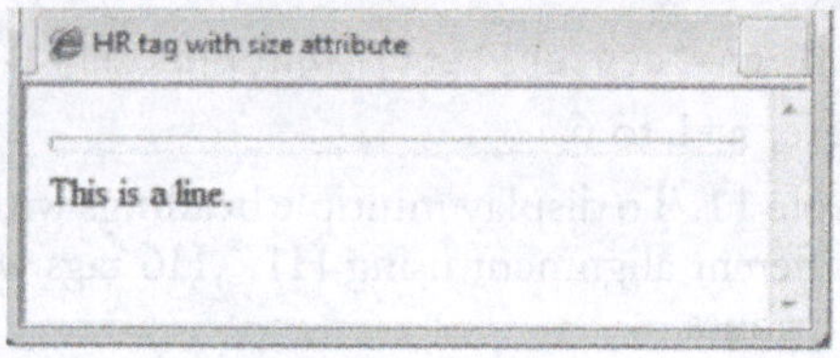

noshade

When this boolean attribute is present, the rule is drawn with a solid black line as a 2D effect instead of the default 3D effect, i.e. without shading.

Syntax

```
<HR noshade>
```

Example 16. To display 2D and 3D horizontal rules.

```
<HTML>
  <HEAD>
    <TITLE>
      Types of Horizontal Rule
    </TITLE>
  </HEAD>
  <BODY>
    <HR size = "5" noshade>
      2D Horizontal rule using noshade attribute
    <HR size= "5">
      3D Horizontal rule without using noshade
      attribute.
  </BODY>
</HTML>
```

Output

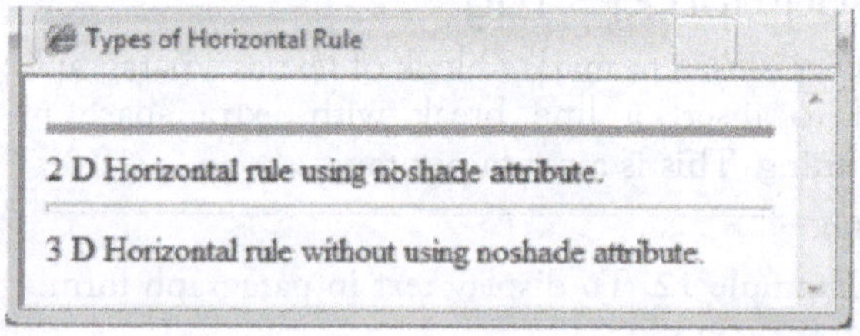

align

This attribute specifies the alignment of a horizontal line.

Syntax

```
<HR align="left|center|right">
```

width

This attribute specifies the width of a horizontal line in pixels or percent. Its default value is 100%.

Syntax

```
<HR width="pixels or %">
```

Attribute Values

Value	Description
pixels	The width in pixels (like '100 px' or just '100').
%	The width in percent of the available space (like '50%').

Example 17. To illustrate the use of align and width attributes in <HR> tag.

```
<HTML>
  <HEAD>
    <TITLE>
      HR tag with align and width attributes
    </TITLE>
  </HEAD>
  <BODY>
    <HR align= "right" width="50%">
      This is a line.
  </BODY>
</HTML>
```

Output

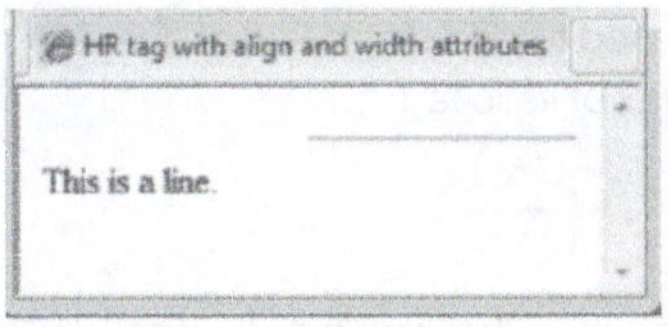

color

This attribute specifies the color of the horizontal line.

Syntax

```
<HR color="color_name|hex_number|rgb_number">
```

Example 18. To display horizontal rule in red color.

```
<HTML>
  <HEAD>
    <TITLE>
      HR tag with color attribute
    </TITLE>
  </HEAD>
  <BODY>
    <HR color="red">
      This is a red line.
  </BODY>
</HTML>
```

Output

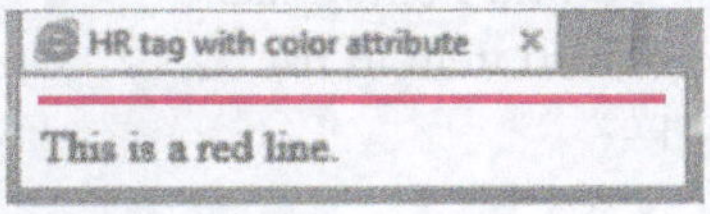

Colors and their Hexadecimal and RGB Values

Color Name	Hexadecimal Value	RGB Value
Aqua	#00FFFF	rgb (0,255,255)
Black	#000000	rgb (0,0,0)
Blue	#0000FF	rgb (0,0,255)
Fuchsia	#FF00FF	rgb (255,0,255)
Gold	#FFD700	rgb (255,215,0)
Gray	#808080	rgb (128,128,128)
Green	#008000	rgb (0,128,0)
Khaki	#F0E68C	rgb (240,230,140)
Lime	#00FF00	rgb (0,255,0)
Maroon	#800000	rgb (128,0,0)
Navy	#000080	rgb (0,0,128)
Olive	#808000	rgb (128,128,0)
Orange	#FFA500	rgb (255,165,0)
Pink	#FFC0CB	rgb (255,192,203)
Purple	#800080	rgb (128,0,128)
Red	#FF0000	rgb (255,0,0)
Silver	#C0C0C0	rgb (192,192,192)
White	#FFFFFF	rgb (255, 255, 255)
Yellow	#FFFF00	rgb (255, 255, 0)

Style Tags

HTML provides various style tags, which are as follows:

Bold <B> Tag

This tag specifies the text into bold text. It is a container element. This tag is used for text formatting.

Syntax

```
<B>........</B>
```

Example 19. To display some text in bold style.

```
<HTML>
  <HEAD>
    <TITLE> Bold </TITLE>
  </HEAD>
  <BODY>
   <P>
    This normal text and <B> this is bold text.</B>
   </P>
  </BODY>
</HTML>
```

Output

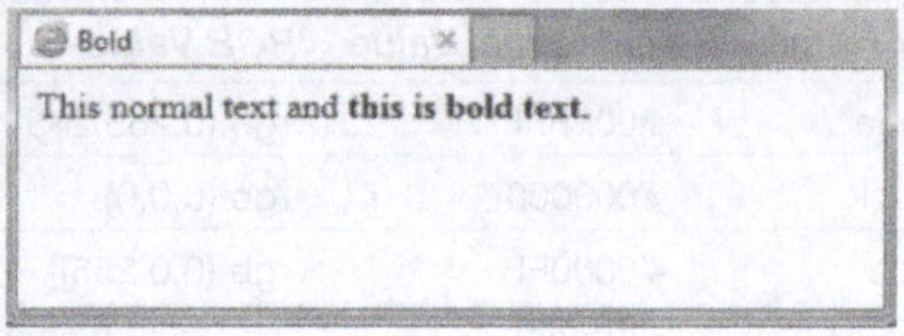

Italic <I> Tag

This tag is used to make the text in italic form. It is also a container element. This is also used for text formatting.

Syntax

```
<I>.....</I>
```

Example 20. To display text in italic style.

```
<HTML>
  <HEAD>
    <TITLE> Italic </TITLE>
  </HEAD>
  <BODY>
    <I> Hello </I>
  </BODY>
</HTML>
```

Output

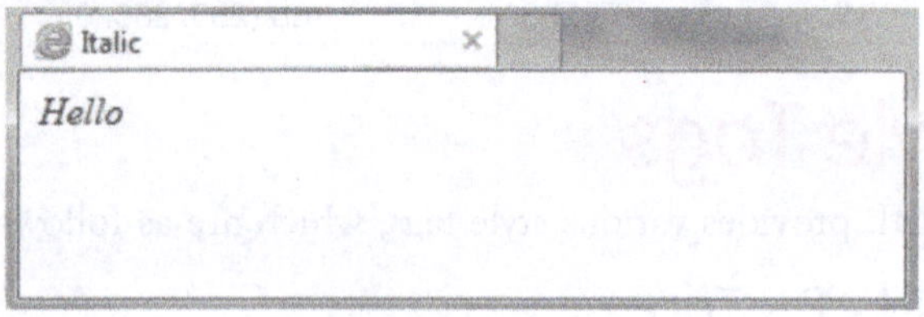

Underline <U> Tag

This tag is used to underline the text. It is also a container element.

Syntax

```
<U> ........ </U>
```

Example 21. To display some underlined text.

```
<HTML>
  <HEAD>
    <TITLE> Underline </TITLE>
  </HEAD>
  <BODY>
    <P> This is a <U> text </U> </P>
  </BODY>
</HTML>
```

Output

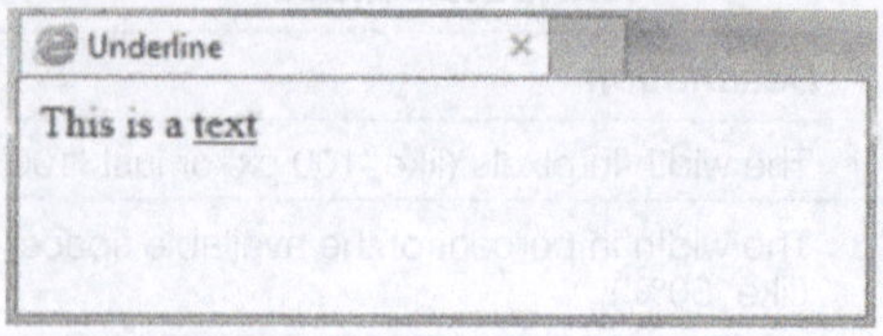

Gigo

- The teletype element (<TT> -- </TT>) renders the enclosed text in teletype font, i.e. typewriter font.
- If the background image is smaller than the browser window then, it will be repeated on the window.
- With background image, you should specify a background color because this background color will be shown until the image loads.

Check Point 02

1 .... attribute specifies the font name or type face of text.

2 Among the following, which is the correct way to specify that the content is a comment?

(a) <! -- (b) !
(c) <comment (d) None of these

3 Which tag is used to add single line of space?

4 Write the syntax of italic tag.

HTML Lists

Sometimes, we are in hurry and do not like to read a lot of text. So, putting important information in the form of a list seems to be helpful. HTML supports several elements for making lists. They can be divided into two types of lists, i.e. Glossary lists and Regular lists. Glossary lists are denoted by the element <DK>, while Regular lists are denoted by the elements <UL>, <OL>, <MENU> and <DIR>. Lists can be nested, i.e. you can have a list within a regular list, a regular list within a glossary list and so on.

List tags are generally HTML containers that are capable of accepting other container and empty tags within their boundaries. These list tags are responsible for affecting the spacing and layout of text, not the emphasis, so they are applied to groups of text and allow individual formatting tags within them.

Most HTML lists are created in the following form:

```
<LIST type>
  <ITEM> First item in list
  <ITEM> Second item in list
  <ITEM> Third item in list
</LIST type>
```

List Item (<LI>) This element is used to indicate a list item as contained in an ordered list or an unordered list. The <LI> tag is an empty tag.

Syntax

```
<LI> Item name </LI>
```

Types of Lists

There are various types of list as follows:

Unordered List <UL>

This list (also known as **unnumbered list**) is an indented list with a bullet symbol in front of each list item.

An unordered list starts with the <UL> tag. Each list item starts with the <LI> tag. The list items are marked with bullets (typically small black circles).

The unordered list tag is a container tag. The default bullet type for most Web browsers is a full disc (black circle).

Syntax

```
<UL>........</UL>
```

Example 22. To display unordered list.

```
<HTML>
  <HEAD>
    <TITLE> Unordered List </TITLE>
  </HEAD>
  <BODY>
    <UL>
      <LI>My first item on the list.</LI>
      <LI>My second item on the list.</LI>
      <LI>My third item on the list.</LI>
      <LI> My fourth item on the list.</LI>
    </UL>
  </BODY>
</HTML>
```

Output

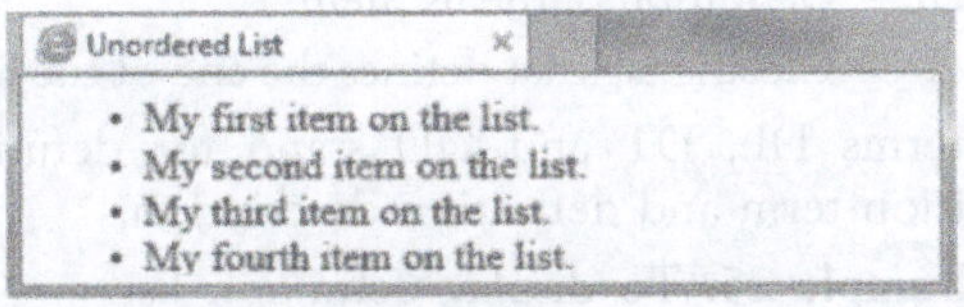

Attribute of Unordered List Tag

Following is the attribute of <UL> tag:

type

This attribute is used to change the bulleted symbol in a list. The attribute may have a value of circle, disc or square.

Syntax

```
<UL type="value">
```

HTML Unordered List Types Value

Value	*Description*
Square	Use black square bullet (■)
Disc	Use solid circle bullet (•)
Circle	Use a hollow bullet (○)

Here, we are using <UL> tag in the below example and we get various output as follows:

```
<UL type="square">
<UL type="disc">
<UL type="circle">
```

HTML Unordered List Types Output

Square	*Disc*	*Circle*
▪ Rose	• Rose	○ Rose
▪ Lotus	• Lotus	○ Lotus
▪ Lily	• Lily	○ Lily

Ordered List <OL>

This list starts with the <OL> tag. Each list item starts with the <LI> tag. The list items are marked with numbers. The ordered list tag is a container tag which is used for numbered lists. By default, the numbering will be 1, 2, 3 .... You can also adjust the numbering using **type** attribute.

Syntax

```
<OL>......</OL>
```

Example 23. To display ordered list.

```
<HTML>
  <HEAD>
    <TITLE> Ordered List </TITLE>
  </HEAD>
  <BODY>
    <OL>
      <LI> Rose </LI>
      <LI> Lotus </LI>
      <LI> Lily </LI>
    </OL>
  </BODY>
</HTML>
```

Output

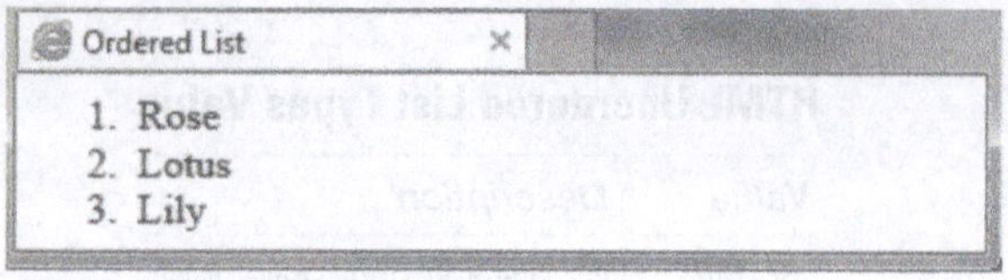

Attributes of Ordered List Tag

Following are the attributes of <OL> tag:

type

The numbering of an HTML list can be changed to letters or roman numerals by the type attribute.

Syntax

```
<OL type="value">
```

HTML Ordered List Types Value

Value	Description
1	The default, uses arabic numerals
I	Uses uppercase roman numerals
i	Uses lowercase roman numerals
A	Uses uppercase letters
a	Uses lowercase letters

Here, we are using <OL> tag in the below example and we get various output as follows:

```
<OL type="a">
<OL type="A">
<OL type="i">
<OL type="I">
```

HTML Ordered List Types Output

Lowercase roman numerals	*Uppercase roman numerals*
i. Rose	I. Rose
ii. Lotus	II. Lotus
iii. Lily	III. Lily
Lowercase letters	***Uppercase letters***
a. Rose	A. Rose
b. Lotus	B. Lotus
c. Lily	C. Lily

start

This attribute is used to change the beginning value of an ordered list. Normally, the ordered list begins with 1. It lets you further customise an HTML ordered list by setting a new starting digit for the ordered list element.

Syntax

```
<OL start="number" type = "value">
```

Example 24. To illustrate the use of type and start attributes of ordered list.

```
<HTML>
  <HEAD>
    <TITLE>
      Ordered List with type and start attributes
    </TITLE>
  </HEAD>
  <BODY>
    <OL start="4" type="1" >
      <LI> Rose </LI>
      <LI> Lotus </LI>
      <LI> Lily </LI>
    </OL>
  </BODY>
</HTML>
```

Output

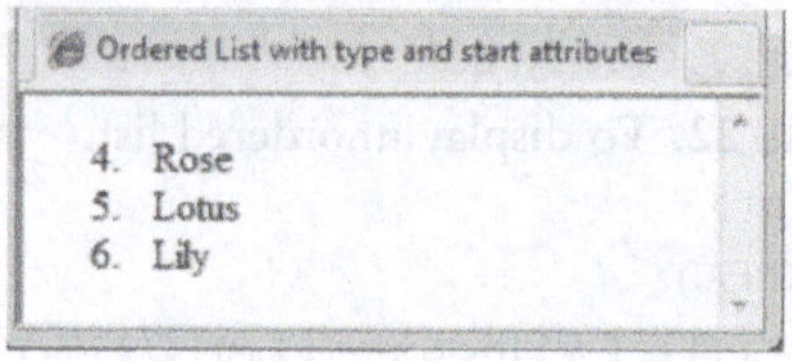

Definition List

This is a list of items, with a description of each item. HTML definition lists (<DL>) are indented list without any bullet symbol or any number in front of each item. This list elements have a unique array of tags or elements; the resulting lists are similar to those you would see in a dictionary.

Tags used in definition lists are as follows:

- <DL> Opening tag that defines the start of the list.
- <DT> List item that defines the definition term.
- <DD> Definition of the list item.
- </DL> Closing tag that defines the end of the list.

The terms DL, DT and DD stand for definition list, definition term and definition description.

Example 25. To display definition list.

```
<HTML>
  <HEAD>
    <TITLE> Definition List </TITLE>
  </HEAD>
  <BODY>
  <DL>
    <DT><B> Fromage </B>
    <DD> French word for cheese
```

```
      <DT><B> Voiture </B>
      <DD> French word for car
    </DL>
  </BODY>
</HTML>
```

Output

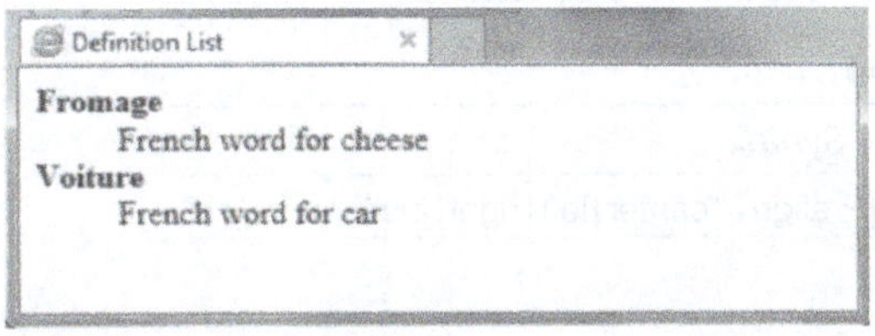

Nested List

List can be nested that means one list can be placed inside another. In the nested list, one or more items can contain sub-items.

Example 26. To display nested list.

```
<HTML>
  <HEAD>
    <TITLE> Nested List </TITLE>
  </HEAD>
  <BODY>
    <UL>
      <LI> Fruits </LI>
        <OL type="1">
          <LI> Mango </LI>
          <LI> Apple </LI>
        </OL>
        <LI> Vegetables </LI>
        <OL type="1">
          <LI> Onion </LI>
          <LI> Tomato </LI>
        </OL>
    </UL>
  </BODY>
</HTML>
```

Output

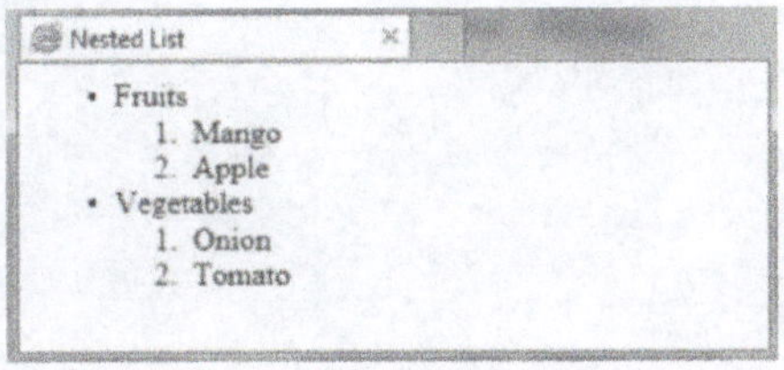

Check Point 03

1. Mention the answer in True/False: <DIR> tag represents the regular lists.
2. Each list item should start with which tag?
3. Which attribute is used to change the beginning value of an ordered list?
4. You can create definition list with the .... tag.
   (a) <DL> (b) <UL>
   (c) <OL> (d) <LI>

Attributes of <HTML> Tag

Attributes	*Explanation*	*Syntax*
dir	Specifies the text direction for the content in an element	`<HTML dir="ltr|rtl">`
lang	Specifies the language of the element's content	`<HTML lang="language_code">`

Attributes of <BODY> Tag

Attributes	*Explanation*	*Syntax*
background	Specifies a background image for a document	`<Body background ="URL">`
text	Specifies the color of the text in a document	`<Body text ="color_name|hex_number|rgb_number">`
bgcolor	Specifies the background color of a document	`<Body bgcolor ="color_name|hex_number|rgb_number">`
link	Specifies the color of unvisited links in a document	`<Body link ="color_name|hex_number|rgb_number">`
vlink	Specifies the color of visited links in a document	`<Body vlink ="color_name|hex_number|rgb_number">`
alink	Specifies the color of an active link in a document	`<Body alink ="color_name|hex_number|rgb_number">`
topmargin	Set a margin above the body of a document	`<Body topmargin ="value">`
leftmargin	Set a margin of the left of the body of a document	`<Body leftmargin ="value">`

Attributes of <FONT> and <BASEFONT> Tags

<table>
<tr><th>Attributes</th><th>Explanation</th><th>Syntax</th></tr>
<tr><td>size</td><td>Specifies the size of text</td><td><FONT|BASEFONT size="number"></td></tr>
<tr><td>face</td><td>Specifies the font of text</td><td><FONT|BASEFONT face="font_family"></td></tr>
<tr><td>color</td><td>Specifies the color of text</td><td><FONT|BASEFONT color="color_name|hex_number|rgb_number"></td></tr>
</table>

Attribute of <H1>...<H6> and <P>Tag

<table>
<tr><th>Attribute</th><th>Explanation</th><th>Syntax</th></tr>
<tr><td>align</td><td>Specifies the alignment of a heading or paragraph</td><td><H<i>n</i>|P align="center|left|right|justify"></td></tr>
</table>

Attributes of <HR> Tag

<table>
<tr><th>Attributes</th><th>Explanation</th><th>Syntax</th></tr>
<tr><td>size</td><td>Specifies the height of horizontal rule</td><td><HR size="pixel"></td></tr>
<tr><td>noshade</td><td>Specifies that a horizontal rule should render in one solid color (noshaded), instead of a shaded color</td><td><HR noshade></td></tr>
<tr><td>align</td><td>Specifies the alignment of horizontal rule</td><td><HR align ="center|left|right"></td></tr>
<tr><td>width</td><td>Specifies the width of horizontal rule</td><td><HR width ="pixel|percentage"></td></tr>
<tr><td>color</td><td>Specifies the color of horizontal rule</td><td><HR color ="color_name|hex_number|rgb_number"></td></tr>
</table>

Attribute of <UL> Tag

<table>
<tr><th>Attribute</th><th>Explanation</th><th>Syntax</th></tr>
<tr><td>type</td><td>Specifies the kind of marker to use in the list</td><td><UL type ="disc|square|circle"></td></tr>
</table>

Attributes of <OL> Tag

<table>
<tr><th>Attributes</th><th>Explanation</th><th>Syntax</th></tr>
<tr><td>type</td><td>Specifies the kind of marker to use in the list</td><td><UL type="1|A|a|i|I|"></td></tr>
<tr><td>start</td><td>Specifies the start value of an ordered list</td><td><UL start="number"></td></tr>
</table>

SUMMARY

- On WWW, the documents are written in markup language called HTML.
- HTML is not case sensitive markup language.
- HTML provides predefined tags and these are kept inside the angular brackets < and >.
- HTML tags or elements define the two different parts, i.e. Container Elements and Empty Elements.
- An HTML document must consists of four basic elements, i.e. <HTML>, <HEAD>, <TITLE> and <BODY>.
- <HEAD> and <TITLE> tags specify the header part and <BODY> tag specifies the body part of an HTML document.
- HTML documents are saved with the extension .htm or .html.
- Each tag provides various attributes such as <BODY> tag that has attributes like background, text, bgcolor, link, topmargin etc.
- link attribute is used for unvisited links, alink for links being clicked and vlink for links already visited.
- The <FONT> tag is used to change the size, style and color of the text in a Web page.
- Comment tag is included in HTML documents by the user for his own understanding.
- HTML provides six levels of heading, i.e. <H1>, <H2>, <H3>, <H4>, <H5> and <H6>.
- The <P> tag is used to make the paragraph. By default, alignment of paragraph text is left.
- The text in a Web page appears as a single line by default. To break the text, HTML provides <BR> tag.
- The <HR> tag is used to insert a horizontal line in a Web page.
- <B>, <I>, <U> tags are used to set the style of text.
- HTML provides various types of list, i.e. Unordered list, Ordered list, Definition list and Nested List.
- The <LI> tag is used to display the items in a list format in a Web page.
- The <UL> tag is used to display Unordered list. It displays the item in a bulleted format.
- The <OL> tag is used to display Ordered list. It displays the item in a sequential manner as 1, 2, 3.... .
- The <DL> tag defines a description list. This tag is used in conjunction with <DT> (defines terms) and <DD> (describes each term).

Exam Practice

Multiple Choice Questions

1 HTML is a **CBSE 2011**

(a) package (b) software

(c) markup language (d) None of these

Ans. (*c*) HTML is a markup language which is used to define the layout and attributes of WWW document.

2 HTML tags are enclosed in

(a) curly brackets (b) square brackets

(c) double quotes (d) angular brackets

Ans. (*d*) HTML tags are enclosed within angular brackets (< and >).

3 HTML tags are

(a) in uppercase

(b) case sensitive

(c) in lowercase

(d) not case sensitive

Ans. (*d*) HTML tags are not case sensitive means we can write tags either in uppercase or lowercase.

4 Which type of tags used by HTML?

(a) tags only for image

(b) user defined tags

(c) tags only for linking

(d) fixed tags defined by the language

Ans. (*d*) HTML provides predefined and fixed tags.

5 Container elements in HTML require **CBSE 2015**

(a) starting tag

(b) ending tag

(c) starting and ending tags

(d) None of the above

Ans. (*c*) In HTML, container elements are required as both starting and ending tags.

6 Which of the following is not a container element? **CBSE 2013**

(a) P (b) B

(c) OL (d) HR

Ans. (*d*) HR is an empty tag because it has no closing tag.

7 To create an HTML page, you need

(a) text editor (b) Web browser

(c) Both (a) and (b) (d) None of these

Ans. (*c*) Because text editor is required to write HTML code and Web browser is needed to display the page.

8 Which program do you need to write HTML code?

(a) Spreadsheet (b) Access

(c) Notepad (d) None of these

Ans. (*c*) From the given options, Notepad is useful program to write HTML code.

9 An example of HTML editor is

(a) Notepad (b) Dreamweaver

(c) Microsoft frontpage (d) All of these

Ans. (*d*) HTML provides various text editors like Notepad, Microsoft frontpage, Dreamweaver etc.

10 M in HTML stands for **CBSE 2019**

(a) MANAGEMENT (b) MARKUP

(c) MODIFIED (d) MACHINE

Ans. (*b*) M in HTML stands for MARKUP.

11 Which of the following is the correct code of HTML page?

(a)
```
<HTML>
<TITLE> Hello
</TITLE>
</HTML>
```

(b)
```
<HTML>
<HEAD>
<TITLE> Hello
</TITLE>
</HEAD>
</HTML>
```

(c)
```
<HTML>
<BODY> Hello
</HTML>
```

(d)
```
<HTML>
<HEAD> Hello
<BODY>
</HTML>
```

Ans. (*b*) Because <TITLE> tag must close inside the <HEAD> tag.

12 Tags and text that do not display directly on the Web page are placed in

(a) body (b) table (c) head (d) title

Ans. (*c*) Information in <HEAD> tag is not displayed directly in Web page. It is used to identify the matter (tags) used in a Web page.

13 A Web page normally consists of

(a) head and body

(b) top and bottom

(c) body and font

(d) body and title

Ans. (*a*) From the given options, a Web page normally consists of head and body.

14 Where do you place the <TITLE> tag in a HTML?

(a) BODY (b) HEAD
(c) TITLE (d) FONT

Ans. (*b*) <TITLE> tag is placed in the <HEAD> tag.

15 Which section is used for text and tags that are shown directly on your Web pages?

(a) Meta (b) Head
(c) Body (d) Table

Ans. (*c*) Information in <BODY> tag is directly displayed on Web pages.

16 Which attribute is not supported by a <BODY> tag? **CBSE 2013**

(a) bgcolor (b) size
(c) text (d) link

Ans. (*b*) size is not an attribute of <BODY> tag.

17 What will happen if the background image is smaller than the browser's window?

(a) It will leave a blank space at the bottom of your page
(b) It will be repeated
(c) It will be stretched
(d) It will not be displayed

Ans. (*b*) When the background image is smaller than the browser's window then it will be shown in boxes in repeated pattern.

18 Why should you specify a background color, if you are using an image for the actual background of your page?

(a) So the text shows up better
(b) The background color will be shown until the image loads
(c) In case the image does not fit right
(d) None of the above

Ans. (*b*) We have to use background color because if in any case image is not displayed then atleast background color will be shown on that place.

19 ......attribute is used to set the color of a link while it is active.

(a) vlink (b) alink
(c) Both (a) and (b) (d) None of these

Ans. (*b*) alink attribute is used to set the color of link while it is active.

20 Which attribute of <BODY> tag specifies the color of visited links in a document?

(a) vlink (b) alink
(c) link (d) None of these

Ans. (*a*) vlink attribute specifies the color of visited links in a HTML document.

21 Heading tags in HTML are **CBSE 2019**

(a) H1...H6 (b) H1...H5
(c) H1...H10 (d) H1...H8

Ans. (*a*) H1...H6 are headings tag in HTML.

22 Choose the correct HTML tag for the largest heading.

(a) <H2> (b) <H4>
(c) <H6> (d) <H1>

Ans. (*d*) <H1> tag provides the largest heading in HTML.

23 Which of the following will give smallest size of the text? **CBSE 2014**

(a) <H3> (b) <H6> (c) <H2> (d) <H4>

Ans. (*b*) From the given options, <H6> tag displays the smallest size of heading text.

24 In a Web page, you can place

(a) 2 levels of headings
(b) 6 levels of headings
(c) 4 levels of headings
(d) 7 levels of headings

Ans. (*b*) Web page provides six levels of headings.

25 The default alignment for paragraph is

(a) left (b) right
(c) center (d) justified

Ans. (*a*) The align attribute of <P> tag provides various alignments like left, right, center and justify. But by default, its alignment is left.

26 Which of the following HTML container tags do you apply to text for formatting the text as a paragraph?

(a) <PARAGRAPH> .... </PARAGRAPH>
(b) <PARA> .... </PARA>
(c) <P> .... </P>
(d) None of the above

Ans. (*c*) <P> .... </P> is a container tag, which is used for formatting text.

27 The tags used for specifying the style in HTML are

(*i*) <B> (*ii*) <I> (*iii*) <M> (*iv*) <L>

Choose the correct one

(a) (i) and (ii) (b) (i) and (iii)
(c) (ii) and (iv) (d) (i), (ii) and (iii)

Ans. (*a*) Because these two tags are text formatting/styling tags.

28 Which of the following is not HTML list? **CBSE 2013**

(a) Ordered (b) Unordered
(c) Definition (d) Detailed

Ans. (*d*) Detailed list is not a type of HTML list.

29 In an unordered list, it is necessary to enclose each item in **CBSE 2013**

(a) <LI> tag (b) <UL> tag
(c) <I> tag (d) <OL> tag

Ans. (*a*) Each item must be enclosed in <LI> tag either in ordered list or unordered list.

30 Which one of the following list type that will create a bulleted list? **CBSE 2014**

(a) Unordered (b) Ordered
(c) Definition (d) All of these

Ans. (*a*) Unordered list provides various types of bullets like square, disc and circle.

31 In an ordered list, each item cannot be preceded with **CBSE 2013**

(a) counting numbers (b) arabic numbers
(c) roman numerals (d) bullets

Ans. (*d*) In unordered list, bullets are used while counting numbers, arabic numbers and roman numbers are used in an ordered list.

32 To create a numbered list with A, B, ... use

(a) `<ol type="A">` (b) `<OL start="A">`
(c) `<OL begin="A">` (d) `<OL starts="a">`

Ans. (*a*) The given list uses the uppercase letter for each item so, the correct syntax is

```
<OL type="A">
```

33 To start a list with number 3, we should write **CBSE 2015**

(a) `<OL start="3">` (b) `<OL type="3">`
(c) `<OL value="3">` (d) All of these

Ans. (*a*) The correct syntax for start a list with number 3 is `<OL start = "3">`.

34 To start a numbered list with regular numerals, use

(a) `<OL type="A">` (b) `<OL type="1">`
(c) `<OL type="I">` (d) `<OL type="U">`

Ans. (*b*) Because regular numbering is the natural numbers starting from 1, 2, 3, ... etc.

35 HTML tag to draw horizontal line **CBSE SQP Term-I**

(a) <HL> (b) <HR>
(c) <HLINE> (d) None of these

Ans. (*b*) <HR>

36 The correct HTML code to display $(P+Q)^2$ is **CBSE SQP Term-I**

(a) `<SUB>(P+Q) 2</SUB>`
(b) `P+Q <SUP> 2 </SUP>`
(c) `(P + Q)<SUP> 2 </SUP>`
(d) `<SUP> (P+Q) 2</SUP>`

Ans. (*c*) `(P + Q)<SUP> 2 </SUP>`

37 Which of these is not an attribute of the FONT tag? **CBSE SQP Term-I**

(a) color (b) face (c) type (d) size

Ans. (*c*) type

38 Consider the following HTML code:

```
<OL type="i">
<LI>First</LI>
<LI>Second</LI>
<LI>Third</LI>
<LI>Fourth</LI>
</OL>
```

Choose the correct output that would be shown upon execution of the above code , from the choices given below. **CBSE SQP Term-I**

(a)
I. First
II. Second
III. Third
IV. Fourth

(b)
i. First
ii. Second
iii. Third
iv. Fourth

(c)
I First
II Second
III Third
IV Fourth

(d)
i First
ii Second
iii Third
iv Fourth

Ans. (*b*) i. First
ii. Second
iii. Third
iv. Fourth

39 Identify invalid HTML tag from the following list. **CBSE 2021 Term-I**

(a) <H6> ... </H6> (b) <H4>...</H4>
(c) <H5> ... </H5> (d) <H7>...</H7>

Ans. (*d*) <H7>...</H7>

40 Identify the correct statement with reference to <P> tag. **CBSE 2021 Term-I**

(a) It is used within the <BODY> tag.
(b) The <P> tag defines a paragraph.
(c) Browsers automatically add a single blank line before and after each <P> element.
(d) All of the above

Ans. (*d*) All of the above

41 OL stands for **CBSE 2021 Term-I**

(a) Organised List (b) Outstanding List
(c) Ordered List (d) Overall List

Ans. (*c*) Ordered List

42 The .... tag defines the terms in the description list. **CBSE 2021 Term-I**

(a) <DL> (b) <DT>
(c) <DD> (d) All of these

Ans. (*b*) <DT>

43 The <TITLE> element **CBSE 2021 Term-I**
(a) defines a title in the browser toolbar
(b) provides a title for the page when it is added to favourites
(c) displays a title for the page in search-engine results
(d) All of the above

Ans. (*d*) All of the above

44 H in <HR> tag stands for **CBSE 2021 Term-I**
(a) Height (b) Horizontal
(c) Hollow (d) None of these

Ans. (*b*) Horizontal

45 The .... tag inserts a single line break. **CBSE 2021 Term-I**
(a) <BREAK> (b)
(c) <LINE> (d) <NEW LINE>

Ans. (*b*)

46 Razia, a Class X student, is a beginner in the field of web designing. Help her in identifying the attribute which is not related to <BODY> tag. **CBSE 2021 Term-I**
(a) src (b) background
(c) bgcolor (d) text

Ans. (*a*) src

47 By mistake, Raj has jumbled up a few tags and their attributes. Help him by choosing correct option for tags and their corresponding attributes. **CBSE 2021 Term-I**

	Tags		Attributes
1.	FONT	i.	src
2.	BODY	ii.	face
3.	IMG	iii.	text

	1	2	3		1	2	3
(a)	ii	iii	i	(b)	iii	i	ii
(c)	iii	ii	i	(d)	i	ii	iii

Ans. (*a*) ii iii i

48 The .... tag represents the root of an HTML document. **CBSE 2021 Term-I**
(a) <ROOT> (b) <HTML>
(c) <FIRST> (d) <MAIN>

Ans. (*b*) <HTML>

49 The .... tag is an empty tag and it does not require closing tag. **CBSE 2021 Term-I**
(a) <TAG> (b) <HR>
(c) <FORM> (d) <FONT>

Ans. (*b*) <HR>

Fill in the Blanks

1 HTML is a subset of ....

Ans. SGML

2 The tag that requires a opening as well as closing tag is called ....

Ans. container tag

3 An element that only has a starting tag and no ending tag is .... element.

Ans. empty

4 .... attribute of <BODY> tag helps to set background color.

Ans. bgcolor

5 The default color of a link attribute is ....

Ans. blue

6 .... is used to change the color of a visited link. **CBSE 2016**

Ans. vlink

7 A visited link on a Website is generally underlined and .... in color.

Ans. purple

8 The attribute topmargin sets a margin alongwith the top of your .... element.

Ans. BODY

9 The .... tag is used to define basic font size for the HTML page.

Ans. <BASEFONT>

10 The .... tag is used to make the Web browser ignore anything that the tag contains.

Ans. <!--....-->

11 .... tag is used to bring the text to new line. **CBSE 2014**

Ans.

12 HR tag is used for .... **CBSE 2014**

Ans. horizontal line

13 .... and .... tags break the line flow.

Ans.
, <HR>

14 noshade is an attribute of .... tag.

Ans. <HR>

EXAM PRACTICE

15 .... attribute of <HR> tag specifies the width of a horizontal line.

Ans. width

16 .... tag is used to make the text bold.

Ans. <B>

17 To display the text in italics, ... tag is used and to display in type writer font, ... tag is used. **CBSE 2013**

Ans. <I>, <TT>

18 .... tag is used to underline the text.

Ans. <U>

19 <LI> tag is an .... tag.

Ans. empty

20 .... tag creates a bulleted list. **CBSE 2015**

Ans. <UL>

21 The unordered list starts with .... tag.

Ans. <UL>

22 ....value of type attribute displays a hollow circle for an unordered lists.

Ans. circle

23 If you want to display uppercase alphabets instead of numbers, ... ordered type should you use.

Ans. A

True or False

1 HTML is a programming language **CBSE 2015**

Ans. **False** Because it is a markup language.

2 HTML is a case sensitive Web language.

Ans. **False** No, you can write your text in both uppercase and lowercase. So, HTML is not a case sensitive Web language.

3 <HEAD> tag is used to define document body.

Ans. **False** <HEAD> tag is used to define the document head.

4 <TITLE> tag is one of the structural tags of HTML document. **CBSE 2015**

Ans. **True** HTML provides four structural tags, these are as follows: <HTML>, <HEAD>, <TITLE>, <BODY>.

5 There should be only one <BODY> tag in each Web page. **CBSE 2014**

Ans. **True** A Web page contains necessarily one <BODY> tag.

6 All HTML document contains only <BODY> tag.

Ans. **False** All HTML document contains various tags.

7 background attribute is used to display image.

Ans. **True** It is an attribute of <BODY> tag, used to display background image.

8 The default color of link attribute is #0000FF.

Ans. **True** The default color of link attribute is blue and #0000FF is the hex_number of blue.

9 topmargin is used to specify the distance between the top of the document and top of the browser window.

Ans. **True** topmargin is an attribute of <BODY> tag, which is used to specify the distance between the top of the document and top of the browser window.

10 The default font size is 5. **CBSE 2015**

Ans. **False** The size attribute of <FONT> tag provides 1 to 7 range. By default, size value is 3.

11 bgcolor is an attribute of <FONT> tag.

Ans. **False** bgcolor is an attribute of <BODY> tag.

12 color is an attribute of <FONT> tag.

Ans. **True** It defines color of the text.

13 The heading tag always starts new line.

Ans. **True** Yes, heading tag always starts new line and it is of size types say H1, H2, H3, H4, H5 and H6.

14 <P> tag has no closing tag. **CBSE 2014**

Ans. **False** <P> is a container tag. As we know container tag must contain both opening and closing tags.

15 color attribute is used with <P> tag.

Ans. **False** <P> tag has only one attribute name align so, color attribute can't be used with <P> tag.

16
 tag has its closing tag as </BR>.

Ans. **False**
 tag need not have closing tag because it is an empty element.

17 Line breaks are given through
tag. **CBSE 2015**

Ans. **True**
 tag will insert a line break.

18 <HR> tag is not used to align the horizontal lines in a Web page.

Ans. **False** <HR> tag is used to display horizontal lines in a Web page.

19 A list item is designed with the empty tag <LI>.

Ans. **True** It is the standard format of HTML that designed with the empty tag <LI>.

20 An ordered list starts with the <UL> tag.

Ans. **False** An ordered list starts with the <OL> tag. <UL> tag is used to start an unordered list.

21 Can you use the unordered type option in ordered type?

Ans. **True** Using the nested list, we can use the unordered type option inside ordered type.

22 We cannot number a list as A, B, C, D etc.

Ans. **False** We can number a list alphabetically either lowercase or uppercase.

23 The <DL> tag shows elements without any bullet symbols or any number in the front of items.

Ans. **True** It is a definition list that shows elements without any bullet symbols or any number in the front of items.

Very Short Answer (VSA) Type Questions

1 HTML is a markup language. Expand the term HTML. **CBSE 2002**

Ans. HyperText Markup Language.

2 Give examples of a container element in HTML. **CBSE 2009**

Ans. <HEAD>, <TITLE>, <BODY>.

3 Give the examples of an empty element in HTML. **CBSE 2010, 09**

Ans.
, <HR>

4 Write the extension of HTML code file. **CBSE 2005**

Ans. .html or .htm

5 While writing HTML code, how do you find out how your Web page would look like? **CBSE 2007**

Ans. For this, open the HTML code file in a Web browser.

6 What is the method of viewing the source code of the current page in the Web browser?

Ans. Right click on the Web page and then select View Source from the context menu.

7 How would you display text in the title bar of a browser? **CBSE 2005**

Ans. To display text in a title bar of a browser, use the <TITLE> tag inside the <HEAD> tag in the HTML document.

e.g.

```
<HTML>
   <HEAD>
      <TITLE> HTML document </TITLE>
   </HEAD>
</HTML>
```

8 Write HTML code to set the image 'Pen.jpg' stored in 'My Pictures' folder in C: as the background of your Web page. **CBSE 2007**

Ans. The HTML code is <BODY background="C:\My Pictures \Pen.jpg">.

9 Name two common graphic files formats that most browser recognise. **CBSE 2007**

Ans. The two common graphic file formats are: .gif and .jpg.

10 Write one basic difference between bgcolor and background attributes.

Ans. The bgcolor attribute is used for coloring the background of the document while background attribute specifies a background image for a document.

11 Explain the following statement:

```
<BODY bgcolor="yellow" text="red"
vlink="blue">
```

CBSE 2010

Ans. The code will set the Web page background color as yellow, text color as red and visited link color as blue.

12 Identify the error(s) in the following HTML code. Also, write the correct code. **CBSE 2008**

```
<BODY color="red" background
="school.jpg">
```

Ans. The error in the code is that in place of color attribute there should be bgcolor.

The correct code is

```
<BODY bgcolor="red" background
          ="school.jpg">
```

13 What do you understand by option alink used with <BODY> tag? **CBSE 2010, 04**

Ans. alink attribute defines the color of the link as it is being clicked on the Web page. The default color of alink is red.

14 What do you understand by option vlink used with <BODY> tag? **CBSE 2005, 04**

Ans. vlink attribute defines the color of a link after it has been visited. The default color of vlink attribute is purple.

15 What is the use of <FONT> tag in HTML code? Write any two options used with this tag. **CBSE 2002**

Ans. The <FONT> tag is used to change the size, color and type face of the text on HTML page. It uses attributes such as size, face etc.

16 How the font size of a single line on a Web page be changed? **CBSE 2005**

Ans. The font size of a single line can be changed by using the following HTML code:

`<FONT size =+1>` This is a HTML text `</FONT>`.

17 Identify the errors and write the correct HTML code **CBSE 2011**

(a) `<BODY background = "red">`
(b) `<FONT type="arial">`

Ans. (a) `<BODY bgcolor="red">`
(b) `<FONT face="arial">`

18 Why do we insert comments in an HTML document, even though they are not displayed on a Web page? **CBSE 2005**

Ans. So, that user will be able to understand coding effects and meaning.

19 What is the method of using comment line in the HTML code? **CBSE 2005, 03**

Ans. In HTML code, the comment line is declared as `<!--Any text-->`.

20 Which heading element gives the most prominent headings? **CBSE 2007**

Ans. <H1>

21 Which tag is used to insert heading of third level on a Web page? **CBSE 2007**

Ans. <H3>

22 What is the purpose of using the tags <H1>...<H6>? **CBSE 2004**

or What is the method of using headings in HTML? **CBSE 2004**

or Write the difference between <H1> and <H6> heading tags. **CBSE 2008**

Ans. <HTML> provides six levels of headings. <H1> is the largest heading level while <H6> is the smallest heading level. These headings help us in obtaining a uniform look and feel for the document.

Syntax `<Hn>.........</Hn>`

23 How can anyone insert horizontal line in a Web page? **CBSE 2005**

Ans. Using <HR> tag, anyone can insert horizontal line in a Web page.

24 What is the use of width attribute of <HR> in HTML? **CBSE 2002**

Ans. width attribute specifies the width of a horizontal line in pixels or percent. Its default value is 100%.

25 Explain the following statement:

`<HR size="5" align="right" width="60">` **CBSE 2004**

Ans. The given HTML code produces a horizontal rule with size 5, aligning right on page and of width 60.

26 Write the HTML code to display horizontal line of red color. **CBSE 2015**

Ans. `<HR color = "red">`

27 Write the expansions of the following tags used in HTML. **CBSE 2004**

(a)
 (b) <I> (c) <HR> (d) <U>

Ans. (a)
 – Break line
(b) <I> – Italic
(c) <HR> – Horizontal Rule
(d) <U> – Underline

28 What are the different forms of list used in HTML? Name any two. **CBSE 2004**

Ans. The different forms of list are ordered list and unordered list.

29 What are two basic tags in HTML lists?

Ans. <OL> and <UL>

30 What does a <LI> create when used in an unordered list?

Ans. <LI> creates bulleted points for each list item.

31 Find error(s) in the following HTML code segment. Rewrite the correct code. **CBSE 2007**

```
<UL style = square>
<LI> Water Bottles
<LI> Lunch Box
<LI> Handkerchief
</UL>
```

Ans. There should be type instead of style. So, correct line is <UL type ="square">

32 Can you change the style of numbers in an ordered list?

Ans. Yes, we can change the style of numbers in an ordered list.

33 Write the expansions of the following tags. **CBSE 2002**

(a) <P> (b) <UL> (c) <OL> (d) <B>

Ans. (a) <P>-Paragraph (b) <UL>-Unordered list
(c) <O>-Ordered list (d) <B >-Bold

Short Answer (SA) Type Questions

1 What is the purpose of HTML? **CBSE 2008**

Ans. HTML (HyperText Markup Language) is used to create Web pages and tells the browser how to display them. It designs the basic layout and formatting of Web pages. HTML is made up of elements or tags and attributes, which work together to identify document parts and tell browser how to display them.

2 What is the purpose of using HTML tags and attributes for Web designing? **CBSE 2013**

Ans. HTML is used to create Web pages. It designs the basic layout and formatting of Web pages by using tags and attributes. The tag's name tells the tag's purpose and the attributes that follow the tag name give the additional information of the Web browser.

3 Differentiate between container and empty elements used in HTML. **CBSE 2011, 10, 02**

or

Distinguish between container and empty tags. **CBSE 2007**

or

Sriram software solution has used different tags in its Website some are empty while majority are container. Give the detailed difference between container and empty elements. **CBSE 2013**

Ans. **Container elements** HTML container elements require a starting as well as an ending tags.
e.g
<HTML>, <HEAD>, <BODY>.
They affect the text appearing between their starting and ending tags.
Empty elements HTML empty elements require just a starting tag and not an ending tag.
e.g.
<IMG>, <BR>, <HR>.
They just carry out the job assigned to them.

4 What is the <TITLE> tag? **CBSE 2006**

Ans. Refer to text on Page No. 44.

5 Find the error(s) in the following code and underline those errors.

```
<HTML>
  <HEAD>
    <TITLE> Example
  </HEAD>
    </TITLE>
  <BODY>.....</BODY>
</HTML>
```

Ans. </TITLE> should be placed before </HEAD>
The correct code is

```
<HTML>
  <HEAD>
    <TITLE> Example </TITLE>
  </HEAD>
  <BODY>.....</BODY>
</HTML>
```

6 What is the use of <BODY> tag in HTML code? Write any two attributes used with this tag. **CBSE 2010, 03**

or

What does <BODY> tag in HTML contain? Write any two attributes used with this tag. **CBSE 2008, 03**

Ans. The <BODY> tag encloses the main part of the document. It contains all the contents of a document. Various markup elements are allowed within the body to indicate heading, paragraphs, lists, hypertext links, images and so on. The <BODY> tag uses various attributes such as background, bgcolor etc.

7 Which tag do we use to change the size and style (face) of the text of an HTML file viewed on a Web browser? Also, explain any two attributes used with this tag. **CBSE 2004**

Ans. <FONT> tag is used to change the size and style (face) of the text of an HTML file displayed on a Web browser.
Two attributes of <FONT> tag are as follows:
size It specifies the size of the text inside a <FONT> tag.

Syntax

```
<FONT size="number">
```

face It specifies the font name of the text inside a <FONT> tag.

Syntax

```
<FONT face="Font_family">
```

8 What is a <BASEFONT> tag? Name any two attributes used with this tag. **CBSE 2009**

Ans. <BASEFONT> tag specifies a default font size, color and face for the font, the browser will use to render normal document text, i.e. the text, for which no other font setting has been provided. It occurs only for one time in the document. The attributes of this tag are size and face.

9 Where can a comment be placed in an HTML document? How is it useful? **CBSE 2008**

or

How do you give a comment in HTML?

or

Why are comment included in HTML document? With the help of an example, explain how they are included in HTML code?

or

How are comments inserted in HTML code? Explain with an example. **CBSE 2007, 06, 05**

Ans. Comments are inserted in HTML code with the help of <!--....--> tag. To insert the text as comment, type the text between <!-- and --> tag, then that text will be ignored by the browser and invisible for the user.

e.g.

```
<HTML><BODY>
<!--This is a comment.-->
This is a book
</BODY></HTML>
```

10 Sumit has to create following list through HTML as a part of his social science project. Help him in writing HTML code for the same. **CBSE 2019**

ASIAN COUNTRIES AND THEIR CAPITALS

1. INDIA
   - New Delhi
2. PAKISTAN
   - Islamabad
3. THAILAND
   - Bangkok

Ans.

```
<HTML>
<BODY>
ASIAN COUNTRIES AND THEIR CAPITALS
<OL>
<LI> INDIA
<UL type = "circle">
<LI> New Delhi
</UL>
<LI> PAKISTAN
<UL type ="circle">
<LI> Islamabad
</UL>
<LI> THAILAND
<UL type = "circle">
<LI> Bangkok
</UL>
</OL>
</BODY>
</HTML>
```

11 List any two types of alignment that can be applied to a paragraph in HTML. **CBSE 2008**

Ans. Any two types of alignment that can be applied to a paragraph are as follows:

Left alignment This type of alignment aligns text in left. This is the default alignment.

Syntax

```
<P align="left">.......</P>
```

Right alignment This type of alignment aligns text in right within the paragraph.

Syntax

```
<P align="right">.......</P>
```

12 Write the HTML code to create a paragraph whose text color is blue. **CBSE 2015**

Ans.

```
<P>
<FONT color="blue">
</FONT>
</P>
```

or

```
<P style = "color : blue"> </P>
```

13 What is the function of <HR> tag in HTML? Give any two attributes used with it.

or

List any two attributes of <HR> tag. **CBSE 2008, 09**

Ans. <HR> tag is used to draw horizontal lines in the Web page. This horizontal line divides the screen horizontally. <HR> tag creates a shaded horizontal line between text. Attributes of <HR> tag are size, align and width.

14 Difference between <BR> and <HR> tags.

Ans.
 tag is used to insert a line break which means the text/image following the tag will be moved to the next line while <HR> tag is used to insert horizontal line that can divide the information into sections.

15 Explain the following with the help of an example: **CBSE 2010**

(a) <U>......</U>

(b) <I>......</I>

Ans. (a) <U> ......</U> This element is used to underline the text.

e.g.

```
<U> School </U>
```

Output

<u>School</u>

(b) <I> ...... </I> This element marks up text in italic form.

e.g.

```
<I> Hello </I>
```

Output

Hello

16 What is the output of the following segment of the HTML code? **CBSE 2010**

```
<BODY>
    <HR width="50%">
        <UL>
            <LI> MANGO </LI>
            <LI> APPLE </LI>
            <LI> GRAPES </LI>
        </UL>
</BODY>
```

Ans. **Output**

- MANGO
- APPLE
- GRAPES

17 Write HTML code to generate the Web page as shown below having lists in the given style:

Career Options **CBSE 2018**

- Medical
  1. Medicine
  2. Research
- Engineering
- Marketing

Ans. The code is

```
<HTML>
<HEAD><TITLE> List </TITLE></HEAD>
<BODY>
Career Options
<UL>
<LI>Medical
<OL type = "1">
<LI>Medicine
<LI>Research
</OL>
<LI>Engineering
<LI>Marketing
</UL>
</BODY>
</HTML>
```

18 Discuss the use of <UL> and <LI> tag with suitable example of each. **CBSE 2018**

Ans. <UL>tag

This list (also known as unnumbered list) is an indented list with a bullet symbol in front of each list item.

<LI>tag

This element is used to indicate a list item as contained in an ordered list or an unordered list.

e.g.

```
<HTML>
<HEAD><TITLE> Unordered List </TITLE></HEAD>
<BODY>
<UL>
<LI>First
<LI>Second
<LI>Third
</UL>
</BODY>
</HTML>
```

19 Explain the following with the help of an example.

(a) <B>......</B> (b) <OL type ="1">

Ans. (a) <B> tag makes the text bold.

e.g. <B>This is a bold text</B>

Output

This is a bold text

(b) <OL> tag with attribute type of value "1" displays the lists of items with arabic numerals.

e.g.

```
<OL type="1">
    <LI> Mango </LI>
    <LI> Apple </LI>
    <LI> Banana </LI>
</OL>
```

Output

1. Mango
2. Apple
3. Banana

20 What is the <OL>......</OL> tag? Name any two attributes used with this tag. **CBSE 2009**

Ans. <OL>......</OL> tag is used for the ordered list, i.e. a list of items to be displayed in a particular order. An ordered list is also a list of items. An ordered list starts with the

<OL> tag. Each list item starts with the <LI> tag.

e.g.

```
<OL>
   <LI> A </LI>
   <LI> B </LI>
</OL>
```

Two attributes of <OL> tag are : start and type.

21 Identify error(s) in the following HTML code. Also, write the correct code. **CBSE 2008**

```
<OL> type="a" start="d">
```

Ans. <OL> tag's attributes should be placed in between < and >. In <OL> list, the start attribute must be set to a numeric value and type attribute specifies 'A', 'a', 'I' 'i' or '1'. So, the correct code is

```
<OL type="a" start="4">
```

22 What is definition list?

Ans. Refer to text on Page No. 54.

23 Write a code to produce the following output.

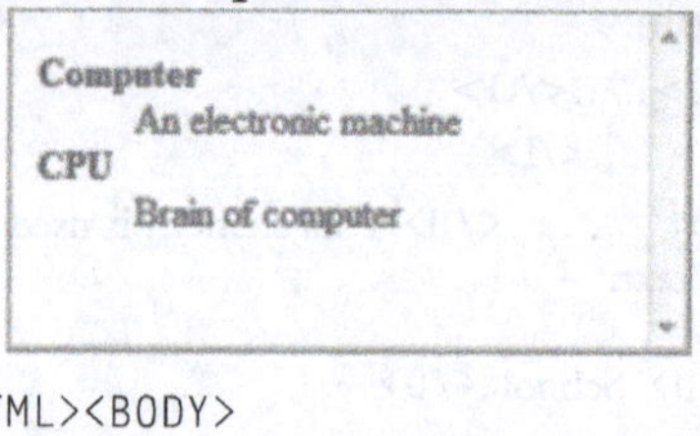

Ans.

```
<HTML><BODY>
   <DL><DT><B>Computer</B>
   <DD>An electronic machine
   <DT><B>CPU</B>
   <DD> Brain of computer</DL>
</BODY></HTML>
```

Long Answer (LA) Type Questions

1 What are the role of <HTML> .....</HTML> tags in HTML? **CBSE 2009**

Ans. The <HTML> and </HTML> tags are used to mark the beginning and end of the HTML document. The basic purpose of this tag is to make the browser and text editor identify that the document is an HTML document.This is a container element and does not affect the appearance of the document. The <HTML> element contains only the <HEAD> and <BODY> elements, which in turn contains a number of other elements.

Syntax

```
<HTML>
  :
</HTML>
```

2 Explain the <HEAD> tag. **CBSE 2006**

Ans. Refer to text on Page No. 44.

3 Explain the topmargin and leftmargin attributes of <BODY> tag. **CBSE 2006**

Ans. Refer to text on Page No. 46.

4 Identify which one is an attribute or a tag?

(*i*) Body (*ii*) Type (*iii*) Br (*iv*) Link (v) Face

Ans. (*i*) Body - Tag (*ii*) Type - Attribute
(*iii*) Br - Tag (*iv*) Link - Attribute
(*v*) Face - Attribute

5 Distinguish between <BASEFONT> tag and <FONT> tag with the help of an example of each. **CBSE 2009, 08**

Ans. <BASEFONT> tag is used to specify the default setting of the text. It takes the same attributes as <FONT> tag. The only difference is that the <BASEFONT> tag affects all the text that follows until a new tag affect that is encountered. <FONT> tag affects the text that comes upto its closing </FONT> tag.

e.g.

```
<HTML>
   <BODY>
      <BASEFONT size="2" color="red">
      Hi Everyone
      <FONT size="4">
      HTML is a Web language </FONT>
      It is used for creating Web pages.
   </BODY>
</HTML>
```

Here, in the above example only the text enclosed in <FONT> ..... </FONT> is affected by font setting, rest of the text gets affected by BASEFONT setting.

6 Distinguish between <P> tag and <BR> tag with the help of an example. **CBSE 2005**

Ans. Distinguishing between <P> tag and <BR> tag are as follows:

<P> tag	 tag
It is a container element.	It is an empty element.
It is used to define a paragraph of the text on the Web page.	It is used to insert the line break.
It inserts line break with extra space in the beginning.	It does not insert any extra space.
This tag has an attribute align.	This tag has no attribute.

EXAM PRACTICE

<P> tag	* tag*
e.g. <HTML> <BODY> <P> This is a paragraph. </p> </BODY> </HTML>	e.g. <HTML> <BODY> This is a line break into the Web document. </BODY> </HTML>

7 Carefully study the Web page given here. Identify 10 tags (Structural as well as formatting tags) that have been utilised in creating this Web page and write usage of each of them. **CBSE 2013**

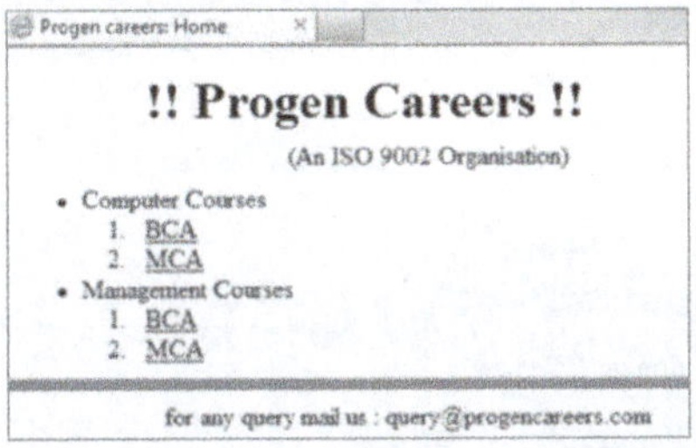

Ans. (*i*) <HTML> - - - </HTML> It encloses the entire HTML document and tells the browser that it is reading an HTML document and to display as such.

(*ii*) <HEAD> - - - </HEAD> It encloses the head of the HTML document and it is used to contain face information about the document.

(*iii*) <TITLE> - - - - </TITLE> It indicates the title of the document and appears in a browser's bookmark file.

(*iv*) <BODY> - - - - </BODY> It is used to enclose the body (text, images, tags, links) of the HTML document.

(*v*) <H1> - - - - </H1> It is used to define the heading level 1.

(*vi*) <UL> - - - - </UL> It is used to create an unordered list.

(*vii*) <LI> - - - - </LI> It is used to define each list item in the list.

(*viii*) <U> - - - - </U> It is used to underline the text.

(*ix*) <HR> It is used to insert a horizontal line.

(*x*) <CENTER> ... </CENTER> This tag is used to align the text centrally.

8 Write HTML code to display various bullet types.

Ans.
```
<HTML>
  <HEAD>
    <TITLE>Various Bullet Styles
    </TITLE>
  </HEAD>
  <BODY>
    <UL type="disc">
      <LI>Mango</LI>
      <LI>Grapes</LI>
    </UL>
    <UL type = "circle">
      <LI>Lotus</LI>
      <LI>Rose</LI>
    </UL>
    <UL type = "square">
      <LI>Sun</LI>
      <LI>Moon</LI>
    </UL>
  </BODY>
</HTML>
```

Output

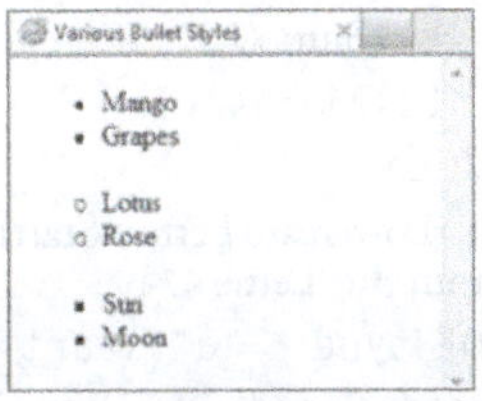

9 Give HTML code for the following output

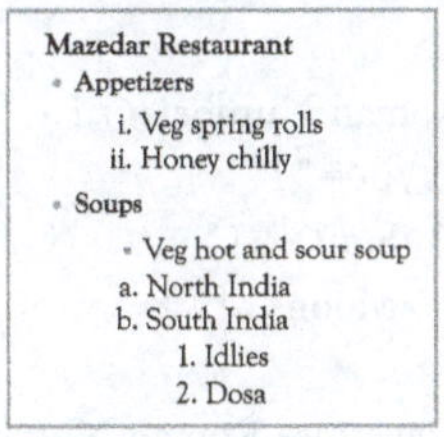

Ans.
```
<HTML>
  <BODY>
  <UL type="disc"><B>Mazedar Restaurant
  </B><LI><B>Appetizers</B>
    <OL type ="i">
      <LI> Veg spring rolls
      <LI> Honey chilly
    </OL>
    <LI><B>Soups</B>
    <UL type = "square">
      <LI> Veg hot and Sour soup
    </UL>
    <OL type = "a">
      <LI> North India
      <LI> South India
    <OL type = "1">
      <LI> Idlies
      <LI> Dosa
    </OL>
    </OL>
    </UL>
  </BODY>
</HTML>
```

10 **Write HTML code to display ordered lists.**

Ans.

```
<HTML>
  <HEAD>
    <TITLE>Many Ordered List</TITLE>
  </HEAD>
  <BODY>
    <I>Numbered List</I>
    <OL>
      <LI>Sun</LI>
      <LI>Moon</LI>
    </OL>
    <I>Letters List</I>
    <OL type = "A">
      <LI>Sun</LI>
      <LI>Moon</LI>
    </OL>
    <I>Lowercase Letters Starting
    From 3rd Letter</I>
    <OL type = "a" start = "3">
      <LI>Sun</LI>
      <LI>Moon</LI>
    </OL>
    <I>Roman Numbers</I>
    <OL type="I">
      <LI>Sun</LI>
      <LI>Moon</LI>
    </OL>
    <I>Lowercase Roman Number List
    Starting From 5th Number</I>
    <OL type = "i" start= "5">
      <LI>Sun</LI>
      <LI>Moon</LI>
    </OL>
  </BODY>
</HTML>
```

Output

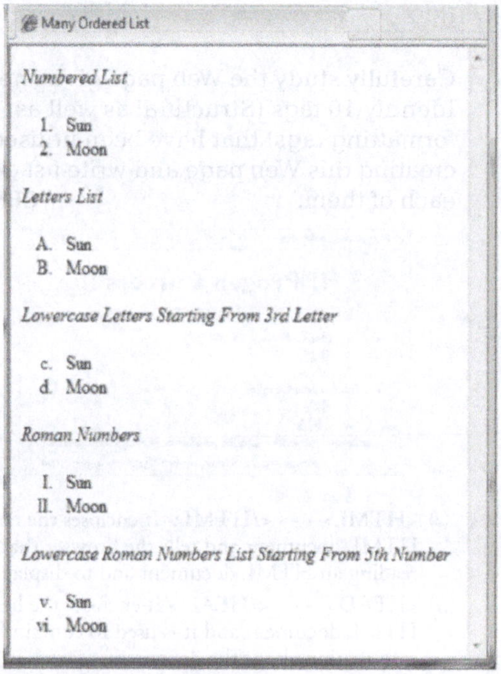

Application Oriented Questions

1 Consider the HTML code given below

```
<HTML>
<HEAD>
<TITLE> First Page </TITLE>
</HEAD>
<BODY bgcolor="red" text="white">
<FONT size="10" color="black" face ="arial">
This is my first Web page </FONT>
</BODY>
</HTML>
```

Now, answer the following questions:

(*i*) What will be displayed in the title bar of the browser?

(*ii*) Name the attributes of FONT tag used in the given code.

(*iii*) What will be displayed in the browser window and in which color?

(*iv*) What will be color of background?

Ans. (*i*) First Page

(*ii*) size, color and face

(*iii*) This is my first Web page
It will be displayed in black color.

(*iv*) Background color will be red.

2 **Write the HTML code to display the text in red color and arial font. Give the background image of your choice.**

Ans.

```
<HTML>
  <BODY background
    = "C:\My pictures\computer.jpg">
    <FONT color = "red" face = "arial">
    Learning HTML is quite easy.
```

```
HTML is a markup language.
</FONT>
</BODY>
</HTML>
```

3 Write the HTML code to generate a Web page in the format shown below:

(*i*) Title of the page as HTML code.

(*ii*) The bgcolor as golden with red text, font size 10 and color as purple with Times New Roman face.

(*iii*) Heading one as "Welcome to HTML".

(*iv*) Heading two as "Web language".

(*v*) A text line as "HyperText Markup Language".

(*vi*) A bold text line "Markup text"

Ans.

```
<HTML>
  <HEAD>
    <TITLE> HTML code </TITLE>
  </HEAD>
  <BODY bgcolor = "golden" text="red">
    <FONT size="10" color = "purple"
    face = "Times New Roman">
    <H1> Welcome to HTML </H1>
    <H2> Web language </H2>
    HyperText Markup Language
    <B> Markup text </B>
    </FONT>
  </BODY>
</HTML>
```

4 Use the following information to answer the questions (*i*) and (*ii*)

Janine used an HTML editor to edit the code of a Web page she developed for an assignment.

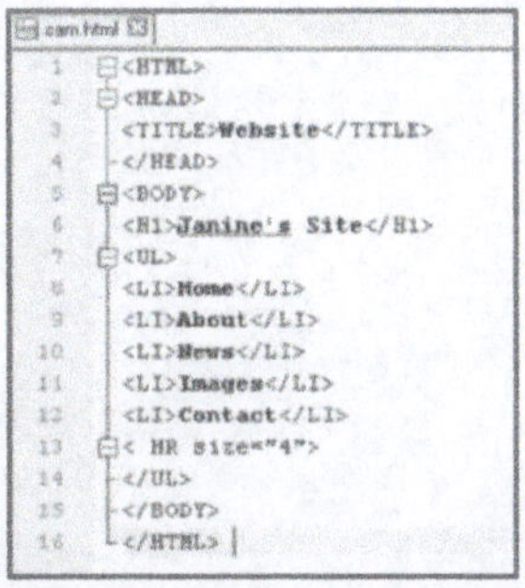

Janine found that her horizontal ruler did not display correctly on her Web page.

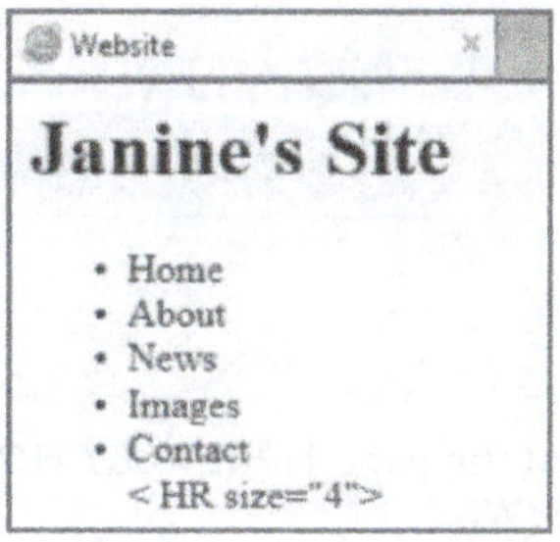

(*i*) What is the most likely reason for this?

(*ii*) The tag <HEAD> specifies

Ans. (*i*) Space between angular bracket and HR.

(*ii*) The container of all the header element.

5 Write HTML code to generate a Web page in the format shown

(*i*) The title should be 'My first Web page'.

(*ii*) The body of the text should be 'Creating Web page using HTML'

(*iii*) A horizontal line after the body text.

(*iv*) A message line 'The above line is a horizontal line'.

(*v*) At last print your name and address, make your name italic and bold. Make sure that a line break after every line.

Ans.

```
<HTML>
  <HEAD>
    <TITLE>
      My first Web page
    </TITLE>
  </HEAD>
  <BODY>
    Creating Web page using HTML<HR>
    The above line is a horizontal line.
    <P>
      <I> <B> Samarth Das </B> </I>
      <BR>
      112, Akash Nagar <BR>
      Meerut <BR>
    </P>
  </BODY>
</HTML>
```

6 Write the HTML code to generate the following Web page. **CBSE 2013**

Note Tags and attributes needed to generate Web page based on notes must appear in the code. You may use any tags as needed.

(*i*) Title of the page is "REALLY HONEST BOOK REVIEWS."

(*ii*) Background color of the page is "aqua" and the text color is "blue".

(*iii*) The links are in "green". The active and visited links are in "red".

(*iv*) 'News Gothic MT' font has been used everywhere.

(*v*) Use Horizontal Ruler wherever required. Their color is blue.

(*vi*) Use ordered/ unordered lists wherever required.

(*vii*) The style of following are

(a) "The Rainbow Returns" by E. Smith. - it must appear in green, bold and underline.

(b) "Seven steps to immeasurable wealth" by R.U. Needy. - purple color, arial font.

(c) "The Food_Lover's Guide to Weight Loss" by L. Goode. - black color, italics.

(d) "A Silly Person's Guide to Seriousness" by M. Nott. - yellow color, underlined.

Ans.
```
<HTML>
  <HEAD>
    <TITLE>
    REALLY HONEST BOOK REVIEWS
    </TITLE>
  </HEAD>
  <BODY bgcolor="aqua" text="blue" link=
  "green" alink="red" vlink="red">
    <BASEFONT face= "News Gothic MT">
    <CENTER> <H1> REALLY HONEST
    </H1></CENTER>
    <H1 align="right"> BOOK REVIEWS
    </H1>
    <HR color="blue">
I read a lot of books about many different subjects,here is
a list of books that I have read recently
    <UL type ="square"><LI><B><U>
    <FONT color="green">"
    The Rainbow Returns"
    by E.Smith</FONT></U></B>
    <LI><FONT face="arial" color="purple">
     "Seven steps to immeasurable wealth" by
       R.U. Needy.</FONT>
    <LI> <I><FONT color = "black"> "The
       Food_Lover's Guide to Weight Loss" by L.
       Goode. </FONT> </I>
    <LI><U><FONT color="yellow">"A Silly
     Person's Guide to Seriousness" by M.
       Nott.</FONT></U>
    </UL>
  </BODY>
</HTML>
```

CHAPTER

04

Inserting Images and Links in HTML

Chapter Checklist

- Inserting an Image in a Web Page
- Linking
  - External Linking
  - Internal Linking
- Sending E-Mail from a Browser (mailto)
- Superscript and Subscript in HTML

When we open a Website, it provides information in the two different formats, i.e. information through text and information through images. Information through images can be easily gathered by the user as compared to the information written in text. Thus, it becomes important for a Web developer to know how to insert images in an HTML Web pages, because an image not only makes the Web page attractive, it helps to break the monotony of text and maintain the user's interest in the Web page. Another, interesting element within an HTML Web page is hyperlink (or simply link). It is a word or group of words or image that you can click on, to jump to another Web page or within the same Web page.

Inserting an Image in a Web Page

HTML can be used to insert images in the following formats:

(*i*) GIF (Graphics Interchange Format) (*ii*) XBM (X Bitmap)

(*iii*) JPG or JPEG (Joint Photographic Experts Group)

(*iv*) PNG (Portable Network Graphics)

The <IMG> tag is used to insert an image in a Web page. It is very important to know that images are not technical part of the Web page file, they are separate files which are inserted into the Web page, when it is viewed by a browser.

So, a simple Web page with one image is actually two files. When an HTML file is displayed in a browser, it requests the image file and places it on the Web page where the tag appears.

Syntax

```
<IMG src = "image URL" [various attributes]>
```

Here, src attribute is used because it provides the information about the path of an image file to the Web browser.

<IMG> tag is an empty element, which means it has no closing tag.

Attributes of <IMG> Tag

Following are the various attributes of <IMG> tag:

src Attribute

The src (source) attribute takes URL (Universal Resource Locator) of an image file as value, which points to the direct location of an image to be displayed.

The image that you specify in your <IMG> tag should be in your computer otherwise the image will not be displayed and in place of image a cross mark in a box (×) will appear.

Example 1. *To display an image.*

```
<HTML>
  <HEAD><TITLE> Image </TITLE></HEAD>
  <BODY>
    <H1> Look at the image </H1><BR>
    <IMG src = "D:\image.jpg">
  </BODY>
</HTML>
```

Output

Absolute and Relative URL of an Image

An **Absolute URL** is a full path to an image. If the HTML file and image are placed in different folder then in coding defining the full path of an image has to be defined as the value of src attribute.

e.g. <IMG src = "E:\AIO IT Term-2\images\image.jpg" >

A **Relative URL** is a path to an image relative to the current location. If the HTML file and image are placed in same folder then in coding defining the full path of an image is not necessary, thus we have to just write an image name with extension as the value of src attribute.

e.g. <IMG src = "image.jpg" >

alt Attribute

This attribute of <IMG> tag is used to provide alternate text when an image on a Web page cannot be displayed.

The alternate text is the text associated with an image that serves the same purpose and conveys the same essential message. As per HTML standard, alt attribute is optional but is highly recommended.

Sometimes, the Web browser you are using does not display an image that is inserted in the Web page because of slow connection, error in src attribute or if the user uses a screen reader. In such cases, this attribute is specified to provides alternate information for an image. Generally, it is a short description of an image. The value for alt attribute is a text string of upto 1024 characters including spaces and punctuations. The string must be enclosed in quotation marks.

Example 2. *To display an image with some alternate text.*

```
<HTML>
  <HEAD> <TITLE> Image </TITLE> </HEAD>
  <BODY>
    <H1> Look at the image </H1><BR>
    <IMG src = "D:\image.jpg" alt ="It is a
    beautiful flower">
  </BODY>
</HTML>
```

Output

When mouse pointer is moved on the image, the text specified in alt attribute displayed as a tooltip in Internet Explorer only. If you want to provide a tooltip for other browsers such as Mozilla Firefox, Google Chrome etc., use title attribute in place of alt attribute, since it is supported in most of the browsers.

e.g.

```
<IMG src="image1.jpg" title="Flower Picture">
```

Inline Image

An image that is displayed in the same line of the text is called an inline image. Inline images can occur within headings and paragraphs. The <IMG> tag is used to insert inline images into paragraphs and headings.

The browser separately loads images and places them into the text flow as if the images are some special character.

Example 3. *To insert inline image.*

```
<HTML>
   <HEAD> <TITLE>Inline Image</TITLE> </HEAD>
   <BODY>
      <H1>Inline Image</H1><BR>
      This image is placed in the
      <IMG src="flower1.jpg">
      middle section of the sentence.
   </BODY>
</HTML>
```

Output

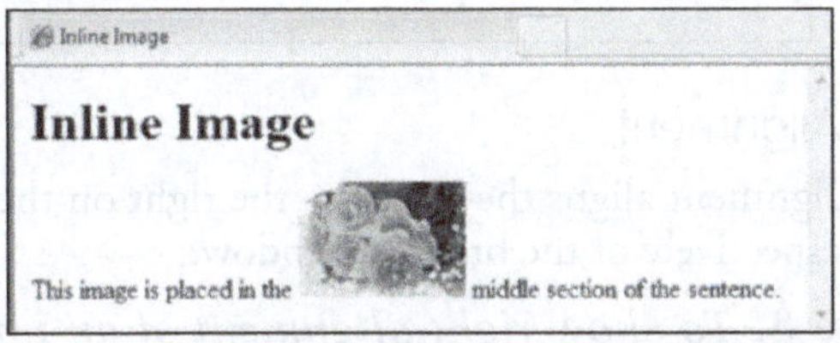

By default, an image, inserted using <IMG> tag, is placed inline with text. However, if you put a <P> tag (paragraph tag) before <IMG> tag, a blank line will appear before and after the image.

e.g. `<P> <IMG src="image1.jpg"> </P>`

align Attribute

This attribute is used to set the position of an image in a Web page according to the user's requirements. In HTML, images appear inline with a single line of the text. But, HTML standard does not define a default alignment for the images with respect to other text and images in the same line.

Hence, the absolute output regarding the placement of image cannot be predicted in advance. So, to control the image alignment, align attribute is used. The alignment of the image depends upon the Web browser that you are using to view the Web page. This implies that the Web page can be different according to the Web browser such as Internet Explorer and Mozilla Firefox. There are some values of image alignment attribute as follows:

1. Top Alignment

This alignment aligns the top of an image with the top edge of the tallest item in the text line. If there are no other images in the current line, then the image is aligned to top of the text. Both Internet Explorer and Mozilla Firefox treat this alignment in same manner.

Example 4. *To show top alignment of an image.*

```
<HTML>
   <HEAD> <TITLE> Alignment </TITLE> </HEAD>
   <BODY>
      <H1> Top Alignment </H1>
      <IMG src="flower2.jpg" align="top">
      A flower, sometimes known as a bloom or
      blossom, is the reproductive structure found in
      flowering plants. The biological function of a
      flower is to effect reproduction, usually by
      providing a mechanism for the union of sperm
      with eggs.
   </BODY>
</HTML>
```

Output

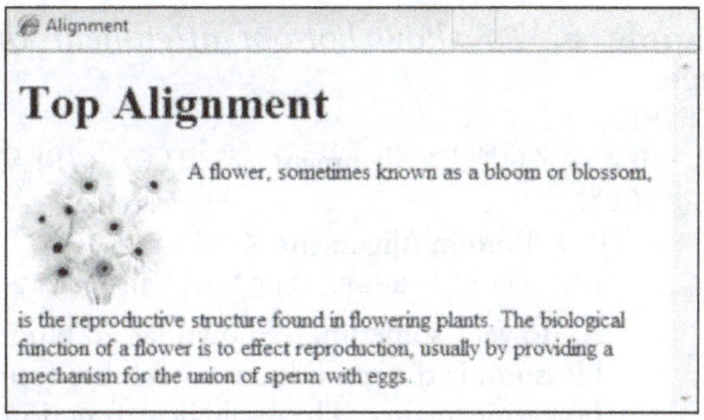

2. Middle Alignment

This alignment is different in both Internet Explorer and Mozilla Firefox. In Internet Explorer, this alignment aligns the image to the middle of the tallest item in the current line. While in Mozilla Firefox, this alignment aligns the image to the baseline of the current line in which it is placed.

Example 5. *To show middle alignment of an image.*

```
<HTML>
   <HEAD>
      <TITLE> Alignment </TITLE>
   </HEAD>
   <BODY>
      <H1> Middle Alignment </H1>
      <IMG src="flower2.jpg" align="middle">
      A flower, sometimes known as a bloom or blossom,
      is the reproductive structure found in flowering
      plants. The biological function of a flower is to
      effect reproduction, usually by providing a
      mechanism for the union of sperm with eggs.
   </BODY>
</HTML>
```

Output

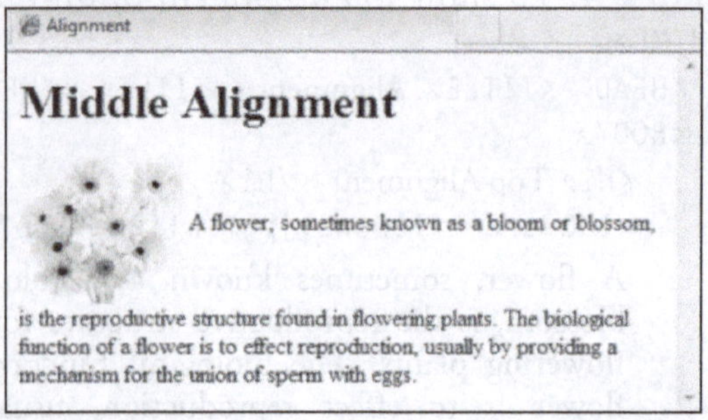

3. Bottom Alignment

This alignment aligns the bottom edge of the image, to the same horizontal plane as the baseline of the text. Both Internet Explorer and Mozilla Firefox treat this alignment in the same manner.

Example 6. *To show bottom alignment of an image.*

```
<HTML>
  <HEAD> <TITLE> Alignment </TITLE> </HEAD>
  <BODY>
    <H1> Bottom Alignment </H1>
    <IMG src="flower2.jpg" align="bottom">
      A flower, sometimes known as a bloom or
      blossom, is the reproductive structure found in
      flowering plants. The biological function of a
      flower is to effect reproduction, usually by
      providing a mechanism for the union of sperm
      with eggs.
  </BODY>
</HTML>
```

Output

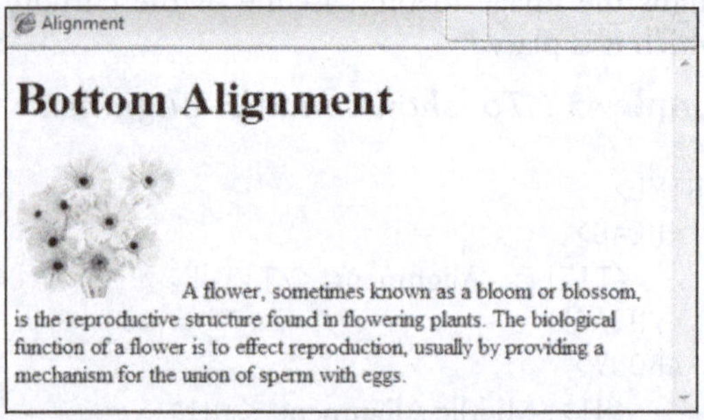

4. Left Alignment

This alignment aligns the image to the left on the Web page respectively of the browser window.

Example 7. *To show left alignment of an image.*

```
<HTML>
  <HEAD> <TITLE> Alignment </TITLE> </HEAD>
    <BODY>
      <H1> Left Alignment </H1>
      <IMG src="flower2.jpg" align="left">
        A flower, sometimes known as a bloom or
        blossom, is the reproductive structure found in
        flowering plants. The biological function of a
        flower is to effect reproduction, usually by
        providing a mechanism for the union of sperm
        with eggs.
    </BODY>
</HTML>
```

Output

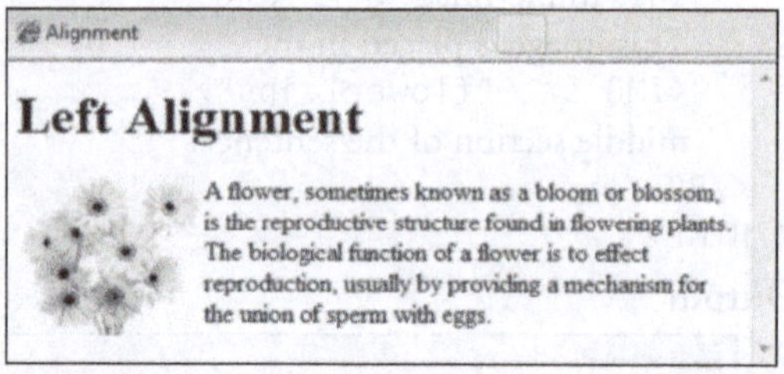

5. Right Alignment

This alignment aligns the image to the right on the Web page respectively of the browser window.

Example 8. *To show right alignment of an image.*

```
<HTML>
  <HEAD> <TITLE> Alignment </TITLE> </HEAD>
  <BODY>
    <H1> Right Alignment </H1>
    <IMG src="flower2.jpg" align="right">
      A flower, sometimes known as a bloom or
      blossom, is the reproductive structure found in
      flowering plants. The biological function of a
      flower is to effect reproduction, usually by
      providing a mechanism for the union of sperm
      with eggs.
  </BODY>
</HTML>
```

Output

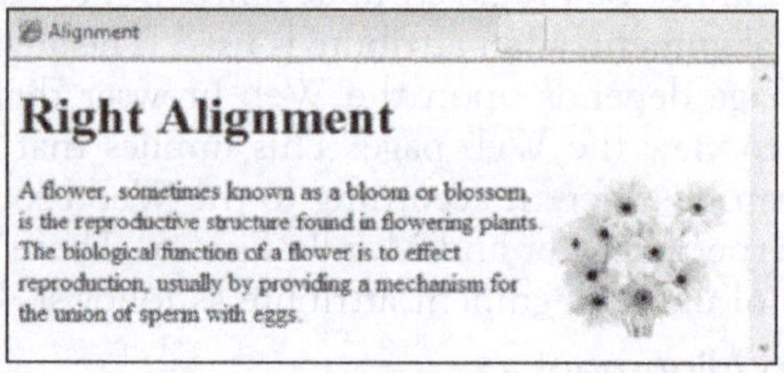

Note In align attribute, you cannot center align an image horizontally. The middle align, aligns the image vertically with the line of text in which the image is presented. For this purpose (i.e. to center align the image horizontally), <CENTER> tag can be used. In its simplest form, center alignment may be specified as follows:

```
<CENTER><IMG src="img1.jpg"></CENTER>
```

width and height Attributes

When an image is added to a Web page, it is not mandatory to specify width and height of the image. At the time of loading an image, a box will appear on the place where the image will be loaded. This box may be of any size and often of the wrong size.

Then, when the image finally begins to load, it is suddenly found to be too big for the given space. So, everything shifts around to make place for the image and this cause obstruction.

To prevent this situation, width and height attributes are used. The width and height attributes tell the dimensions of an image to the browser.

If height and width are set, the space required for image is reserved before loading the page.

Both (height and width) attributes require integer values (dimension of image in terms of either pixels or percentage of its actual size). It is also noticeable that the order in which these attributes appear, is not important.

Example 9. ***To illustrate the use of width and height attributes.***

```
<HTML>
   <HEAD>
      <TITLE> Resize </TITLE>
   </HEAD>
   <BODY>
      <H1> Height and Width </H1>
   Original Image <IMG src ="picture1.jpg">
   After Resizing <IMG src="picture1.jpg"
   height = "50" width = "50">
   </BODY>
</HTML>
```

Output

border Attribute

You can set the border of an image that you want to use in your Web page. The border attribute of the <IMG> tag specifies the width of the border around an image. By default, an image has no border in HTML.

Example 10. ***To set the border around an image using border attribute.***

```
<HTML>
   <HEAD><TITLE> Setting Image Border </TITLE>
   </HEAD>
   <BODY>
      <H1> Setting Image Border </H1>
      <CENTER>
         <IMG src="flower1.jpg" height="120"
          width="200" border="5">
      </CENTER>
   </BODY>
</HTML>
```

Output

Check Point 01

1. Name some common image formats used in HTML Web pages.
2. The .... attribute of the <IMG> tag is used to specify the location of an image.
3. Sahil wants to display the image on Web page. When image finally begins to load, it is found to be too big for the given space. Then, which attribute(s) will you suggest him for this situation?

Linking

A key feature of the HTML is its ability to link text and/or an image to another document or within a document. If you are on a Web page and see the colored and/or an underlined text, it is a **hyperlink**. It is also known as **hypertext link** or just **link**. By default, color of a hyperlink is blue. The main objectives of linking are as follows:

(*i*) To add more pages to the Website and link them together.

(*ii*) Using internal links (anchors) to save scrolling for visitors.

(*iii*) To indirect the user to Web page of different Website.

In other words, hyperlinks are the links that carry user from one Web page to another (within or on another Website). It is activated by clicking on an underlined text or image. And, when the mouse pointer is brought over a hyperlink, the pointer changes to a hand. In HTML, links can be created by using **<A> anchor tag.** <A> tag is a container tag that means it requires a starting as well as ending tags.

To include an anchor in your document, you should do the following:

(*i*) Start the anchor tag with <A.

(*ii*) Specify the document you are linking to, by entering the parameter href = "file name with extension".

(*iii*) Place closing right angle bracket (>).

(*iv*) Enter the text that will serve as the hypertext link after the opening <A> tag.

(*v*) Enter the closing anchor tag </A>.

More precisely, it can be seen as:

```
<A href ="mypage.html">My another page</A>
```

Here, it is noticeable that the final </A> tag is required. If it is not included, everything following that link will also be linked to another document, until the tag is closed.

Types of Linking

There are two types of linking in a Web page, which are as follows:

1. External Linking

This leads to a link that go to another Website. In other words, it refers to a different page on a different Website. When a user click on a hyperlink on a Web page, user is directed on the location, which is specified in that hyperlink. To create an external link with <A> tag and its href attribute (to define URL of target document), a title attribute also needed.

href Attribute

The href stands for Hypertext REFerence. The href attribute is used to specify the URL of the target document. It is used to specify the destination of Web page, which is linked. Notice, the pages on Internet should give a complete URL, i.e. alongwith http://.

Example 11. ***To show external linking.***

```
<HTML>
  <HEAD> <TITLE> Creating a Hyperlink </TITLE>
  </HEAD>
  <BODY> <H1> Look at the image </H1>
  <BR><IMG src ="D:\images.jpg"
     alt = "It is a beautiful picture">
     <A href= "http://www.google.com">
     Click Here </A> to get more flower images.
  </BODY>
</HTML>
```

Output

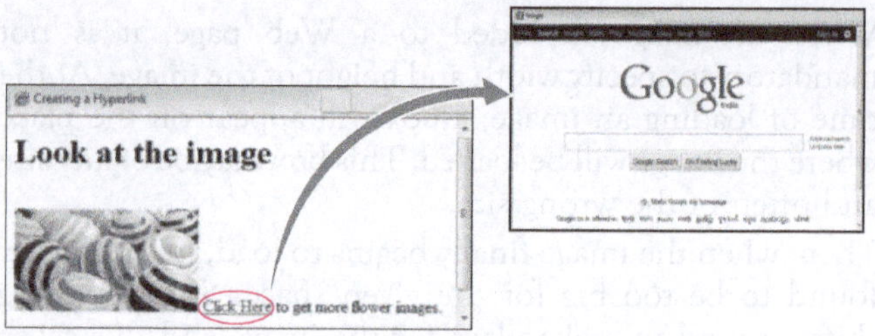

Images as Links

Images can also be used as hyperlinks. To create image as a link, following syntax is used:

```
<A href = "URL"> <IMG src="image1.jpg"> </A>
```

Example 12. ***To show image as link.***

```
<HTML>
  <HEAD>
     <TITLE>Image as Link</TITLE>
  </HEAD>
  <BODY>
     <A href="http://en.wikipedia.org/wiki
     /Tweety">
     <IMG src="D:\Class10\computer
     \tweety1.jpg"></A>
  </BODY>
</HTML>
```

Output

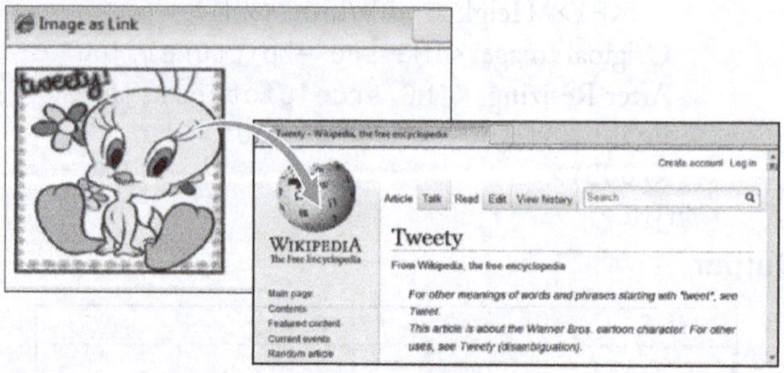

Listed Hyperlinks

It is noticeable that <A> tag can also be used for more complex task (as with images or with lists etc.)

Example 13. ***To show listed hyperlinks.***

```
<HTML>
  <HEAD> <TITLE> List </TITLE> </HEAD>
  <BODY> <H1> List </H1>
     <UL>
     <LI><A href="link1.html"><IMG src="F:
     \Fruits-wallpaper-91.jpg"
     align="middle" height="75" width="75">
     Fruit Chart </A></LI><BR><BR>
```

```
<LI> <A href= "link2.html">
<IMG src="F:\vegetable.jpg"
align="middle" width="75" height="75">
Vegetable Chart </A> </LI> </UL>
</BODY>
</HTML>
```

Output

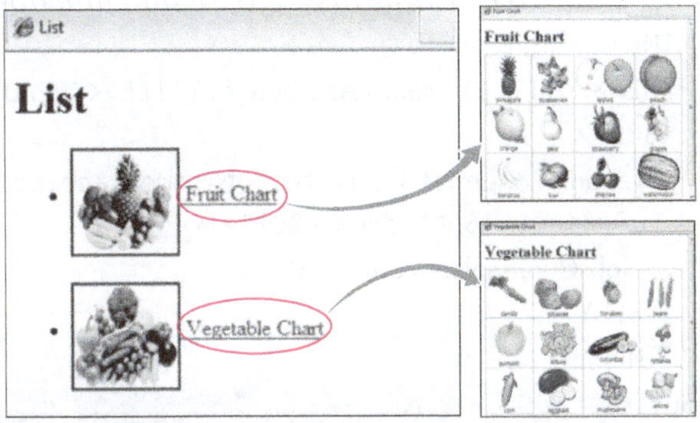

title Attribute

The title attribute of anchor <A> tag is used to specify the title of the document to which, we are linking. The value of the title attribute can be any string enclosed within double (or single) quotes. It is used for referencing an unlabeled resource (like an image or a non-HTML document). The value specified for this attribute appears as a tooltip when the mouse pointer is placed over the hyperlink. The title attribute can also be used by the browser, when adding the link to the user's hotlist.

Example 14. *To illustrate the use of title attribute.*

```
<HTML>
<HEAD><TITLE>Creating Hyperlink </TITLE></HEAD>
<BODY>
<A href ="http://www.google.com" title
="It is a hyperlink"> Click Here </A>
</BODY>
</HTML>
```

Output

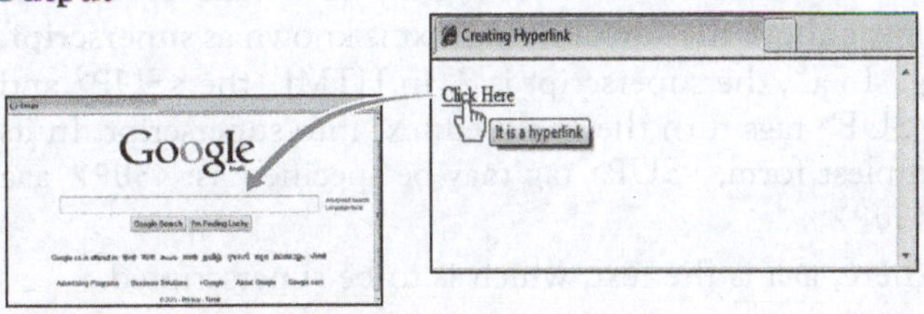

2. Internal Linking

This is a type of HTML linking that links pages within a single Website, various sections of same document or different document.

Linking on the Same Web Page

To create an internal link, you need to use a pair of <A> tags. The first <A> tag is used to specify the name of the target location for identification purpose. It is known as **target fragment**. You can use the <A> tag with its name or id attribute to identify a fragment. This type of anchor is commonly called as **named anchor**.

The first step is to make the target fragment. The simple syntax to do so is written below:

```
<A name ="aa"> Part A </A>
```

Where, "aa" is the name of fragment/segment that you want to refer (like top, bottom etc.). The second <A> tag is used to create a link to the target fragment. The simple syntax to link to the target segment is written below:

```
<A href = "#aa"> Click Here </A>
```

In the second <A> tag, the value of href attribute with # symbol is to be specified.

Example 15. *To show the internal linking in an HTML document.*

```
<HTML>
<HEAD><TITLE>Internal Linking</TITLE></HEAD>
<BODY>
<H1>Linking in a page </H1>
<H3>Click here to go to the
<A href="#bottom">bottom</A>of the
page.</H3>
<BR><BR><BR><BR><BR><BR><BR><BR><BR>
<BR><BR>
<BR><BR><BR><BR><BR><BR><BR><BR><BR>
<BR>
<BR><BR><BR><BR><BR><BR><BR><BR><BR>
<BR><BR>
<A name="bottom"><H3> You are at the bottom
of the page.</H3></A>
</BODY>
</HTML>
```

Output

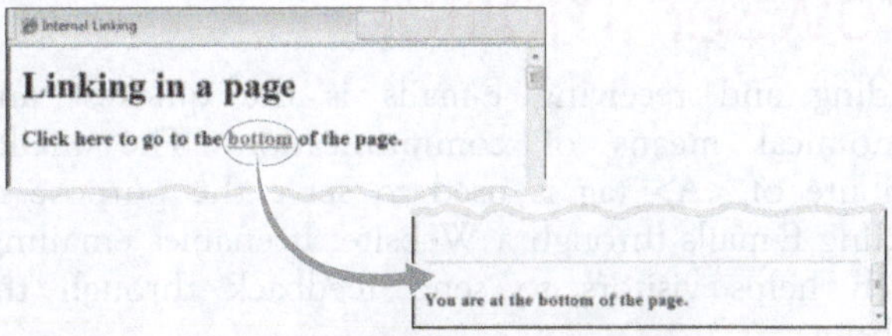

Linking Sections of Different Web Pages

Internal linking enables us to link sections of different Web pages also. It can be done by specifying the name of the Web page and the section which is to be linked. To link two Web pages, you first need name to the section by using name attribute of <A> tag that you want to link. Suppose, we need to link a section of HTML1.html to HTML2.html. Create a named anchor in HTML1.html. The syntax is given below:

```
<A name ="link"> Different Page </A>
```

After this, you have to write the code to refer to it, from Web page HTML2.html. Following is the code to do so:

```
<A href ="HTML1.html#link">
```

Here, HTML1.html is the name of HTML file to the section of which you want to link and # link is the segment name you want to link in that html file.

Significance of Linking

Links on a Web page allow user to jump to another document. It is a very useful feature of HTML as when you click on a hypertext, it carries you to other document.

It enables the Web page writer to refer to other documents and thus prevent the need of creating large document.

e.g. if you are reading an E-book, where many chapters are explained. Now, if you want to read the last chapter of the book, then by using hyperlink, you can go to that chapter directly without scrolling down to whole book.

Check Point 02

1. Write only the code fragment for an image named 'hills.jpg', which when clicked opens the Web page www.hillsofindia.in?
2. What is the correct syntax in HTML for creating a link on a Web page?
3. Which attribute of the <A> tag takes the URL of the linked file?
4. <A> tag enables us to link sections of different Web pages. (True/False)

Sending E-Mail from a Browser (mailto)

Sending and receiving E-mails is the quickest and economical means of communication. The mailto attribute of <A> tag is used to serve the purpose of sending E-mails through a Website. It enables emailing, which helps visitors to send feedback through the Website.

The mailto value when used alongwith an E-mail address in href attribute of anchor tag, will create a link. When this link will be clicked, it will open default E-mail client. You can also add a header to E-mail sent from a mailto link. Using "?Subject = Subject line", we can add subject line of the E-mail window.

Example 16. *To illustrate the use of mailto function.*

```
<HTML>
  <HEAD><TITLE> Mailto Attribute </TITLE></HEAD>
  <BODY>
     Send to <A href="mailto:job@someplace.com?
     Subject='Sent from ABC'">
     jobs@someplace.com </A>
  </BODY>
</HTML>
```

Output

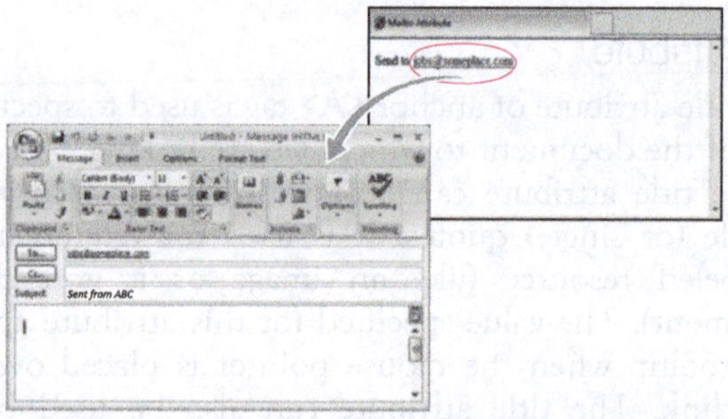

Note It is noticeable that through mailto function E-mail messages can be send to multiple recipients. For this, only E-mail addresses of the recipients are to be typed in the same link separated with commas.

Superscript and Subscript in HTML

<SUP> Tag

The text which is elevated slightly above the baseline to appear above the surrounding text is known as **superscript**. e.g. In a^2, the superscript is 2. In HTML, the ^{and} tags turn the enclosed text into superscript. In its simplest form, <SUP> tag may be specified as: `<SUP> aaa </SUP>`

Where, aaa is the text, which is to be superscripted.

Example 17. *To show the use of superscript.*

```
<HTML>
   <HEAD><TITLE> Superscripted </TITLE></HEAD>
   <BODY>
      <H1> Some Examples of Superscript are </H1>
      2<SUP>3</SUP>=8<BR>
      14<SUP>x</SUP>=8<BR>
      e<SUP>x</SUP>=8<BR>
   </BODY>
</HTML>
```

Output

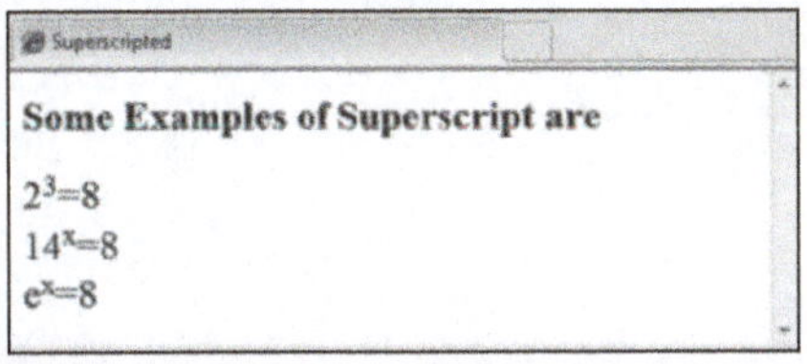

Example 18. *To show the use of subscript.*

```
<HTML>
   <HEAD><TITLE> Subscripted </TITLE></HEAD>
   <BODY>
      <H1> Some Examples of Subscript are </H1>
      <P>H<SUB>2</SUB>O - Water </P><BR>
      <P>log <SUB>2</SUB>x</P><BR>
      <P>CO<SUB>2</SUB> - Carbon Dioxide</P>
   </BODY>
</HTML>
```

Output

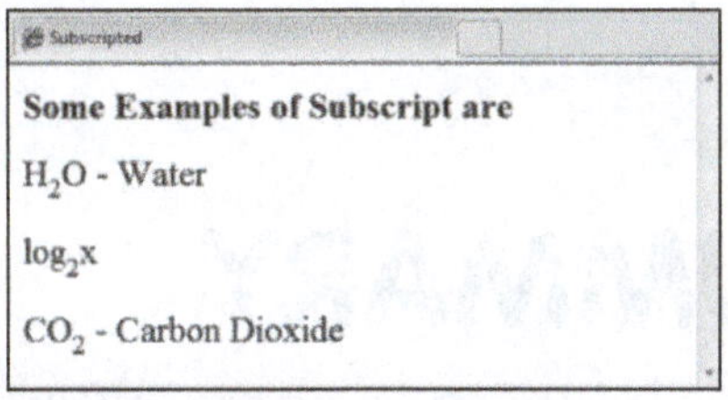

<SUB> Tag

The text which is lowered slightly below the baseline to appear below the surrounding text is known as **subscript**. e.g. in H_2O, 2 is the subscripted text.

In HTML, the _{and} tags turn the enclosed text into subscript. In its simplest form, <SUB> tag may be specified as:

```
<SUB> aaa </SUB>
```

Where, aaa is the text, which is to be subscripted.

Check Point 03

1. With the help of which tag of HTML, you can display $(a^2 + b^2)$ in your Web page?
2. Shreya is making a Web page on chemical compound, in which she wants to write H_2SO_4 but she is unable to get 2 and 4 in right position. Which feature of HTML will help her to get 2 and 4 in its right position?
3. ....tag helps to display text in superscript manner.

Attributes of <IMG> Tag

Attributes	*Description*	*Syntax*
src	Takes the URL of the image file that you want to insert in the Web page.	<IMG src="path/file name">
alt	Provides an alternate text to an image, in case of someone using a text-only browser or using a graphical browser with images turned OFF.	<IMG src="path/file name" alt="text">
align	Allows to position an inline image relative to the line of the text that it is ON. Values that align attribute can have: top, middle, bottom, left and right	<IMG src="path/file name" align="left/right/middle/top/bottom">
height	Specifies the height of an image.	<IMG src="path/file name" height ="pixels/percentage">
width	Specifies the width of an image.	<IMG src="path/file name" width="pixels/percentage">
border	Specifies the width of an image border.	<IMG src="path/file name" border="number">

Attributes of <A> Tag

Attributes	*Description*	*Syntax*
href	Specifies the URL of the page link goes to.	<A href="URL"> Some Text</A>
name	Specifies the name of an anchor. Used to link to different segments within the same html document or of different html document.	<A name="name of segment"> Some Text </A>
title	To give title to the document to which you are linking.	<A href ="URL" title="text">Some Text</A>
mailto	This function is used in href which creates a mail link upon clicking at which the mail software gets opened.	<A href="mailto: emailaddress?Subject="Subject Line"> Some Text </A>

SUMMARY

- The <IMG> tag is used to place an image on the Web page. HTML supports various types of image formats such as .jpeg, .png, .gif to display in Web browsers.
- Internet Explorer displays the value of the alt attribute as a tooltip, when mouse pointer goes over the image. Unlike the Internet Explorer browser, other browsers do not display the text used in the alt attribute, for this use title attribute in place of alt attribute.
- The <IMG> tag is an inline element (it does not insert a new line on a page), that means text and other elements can wrap around it.
- Linking is done using anchor <A> tag with href, alt and name attributes.
- External links are those HTML links that go to another Website. If you place HTML links to About.com, or another Website you like, on your Web page that would be an example of external HTML links.
- An internal link is a type of hyperlink on a Web page to another page or resource, such as an image or a document, on the same Website or domain.
- If you want to make an image into a hyperlink without a border, specify a zero value to the border attribute.
- mailto is an easy and a fast way by which a visitor at a Website can directly send mail to the Website owner or send the information on the Website to another E-mail address.
- The <SUP> tag defines superscript text, which appears half a character above the normal line, and is sometimes rendered in a smaller font.
- The <SUB> tag defines subscript text, which appears half a character below the normal line and is sometimes rendered in a smaller font.

Exam Practice

Multiple Choice Questions

1 Web browsers display images in the following format
(a) XBM (b) JPEG
(c) GIF (d) All of these

Ans. (*d*) Web browsers display images in XBM, JPEG, GIF, etc. format.

2 Which tag is used to insert an image in Web page?
(a) <A> (b) <TABLE>
(c) <IMG> (d) <P>

Ans. (*c*) <IMG> tag is used to insert an inline image in a Web page.

3 The correct HTML code for inserting an image is **CBSE 2012**
(a) <IMG href="image.gif">
(b) <IMG> image.gif</gif>
(c) <IMG src = "image.gif">
(d) <IMAGE src = "image.gif">

Ans. (*c*) <IMG src="image.gif ">

4 src attribute used with <IMG> tag stands for **CBSE 2013**
(a) screen (b) screen resolution count
(c) source (d) structure

Ans. (*c*) src (source) attribute takes URL of an image file.

5 ...... attribute is used to specify the location of an image file.
(a) alt (b) src
(c) align (d) name

Ans. (*b*) src attribute is used to specify the location of an image file.

6 The alternate text of an image can be displayed by using .... attribute of the <IMG> tag.
(a) src (b) alt
(c) align (d) None of these

Ans. (*b*) alt attribute of the <IMG> tag is used to display the alternate text of an image.

7 alt attribute allows **CBSE 2016**
(a) addition of an alternate hyperlink
(b) addition of a border to image
(c) use of an alternate image in place of the specified image
(d) addition of alternate text about an image

Ans. (*d*) alt attribute allows addition of alternate text about an image.

8 The text specified in the alt attribute is displayed as tooltip in
(a) Internet Explorer (b) Google Chrome
(c) Both (a) and (b) (d) None of these

Ans. (*a*) The text specified in alt attribute is displayed as tooltip in Internet Explorer only.

9 The default alignment of images, that are inserted in Web page, is
(a) left (b) right
(c) inline with text (d) middle

Ans. (*c*) An image which is inserted in Web page by default placed inline with text.

10 Which is not a valid value in the align attribute of <IMG> tag? **CBSE 2014, 2013**
(a) top (b) center (c) bottom (d) right

Ans. (*b*) center is not a valid value in the align attribute of <IMG> tag. To align in center, <CENTER> tag can be used.

11 Why is it important to specify width and height attributes in <IMG> tag? **CBSE 2013**
(a) To ensure that image is not copied
(b) The image will not render without these
(c) To stop the image from loading
(d) Helps the browser to load the Web page faster

Ans. (*d*) Helps the browser to load the Web page faster.

12 When creating a Web document, which unit is used to express an image's height and width? **CBSE 2013**
(a) Centimetres (b) Pixels
(c) Dots per inch (d) Inches

Ans. (*b*) Image's height and width units are expressed in pixels or in per cent form.

13 .... is the default color of a hyperlink.
(a) Red (b) Blue (c) Green (d) Black

Ans. (*b*) By default, color of a hyperlink is blue.

14 Which of the following is not the attribute of <A> tag? **CBSE 2019**
(a) NAME (b) TITLE
(c) HREF (d) SRC

Ans. (*b*) TITLE is not the attribute of <A> tag.

15 The tag used in HTML to link a Web page with other Web page is **CBSE 2013**
(a) <A> (b) <H> (c) <U> (d) <L>

Ans. (*a*) <A> anchor tag is used to create links.

16 Which tag tells, where a link starts? **CBSE 2014**
(a) <L> (b) <START>
(c) <A> (d) None of these

Ans. (*c*) <A> tag specifies that a link starts, in which, href creates a hyperlink.

17 Which command should be use to link a page with HTML page? **CBSE 2013**
(a) <A link = "page.htm"></A>
(b) <A href = "page.htm">page</A>
(c) <A connect = "page.htm"></A>
(d) <A attach = "page.htm"></A>

Ans. (*b*) <A href="page.htm">page</A>

18 With which code you can make an image works as link? **CBSE 2016**
(a) <A href = "URL">Text</A>
(b) <A href="ABC.html"><IMG src = "graphic.gif">Click Here</A>
(c) <A ref=mailto:<IMG src ="graphic.gif">Click Here</A>
(d) None of the above

Ans. (*b*) With <A href="ABC.html"><IMG src="graphic.gif">Click Here</A> image works as link.

19 To create a hyperlinked image
(a) the image tag should be within anchor tag
(b) the anchor tag should be within image tag
(c) the image tag should be before the anchor tag
(d) the image tag should be after the anchor tag

Ans. (*a*) The <IMG> tag should be within anchor tag to create hyperlinked image.

20 Is it possible to link within the current page?
(a) No (b) Only in framesets
(c) Yes (d) Can't say

Ans. (*c*) Yes, it is possible to link within the current page, which is called internal linking.

21 For internal linking, the section names are provided by .... attribute of <A> tag.
(a) title (b) href
(c) name (d) None of these

Ans. (*c*) For internal linking, section names are provided by name attribute.

22 ...... attribute of the <A> tag is used to name a section in a Web page to create an internal link.
(a) href (b) name (c) align (d) link

Ans. (*b*) name attribute is used to create an internal link.

23 The attribute which is used to send E-mails through a Website.
(a) tomail (b) mailto
(c) Both (a) and (b) (d) None of these

Ans. (*b*) mailto attribute is used to send E-mails through a Website.

24 Choose the correct syntax to create an E-mail link. **CBSE 2014**
(a) <A href = "abc@xyz.com">
(b) <A href = "mailto:abc@xyz.com">
(c) <mail = "abc@xyz.com">
(d) <A mail = "abc@xyz.com">

Ans. (*b*) <A href ="mailto:abc@xyz.com">

25 To display $(X + Y)^2$, correct HTML code is **CBSE 2013**
(a) _{(X +Y)2}
(b) X+Y²
(c) (X+Y)²
(d) ^{(X +Y)2}

Ans. (*c*) (X+Y) ² code is correct because superscript text have to be placed in between ^{and} tags.

26 The.............. attribute of <IMG> tag specifies an alternate text for an image, if the image cannot be displayed due to any reason. **CBSE SQP Term-I**
(a) alt (b) alternate
(c) tooltip (d) text

Ans. (*a*) alt

27 While creating a web document, which unit is used to express an image's height and width? **CBSE SQP Term-I**
(a) Centimetres (b) Pixels
(c) Dots per inch (d) Inches

Ans. (*b*) Pixels

28 The default alignment of images, that are inserted in web page, is **CBSE SQP Term-I**
(a) left (b) right
(c) inline with text (d) middle

Ans. (*c*) inline with text

29 Consider the following code:

```
<IMG src="Computers.jpg" width="
________ " height="________ ">
```

Fill in the blanks to set the image size to be 250 pixels wide and 400 pixels tall. **CBSE SQP Term-I**
(a) 250, 400
(b)400, 250
(c) <250><400>
(d) <400><250>

Ans. (*a*) 250, 400

30 Gagandeep has written the following code to display an image in the background of HTML document: **CBSE SQP Term-I**

```
<BODY BgGround= "Animals.jpeg">
```

But he is not getting the desired output. Help him to identify correct code.

EXAM PRACTICE

(a) <BODY Bg= "Animals.jpeg">
(b) <BODY BACK= "Animals.jpeg">
(c) <BODY BGIMAGE= "Animals.jpeg">
(d) <BODY BACKGROUND= "Animals.jpeg">

Ans. (*d*) <BODY BACKGROUND= "Animals.jpeg">

31 Rajesh, an IT club volunteer of the school, needs to add a picture of 'Green Earth' in the center of a web page designed to spread awareness on saving the environment. Help him in choosing the correct HTML command for the same. **CBSE 2021 Term-I**

(a) <PICTURE> (b) <IMAGE>
(c) <IMG> (d) <PICT>

Ans. (*c*) <IMG>

32 Romal, a chemical analyst, is designing a web page of the company, which may contain the chemical formula of water H_2O. Which tag should she use to display 2 little bits below the normal line? **CBSE 2021 Term-I**

(a) <LOWER>
(b) <SUBSCRIPT>
(c) <SUB>
(d) No tag is available in HTML for it

Ans. (*c*) <SUB>

Fill in the Blanks

1 <IMG> tag is used for .... images. **CBSE 2014**

Ans. displaying

2 .... is an attribute of the <IMG> tag which specifies the location or URL of the image to be displayed.

Ans. src

3 The <IMG> tag is an .... tag, that means it has no closing tag.

Ans. empty

4 The alt attribute provides .... for an image.

Ans. alternate information

5 The value for alt attribute is a text string of upto .... characters.

Ans. 1024

6 .... tag is used to create inline images. **CBSE 2013, 2012**

Ans. <IMG>

7 An image to be displayed in a Web page has to cover 25% of the browser window horizontally and 50% vertically. The attributes .... and .... of the <IMG> tag would be used for achieving this.

Ans. height, width

8 .... attribute is used to give border to an image. **CBSE 2016**

Ans. border

9 .... is a word or an image that when clicked take us to another Web page. **CBSE 2013**

Ans. Hyperlink

10 .... tag is used to connect Web pages. **CBSE 2014**

Ans. <A>

11 .... are used to connect Web pages. They are created with <A> tag. **CBSE 2016**

Ans. Hyperlinks

12 The .... tag is considered to establish a hypertext relationship between the current document and another URL.

Ans. <A>

13 An .... linking allows a link to another Web page or another Website. **CBSE 2011**

Ans. external

14 The .... attribute is used for specifying the URL of the anchor tag.

Ans. href

15 The .... attribute of <A> tag is used to provide information or a title for the linked document or Web page.

Ans. title

16 An .... linking allows a link to another section on the same or different Web page.

Ans. internal

17 Using the .... type URL, you can create the E-mail hyperlink.

Ans. mailto

18 The tag .... is used to create superscripts and .... tag is used to create subscripts on a Web page.

Ans. <SUP>, <SUB>

True or False

1 You can have inserted an image in your Web page which is physically present in your computer.

Ans. **True** With the help of <IMG src="image URL">, we can insert an image in Web page which is present in our computer.

2 If the image you are loading in the Web page is not available, then you want a text to appear in the image placeholder, text attribute lets you define this text.

Ans. **False** The alt attribute is used to define text to appear in the image placeholder, if image is not visible for any reason.

3 No value is specified with alt attribute of <IMG> tag. **CBSE 2012**

Ans. **False** alt attribute provides alternate text for an image if the image is not visible on Web page for any reason.

4 String as a value of alt attribute must be enclosed in quotation marks.

Ans. **True** alt attribute contains string which must be enclosed in quotation marks.

5 The align attribute of the <IMG> tag is used to specify the text that is to be displayed in case the browser that does not support graphics.

Ans. **False** alt attribute is used to specify the text that is to be displayed in case the browser which does not support graphics.

6 The general syntax for inline image is <IMG src = "file name">.

Ans. **False** At the place of file name, path of the image is specified. If the image is in the same folder as HTML file, it is not needed to specify full path of an image.

7 The default alignment of image is right. **CBSE 2014**

Ans. **False** There is no default alignment of image with respect to text in HTML.

8 It is not important to specify an integer value as the width of the border of an image.

Ans. **False** Width takes an integer values that are in pixels.

9 We can put a border around an image by using width attribute. **CBSE 2013**

Ans. **False** We can put a border around an image by using border attribute.

10 Border is an attribute of <A> tag. **CBSE 2012**

Ans. **False** border is an attribute of <IMG> tag.

11 The <A> tag is called the align tag. **CBSE 2011**

Ans. **False** The <A> tag is called anchor tag.

12 The anchor tag <A> signals the beginning of the text.

Ans. **False** Anchor tag is used to create hyperlinks not text.

13 The color of the hyperlinks in an HTML document can be changed.

Ans. **True** We can change the color of hyperlinks in HTML document.

14 Hyperlinks can also be created for links within the same document. Linking within the same document is called external linking.

Ans. **False** Linking within the same document is called internal linking.

15 It is not possible to create link within current document. **CBSE 2012**

Ans. **False** You can link various sections of the current document together, which is called internal linking.

16 The name attribute of the <A> tag allows the user to create links within the same document. **CBSE 2011**

Ans. **True** Because name attribute defines a name of a section in a document.

17 You should include a mailto function in the body of your document to allow user to respond to your Web page.

Ans. **True** The mailto function is used to send E-mails from the Website.

EXAM PRACTICE

Very Short Answer (VSA) Type Questions

1 Which HTML tag is used to insert an image in a Web page? Write an option used with this tag. **CBSE 2002**

Ans. The <IMG> tag is used to insert an image in a Web page. This tag uses the options like src, alt etc.

2 What do you mean by src? **CBSE 2007**

Ans. The src is an attribute of <IMG> tag. It gives the URL of the image document.

3 Write the full form of the following tags: **CBSE 2008**

(a) <LI>
(b) <IMG>

Ans. (a) <LI> List item
(b) <IMG> Image

4 Write a statement in HTML that inserts an image named 'school.jpg' found in the 'images' folder of the current folder. In case the image cannot be found, it should display 'Schools in India'.

Ans. <IMG src ="images\school.jpg" alt="Schools in India">

5 How can text be displayed in place of image for users whose browser do not support images? **CBSE 2007**

Ans. The alt attribute of <IMG> tag is used to display the text in place of image for the users whose browser do not support images.

6 The following code is written to align the image in center in the browser's window. However, the desired result is not achieved. Mention the reason.

```
<IMG src = "image.jpg" align = "center">
```

Ans. The reason for not getting the desired result is that center is not a value of align attribute in <IMG> tag.

7 Why width and height attributes are used?

Ans. The width and height attributes are used, such that downloading of an image will be faster after knowing the dimensions of the images in the browser.

8 Explain linking.

Ans. When one Web page or a text fragment is connected to another Web page, then it is called linking. It is of two types– internal linking and external linking.

9 What do you mean by hypertext?

Ans. Hypertext acts as a link on which you click to navigate to the desired content.

10 What happens when we click on a hyperlink in a Web page? **CBSE 2008**

Ans. When we click on a hyperlink in a Web page, it carry user from one Web page to another Web page(within or on another Website).

11 In HTML, how linking can be done?

Ans. In HTML, linking can be done by using anchor <A> tag followed by href attribute.

12 Give the expansion of the following

(*a*) alt (*b*) <A>

Ans. (*a*) alt is used for alternate text attribute.
(*b*) <A> is used for anchor tag.

13 $6CO_2 + 6H_2O \longrightarrow C_6H_{12}O_6 + 6O_2$ **CBSE 2018**

To display above given chemical expression on a Web page, following HTML code was written:

6CO²6H²→ ⁶H¹²O⁶+ 60²

But its not displaying the expression in desired format. Identify the fault(s) and suggest the required correction(s).

Ans. <SUP>tag will not be use in the given expression because it is a superscript tag. In this expression, subscript tag, i.e. <SUB> tag will be use.

14 Write the HTML command to display the following in your Web page.

$A^2 + B^2$ **CBSE 2006**

Ans. The HTML command is

```
A<SUP>2</SUP> + B<SUP>2</SUP>
```

15 Mention the suitable HTML tag and the attribute to insert an image named globe.jpg in the background of a Web page. **CBSE 2019**

Ans.
```
<HTML>
<BODY background ="globe.jpg">
</BODY>
</HTML>
```

EXAM PRACTICE

Short Answer (SA) Type Questions

1 Describe the use of alt attribute with <IMG> tag.

Ans. The alt attribute is used to define 'alternate text' for an image. It tells the Website visitor, what he/she is missing on the page if the browser cannot load images. The browser will then display the altertnate text instead of the image. It is good to include alt attribute for each image on a page to improve the appearance and usefulness of the document.

2 Write the HTML code to display an inline image named pencil.jpg located at C:\ in the center of your Web page. **CBSE 2013**

Ans.
```
<HTML>
  <BODY>
    <CENTER>
      <IMG src="C:\pencil.jpg">
    </CENTER>
  </BODY>
</HTML>
```

3 Write the HTML code to display an image on the right side of the page. **CBSE 2016**

Ans.
```
<HTML>
  <BODY>
    <IMG src="image.jpg" align="right">
  </BODY>
</HTML>
```

4 Name the values that can be assigned to align attribute of <IMG> tag.

Ans. The values that can be assigned to align attribute of <IMG> tag are as follows:

(*i*) top (*ii*) bottom (*iii*) left
(*iv*) right (*v*) middle

5 Define height and width attributes of <IMG> tag.

Ans. Refer to text on Page No. 77.

6 Explain the need of linking between Web pages.

Ans. Linking between different Web pages is required, as when we create Websites, different html files (Web pages) are created. These files contain different modules and cannot be open individually. If we link between them, the Website becomes more productive and informative.

7 How is external linking different from internal linking? **CBSE 2004, 05**

Ans. External link is a type of linking that goes to another Website. It is a linking of two different documents. While, internal linking is a type of linking that links pages within a single Website, various sections of same document or different document.

8 Explain the given command
`<A href ="wild.html">Click Here for wild animals </A>` **CBSE 2006**

Ans. In this command, anchor <A> tag and its href attribute is included. The text (Click Here for wild animals) will appear underlined and indicates that clicking the text activates the hypertext link. The address of the referenced document can be specified by an absolute or relative URL.

Thus, "wild.html" is an URL or Web page address and Click Here for wild animals is the hyperlinked text.

9 Name the attributes of <A> tag which are used for internal linking in a Web page. **CBSE 2014, 13**

Ans. The attributes of <A> tag which are used for internal linking in a Web page as follows:

(*i*) **href** is used to specify the URL of the segment the link goes to.

(*ii*) **name** gives the name to the segment.

10 Gaurav, a Web designer in a company named "International Designers" has just created a Web page in which different sections of the Web page are linked and can be traversed by clicking on the text given as "Top", "Middle" and "Bottom". Is the internal linking or external linking and why? Additionally tell him about the suitable tag and its attribute(s) to open another Web page named 'second.html' by clicking on the text "Next". **CBSE 2018**

Ans. It is internal linking because links pages are within a single website, various sections of same document or different document.

To open another web page, user will be need to use external linking with <A> tag and href attribute.

Suitable code to open web page named 'Second.html':
<A href="second.html"> Next </A>

11 Write the HTML code to create a link for school.jpg located at C:\. **CBSE 2014**

Ans.
```
<HTML>
  <BODY>
    <A href = "C:\school.jpg">Image</A>
  </BODY>
</HTML>
```

12 Write an simple HTML code to show an example of internal linking.

EXAM PRACTICE

Ans.
```
<HTML>
  <HEAD><TITLE>Internal Linking</TITLE>
  </HEAD>
  <BODY>
     <H1> It is <A name ="top">top</A>
     of the page </H1>
     <BR><BR><BR><BR><BR><BR><BR><BR><BR>
     <BR>
     <BR><BR><BR><BR><BR><BR><BR><BR><BR>
     <BR>
     <BR><BR><BR><BR>
     <H1><A href ="#top">Top</A></H1>
  </BODY>
</HTML>
```

13 What is the purpose of mailto function?

Ans. The mailto function is used to send E-mail messages to multiple recipients. For this, we only need to type the E-mail address of the recipients in the same link separated by commas.

14 Write an HTML code to show the use of mailto function.

Ans.
```
<HTML>
  <HEAD>
     <TITLE> Use of mailto </TITLE>
  </HEAD>
  <BODY>Send your views to
     <A href= "mailto:aaa_rr@gmail.com">
     aaa_rr@gmail.com</A>
  </BODY>
</HTML>
```

15 Write the HTML code to send an E-mail to abc@xyz.com from your Web page. **CBSE 2013**

Ans.
```
<HTML>
  <BODY>
   <A href="mailto:abc@xyz.com">abc@xyz.com</A>
  </BODY>
</HTML>
```

16 Distinguish between <SUP> and <SUB> tags with example.

Ans. Distinguishes between <SUP> and <SUB> tags are as follows:

<SUP> Tag	<SUB> Tag
The <SUP> tag is known as superscript tag.	The <SUB> tag is known as subscript tag.
It is used to define superscripted text.	It is used to define subscripted text.
Tags that are used to specify superscripted written as ^{text}	Tags that are used to specify subscripted written as _{text}
e.g. HTML command to display $(a + b)^2$ is (a + b)²	e.g. HTML command to display $\log_2 + \log_x$ is log ₂+log _x

17 Write the full forms of: **CBSE 2013**

(*i*) <SUP> (*ii*) <A>
(*iii*) <IMG> (*iv*) <SUB>

Ans. (*i*) <SUP> Superscript (*ii*) <A> Anchor
(*iii*) <IMG> Image (*iv*) <SUB> Subscript

18 Shreya, has just started learning HTML. She has made a list of few HTML tags which she will be using in creating a Web page but by mistake she has mentioned wrong attributes in front of the tags. Help her in selecting correct attributes from 'Column B' for the tags given in 'Column A'. **CBSE 2019**

Column A (TAGS)	*Column B (ATTRIBUTES)*
BODY	NAME
IMG	TEXT
OL	ALT
A	START

Ans. Correct Matching

TAGS	*ATTRIBUTES*
BODY	TEXT
IMG	ALT
OL	START
A	NAME

19 Mention any two attributes of <IMG> tag along with their significance. **CBSE 2019**

Ans. Two attributes of <IMG> tag are

(i) src-takes the URL of the image file that you want to insert in the Web page.

(ii) alt-provides an alternate text to an image, in case of someone using a text-only browser or using a graphical browser with images turned OFF.

Long Answer (LA) Type Questions

1 Explain various attributes of <IMG> tag.

Ans. Refer to text on Page No. 81.

2 Which attribute is used to specify the location of an image file in <IMG> tag? Explain.

Ans. The attribute you need to get an image to display on a Web page is the src attribute.

In the src attribute of the <IMG> tag, you can specify the path of the image that you want to add to the Web page. This may be an image in the same directory, an image somewhere else on the same server, or an image stored on another server.

The syntax for src attribute is `<IMG src ="image1.jpg">`

3 Define various alignments of align attribute with example.

Ans. Refer to text on Page No. 75-76.

4 Identify the errors in the following HTML code and write the correct code with each correction underlined. **CBSE 2011**

```
<HTML>
  <TITLE>IMAGES</HEAD>
    <BODY bgcolor="PICI.JPG">
    <IMG href="ABC.JPG">
    HERE IS MY IMAGE FILE
    </BGCOLOR>
</HTML>
```

Ans. **Error 1** The <TITLE> tag must be within <HEAD> tag.

Error 2 bgcolor attribute of BODY element supports a color like red, green or its color value.

Error 3 <IMG> tag needs a source attribute src to place an href.

Error 4 BODY element must be closed not bgcolor attribute.

The correct code is as follows:

```
<HTML>
  <HEAD>
    <TITLE>IMAGES</TITLE>
  </HEAD>
  <BODY bgcolor = "yellow">
    <IMG src= "ABC.JPG">
    HERE IS MY IMAGE FILE
    </BODY>
  </HTML>
```

5 Write HTML code to illustrate

(*i*) listed hyperlinks (*ii*) image hyperlinks

Ans. Refer to text on Page No. 78-79.

6 Explain the following (with example):

(*i*) linking on same Web page.

(*ii*) linking on different Web page.

Ans. Refer to text on Page No. 79-80.

Application Oriented Questions

1 Consider the following HTML code given below:

```
<HTML>
   <HEAD>
       <TITLE>
           My First Web page
       </TITLE>
   </HEAD>
   <BODY bgcolor = "red">
       <H1>Look at the image</H1><BR>
       <IMG src ="D:\images.jpg" alt ="
                   Rose Flower">
   </BODY>
</HTML>
```

Now, answer the following questions:

(*i*) What will be displayed in the title bar of the browser?

(*ii*) What will be the alternate text if the image linked in this Web page will not open?

(*iii*) Name the attributes of <IMG> tag which are being used in the above given code.

(*iv*) Name the tags that are used in the above code.

(*v*) What will be the color of background?

Ans. (*i*) My First Web page

(*ii*) Rose Flower

(*iii*) src, alt

(*iv*) <HTML>, <HEAD>, <TITLE>, <BODY> <H1>, <IMG>,

(*v*) red

2 Write an HTML code to produce the following: **CBSE 2006**

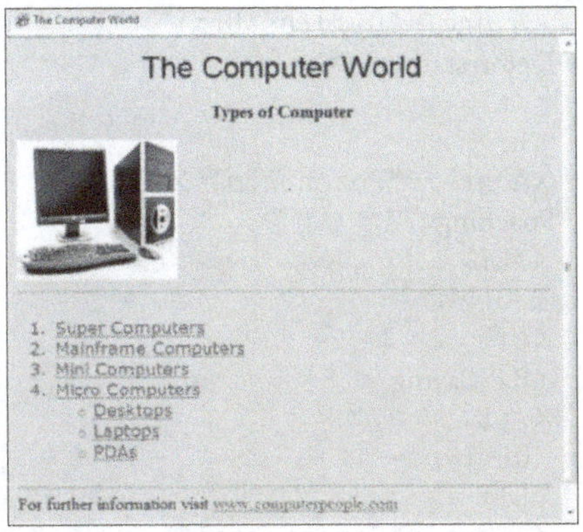

Consider the following points while writingthe code:

(*i*) Title of the page is "The Computer World".
(*ii*) Background color of the page is "Yellow".
(*iii*) Active link color is Green and Visiting link color is Red.
(*iv*) All font face in the page is Verdana but heading is in Arial and Black.
(*v*) Image is from the file "computer.jpg"
(*vi*) Use horizontal rule wherever required.
(*vii*) Use ordered and unordered lists wherever required.
(*viii*) Pages linked with

Super Computers	:Super.html
Mainframe Computers	:Main.html
Mini Computers	:Mini.html
Micro Computers	:Micro.html
Desktops	:Desk.html
Laptops	:Laptop.html
PDAs	:PDA.html

Note You can use any other attributes that are not mentioned above to produce a similar output.

Ans. The HTML code is

```
<HTML>
   <HEAD>
      <TITLE>The Computer World</TITLE>
</HEAD>
   <BODY bgcolor="yellow" alink ="green"
   vlink="red">
     <FONT face="arial"color="black">
     <H1>
     <CENTER>The Computer World</CENTER>
     </H1>
     </FONT>
     <BASEFONT face="verdana">
     <P align="center"><B>
     Types of Computer
     </B></P>
     <IMG src="computer.jpg">
     <HR>
     <OL type="1">
     <LI><A href="Super.html">
     Super Computers </A></LI>
     <LI><A href="Main.html">
      Mainframe Computers</A></LI>
     <LI><A href="Mini.html">
      Mini Computers</A></LI>
     <LI><A href="Micro.html">
      Micro Computers</A></LI>
     <UL>
     <LI><A href="Desk.html">Desktops
     </A></LI>
     <LI><A href="Laptop.html">Laptops
     </A></LI>
     <LI><A href="PDA.html">PDAs
     </A></LI>
     </UL> </OL> <HR>
     <FONT size="4">
     For further information visit
     <A href="www.computerpeople.com">
      www.computerpeople.com</A>
     </FONT>
   </BODY>
</HTML>
```

3 Write an HTML code to produce the following: **CBSE 2005**

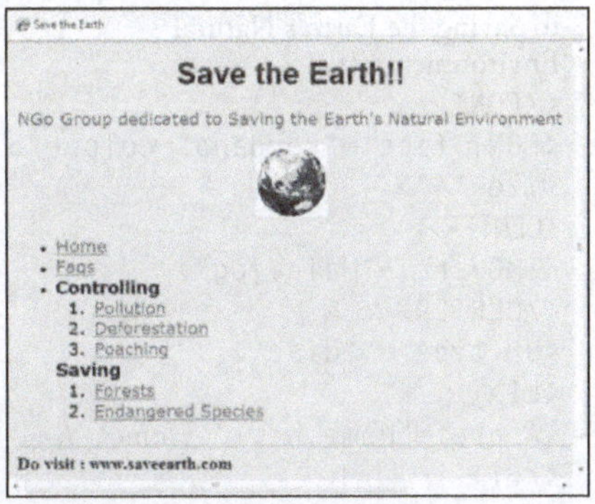

Consider the following points while writing the code:

(*i*) Title of the page is "Save the Earth"
(*ii*) The background color of the page is Silver.
(*iii*) The font used for heading is "Arial", size is 6 and color is Black.
(*iv*) The sub heading is in "Verdana" font, font size is 4 and color is Brown.

(v) Rest of the text is in "Verdana" font, font size 4 and black color.

(vi) Image used is from file "Main.jpg"

(vii) The links are provided in an unordered list with ordered list used in between.

(viii) The pages are linked as follows

Home	Home.html
Faqs	Faq.html
Pollution	Poll.html
Deforestation	Defores.html
Poaching	Poach.html
Forests	Forest.html
Endangered Species	Specie.html

(ix) The categories 'Controlling' and 'Saving' in the unordered list are not linked to any page.

(x) The width and height of horizontal line is 820 and 80, respectively.

Note You can use any other attributes that are not mentioned above to produce a similar output.

Ans. The HTML code is

```
<HTML>
  <HEAD>   <TITLE> Save the Earth </TITLE>
  </HEAD>
  <BODY bgcolor ="silver">
    <H1>
    <FONT face="arial" color="black"
    size="6">
    <CENTER>Save the Earth!! </CENTER>
    </FONT>
    </H1>
    <FONT face="verdana" color="brown"
    size="4">
    <P align="center">NGo Group dedicated
    to Saving the Earth's Natural
    Environment</P>
    </FONT>
    <FONT face ="verdana" color="black"
    size="4">
    <CENTER>
    <IMG src ="Main.jpg">
    </CENTER>
    <UL type = "disc">
    <LI>
    <A href="Home.html">Home</A>
    </LI>
    <LI>
    <A href="Faq.html">Faqs</A>
    </LI>
    <LI>
    <B> Controlling </B>
    </LI>
    <OL type="1">
    <LI>
    <A href="Poll.html">
    Pollution</A>
    </LI>
    <LI>
    <A href="Defores.html">
    Deforestation</A>
    </LI>
    <LI>
    <A href="Poach.html">
    Poaching</A>
    </LI>
    </OL>
    <LI>
    <B> Saving </B>
    </LI>
    <OL type="1">
    <LI>
    <A href="Forest.html">
    Forests</A>
    </LI>
    <LI>
    <A href="Specie.html">
    Endangered Species</A>
    </LI>
    </OL>
    </UL>
    </FONT>
    <HR noshade width="820"
    height="80" size="2">
    <B><FONT size="4">Do visit:
    www.saveearth.com</FONT></B>
  </BODY>
</HTML>
```

4 Sushila, a web designer working with Global Designers, is supposed to design a Web page shown below: **CBSE 2019**

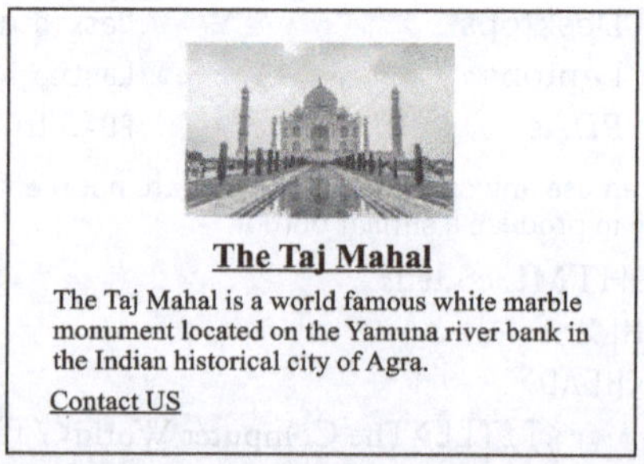

Write the HTML code to design the above shown Web page considering the specifications as given below:

(i) Background colour of the page should be pink and all the hyperlinked text should be green in colour.

(ii) Image named "taj.jpg" should be placed in the centre of the Web page.

(*iii*) Heading "The Taj Mahal" should be first level of the heading and underlined.

(*iv*) Paragraph should have following formatting styles applicable:
Colour-Blue;
Size-5;
Font style-Times New Roman.

(*v*) At the bottom of the page, "Contact Us" text should be linked with admin@taj.com E-mail id.

Ans.

```
<HTML>
  <HEAD>
    <TITLE>Taj Mahal</TITLE>
  </HEAD>
  <BODY bgcolor="pink">
  <CENTER>
  <IMG src="taj.jpeg" height="100"
                  width="150">
  <H1><U>The Taj Mahal</U></H1>
  </CENTER>
  <P><FONT color="blue"size="5"
  face="Times New Roman">
  The Taj Mahal is a world famous white marble<BR>
  monument located on the Yamuna river bank in <BR>
  the Indian historical city of Agra.
  </FONT>
  </P>
  <FONT color = "green">
  <A href = "mailto:admin@taj.com">
  Contact Us</A>
  </FONT>
  </BODY>
</HTML>
```

5 Differentiate between Container and Empty elements in HTML. Also, give any two examples of HTML tags from each category. **CBSE 2019**

Ans. Differences between container and empty elements in HTML are as follows:

Container elements	*Empty elements*
These types of HTML elements always wrap around the text or graphics which come in a set with an opening as well as closing tag.	Empty elements are standalone tags, i.e. empty tags do not have to wrapped around text or graphics and do not require a closing tag.
HTML tags that include both ON and OFF tags are known as container tags **e.g.** <HTML> ...... </HTML> <HEAD>...... </HEAD>	HTML tags that include only ON tag and there is no OFF tag then , these tags are known as empty tags. **e.g.** <HR>

6 Observe following output and write HTML code to generate it. **CBSE 2018**

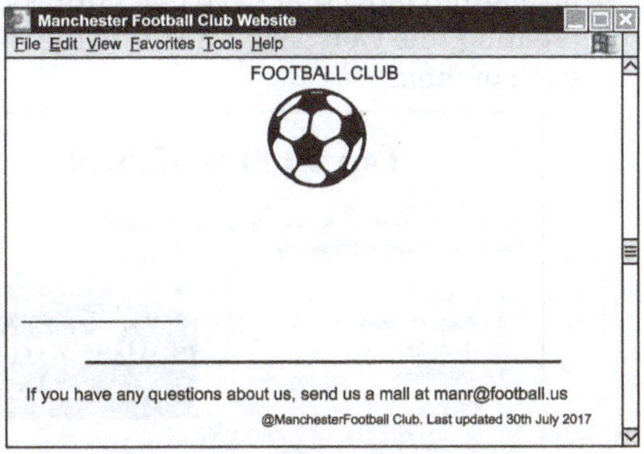

Consider the following points while generating the Web page:

(*i*) The title of the page is "FOOTBALL CLUB"
(*ii*) The heading is blue color
(*iii*) Font of entire document is arial
(*iv*) Image used is "football.jpeg"
(*v*) The page is linked to:
Proud history to "history.html"
(*vi*) Bottom message is of size 2.

Ans. The code is

```
<HTML>
<HEAD><TITLE>FOOTBALL
CLUB</TITLE></HEAD>
<BODY>
<FONT face="arial" size="3">
<H1 align="center"><FONT
color="blue">FOOTBALL CLUB</FONT></H1>
<CENTER><IMG src="football.jpg"
height="150" width="150"></CENTER>
<H3>Welcome to the website of the Manchester Football
Club</H3>
<P>The Manchester Football Club is based in United
States of America and has a long <BR>
and <A href="history.html">proud
history</A>. We have several teams in various age
groups from kids to grown-<BR>ups so there is a team to
suit any player. <BR><BR>
<U>This year's motto:</U><BR>
We are the BEST:<BR>
<HR size="3" noshade size ="75%">
<FONT size="2"><B>If you have any questions about
us, send us a mail at
manr@football.us</B></FONT><BR>
<H5 align="right">
<IMG src="copy.jpg" height="20"
width="30">Manchester Football Club. Last updated
30<SUP>th</SUP>July 2017</H5>
</FONT>
</BODY>
</HTML>
```

7 Carefully study the Web page given below. Identify 10 tags (structural as well as formatting tags) that have been utilised in creating this Web page and write the usage of each of them.

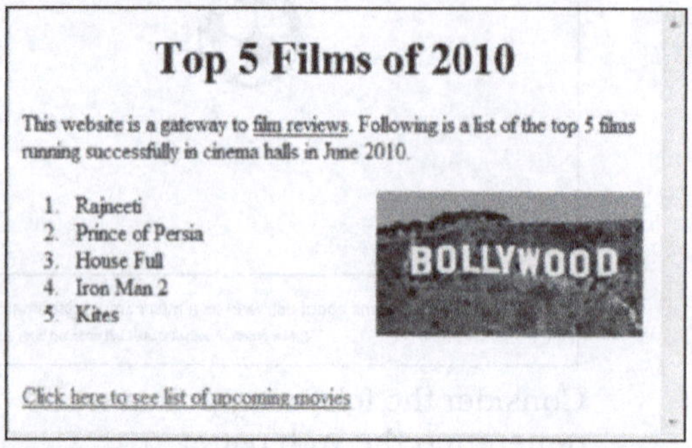

Ans. Following tags are used:

(*i*) <HTML> Container of all the HTML elements. Tells the browser that it is dealing with an HTML document.

(*ii*) <BODY> It defines the document's body. It contains all the necessary contents of HTML document that is to be displayed on Web browser.

(*iii*) <H1> Top level of heading.

(*iv*) <CENTER> Used to centralise a segment of text to be displayed.

(*v*) <P> It is used to define the paragraph.

(*vi*) <OL> To insert an ordered list in the Web page.

(*vii*) <LI> It is used to indicate a list item as contained in an ordered.

(*viii*)
 Break line tag is used to move all the text/image that follows the tag to the next line.

(*ix*) <IMG> This tag is used to insert the desired image into the Web page.

(*x*) <A> Anchor tag is used to create the hyperlink.

8 Observe the following Web page and write HTML code to generate it. **CBSE 2013**

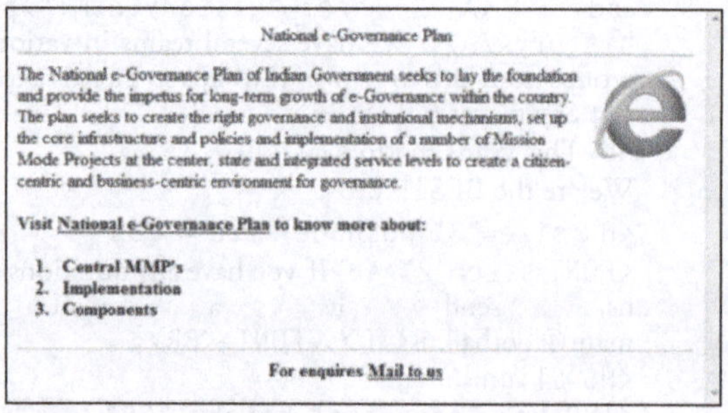

Note The following points while generating the Web page:

(*i*) Background color of page is yellow.
(*ii*) Link color is black and visited link color is green.
(*iii*) Font style for the page is arial.
(*iv*) Heading of the page is maroon.
(*v*) Image used is gov.jpeg.
(*vi*) Text color of the paragraph is red.
(*vii*) Link for 'National e-Governance Plan' is nation.html.
(*viii*) E-mail id for bottom message is abc@xyz.com.

Ans. The HTML code is

```
<HTML>
  <BODY bgcolor="yellow" link ="black"
   vlink="green">
    <BASEFONT face = "arial">
    <CENTER>
    <FONT color="maroon"><H1>
    National e-Governance Plan</H1>
    </FONT></CENTER><HR>
    <P> <FONT color="red">
    <IMG src="gov.jpeg" alt="gov"
    align="right">
The National e-Governance Plan of Indian Government
seeks to lay the foundation and provide the impetus for
long-term growth of e-Governance within the country.
The plan seeks to create the right governance and
institutional mechanisms, set up the core infrastructure
and policies and implementation of a number of
Mission Mode Projects at the center, state and
integrated service levels to create a citizen-centric and
business-centric environment for governance.
    </FONT></P>
    <BR>
    <B>Visit<A href ="nation.html">
    National e-Governance Plan</A> to know
    more about:<BR>
    <OL type ="1">
    <LI>Central MMP's</LI>
    <LI>Implementation</LI>
    <LI>Components</LI>
    </OL></B><HR>
    <CENTER>For enquires
    <A href="mailto:abc@xyz.com">Mail to us
    </A>
    </CENTER>
  </BODY>
</HTML>
```

9 Write the HTML code for the following output: **CBSE 2011**

Note The following points while generating the Web page:

(*i*) Title of the page should be "Dubai Tourism".
(*ii*) The heading text "WELCOME TO DUBAI" is in arial font and is of maroon color.
(*iii*) The horizontal lines below the heading are 5 pixels thick and of red color.
(*iv*) Image used in the page is burj.jpg.
(*v*) The bulleted list contains links as specified below:
- The text Morning is a link to the Web page "morning.html"
- The text Evening is a link to the Web page "evening.html"

Ans. The HTML code is

```
<HTML>
 <HEAD>
   <TITLE>Dubai Tourism</TITLE>
 </HEAD>
 <BODY>
   <CENTER>
   <H1>
   <FONT face="arial" color="maroon">
    WELCOME TO DUBAI</FONT>
   </H1>
   </CENTER>
   <HR width=80% size="5" color="red"
   noshade>
   <HR width=60% size="5" color="red"
   noshade>
   <P>
   <FONT size="5">
    Enjoy the world of pure travel masti
   </FONT>
   <IMG src="burj.jpg" align="bottom"
   width="110">
   </P>
   The following is alist of major tourist
   attractions in Dubai:<BR><BR>
   <UL type="disc">
   <LI>
   <A href="morning.html">
   Morning</A>
   - Dolphinarium and Palm Dubai
   </LI>
   <LI>
   <A href="evening.html">
   Evening</A>
   - Ski Dubai and Cruise
   </LI>
   </UL>
   <CENTER>
    For enquires write at dubai@gmail.com
   </CENTER>
 </BODY>
</HTML>
```

10 Write HTML code for the following output:

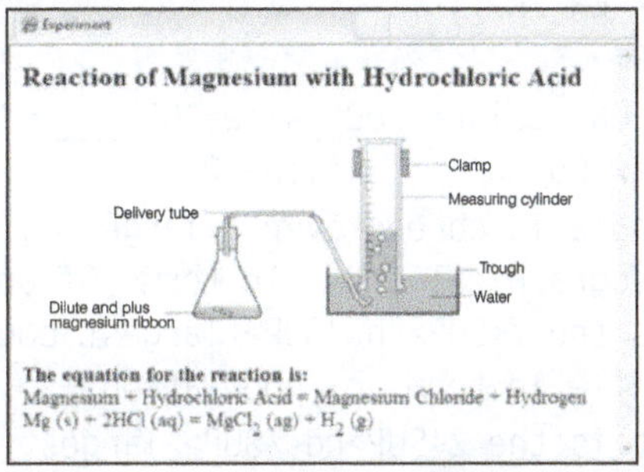

Note Consider the following points while generating output:

(*i*) Title of the page should be Experiment.
(*ii*) In whole Web page font face is "Times New Roman" and size is "4".
(*iii*) The second heading text "Reaction of Magnesium with Hydrochloric Acid".
(*iv*) The image used in the page is reaction.jpg with alternate text is "magnesium with hydrochloric acid", width is 500 pixels and height is 200 pixels.

Ans. The HTML code is

```
<HTML>
 <HEAD>
   <TITLE>Experiment</TITLE></HEAD>
 <BODY>
   <BASEFONT face="Times New Roman"
   size="4">
   <H2>Reaction of Magnesium with
   Hydrochloric Acid</H2>
   <IMG src= "reaction.jpg" alt=
   "magnesium with hydrochloric
   acid" width="500" height="200">
   <BR><BR>
   <B>The equation for the reaction is:</B><BR>
   Magnesium + Hydrochloric Acid =
   Magnesium Chloride + Hydrogen <BR>
   Mg(s) + 2HCl(aq) = MgCl<SUB>2</SUB>(ag) +
   H<SUB>2</SUB>(g)
 </BODY>
</HTML>
```

11 Consider the following code created by Sumantha for a webpage:

```
<HTML>
<BODY bgcolor="yellow">
<CENTER>
<H1> Our Country : India <_>
#line 1
```

```
<IMG src="india.jpg">
</CENTER>
<P>
<FONT color="red" size="5" ____="Times
New Roman">     #line 2
India is spread over a large
geographical area. In terms of area, it
is the 7<SUP>th</SUP> largest country
while in terms of population,
it is the 2<SUP>nd</SUP> largest
country in the world.
Some facts about India are as
follows___</P> #line 3
<UL>
<LI>Area :Approx 3.28 million sq. km
                  #line 4
<LI>North to South extension :Approx
3,200 km</LI>
<LI>East to West extension :Approx 2900
km</LI>
<__>                          #line 5
</BODY>
</HTML>
```

Based on the given code, answer the questions (i) to (v).

(i) Choose the correct option from the following to fill up in line 1.

(a) \H1 (b) \H6
(c) /H6 (d) /H1

(ii) Choose the correct option from the following to fill up in line 2.

(a) font (b) face
(c) type (d) text

(iii) Choose the correct option from the following to fill up in line 3.

(a) </F> (b) <F>
(c) </FONT> (d) <FONT>

(iv) Choose the correct option from the following to fill up in line 4.

(a) <I> (b) </LI>
(c) <\LI> (d) <\I>

(v) Choose the correct option from the following to fill up in line 5.

(a) UL (b) <\UL>
(c) <UL> (d) /UL

Ans. (i) (d) /H1
(ii) (b) face
(iii) (c) </FONT>
(iv) (b) </LI>
(v) (d) /UL

CHAPTER

05

Working with Tables in HTML

Chapter Checklist

- Basic Table Tags in HTML
- The <TABLE> Tag
- The <TD> Tag
- The <TR> and <TH> Tags
- Table Header, Body and Footer
- Event Handling in HTML Tables

Tables are great way to layout the HTML Web pages. Tables allow a user to display tabular data on Web pages in a very clear and uniform way. It is an orderly arrangement of data that is stored in the form of rows and columns, therefore, Web developers use tables very frequently in their Web pages.

According to W3C (World Wide Web Consortium), "The HTML table model allows authors to arrange data text, preformatted text, images, links, forms, form fields, other tables etc., into rows and columns of cells."

Basic Table Tags in HTML

In HTML, tables are created by <TABLE> tag. Data of tables can be in form of text or graphics. These tables are made up of rows and columns. An intersection of a row and a column is known as cell. The data in tables is contained in cells.

Each table may have an associated caption attribute (it provides a description about the table). Moreover, a summary attribute can also be included (for more precise description).

Basic tags that are used to create a table in HTML are as follows:

(*i*) **Table Tags (<TABLE>....</TABLE>)** It is used to insert a table in a Web page. It is a first tag, which starts and closes a table.

(*ii*) **Row Tags (<TR>....</TR>)** It is used to define a table rows. Table rows are group of the header, footer and body sections that is created by using thead, tfoot and tbody elements. Generally, the first row of a table is referred to as the **header section**, the last row of a table is referred to as the **footer section** and the middle rows in the table are referred to as the **body section.**

(*iii*) **Cell Tags (<TD>....</TD>, <TH>....</TH>)** It is used to define data cells (current cells) or header of the table. These tags are the data containers of the table. They can contain all sorts of HTML elements like text, images, lists, other tables etc.

(*iv*) **Caption Tags (<CAPTION>....</CAPTION>)** It is used to define the title or caption for the table that provides a short description of the table's purpose.

To Create a Table

Here is an example of HTML code for creating a table:

```
<HTML>
  <HEAD> <TITLE> Table </TITLE> </HEAD>
  <BODY>
    <TABLE>
      <CAPTION> Name of Students</CAPTION>
      <TR>
        <TD> Sunita </TD>
        <TD> Amita </TD>
        <TD> Ameesha </TD>
      </TR>
      <TR>
        <TD> Ankita </TD>
        <TD> Prachi </TD>
        <TD> Neha    </TD>
      </TR>
      <TR>
        <TD> Esha </TD>
        <TD> Preeti </TD>
        <TD> Payal </TD>
      </TR>
    </TABLE>
  </BODY>
</HTML>
```

Output

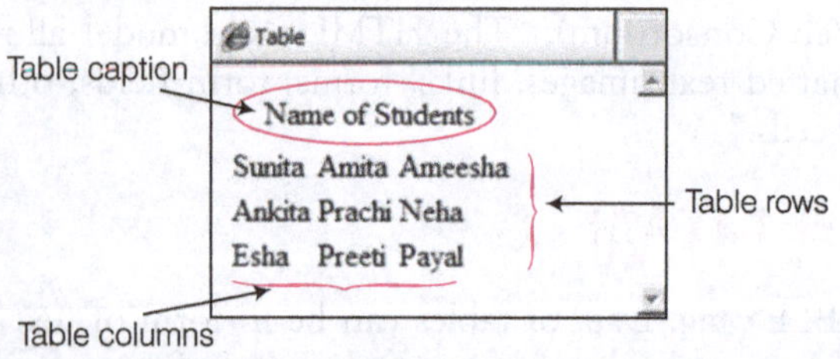

In the above code, we used a <TABLE> tag which specifies a table that is to be inserted. After <TABLE> tag, it arrives a <CAPTION> tag, this <CAPTION> tag is used to add headline in the table. Here, the caption is 'Name of Students'. After <CAPTION> tag, <TR> tag is used which specifies a new table row. There should be a </TR> tag in the end of each row.

Here, <TR> tag is mentioned three times. This means that three rows are added. The next tag is <TD>, which denotes the data cells.

It has been put in front of every piece of information that you want to add in a cell and <TD> tag is mentioned three times in each <TR> tag, i.e. each row will contain three data cells. At the end, the </TABLE> tag closes a table.

The <TABLE> Tag

The <TABLE> tag is used to create tables in HTML. The table tags in HTML are <TABLE> and </TABLE>. Everything to be put in a table, should be enclosed between these two tags. Since, <TABLE> is a container tag thus both the tags are required.

Syntax

```
<TABLE>
   ⋮
</TABLE>
```

Within the <TABLE> tags, a variety of attributes can be added to determine the look of table. You can specify width of the table, add border, background color, spacing between cells (cellspacing) and spacing between border of the cell and its content (cellpadding) in a table. The various attributes of <TABLE> tag discussed in detail are as follows:

1. border Attribute

A border can be added to a table by using border attribute. The border attribute of <TABLE> tag accepts values in pixels. The thickness of border can be adjusted as per the user's requirement. By default, value of the border attribute is 0 (zero), i.e. no border is displayed in your table.

Example 1. *To display border of a table using border attribute.*

```
<HTML>
  <HEAD> <TITLE> Table </TITLE> </HEAD>
  <BODY>
    <TABLE border = "3">
      <CAPTION> Name of Teachers </CAPTION>
      <TR>
        <TD> Shuchi </TD>
        <TD> Shikha </TD>
        <TD> Anita </TD>
      </TR>
      <TR>
        <TD> Manu </TD>
        <TD> Amrita </TD>
        <TD> Aarti </TD>
      </TR>
    </TABLE>
  </BODY>
</HTML>
```

Output

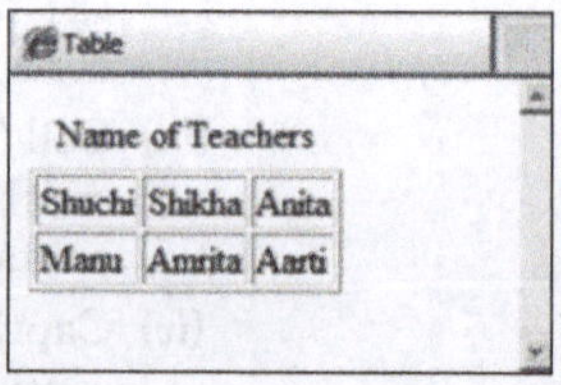

2. bordercolor Attribute

This attribute is used to specify the color of the table's border. Color of your choice for the border to make it more attractive or to make its appearance consistent with the other tables in your Web page.

Example 2. *To display a table with blue border using bordercolor attribute.*

```
<HTML>
  <HEAD> <TITLE> Table </TITLE> </HEAD>
  <BODY>
     <TABLE border="2" bordercolor="blue">
        <TR>
           <TD> One </TD> <TD> Two </TD>
        </TR>
        <TR>
           <TD> Three </TD> <TD> Four </TD>
        </TR>
     </TABLE>
  </BODY>
</HTML>
```

Output

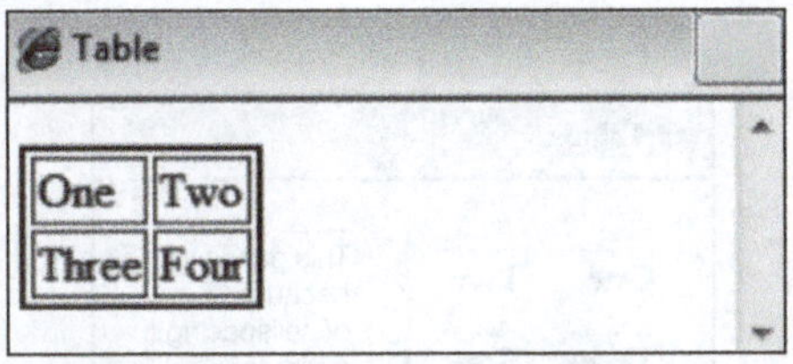

3. frame Attribute

This attribute specifies which part of the table's borders will be visible. Hence, the frame attribute will always be used with the border attribute. The values that can be specified for frames are as follows:

(*i*) **void** outside borders are not shown.

(*ii*) **above** top edge of the border is shown.

(*iii*) **below** bottom edge of the border is shown.

(*iv*) **hsides** top and bottom edges of the border are shown.

(*v*) **lhs** left edge of the border is shown.

(*vi*) **rhs** right edge of the border is shown.

(*vii*) **vsides** left and right edges of the border are shown.

(*viii*) **box** all edges are shown on all four sides (like border).

(*ix*) **border** all edges are shown on all four sides (default).

Thus, frame attribute contains 9 types of values that all can be specified for frames.

Example 3. *To illustrate the use of frame attribute.*

```
<HTML>
  <HEAD><TITLE> Table </TITLE></HEAD>
  <BODY>
     <TABLE border="2" frame="void">
        <TR>
           <TD> One </TD> <TD> Two </TD>
        </TR>
        <TR>
           <TD> Three </TD> <TD> Four </TD>
        </TR>
     </TABLE><BR>
     <TABLE border="2" frame="box">
        <TR>
           <TD> One </TD> <TD> Two </TD>
        </TR>
        <TR>
           <TD> Three </TD> <TD> Four </TD>
        </TR>
     </TABLE>
  </BODY>
</HTML>
```

Output

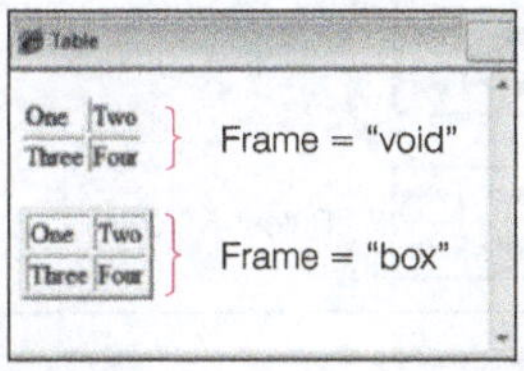

4. rules Attribute

This attribute also works with border attribute of <TABLE> tag. The rules attribute defines which lines or rules to draw between rows and columns in your table. The basic difference between the frame attribute and rules attribute is that the frame attribute is used to display a specific outer portion of a table border while the rules attribute is used to display a specific inside portion of a table border. The values that can be specified for rules attribute are as follows:

(*i*) **none** no rules are drawn or hides all interior borders.

(*ii*) **groups** rules are drawn between row groups and column groups.

(*iii*) **rows** rules are drawn between rows only.

(*iv*) **cols** rules are drawn between columns only.

(*v*) **all** rules are drawn between all rows and all columns.

Thus, rules attribute contains 5 types of values that all can be specified for rules.

Example 4. *To illustrate the use of rules attribute.*

```
<HTML>
  <HEAD> <TITLE> Table </TITLE></HEAD>
  <BODY>
    <TABLE border="2" rules = "groups">
      <TR>
        <TD> One </TD>  <TD> Two </TD>
      </TR>
      <TR>
        <TD> Three </TD>  <TD> Four </TD>
      </TR>
    </TABLE><BR>
    <TABLE border ="2" rules ="rows">
      <TR>
        <TD> One </TD> <TD> Two </TD>
      </TR>
      <TR>
        <TD> Three </TD> <TD> Four </TD>
      </TR>
    </TABLE>
  </BODY>
</HTML>
```

Output

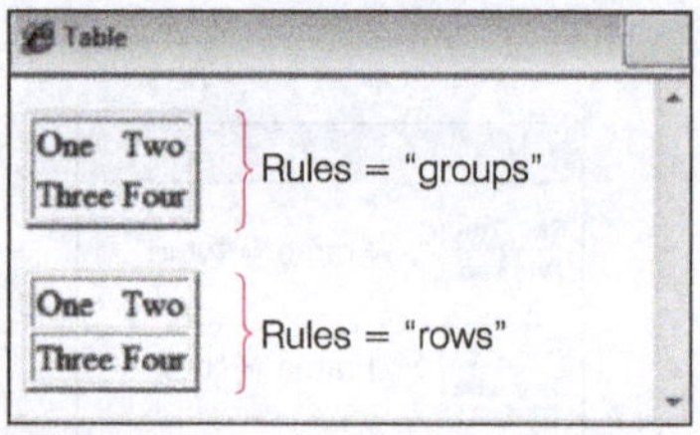

5. cellpadding and cellspacing Attributes

Cellpadding is used to specify the space (in pixels) between the borders of the cell and contents of the cell.

Cellspacing is used to set the distance between two cells.

To control the spacing in the cells, the cellspacing and cellpadding attributes are used.

Example 5. *To illustrate the use of cellpadding attribute.*

```
<HTML>
  <HEAD><TITLE> Table </TITLE></HEAD>
  <BODY>
    <TABLE border="2" cellpadding="10">
      <TR>
        <TD> One </TD> <TD> Two </TD>
      </TR>
      <TR>
        <TD> Three </TD> <TD> Four </TD>
      </TR>
    </TABLE>
  </BODY>
</HTML>
```

Output

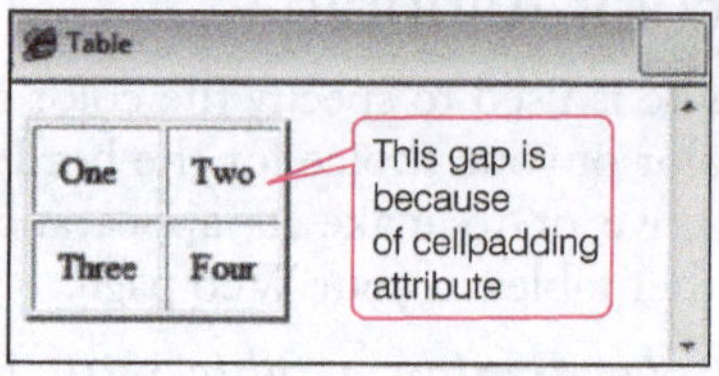

Example 6. *To illustrate the use of cellspacing attribute.*

```
<HTML>
  <HEAD><TITLE> Table </TITLE></HEAD>
  <BODY>
    <TABLE border="2" cellspacing="10">
      <TR>
        <TD> One </TD> <TD> Two </TD>
      </TR>
      <TR>
        <TD> Three </TD> <TD> Four </TD>
      </TR>
    </TABLE>
  </BODY>
</HTML>
```

Output

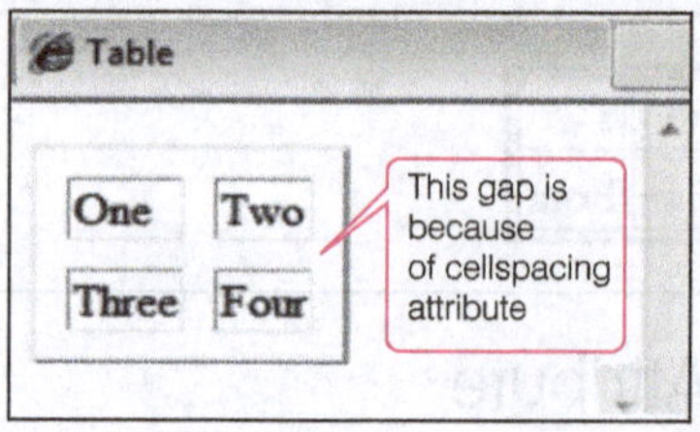

6. align Attribute

This attribute allows you to change the position of the table in a Web page. It can have values left, right and center. The align attribute of <TABLE> tag aligns complete table with respect to the text in the browser.

Example 7. *To illustrate the use of align attribute.*

```
<HTML>
  <HEAD><TITLE> Table </TITLE></HEAD>
  <BODY>
    <TABLE border="2" align="right">
      <TR>
        <TD> One </TD> <TD> Two </TD>
      </TR>
      <TR>
        <TD> Three </TD> <TD> Four </TD>
      </TR>
    </TABLE>
  </BODY>
</HTML>
```

Output

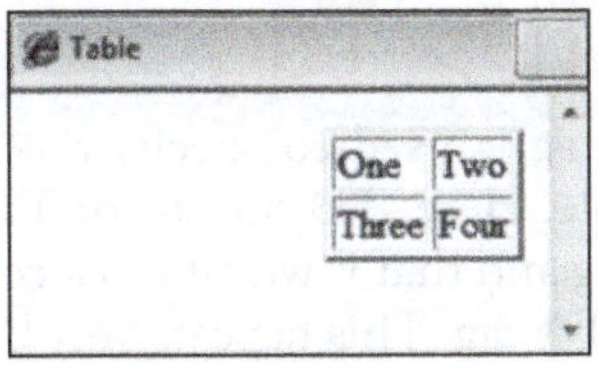

7. background Attribute

This attribute is used to set an image in the background of the table. It enables you to modify the background of your tables in HTML. You can specify an image by putting its path as the value of background attribute to set it as a background of the table.

Example 8. ***To add an image in the background to a table using background attribute.***

```
<HTML>
  <HEAD><TITLE> Table </TITLE></HEAD>
  <BODY>
    <TABLE border="2" cellpadding="15"
    background="D:\images.jpg">
      <TR>
        <TD> One </TD> <TD> Two </TD>
      </TR>
      <TR>
        <TD> Three </TD> <TD> Four </TD>
      </TR>
    </TABLE>
  </BODY>
</HTML>
```

Output

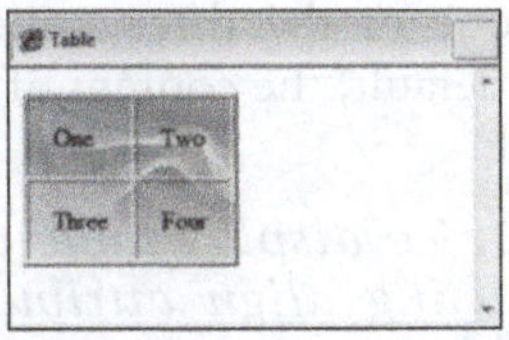

8. bgcolor Attribute

This attribute specifies the background color of a table. With bgcolor, you need to specify the desired background color. By default, background color of the table is white.

Example 9. ***To add pink background color to a table using bgcolor attribute.***

```
<HTML>
  <HEAD><TITLE> Table </TITLE></HEAD>
  <BODY>
    <TABLE border="2" cellpadding="15"
    bgcolor="pink">
      <TR>
        <TD> One </TD> <TD> Two </TD>
      </TR>
      <TR>
        <TD> Three </TD> <TD> Four </TD>
      </TR>
    </TABLE>
  </BODY>
</HTML>
```

Output

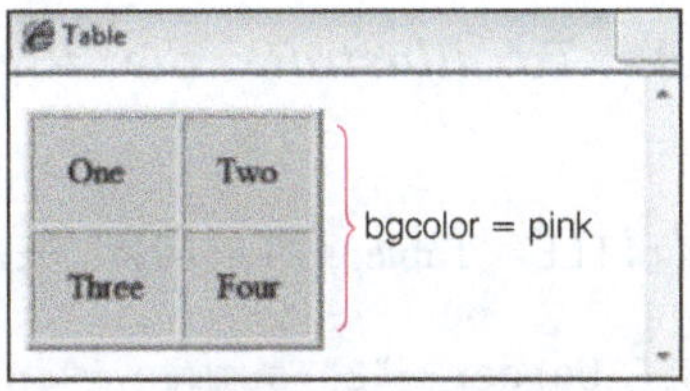

9. height and width Attributes

You can set the height and width of the table using height and width attributes. Height and width are specified in terms of pixels or percentage of the browser window.

Example 10. ***To specify desired height and width of a table using height and width attributes.***

```
<HTML>
  <HEAD><TITLE> Table </TITLE></HEAD>
  <BODY>
    <TABLE border="2" height="100"
    width="50">
      <TR>
        <TD> One </TD> <TD> Two </TD>
      </TR>
      <TR>
        <TD> Three </TD> <TD> Four </TD>
      </TR>
    </TABLE><BR>
    <TABLE border="2" height="50%"
    width="50%">
      <TR>
        <TD> One </TD> <TD> Two</TD>
      </TR>
      <TR>
        <TD> Three </TD> <TD> Four </TD>
      </TR>
    </TABLE>
  </BODY>
</HTML>
```

Output

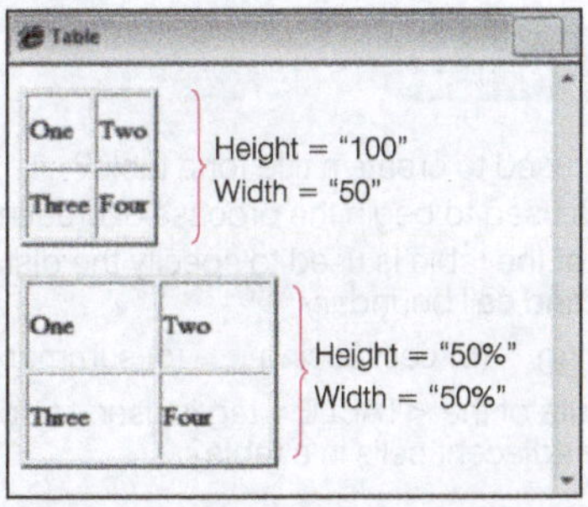

10. summary Attribute

This attribute is used to provide extra information about the table and its contents. It is useful for non-visual Web browsers. This attribute has no visual effect in ordinary Web browsers.

Example 11. ***To illustrate the use of summary attribute.***

```
<HTML>
  <HEAD><TITLE> Table </TITLE></HEAD>
  <BODY>
    <TABLE border ="2" summary="Information
    about students">
       <TR>
          <TD> Student_Name </TD>
          <TD> Roll_No </TD>
          <TD> Division </TD>
       </TR>
       <TR>
          <TD> Ankit </TD> <TD> 15 </TD>
          <TD> Ist </TD>
       </TR>
       <TR>
          <TD> Shikha </TD> <TD> 18 </TD>
          <TD> IInd </TD>
       </TR>
       <TR>
          <TD> Amit </TD> <TD> 21 </TD>
          <TD> Ist </TD>
       </TR>
    </TABLE>
  </BODY>
</HTML>
```

Output

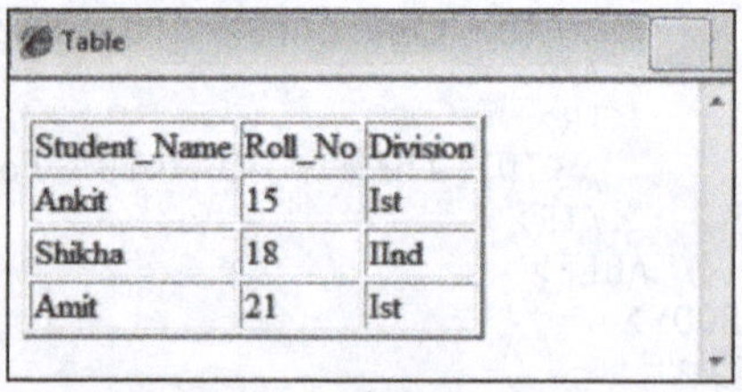

Student_Name	Roll_No	Division
Ankit	15	Ist
Shikha	18	IInd
Amit	21	Ist

Check Point 01

1. Which tag is used to create a title for a table?
2. .... tag is used to begin the process of creating a table in HTML.
3. An attribute of the table is used to specify the distance between the cell content and cell boundary.
   (a) cellpadding (b) cellspacing (c) summary (d) caption
4. Which attribute of the <TABLE> tag is used to specify the distance between the adjacent cells in a table?

The <TD> Tag

The <TD> tag is used to specify a cell or table data within a table. Here, TD stands for Table Data. It is a container tag and that is why it must contain matching closing </TD> tag. This tag can only be present inside <TR> ... </TR> tag.

Note Combining two or more cells in a table on a Web page is called Spanning.

Example 12. ***To show the use of <TD> tag.***

```
<HTML>
  <HEAD><TITLE> TD Tag </TITLE></HEAD>
  <BODY>
    <TABLE>
       <TR> <TD> The td attribute </TD>
       </TR>
    </TABLE>
  </BODY>
</HTML>
```

Output

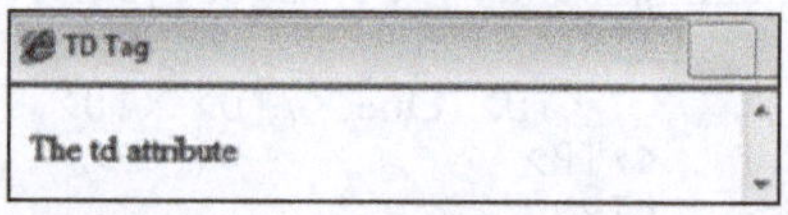

The various attributes of <TD> tag are as follows:

1. align Attribute

The table data can be aligned using align attribute. The align attribute is used with <TD> tag. It can have any one of the three values–left, right and center. By default, the content of a cell in a table is left aligned.

Example 13. ***To display table cells in various alignments using align attribute with <TD> tag.***

```
<HTML>
  <HEAD><TITLE> Table </TITLE></HEAD>
  <BODY>
    <TABLE border="2" height="80%"
    width="70%">
       <TR>
          <TD align="left"> One </TD>
          <TD align="left"> Two </TD>
       </TR>
       <TR>
          <TD align="right"> Three </TD>
          <TD align="right"> Four </TD>
       </TR>
    </TABLE>
  </BODY>
</HTML>
```

Output

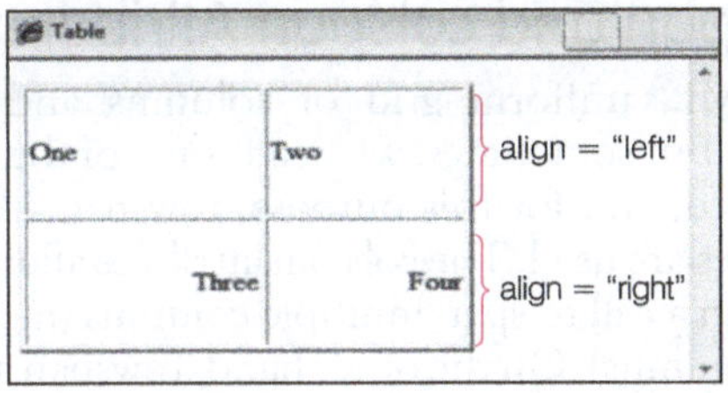

2. width Attribute

This attribute is used to define the width of the cells in the table. It is used with <TD> tag. The width of the cells is defined either in pixels or in percentage.

Example 14. ***To specify individual cell's width using width attribute with <TD> tag.***

```
<HTML>
 <HEAD><TITLE> Table </TITLE></HEAD>
 <BODY>
   <TABLE border="2">
     <TR>
       <TD width="40%"> One </TD>
       <TD width="150"> Two </TD>
     </TR>
     <TR>
       <TD> Three </TD> <TD> Four </TD>
     </TR>
   </TABLE>
 </BODY>
</HTML>
```

Output

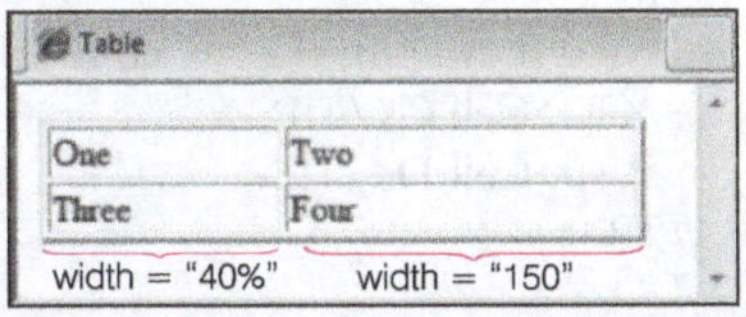

Here, it is noticeable that when the width attribute is used with <TABLE> tag, it specifies the width of the table and when it is used with <TD> tag, it specifies the width of the cells in table.

3. height Attribute

This attribute specifies the height of a cell. Normally, a cell takes up the space it needs to display the content. The height attribute is used to set a predefined height of a cell.

Example 15. ***To specify individual cell's height using height attribute with <TD> tag.***

```
<HTML>
 <HEAD><TITLE> Table </TITLE></HEAD>
 <BODY>
   <TABLE border="2">
     <TR>
       <TD height="100"> one </TD>
       <TD> two </TD>
     </TR>
     <TR>
       <TD height="50"> three </TD>
       <TD> four </TD>
     </TR>
   </TABLE>
 </BODY>
</HTML>
```

Output

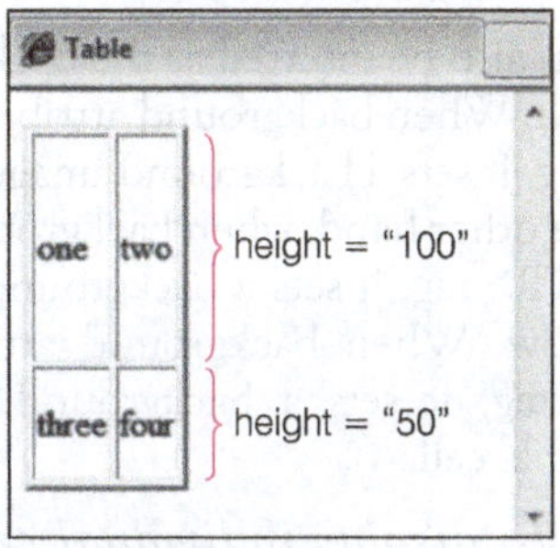

4. bgcolor Attribute

In HTML, background of a table together with colors of rows and columns can be changed.

When bgcolor is used with <TABLE> tag, it sets a background color for the entire table. On the other hand, when bgcolor is used with <TR> tag, it sets a background color for an individual row. When bgcolor is used with <TD> tag, it sets a background color for an individual table cell.

Example 16. ***To display various background colors using bgcolor attribute.***

```
<HTML>
 <HEAD><TITLE> Table </TITLE></HEAD>
 <BODY>
   <TABLE border="2" bordercolor="blue"
   cellpadding="15">
     <TR bgcolor="pink">
       <TD> One </TD><TD> Two </TD>
     </TR>
     <TR bgcolor="red">
       <TD bgcolor="grey"> Three </TD>
       <TD> Four </TD>
     </TR>
   </TABLE>
 </BODY>
</HTML>
```

Output

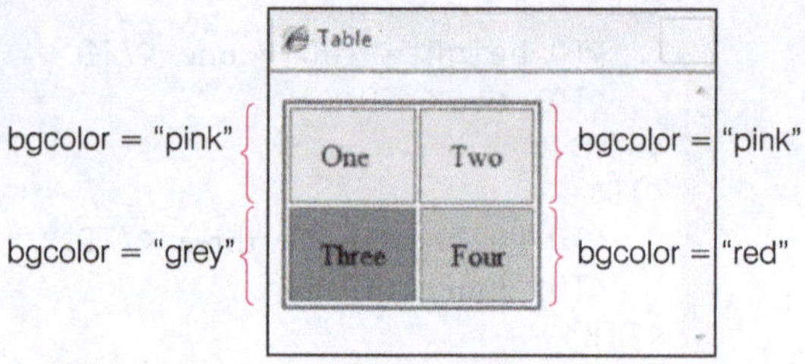

Note Changing the color of any particular row or cell does not affect the background color of rest of the table.

5. background Attribute

An image can also be inserted as the background image of a single cell. When background attribute is used with <TABLE> tag, it sets a background image for the entire table. On the other hand, when background attribute is used with <TR> tag, it sets a background image for an individual row. When background attribute is used with <TD> tag, it sets a background image for an individual table cell.

Example 17. ***To display individual cell's background image using background attribute.***

```
<HTML>
  <HEAD><TITLE> Table </TITLE></HEAD>
  <BODY>
    <TABLE border="2" height="80%"
    width="80%">
        <TR>
          <TD background="birds. jpg">
          Birds</TD>
          <TD background="nature.jpg">
          Nature</TD>
        </TR>
        <TR>
          <TD background="flowers.jpg">
          Flowers</TD>
          <TD backgroud="beverages.jpg">
          Beverages</TD>
        </TR>
    </TABLE>
  </BODY>
</HTML>
```

Output

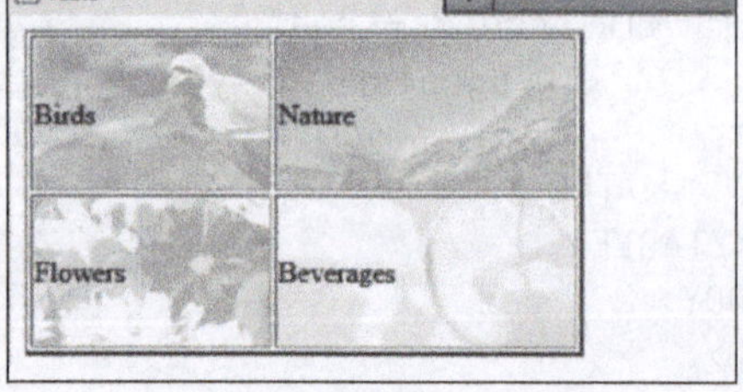

6. rowspan and colspan Attributes

In HTML, uniform grid of columns and rows are created. But sometimes, we need some of the cells to be combined, and for this purpose, rowspan and colspan attributes are used. The colspan attribute allows the user to stretch a cell to span multiple columns (merge two or more columns). On the other hand, rowspan attribute is used to span multiple rows (merge two or more rows). The attributes, colspan (how many across) and rowspan (how many down) indicate, how many columns or rows, a cell should take up.

Example of rowspan and colspan attributes is shown below:

```
<TD rowspan = "2"> </TD>
<TD colspan = "2"> </TD>
```

Here, the rowspan attribute will merge two rows and colspan attribute will merge two columns.

Example 18. ***To create a table with cells having different row and column spans using rowspan and colspan attributes.***

```
<HTML>
  <HEAD><TITLE> Table </TITLE></HEAD>
  <BODY>
    <TABLE border="3" cellpadding="6"
    cellspacing="6">
        <TR>
          <TD align="center"
          colspan="3">Cell A</TD>
        </TR>
        <TR>
          <TD rowspan="2">Cell B</TD>
          <TD>Cell C</TD>
          <TD>Cell D</TD>
        </TR>
        <TR>
          <TD>Cell E</TD>
          <TD>Cell F</TD>
        </TR>
    </TABLE>
  </BODY>
</HTML>
```

Output

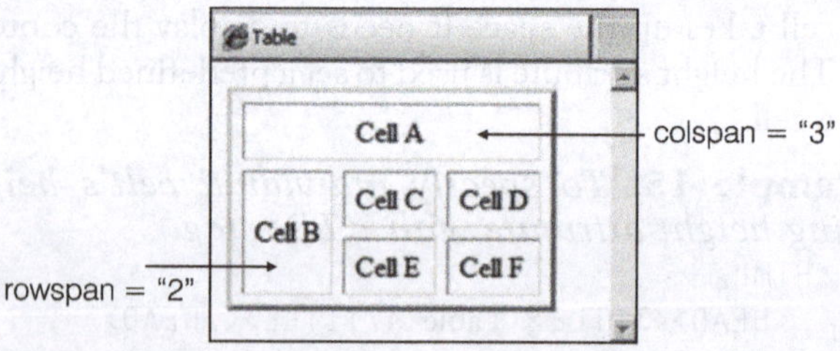

7. valign Attribute

This attribute determines the placement of content in a cell. This attribute is used in <TD> tag to set the vertical alignment of that particular cell's content, when the cell have span of more than one rows. The values that can be used are as follows:

(*i*) **Top** It will put the text as close to the top of the cell as it is possible.

(*ii*) **Middle** It will center the text in the cell.

(*iii*) **Bottom** It will put the text as close to the bottom of the cell as it is possible.

Example 19. *To vertically align a cell's content using valign attribute.*

```
<HTML>
  <HEAD><TITLE> Table </TITLE> </HEAD>
  <BODY>
    <TABLE border="1">
       <TR>
          <TD valign="bottom"
          rowspan="3">One </TD>
          <TD> A </TD> <TD> B </TD>
          <TD> C </TD>
       </TR>
       <TR>
          <TD> D </TD> <TD> E </TD>
          <TD> F </TD>
       </TR>
       <TR>
          <TD> G </TD> <TD> H </TD>
          <TD> I </TD>
       </TR>
    </TABLE>
  </BODY>
</HTML>
```

Output

valign= "bottom"

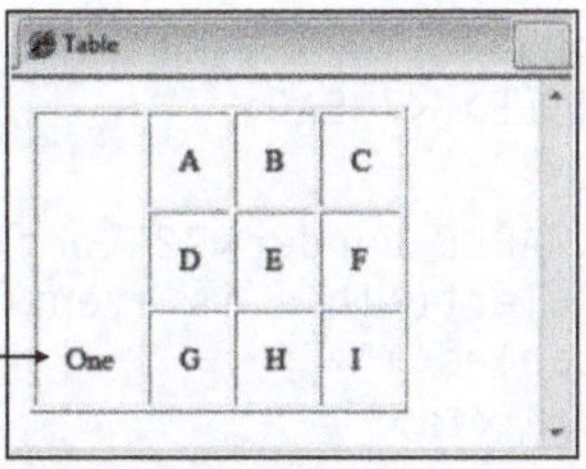

Check Point 02

1 By default, the table data is left-aligned. (True/False).

2 Which attribute helps to align data vertically in a single cell?

3 Which attribute tells that how many columns a cell should span?

The <TR> and <TH> Tags

The <TR> tag stands for Table Row. This tag is used to create a new row of data in a table. The <TR> tag also uses similar attributes as that of <TD> tag except rowspan and colspan. This tag can only be present inside <TABLE> tag. The <TD> tag have higher priority than <TR> tag.

The <TH> tag stands for Table Header. This tag is used for specifying a table's header. It displays the content of a table in heading style and this content appears in bold. This is the only difference between <TH> and <TD> tags. <TH> accepts the similar attributes as that of <TD> tag.

Example 20. *To show the use of <TR> and <TH> tags.*

```
<HTML>
  <HEAD><TITLE> Table </TITLE></HEAD>
  <BODY>
     <TABLE border="1" cellpadding="15">
        <TR>
           <TH> Tag </TH> <TH> Stands For </TH>
        </TR>
        <TR>
           <TD> tr </TD>  <TD> Table Row </TD>
        </TR>
        <TR>
           <TD> th </TD> <TD> Table Header </TD>
        </TR>
     </TABLE>
  </BODY>
</HTML>
```

Output

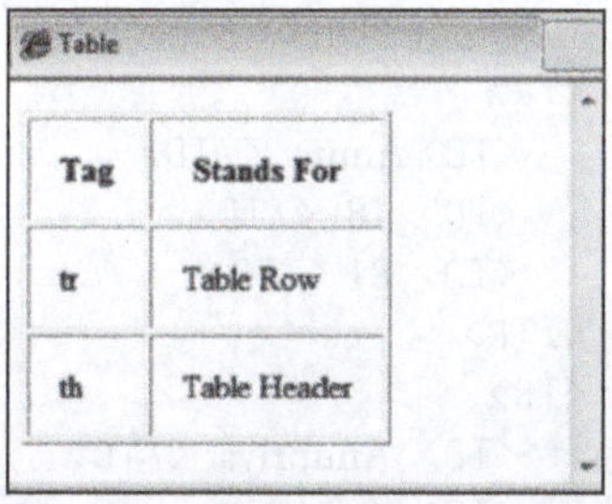

Table Header, Body and Footer

Tables can be divided into three portions as a head, a body and a foot. The head and foot are rather similar to headers and footers in a Word processor document that remain the same for every page, while the body is the main content holder of the table.

The three elements for separating the head, body and foot of a table are as follows:

(*i*) **<THEAD>** indicates that a group of rows are the header rows at the top of the table.

(*ii*) **<TBODY>** indicates that a group of rows are body rows or main body of the table.

(*iii*) **<TFOOT>** indicates that a group of rows are the footer rows at the bottom of the table.

A table may contain several <TBODY> elements to indicate different pages or groups of data.

Browsers can use these elements to enable scrolling of the table body independently of the header and footer. Also, when printing a large table that spans multiple pages, these elements can enable the table header and footer to be printed at the top and bottom of each page.

The <THEAD>, <TBODY> and <TFOOT> tags contain various attributes such as align, bgcolor and valign.

Example 21. *To show the use of <THEAD>, <TBODY> and <TFOOT> tags.*

```
<HTML>
  <HEAD> <TITLE> Table </TITLE> </HEAD>
  <BODY>
    <TABLE border="2">
       <THEAD bgcolor="grey">
         <TR>
           <TD> Student_Name </TD>
           <TD> Roll_No </TD>
           <TD> Percentage </TD>
         </TR>
       </THEAD>
       <TBODY bgcolor="pink">
         <TR>
           <TD> Amita </TD>
           <TD> 18 </TD>
           <TD> 81 </TD>
         </TR>
         <TR>
           <TD> Anupriya </TD>
           <TD> 20 </TD>
           <TD> 89 </TD>
         </TR>
       </TBODY>
       <TFOOT bgcolor="yellow">
         <TR>
           <TD> Sanjay </TD>
           <TD> 21 </TD>
           <TD> 79 </TD>
         </TR>
       </TFOOT>
    </TABLE>
  </BODY>
</HTML>
```

Output

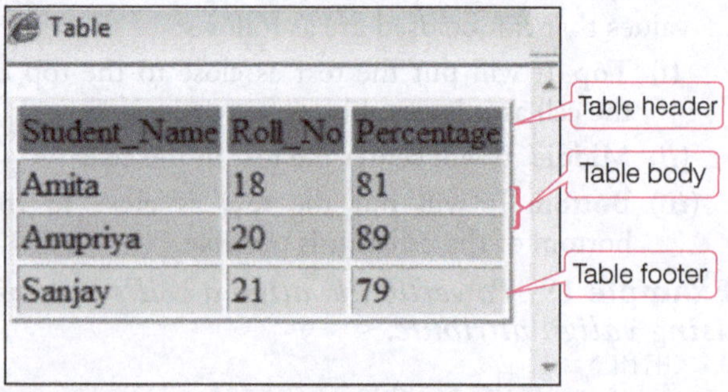

Event Handling in HTML Tables

In HTML, events are features that allow users to add interactivity between the Web page and its visitor. An event is an action that is performed by the user, such as by pressing a key or on mouse click. An event handler allows you to run a particular code, which is associated with that particular event. An event is activated, when you click the object, on which you apply the event. Some of the events available for HTML are given below:

offline, onchange, onclick, ondrag, onerror, onfocus, oninput, oninvalid, ononline, onselect, onwaiting etc.

Example 22. *To illustrate the use of event handling.*

```
<HTML>
  <HEAD> <TITLE> Table with Event Handling
  </TITLE> </HEAD>
  <BODY>
    <TABLE border="2" onclick=
    "alert('This is event handling in HTML
    tables')">
       <TR>
         <TD> One </TD> <TD> Two </TD>
       </TR>
       <TR>
         <TD> Three </TD> <TD> Four </TD>
       </TR>
    </TABLE>
  </BODY>
</HTML>
```

Output

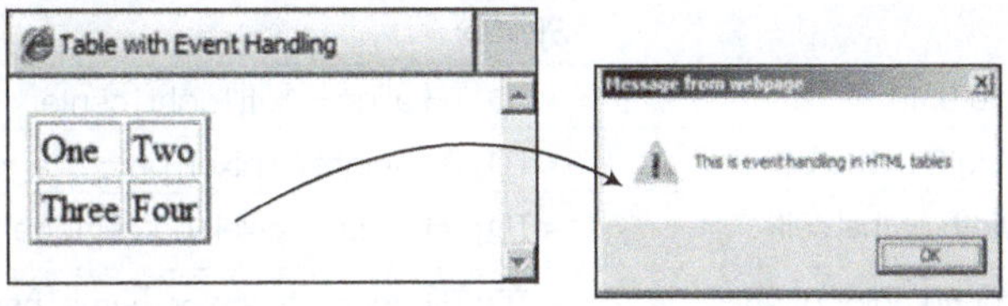

onclick event is activated when you click the object (table) on which you apply the event.

Note When you click anywhere on the table, a message box will appear. In this message box, the message you wrote in the alert, will be display.

Check Point 03

1. The <TR> tag also uses similar attributes as that of <TD> tag except which types of attribute?
2. Name the elements are used for separating body and footer of a table.
3. The......... tag is used to define the header of a table.

Attributes of <TABLE> Tag

Attributes	*Explanation*	*Syntax*
border	Add border to the table. (Takes value in pixel)	<TABLE border="pixel">
bordercolor	Specifies the color of table's border.	<TABLE bordercolor="color_name | hex_number | rgb_number">
frame	Specifies which part of the table's border will be visible. (Outer border)	<TABLE frame="void | above | below | hsides | lhs | rhs | vsides | box | border">
rules	Specifies which lines or rules to draw between rows and columns.	<TABLE rules="none | groups | rows | cols | all">
cellpadding	Specifies the space (in pixel) needed between the edges of cells and its contents.	<TABLE cellpadding="pixel">
cellspacing	Specifies the space (in pixel) between two cells.	<TABLE cellspacing="pixel">
align	Specifies the alignment of the table in a Web browser.	<TABLE align="left | right | center">
background	Used to set an image in background of the table.	<TABLE background="path | image name">
bgcolor	Specifies the background color of the table.	<TABLE bgcolor="color_name | hex_number | rgb_number">
height	Set the height of the table. (in pixel or percentage)	<TABLE height="pixel | percentage">
width	Set the width of the table. (in pixel or percentage)	<TABLE width="pixel | percentage">
summary	Provides information about the table.	<TABLE summary="text">

Attributes of <TD> and <TH> Tags

Attributes	*Explanation*	*Syntax*
align	Used to align the table data.	<TD|TH align= "left|right|center">
height	Used to define the height of the cell.	<TD|TH height=" pixel|percentage">
width	Used to define the width of the cell.	<TD|TH width="pixel|percentage">
bgcolor	Specifies the background color of an individual cell.	<TD|TH bgcolor="color_name|hex_number|rgb_number">
background	Specifies the background image of an individual cell.	<TD|TH background="path|image_name">
rowspan	Used to span multiple rows, i.e. how many rows a cell should take.	<TD|TH rowspan="number">
colspan	How many columns a cell should span across.	<TD|TH colspan="number">
valign	Set the vertical alignment of that particular cell's content (when rowspan is more than one row).	<TD|TH valign="top|bottom|middle">

Attributes of <TR> Tag

Attributes	*Explanation*	*Syntax*
align	Specifies the alignment of the row content.	<TR align= "left|right|center">
bgcolor	Specifies the background color of an individual row.	<TR bgcolor="color_name|hex_number|rgb_number">
background	Specifies a background image for that particular row.	<TR background="path|image_name">
valign	Set the vertical alignment of the text of the cells inside the element.	<TR valign="top|bottom|middle">

SUMMARY

- HTML table allows one to arrange data into rows and columns.
- Each row is divided into data cell that can contain text, images, lists, paragraphs, horizontal rules etc.
- An HTML table can represented and manipulated using <TABLE>, <TR>, <TH>, <TD>, <TBODY>, <THEAD> and <TFOOT> tags.
- The <TABLE> tag begins the process of building a table.
- <CAPTION> tag places a horizontally centered title at the top or at the bottom of a table.
- If a caption of a table is wider than the table, the caption will break and continue onto the next line(s), so as to remain within the left and right boundaries of the table.
- colspan="C": specifies how many columns "C" of a table a heading cell will span. colspan="1" is the default.
- rowspan="R": specifies how many rows "R" of a table a heading cell will span. rowspan="1" is the default.
- A rowspan made to extend into rows which have not been created with <TR> and </TR> tags will be truncated.
- cellspacing="S": causes the non-colored portion of the border (whether visible or invisible) around a table and between adjacent cells of the table to be "S" pixels in width. The default cellspacing width is 2 pixels.
- cellpadding="P": creates a minimum distance of "P" pixels between the contents of each table cell and the closest (whether visible or invisible) border of the cell. The default cellpadding is 1 pixel.

Exam Practice

Multiple Choice Questions

1 Which of these tags belong to table? **CBSE 2016**
(a) <THEAD>,<BODY>,<TR>
(b) <TABLE>,<HEAD>,<TFOOT>
(c) <TABLE>,<TR>,<TD>
(d) <TABLE>,<TR>,<TT>

Ans. (*c*) <TABLE>, <TR>, <TD> tags are used with table.

2 Which of the following is used to specify the beginning of a table's row?
(a) <TABLE> (b) <TR>
(c) <ROW> (d) <BEGIN>

Ans. (*b*) <TR> tag indicates the beginning of a table's row.

3 HTML tag for row is
(a) <COLSPAN> (b) <TR>
(c) <ROWSPAN> (d) <TD>

Ans. (*b*) HTML tag for row is <TR>.

4 Which tag is used to add columns in the tables? **CBSE 2014**
(a) <COLSPAN> (b) <TD>
(c) <TR> (d) None of these

Ans. (*b*) <TD> tag is used to add columns in the table.

5 The ……… tag is used to specify the individual table data in a table. **CBSE 2011**
(a) <TR> (b) <TD>
(c) <TH> (d) <TABLE>

Ans. (*b*) The <TD> tag is used to specify the individual table data in a table.

6 Which of the following tags gives a caption to the table?
(a) <CAPTION> (b) <SUMMARY>
(c) <FRAME> (d) None of these

Ans. (*a*) <CAPTION> tag is used to give caption to the table.

7 In order to add border to a table, border attribute is specified in which tag? **CBSE 2014**
(a) <TH> (b) <TABLE> (c) <TD> (d) <TR>

Ans. (*b*) border attribute is specified in <TABLE> tag.

8 The attribute used to set the border color of a table is **CBSE 2011**
(a) border (b) bordercolor
(c) color (d) border color

Ans. (*b*) bordercolor is used to set the border color of a table.

9 The frame attribute contains ……… types of values.
(a) 9 (b) 3
(c) 6 (d) 4

Ans. (*a*) The frame attribute contains 9 types of values.

10 Which of the following is an attribute of <TABLE> tag? **CBSE 2011**
(a) src (b) cellpadding
(c) link (d) bold

Ans. (*b*) cellpadding is an attribute of <TABLE> tag.

11 Which one of the following is not an option for aligning data in a table? **CBSE 2016**
(a) justify (b) right
(c) left (d) center

Ans. (*a*) justify option is not used for aligning data in a table.

12 Which attribute of the <TABLE> tag is used to set an image in the background of a table?
(a) bgcolor (b) background
(c) frame (d) rules

Ans. (*b*) background attribute is used to set an image in the background of a table.

13 The attribute used to specify the background color of a table is **CBSE 2011**
(a) color (b) bgtable
(c) backcolor (d) bgcolor

Ans. (*d*) bgcolor attribute is used to specify the background color of a table.

14 The two common attributes of the <IMG> and the <TABLE> tag are **CBSE 2011**
(a) src and height
(b) height and width
(c) border and src
(d) they do not have any common attributes.

Ans. (*b*) height and width are two common attributes of the <IMG> tag and the <TABLE> tag.

15 border, frame, cellspacing, cellpadding, align are the attributes of
(a) <BODY> tag (b) <IMG> tag
(c) <TABLE> tag (d) None of these

Ans. (*c*) border, frame, cellspacing, cellpadding and align are the attributes of <TABLE> tag.

16 Which of the following is not an attribute of <TABLE> tag?
(a) border (b) background
(c) bgcolor (d) src

Ans. (*d*) src (source) is not an attribute of <TABLE> tag.

17 In the <TD> tag, TD stands for
(a) Table Data (b) Table Time and Date
(c) Table Date (d) None of these

Ans. (*a*) TD stands for Table Data, which specifies a cell or table data within a table.

18 Combining two or more cells in a table on a Web page is called **CBSE 2011**
(a) merging (b) spanning
(c) combining (d) None of these

Ans. (*b*) Combining two or more cells in a table on a Web page is called spanning.

19 What is the correct HTML code to left align the content inside a table cell?
(a) <TD valign = "left"> (b) <TD align = "left">
(c) <TD left align> (d) <TD left>

Ans. (*b*) <TD align = "left">

20 Choose the correct HTML code to right align the content inside a table cell.
(a) <TD align = "right">
(b) <TD valign = "right">
(c) <TD rightalign>
(d) <TD right = "align">

Ans. (*a*) <TD align ="right">

21 Which attribute tells, how many rows a cell should span?
(a) colspan = n (b) rowspan = n
(c) Both (a) and (b) (d) None of these

Ans. (*b*) rowspan = n will tell how many rows a cell should span.

22 rowspan = n can be added to only which tag? **CBSE 2014**
(a) <HR> (b) <TABLE>
(c) <TD> (d) <TR>

Ans. (*c*) rowspan = n can be added to only <TD> tag.

23 Which attribute of <TD> tag is used to merge two or more columns to form a single column?
(a) colspan (b) cellspacing
(c) cellpadding (d) rowspan

Ans. (*a*) colspan attribute is used to merge two or more columns to form a single column.

24 colspan = n can be added to …… tag. **CBSE 2013**
(a) <HR> (b) <TABLE>
(c) <TD> (d) <TR>

Ans. (*c*) colspan = n can be added to <TD> tag.

25 The ……… attribute helps to align data vertically in a single cell.
(a) align (b) valign
(c) halign (d) Both (b) and (c)

Ans. (*b*) valign attribute is used to align data vertically in a single cell.

26 In the <TH> tag, TH stands for
(a) Table Heading
(b) Total Heading
(c) Table Header
(d) All of the above

Ans. (*c*) TH stands for Table Header, which is used to specify a table's header.

Fill in the Blanks

1 To insert a table on a Web page, we use ……… tag. **CBSE 2012**

Ans. <TABLE>

2 The tag to start a table is ……. **CBSE 2014**

Ans. <TABLE>

3 ……….. tag is used to insert data into a table.

Ans. <TD>

4 The <TD> tag is a ……….. tag.

Ans. container

5 The ……….. attribute is used to display a specific portion of a table border.

Ans. frame

6 frame attribute is used with ……….. attribute.

Ans. border

7 There are total ……….. values for rules attribute in <TABLE> tag.

Ans. 5

8 In the rules attribute, the ……….. value helps to display a table border only between rows.

Ans. rows

EXAM PRACTICE

9 The .... is an attribute of the <TABLE> tag to set the distance between the cell content and its boundary. **CBSE 2011**

Ans. cellpadding

10 Cellspacing is used to create space between different .... in a table.

Ans. cells

11 To set an image as background in HTML table, you can use .... attribute.

Ans. background

12 By default, color of a table is ....

Ans. white

13 The height and width attributes of <TABLE> tag are specified in terms of .... or percentage.

Ans. pixels

14 The .... attribute is used to provide information about a table.

Ans. summary

15 <TD> tag can only be present inside .... tag.

Ans. <TR>

16 The .... attribute is used to combine the cells vertically. **CBSE 2011**

Ans. rowspan

17 The .... attribute is used to span two or more columns in a table. **CBSE 2012**

Ans. colspan

18 The .... attribute is used to align the data vertically within cells.

Ans. valign

19 The <TR> tag can only be present inside .... tag. **CBSE 2013**

Ans. <TABLE>

20 The <TFOOT> tag is used to specify the ...... part of the table.

Ans. footer

True or False

1 A cell is an intersection of a row and a column.

Ans. **True** A cell is an intersection of a row and a column.

2 <CAPTION> is placed just above the <TABLE> tag. **CBSE 2016**

Ans. **False** <CAPTION> tag is placed inside the <TABLE> tag.

3 <CAPTION> tag gives heading to a Web page.

Ans. **False** <CAPTION> tag gives title or caption for the table.

4 <TD> will make the text bold. **CBSE 2016**

Ans. **False** <TD> is a table data. It is used to define a cell of a table that contains data.

5 The border is an attribute of <A> tag. **CBSE 2011**

Ans. **False** The border is an attribute of <TABLE> tag.

6 The default value of border attribute is 1.

Ans. **False** The default value of border attribute is 0.

7 The cols value in the rules attribute, allows you to display table border only between columns.

Ans. **True** The cols value in the rules attribute is drawn between columns only.

8 The cellpadding attribute is used with <TD> tag. **CBSE 2014**

Ans. **False** The cellpadding attribute is used with <TABLE> tag.

9 The cellspacing attribute tells the browser how much space to include between the walls of the table.

Ans. **False** cellspacing attribute is used to create space between different cells in a table.

10 cellspacing attribute is used with <BODY> tag.

Ans. **False** cellspacing attribute is used with <TABLE> tag.

11 The rowspan attribute with <TABLE> tag is used to merge more than one cells row wise. **CBSE 2011**

Ans. **True** The rowspan attribute merges the cells row wise in a table.

12 The rowspan attribute is used to make a cell span multiple columns. **CBSE 2013**

Ans. **False** The rowspan attribute is used to make a cell span multiple rows.

13 The align and valign are the attributes used with <TD> tag to set the alignment of data in a cell.

Ans. **True** The align and valign attributes are used to set alignment of the data.

14 The <TD> tag (column setting) have higher priority than <TR> tag (row setting).

Ans. **True** The <TD> tag (column setting) have higher priority than <TR> tag (row setting).

15 Table row <TR> tag can accept one attribute.

Ans. **False** The <TR> tag can accept many attributes.

16 <TH> tag is used to specify the column heading in a table. **CBSE 2011**

Ans. **True** <TH> tag is used to specify the column heading in a table.

Very Short Answer (VSA) Type Questions

1 Name the tags which are used with <TABLE> tag.

Ans. <TR>,<TD>,<TH> and <CAPTION> tags are used with <TABLE> tag.

2 Describe the border attribute of <TABLE> tag.

Ans. The border attribute is used to define the thickness of the border, which surrounds the table.

3 Why bordercolor attribute is used?

Ans. The bordercolor attribute is used to specify the color of the table's border.

4 Name any two values specified in frame attribute.

Ans. The values that can be specified for frame attribute are void and above.

5 Which attribute lets you control the display of select border sides of a table?

Ans. frame attribute displays the selected border sides of the table.

6 How many values can be specified in rules attribute of <TABLE> tag?

Ans. There are total five values that can be specified for rules attribute.

7 Define cellspacing.

Ans. The cellspacing is used to create space between different cells in a table.

8 Name two table attributes, which are used to set spacing in and between table cells.

Ans. The cellspacing and cellpadding are the attributes, which are used to set spacing in and between the table cells.

9 What is the use of align attribute in <TABLE> tag?

Ans. The align attribute defines the center, right or left alignment of the <TABLE> tag.

10 With which tag, align attribute is used?

Ans. The align attribute is used with both <TD> tag and <TABLE> tag.

11 Why valign attribute is used? **CBSE 2005**

Ans. The valign attribute is used with <TD> tag which helps to align data in a single cell if the cell span in more than one rows.

12 Name the values that can be used in valign attribute.

Ans. The values that can be used in valign attribute are top, middle and bottom.

13 Which tag is used for giving heading to the columns?

Ans. The <TH> tag is used to display the table heading only once for a table column.

14 Which tags divide HTML tables in multiple section?

Ans. <THEAD>, <TFOOT> and <TBODY>

15 What is the difference between <THEAD> and <TFOOT> tags?

Ans. The <THEAD> tag is used to add a header in a table while <TFOOT> tag is used to add a footer in a table.

16 Can you insert hyperlinks inside table cells?

Ans. Yes, in spite of text we just have to insert the anchor tag between the <TD> and </TD> tags.

e.g.

```
<TD>
  <A href = "www.google.com"> link </A>
</TD>
```

EXAM PRACTICE

Short Answer (SA) Type Questions

1 What is table? Name the basic commands for creating a table.

Ans. Tables are made up of rows and columns. In HTML, tables are used to display tabular data in Web pages. The basic commands for creating tables are as follows:

Table tag <TABLE> </TABLE>
Row tag <TR> </TR>
Cell tag <TD> </TD>, <TH> </TH> and
Caption tag <CAPTION> </CAPTION>.

2 What do you mean by the border attribute?

Ans. Refer to text on Page No. 98.

3 Write HTML code to display a table with border of 5px. **CBSE 2016**

Ans.
```
<HTML><BODY>
    <TABLE border = "5">
      <TR><TD>1</TD></TR>
      <TR><TD>2</TD></TR>
    </TABLE>
</BODY></HTML>
```

4 Describe the various values of rules attribute.

Ans. Refer to text on Page No. 99. **CBSE 2018**

5 Differentiate between cellpadding and cellspacing in HTML table.

Ans. Differences between cellpadding and cellspacing are as follows:

Cellpadding	*Cellspacing*
It is used for formatting purpose which specifies the space needed between the edges of the cells and also in the cell contents.	It is one also used for formatting purpose but it sets space between cells.
The general format of specifying cellpadding in HTML is as follows: <TABLE width="100" border ="2" cellpadding="5">	The general format of specifying cellspacing in HTML is as follows: <TABLE width="100" border="2" cellspacing ="20">
The default value of cellpadding attribute is 1.	The default value of cellspacing attribute is 2.

6 Name the attributes of <TABLE> tag which are used for specifying its dimensions in a Web page. **CBSE 2016**

Ans. width and height attributes of <TABLE> tag are used for specifying its dimensions in a Web page. width and height are specified in terms of pixel or percentage of the browser window.

7 Explain the width attribute of <TABLE> tag.

Ans. The width attribute is used to set the absolute width of the table. The values in width attribute can be either in pixel or in percentage of the browser window.

e.g.
```
<TABLE width = "150">
    <TR><TD>Cell1</TD><TD>Cell2</TD></TR>
    <TR><TD>Cell3</TD><TD>Cell4</TD></TR>
</TABLE>
```

8 What is the function of summary attribute?

Ans. summary attribute of <TABLE> tag is used to provide the detailed information about a table. It enables a user to know the type of information that a table contains. It is useful to provide access to non-visual browsers, which are used by users with visual impairment.

e.g. `<TABLE summary="text">`

9 What is data cell? Name the <TABLE> tag, which is used as data cell.

Ans. The data cell defines a cell of a table that contains data. The table data cell is coded with <TD> tag of <TABLE> tag. Here, TD stands for Table Data. The content in the table data cell is normal and left-aligned by default.

10 Why rowspan and colspan attributes are used?

Ans. Sometimes, a table cell is bigger than other. Its span is spread to more rows or columns. Such cells can be created with the help of rowspan and colspan attributes.

11 Name the attributes that are used to do the following in HTML:

(*i*) merge two or more rows.
(*ii*) change the background color of the cells in a table.
(*iii*) vertically align cell content.
(*iv*) merge two or more columns.

Ans. (*i*) rowspan (*ii*) bgcolor
(*iii*) valign (*iv*) colspan

12 Name the attributes used for following:

(*i*) setting the cell width.
(*ii*) setting cell's background image.
(*iii*) setting cell's background color.
(*iv*) changing the cell span.

Ans. (*i*) width (*ii*) background
(*iii*) bgcolor (*iv*) rowspan and colspan

13 Which attributes can you use with <TABLE> tag but not with <TR> tag?

Ans. summary, rules, frame, border, cellpadding, cellspacing, height, width and bordercolor are the attributes that you can use with <TABLE> tag but not with <TR> tag.

14 Define the <TH> and <TR> tags. Are these two tags similar? If yes, how?

Ans. <TH> tag stands for Table Header. It is used to give headings to the various columns in our table. <TR> tag stands for Table Row. It is used to create a row in a table. <TH> and <TR> tags are not similar. <TH> tag is similar to <TD> tag. Since, <TH> tag also defines a data cell, which is taken as heading to the columns and the data is bold faced.

15 What is header cell? Name the <TABLE> tag, which is used as header cell.

Ans. The header cell specifies the header of the table and displays the content of a table in heading style. The content in the table header cell is rendered in bold and centered horizontally within the cell. The table header cell is coded with <TH> tag.

16 Mr. Ayush, Sports Captain of the school, has to display sequence of events of the upcoming Annual Sports Day on the school website. Help him in writing HTML code to create a table in HTML as shown in the given screenshot: **CBSE 2019**

ANNUAL SPORTS DAY–SEQUENCE OF EVENTS		
8:00 AM–9:00 AM	9:00 AM–1:00 PM	1:00 PM–2:00 PM
CULTURAL EVENTS	TRACK EVENTS	PRIZE DISTRIBUTION

Ans.
```
<HTML>
  <BODY>
    <TABLE border = "1">
      <TR>
    <TH colspan ="3" align ="center" ANNUAL
    SPORTS DAY-SEQUENCE OF EVENTS </TH>
    </TR>
    <TR align ="center">
    <TD>8:00 AM - 9:00 AM</TD>
    <TD>9:00 AM-1:00 PM</TD>
    <TD>1:00 PM-2:00 PM</TD>
    </TR>
    <TR align ="center">
        <TD>CULTURAL EVENTS</TD>
        <TD>TRACK EVENTS</TD>
        <TD>PRIZE DISTRIBUTION</TD>
    </TR>
    </TABLE>
    </BODY>
    </HTML>
```

Long Answer (LA) Type Questions

1 Write the HTML code to create the exact table which is given below: **CBSE 2011**

ADMNO	SNAME	NAME	DOB
1110	MANJIT	RANJIT	4-MAR-1998

Ans. The HTML code is
```
<HTML>
   <BODY>
   <TABLE border="3">
     <TR align="center" valign="middle">
       <TH> ADMNO </TH>
       <TH> SNAME </TH>
       <TH> NAME </TH>
       <TH> DOB </TH>
       </TR>
     <TR align="left" valign="middle">
       <TD> 1110 </TD>
       <TD> MANJIT </TD>
       <TD> RANJIT </TD>
       <TD> 4-MAR-1998 </TD>
     </TR>
   </TABLE>
   </BODY>
</HTML>
```

2 Explain the frame attribute and the various values of it.

Ans. Refer to text on Page No. 99.

3 Write an HTML code to create the following table:

Roll Number	Name	Class
100	Amit	10 A
101	Ankit	10 B
102	Arnab	10 C
Footer 1	Footer 2	Footer 3

Note First row has green background.

Ans. The HTML code is
```
<HTML>
   <BODY>
      <TABLE border="2" align="left">
      <THEAD bgcolor="green">
      <TR>
         <TD> Roll Number </TD>
         <TD> Name </TD>
         <TD> Class </TD>
      </TR>
      </THEAD>
      <TBODY>
      <TR>
         <TD> 100 </TD>
```

EXAM PRACTICE

```
        <TD> Amit </TD>
        <TD> 10 A </TD>
      </TR>
      <TR>
        <TD> 101 </TD>
        <TD> Ankit </TD>
        <TD> 10 B </TD>
      </TR>
      <TR>
        <TD> 102 </TD>
        <TD> Arnab </TD>
        <TD> 10 C </TD>
      </TR>
   </TBODY>
   <TFOOT>
      <TR>
        <TD> Footer 1 </TD>
        <TD> Footer 2 </TD>
        <TD> Footer 3 </TD>
      </TR>
   </TFOOT>
   </TABLE>
   </BODY>
</HTML>
```

4 What is the use of <TR> tag in an HTML table? Give a suitable example.

Ans. The <TR> tag creates a table row in an HTML table. A table must have atleast one row and also, it can have as many table rows as you want. A table row is divided into table cells. A table must have atleast one table cell per table row. e.g.

```
<HTML>
   <HEAD><TITLE> TR Tag </TITLE></HEAD>
   <BODY>
    <TABLE border = "1" cellpadding ="3">
    <TR>
      <TH> Head 1 </TH>
      <TH> Head 2 </TH>
      <TH> Head 3 </TH>
    </TR>
    <TR>
      <TD> A </TD>
      <TD> B </TD>
      <TD> C </TD>
    </TR>
    <TR>
      <TD> D </TD>
      <TD> E </TD>
      <TD> F </TD>
    </TR>
    </TABLE>
   </BODY>
</HTML>
```

Output

Head 1	Head 2	Head 3
A	B	C
D	E	F

5 Observe the following table and write the HTML code to generate it: **CBSE 2014**

question	marks
1	2
	2
	5

Note 1st row has pink background.

Ans. The HTML code is

```
<HTML>
   <BODY>
   <TABLE border = "1">
    <TR bgcolor = "pink" align = "center">
      <TH>question</TH>
      <TH>marks</TH></TR>
    <TR><TD rowspan = "3">1</TD>
      <TD>2</TD>
    </TR>
    <TR>
      <TD>2</TD>
    </TR>
    <TR>
      <TD>5</TD>
    </TR>
   </TABLE>
   </BODY>
</HTML>
```

6 Observe the following table and write the HTML code to generate it: **CBSE 2013**

Period1	Period2
Math	Science
English	SST
Science	SST

Ans. The HTML code is

```
<HTML>
   <BODY>
   <TABLE cellpadding = "10"
   cellspacing="0" border="1">
    <TR align = "center">
```

```
        <TH>Period1</TH>
        <TH>Period2</TH>
      </TR>
      <TR align = "center">
        <TD>Math</TD>
        <TD>Science</TD>
      </TR>
      <TR align="center">
        <TD>English</TD>
        <TD>SST</TD>
      </TR>
      <TR align="center">
        <TD>Science</TD>
        <TD>SST</TD>
      </TR>
    </TABLE>
    </BODY>
</HTML>
```

7 Write the HTML code to generate the following table on a Web page with the contents and alignment exactly as shown below: **CBSE 2011**

MOVID	MOVNAME	ACTORS
M001	HIT FACTORY	4

Ans. The HTML code is

```
<HTML>
    <BODY>
    <TABLE border="1" width = "400">
      <TR align="right">
         <TH>MOVID</TH>
         <TH>MOVNAME</TH>
         <TH>ACTORS</TH>
      </TR>
      <TR align="left">
         <TD>M001</TD>
         <TD>HIT FACTORY</TD>
         <TD>4</TD>
      </TR>
    </TABLE>
    </BODY>
</HTML>
```

8 Write the HTML code to generate the following table with the contents exactly in the same format as shown within the table: **CBSE 2012**

<table>
<tr><th colspan="4">Shopping Mall</th></tr>
<tr><td>Floor</td><td>No. of Toy
Shops</td><td>No. of Food
Shops</td><td>No. of Sports
Shops</td></tr>
</table>

Ans. The HTML code is

```
<HTML><BODY>
    <TABLE border="1">
      <TR>
        <TH colspan="4" align="center">
        Shopping Mall</TH>
      </TR>
      <TR align = "center">
        <TD>Floor</TD>
        <TD>No. of Toy<BR>Shops</TD>
        <TD>No. of Food<BR>Shops</TD>
        <TD>No. of Sports<BR>Shops</TD>
      </TR>
    </TABLE>
    </BODY>
</HTML>
```

9 Write the complete <TABLE>...</TABLE> tags to create a table with the following contents.
Ensure that the background of each data cell should have the color as specified in the corresponding column heading.

Ans.

```
<TABLE>
    <CAPTION>Colors</CAPTION>
    <TR>
      <TH>red</TH>
      <TH>green</TH>
      <TH>blue</TH>
      <TH>orange</TH>
      <TH>cyan</TH>
    </TR>
    <TR>
      <TD bgcolor="red" width="100"
       height="50"></TD>
      <TD bgcolor="green" width="100"
       height="50"></TD>
      <TD bgcolor="blue" width="100"
       height="50"></TD>
      <TD bgcolor="orange" width="100"
       height="50"></TD>
      <TD bgcolor="cyan" width="100"
       height="50"></TD>
    </TR>
</TABLE>
```

10 Observe the following table and write the HTML code to generate it: **CBSE 2016**

<table>
<caption>Activities</caption>
<tr><td rowspan="3">Sr School</td><td>Maths Club</td></tr>
<tr><td>Robotics Club</td></tr>
<tr><td>Photography</td></tr>
<tr><td rowspan="3">Middle School</td><td>Gymnastic</td></tr>
<tr><td>Yoga</td></tr>
<tr><td>Computer Club</td></tr>
<tr><td rowspan="3">Primary School</td><td>Dance</td></tr>
<tr><td>Vocal Music</td></tr>
<tr><td>Swimming</td></tr>
</table>

Ans. The HTML code is:

```
<HTML>
    <BODY><BASEFONT face="cambria">
```

```
<TABLE border="1"
bordercolor="black"
cellspacing="0" width="320">
<CAPTION> Activities </CAPTION>
  <TR>
    <TD rowspan="3"> Sr School </TD>
    <TD> Maths Club </TD>
  </TR>
  <TR>
    <TD> Robotics Club </TD>
  </TR>
  <TR>
    <TD> Photography </TD>
  </TR>
  <TR>
    <TD rowspan="3">Middle School </TD>
    <TD> Gymnastic </TD>
  </TR>
  <TR>
    <TD> Yoga </TD>
  </TR>
  <TR>
    <TD> Computer Club </TD>
  </TR>
  <TR>
  <TD rowspan="3"> Primary School </TD>
    <TD> Dance </TD>
  </TR>
  <TR>
    <TD> Vocal Music </TD>
  </TR>
  <TR>
    <TD> Swimming </TD>
      </TR>
    </TABLE>
    </BODY>
  </HTML>
```

11 Can you perform event handling in HTML tables? If yes, explain it.

Ans. Yes, for explanation refer to text on Page No. 106.

12 Write names of two attributes each for the following tags: **CBSE 2013**

(*i*) <HR> (*ii*) <BODY>
(*iii*) <IMG> (*iv*) <TABLE>
(*v*) <A>

Ans.

Tag	Attributes
<HR>	align, width
<BODY>	bgcolor, text
<IMG>	src, alt
<TABLE>	border, rules
<A>	href, name

13 Identify which of the following is a tag or an attribute? **CBSE 2014**

(*i*) link (*ii*) table
(*iii*) align (*iv*) href
(*v*) br

Ans. (*i*) link — attribute (*ii*) table — tag
(*iii*) align — attribute (*iv*) href — attribute
(*v*) br — tag

Application Oriented Questions

1 If you type

```
<TABLE border="2">
  <TR align="center">
    <TH> Sun
    <TH> Mon
    <TH> Tue
    <TH> Wed
    <TH> Thu
    <TH> Fri
    <TH> Sat
  </TR>
  <TR align = "left">
  <TD colspan = "3" >
    <TD> 1 </TD>
    <TD> 2 </TD>
    <TD> 3 </TD>
    <TD> 4 </TD>
  </TR>
</TABLE>
```

How the ouput will look like?

Ans. The output will look like

Sun	Mon	Tue	Wed	Thu	Fri	Sat
			1	2	3	4

2 Write the HTML code to generate the following output:

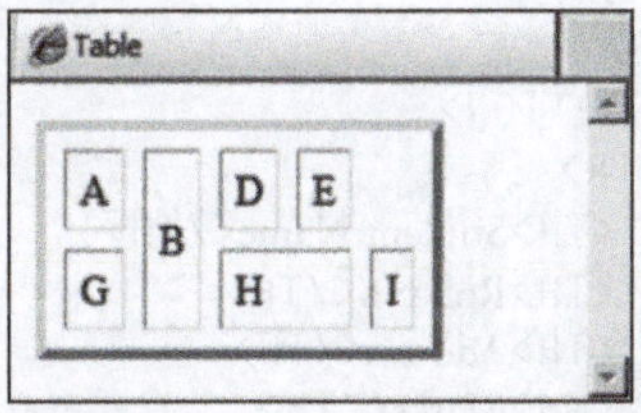

Ans. The HTML code is

```
<HTML>
  <HEAD>
```

```
    <TITLE>Table</TITLE>
  </HEAD>
  <BODY>
  <TABLE border="4" cellspacing="7"
  cellpadding="5">
    <TR>
      <TD>A</TD>
      <TD rowspan="2">B</TD>
      <TD>D</TD> <TD>E</TD>
    </TR>
    <TR>
      <TD>G</TD><TD colspan="2">H</TD>
      <TD>I</TD>
    </TR>
  </TABLE>
  </BODY>
</HTML>
```

3 Write an HTML code to print the following table:

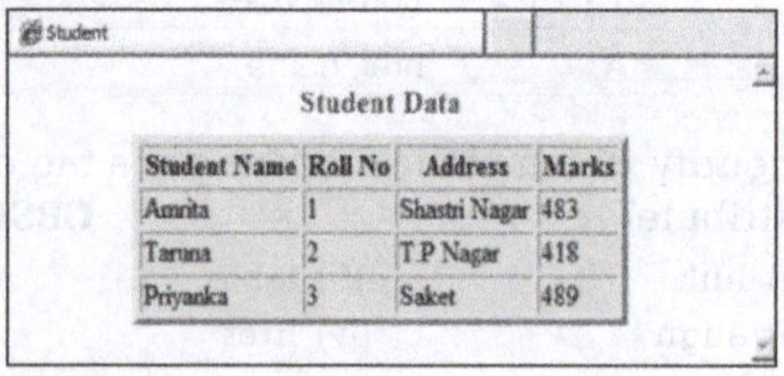

Student Name	Roll No	Address	Marks
Amrita	1	Shastri Nagar	483
Taruna	2	T.P Nagar	418
Priyanka	3	Saket	489

Note • Background color of a table is pink.
• Caption of a table is in red color.

Ans. The HTML code is

```
<HTML>
  <HEAD>
    <TITLE>Student</TITLE>
  </HEAD>
  <BODY>
    <TABLE border="4" bgcolor="pink"
    height="50%" width="70%"
    align="center">
  <CAPTION>
  <B>
    <FONT size="4" color="red">
    Student Data
  </FONT>
  </B>
  </CAPTION>
    <TR>
      <TH>Student Name</TH>
      <TH>Roll No</TH>
      <TH>Address</TH>
      <TH>Marks</TH>
    </TR>
    <TR>
      <TD>Amrita</TD>
      <TD>1</TD>
      <TD>Shastri Nagar</TD>
      <TD>483</TD>
    </TR>
    <TR>
      <TD>Taruna </TD>
      <TD>2</TD>
      <TD>T.P Nagar</TD>
      <TD>418</TD>
    </TR>
    <TR>
      <TD>Priyanka</TD>
      <TD>3</TD>
      <TD>Saket</TD>
      <TD>489</TD>
    </TR>
  </TABLE>
  </BODY>
</HTML>
```

4 Write the HTML code to generate the following Web page:

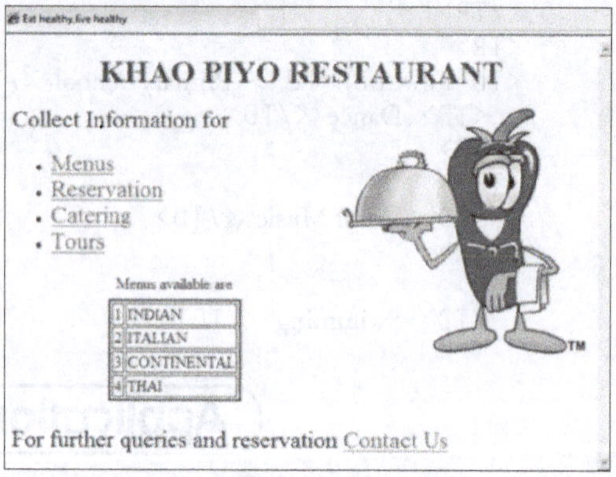

Note The following points while generating the Web page:

- Link color is green, active link color is blue and visited link color is red.
- Title of the page is "Eat healthy, live healthy".
- Heading of the page is maroon.
- Image used is "Restaurant.jpg".
- Caption of table is blue.
- Table border is blue and of size 2.
- The links are one.html, two.html, three.html and four.html.
- The E-mail id for Contact Us is 'abc@xyz.com'. **CBSE 2011**

Ans. The HTML code is

```
<HTML>
  <HEAD>
    <TITLE>Eat healthy, live healthy</TITLE>
  </HEAD>
```

```
<BODY link="green" alink="blue"
vlink="red">
        <CENTER>
        <H1>
        <FONT color="maroon">KHAO PIYO
        RESTAURANT</FONT>
        </H1>
        </CENTER>
        <IMG src="Restaurant.jpg"
        align="right"height="255"
        width="250">
        Collect Information for
        <UL>
        <LI><A
href="one.html">Menus</A></LI>
        <LI><A
href="two.html">Reservation</A></LI>
        <LI><A
href="three.html">Catering</A></LI>
        <LI><A
href="four.html">Tours</A></LI>
        </UL>
        <CENTER>
        <TABLE border="2"
bordercolor="blue">
        <FONT color="blue">
        <CAPTION> Menus available are
</CAPTION>
        </FONT>
        <TR>
           <TD> 1 </TD> <TD> INDIAN </TD>
        </TR>
        <TR>
           <TD> 2 </TD> <TD> ITALIAN </TD>
        </TR>
        <TR>
           <TD> 3 </TD> <TD> CONTINENTAL
           </TD>
        </TR>
        <TR>
           <TD> 4 </TD> <TD> THAI </TD>
        </TR>
        </TABLE>
    </CENTER>
    <BR>
    For further queries and reservation
    <A href="mailto:abc@xyz.com">
    Contact Us</A>
    </BODY></HTML>
```

5 Carefully study the Web page given below. Identify 10 tags (structural as well as formatting tags) that have been utilised in creating this Web page and write the usage of each of them. **CBSE 2012**

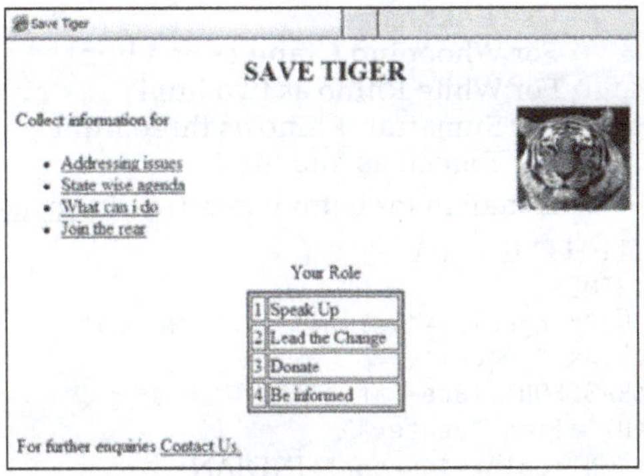

Ans. (*i*) <TITLE> to specify the title of the Web page.

(*ii*) <BODY> contains all the content that is to be displayed on Web page and all the various formatting and structural tags.

(*iii*) <UL> used to create an unordered list.

(*iv*) <LI> to specify the various list items in a list.

(*v*) <CAPTION> to provide caption to the table.

(*vi*) <TABLE> used to create table in HTML document.

(*vii*) <TR> stands for table row, used to create a table row.

(*viii*) <TD> stands for table data, helps to create cells in HTML table.

(*ix*) <IMG> used to insert an image in HTML document.

(*x*) <A> stands for anchor tag. Use the href attribute to provide the reference of the Web page that you want to hyperlink.

6 Observe the following Web page and write HTML code to generate it: **CBSE 2014**

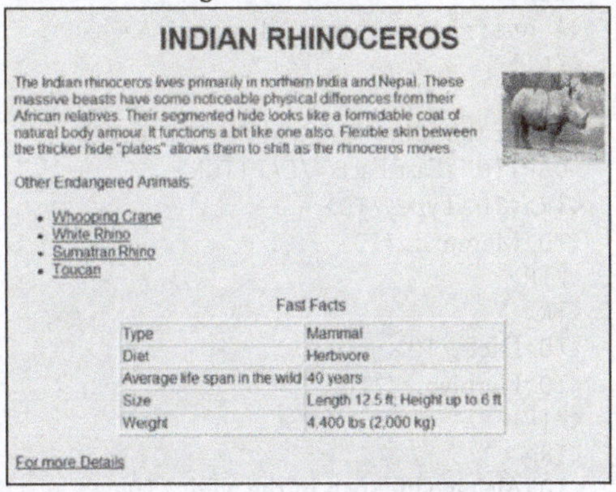

Note The following points while generating the Web page:

- Background color of page is yellow.
- Link color is black and visited link color is green.
- Font style for the page is arial.
- Heading of the page is maroon.
- Image used is mainrhino.jpg.
- Table border is 2px.

- Use links as:
  For Whooping Crane as one.html
  For White Rhino as two.html
  For Sumatran Rhino as three.html
  For Toucan as four.html
- E-mail id for bottom message is abc@xyz.com

Ans. The HTML code is

```
<HTML>
<BODY bgcolor="yellow" link="black"
vlink="green">
<BASEFONT face="arial">
<H1 align="center">
<FONT color="maroon">INDIAN
RHINOCEROS</FONT></H1>
<IMG src="mainrhino.jpg" align="right"
height="100" width="110">
The Indian rhinoceros lives primarily in northern India and Nepal. These massive beasts have some noticeable physical differences from their African relatives. Their segmented hide looks like a formidable coat of natural body armour. It functions a bit like one also. Flexible skin between the thicker hide "plates" allows them to shift as the rhinoceros moves.
<BR><BR>
Other Endangered Animals:
<UL>
<LI>
<A href="one.html">Whooping Crane</A>
</LI>
<LI>
<A href="two.html">White Rhino</A>
</LI>
<LI>
<A href="three.html">Sumatran Rhino</A>
</LI>
<LI>
<A href="four.html">Toucan</A>
</LI>
</UL>
<TABLE border="2" align="center">
<CAPTION>Fast Facts</CAPTION>
<TR><TD>Type</TD>
<TD>Mammal</TD>
</TR>
<TR>
<TD>Diet</TD>
<TD>Herbivore</TD>
</TR>
<TR>
<TD>Average life span in the wild</TD>
<TD>40 years</TD>
</TR>
<TR>
<TD>Size</TD>
<TD>Length 12.5 ft; Height up to 6 ft</TD>
</TR>
<TR>
<TD>Weight</TD>
<TD>4,400 lbs (2,000 kg)</TD>
</TR>
</TABLE>
<BR>
<A href="mailto:abc@xyz.com">
For more Details</A>
</BODY>
</HTML>
```

7 Carefully study the Web page given below. Identify 10 tags (structural as well as formatting tags) that have been utilised in creating this Web page and write the usage of each of them. **CBSE 2012**

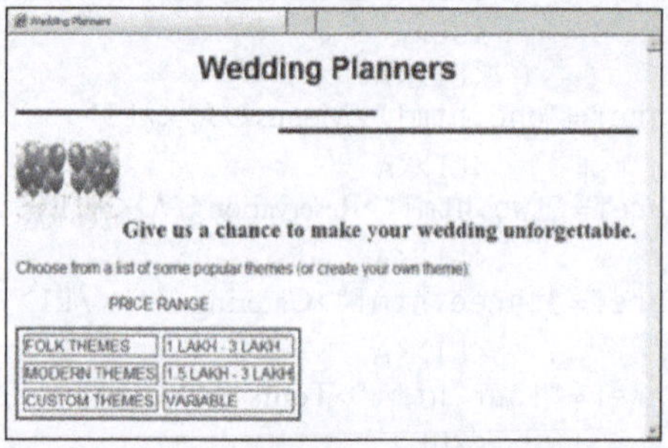

Ans. (*i*) <TITLE> to specify title of the Web page.
(*ii*) <BODY> contains all the text content that is to be displayed on Web page and all the various formatting and structural tags.
(*iii*) <H1> defines the most important and biggest heading.
(*iv*) <HR> used to separate content (or define a change).
(*v*) <IMG> used to insert an image.
(*vi*) <B> used to bold the text.
(*vii*) <TABLE> used to create a table.
(*viii*) <CAPTION> used to provide caption to the table.
(*ix*) <TR> used to create a table row.
(*x*) <TD> used to define data cells.

8 Observe the following Web page and write HTML code to generate it **CBSE 2016**

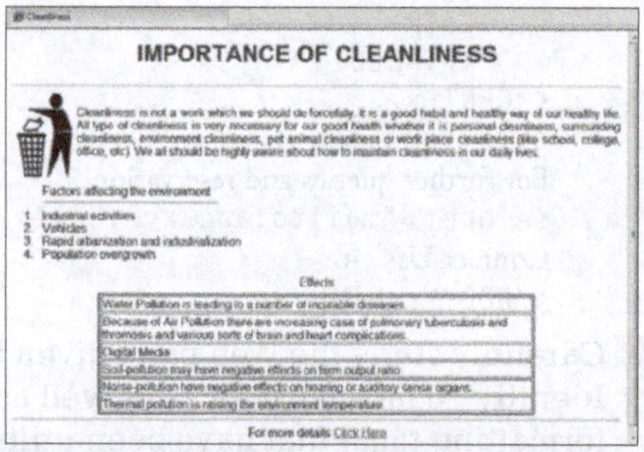

Note The following points while generating the Web page:
- Title of the page is "Cleanliness"
- Link color is green.

EXAM PRACTICE

- Font style for the page is arial.
- Heading of the page is maroon.
- Image used is clean.jpg.
- Table border is 2px and border color is red.
- Link for bottom message is contact.html.

Ans The HTML code is

```
<HTML>
<HEAD> <TITLE> Cleanliness </TITLE>
</HEAD>
<BODY link="green">
<BASEFONT face="arial">
<H1> <FONT color="maroon">
<CENTER> IMPORTANCE OF CLEANLINESS
</CENTER> </FONT> </H1>
<HR>
<IMG src="clean.jpg" align="left"
height="120" width="80">
<P align="justify">
Cleanliness is not a work which we should do forcefully. It
is a good habit and healthy way of our healthy life. All type
of cleanliness is very necessary for our good health whether
it is personal cleanliness, surrounding cleanliness,
environment cleanliness, pet animal cleanliness or work
place cleanliness (like school, college, office, etc). We all
should be highly aware about how to maintain cleanliness
in our daily lives.
</P> <BR>
<OL> Factors affecting the environment
<HR width="240" align="left">
<LI> Industrial activities
<LI> Vehicles
<LI> Rapid urbanization and industrialization
<LI> Population overgrowth
</OL> <BR>
<TABLE border="2" align="center"
bordercolor="red" width="600">
<CAPTION> Effects </CAPTION>
<TR> <TD> Water Pollution is leading to a number of
incurable diseases. </TD> </TR>
<TR> <TD> Because of Air Pollution there are
increasing case of pulmonary tuberculosis and
thromosis and various sorts of brain and heart
complications. </TD> </TR>
<TR> <TD> Digital Media </TD> </TR>
<TR> <TD> Soil-pollution may have negative effects on
farm output ratio. </TD> </TR>
<TR> <TD> Noise-pollution have negative effects on
hearing or auditory sense organs. </TD> </TR>
<TR> <TD> Thermal pollution is raising the
environment temperature. </TD> </TR>
</TABLE>
<HR> <CENTER> For more details
<A href="contact.html"> Click Here </A>
</CENTER>
</BODY>
</HTML>
```

9 Write the HTML code to design the web page as shown below, considering the specifications as given below. Students can write code for any 4 specifications out of the given 5 sepcifications.

HTML Table

<table>
<tr><th>Roll Number</th><th>First Name</th><th>Last Name</th><th>Class</th></tr>
<tr><td>1</td><td>FN1</td><td>LN1</td><td>12th</td></tr>
<tr><td>2</td><td>FN2</td><td>LN2</td><td rowspan="2">11th</td></tr>
<tr><td>3</td><td colspan="2">FN3 LN3</td></tr>
</table>

Specification-1 The HTML code structure should be proper. Heading 'HTML TABLE' should be the first level of heading and background color of the page should be LightCyan.

Specification-2 The value of the table border attribute should be 1. Table header tag should be used wherever required.

Specification-3 The table should exactly contain 4 rows and 4 columns. The data in each cell should be as shown in the above table.

Specification-4 Attribute rowspan should be used wherever required.

Specification-5 Attribute colspan should be used wherever required. **CBSE SQP Term-II**

Ans.

```
<HTML>
<HEAD>
</HEAD>
<BODY bgcolor="LightCyan">
<H1>HTML TABLE</H1>
<TABLE border="1">
<TR>
<TH>Roll Number</TH>
<TH>First Name</TH>
<TH>Last Name</TH>
<TH>Class</TH>
</TR>
<TR>
<TD>1</TD>
<TD>FN1</TD>
<TD>LN1</TD>
<TD>12th</TD>
</TR>
<TR>
<TD>2</TD>
<TD>FN2</TD>
<TD>LN2</TD>
<TD rowspan="2">11th</TD>
</TR>
<TR>
<TD>3</TD>
<TD colspan="2">FN3 LN3</TD>
</TR>
</TABLE>
</BODY>
</HTML>
```

CHAPTER

06

HTML Forms and Cascading Style Sheet

Chapter Checklist

- Basic Form Tags
- Different Controls Supported by HTML Form
- Embed Audio and Video in HTML Page
- Cascading Style Sheet (CSS)

HTML forms are very effective because they can easily collect data from the Internet and utilise that information in other Web page. Form starts with the <FORM> tag and ends with the </FORM> tag.

It contains various attributes these are as follows:

(*i*) **name** It specifies the name of the form. The name attribute is optional if there is only one form on the Web page.

(*ii*) **action** It provides the URL of the program (in the server) that receives the information from the form and processes it.

(*iii*) **method** A method attribute, which is the HTTP method used to submit the form data.

The method attribute of <FORM> tag can take one of the following three values:

(*i*) **GET** method sends the information to the server.

(*ii*) **POST** method sends the form information in the HTTP environment.

(*iii*) **Form** method opens a new form as per the URL specified in the action attribute.

So, a typical <FORM> tag is,

<FORM name= "form_name", action="URL" method= "method">

CSS stands for Cascading Style Sheets, It is a style sheet language which is used to describe the look and formatting of a document written in markup language.

Basic Form Tags

In the form, you can still put any HTML codes as you want. We can also use the following tags in the <FORM> tag.

<INPUT> Tag

It defines text entry fields, check boxes, radio buttons or push buttons. It is an empty element specified by <INPUT> tag. The <INPUT> tag defines an object on the form which can receive user input.

Syntax

```
<INPUT type="fieldtype" name="fieldname"
 value="fieldtext">
```

There are various attributes of <INPUT> tag

Attribute	Use	Syntax
type	This attribute specifies the type of <INPUT> element to display fieldtype can be one of the following: Text, Password, Radio, Checkbox, Submit, Reset Button, Image, Hidden.	<INPUT type ="fieldtype">
name	This attribute specifies the fieldname of <INPUT> tag. It is required for the identification of form.	<INPUT name ="fieldname">
value	This attribute specifies the value of an <INPUT> tag. It is used to represent the default value of any type field.	<INPUT value ="fieldtext">
size	It is used to resize the field such as set the length of text box.	<INPUT size = "value">
height and width	This attribute is used to set the height and width of any field.	<INPUT height ="pixels" width="pixels">

<SELECT> Tag

Use the <SELECT> container tag to create dropdown menus and scrolled lists. Between <SELECT> and </SELECT>, you can only have <OPTION> tag and their text, which define the items in the list.

An <OPTION> tag can have a value attribute, which is what sent to the CGI script, if that item is selected. If there is no value attribute, the value sent is the text following the <OPTION> tag.

To make an item selected by default, use the selected attribute in the <OPTION> tag.

Syntax

```
<SELECT name ="name">
<OPTION value="value 1">Text</OPTION>
<OPTION value="value 2">Text</OPTION>
:
:
More options
</SELECT>
```

There are various attributes of <SELECT> tag

Attribute	Use	Syntax
name	It shows the name of drop-down	<SELECT name ="name">
size	It displays height of the list. If it is 1 (or omitted), the list is a drop-down menu, otherwise it is a scrolled list.	<SELECT size ="value">
disabled	This attribute specifies that a drop-down list should be disabled.	<SELECT disable>

<OPTION> Tag

This tag occurs only within the <SELECT> element (described above) and is used to represent each choice of the select.

Syntax `<OPTION value="value"> Text </OPTION>`

There are various attributes of <OPTION> tag

Attribute	Use	Syntax
label	It specifies a shorter label for an option	<OPTION label = "text">
selected	It defines the default option to be selected when page is loaded.	<OPTION selected>
value	It specifies the value to be sent to the server when form is submitted.	<OPTION value = "value">

<TEXTAREA> Tag

Use the <TEXTAREA> container tag to create multiline, scrollable, text entry boxes. Whatever is between the <TEXTAREA> and </TEXTAREA> tags will be the initial contents of the entry box, so put them right next to each other, if you do not want initial contents. The <TEXTAREA> tag has a name attribute like every input field.

Use the rows and cols (columns) attributes to set the displayed height and width of the text area.

Note The text area scrolls as much as needed, so you are only setting the display size, not the data size.

Syntax

```
<TEXTAREA name= "name" rows="number"
cols="number">Text</TEXTAREA>
```

e.g.

```
<TEXTAREA name = "stuff" rows=10 cols=60>
Enter stuff here </TEXTAREA>
```

There are various attributes of <TEXTAREA> tag

Attribute	Use	Syntax
name	It is used to identify the input field	<TEXTAREA name ="text">
rows ans cols	These attributes are used to arrange the height and width of a row and a column.	<TEXTAREA rows ="number" cols="number">

Different Controls Supported by HTML Form

There are various controls supported by HTML form as follows.

Textbox

It provides a single line text input field where the user can enter text.

e.g.

```
<HTML>
   <HEAD>
      <TITLE> Text Input Control </TITLE>
   </HEAD>
   <BODY>
   <FORM>
      First name: <INPUT type="text" name =
                  "first_name"/> <BR>
      Last name: <INPUT type ="text" name =
      "last_name"/>
   </FORM>
   </BODY>
</HTML>
```

Output

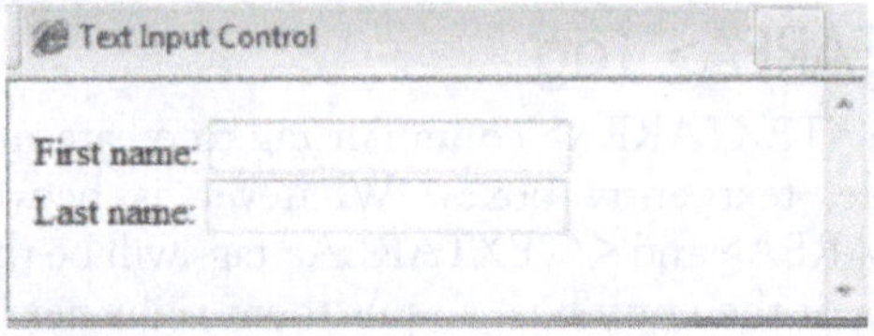

Password

It provides a single line text input field where the user can enter password. A password field shows one dot for each character input by the user. This prevents other from seeing the password.

e.g.

```
<HTML>
   <HEAD>
      <TITLE>Password Input Control</TITLE>
   </HEAD>
   <BODY>
   <FORM>
      User ID: <INPUT type="text"
      name="user_id" value="Enter your name"/> <BR>
      Password: <INPUT type="password" name="password"
      value="Pass"/>
   </FORM>
   </BODY>
</HTML>
```

Output

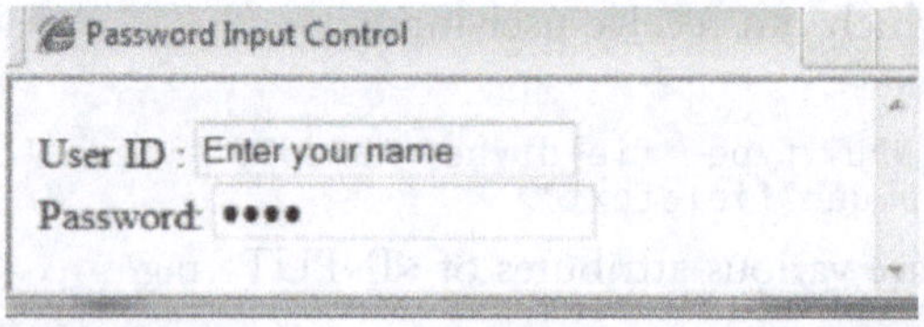

Checkbox

It provides a checkbox on the form. With checkboxes, we can give the users a list of items to choose from. The user can choose more than one items from the list. When a form is submitted, selected checkboxes' values (specified by the value attribute) are submitted to the destination.

The additional attribute of checkbox is **checked** that indicates the checkbox is to be displayed with a tick mark to show selection. This attribute is optional.

e.g.

```
<HTML>
   <HEAD>
      <TITLE> Checkbox Control</TITLE>
   </HEAD>
   <BODY>
      <FORM>
         <INPUT type = "checkbox" name = "maths"
         value = "on"> Maths
         <INPUT type = "checkbox" name = "physics"
         value = "on"> Physics
      </FORM>
   </BODY>
</HTML>
```

Output

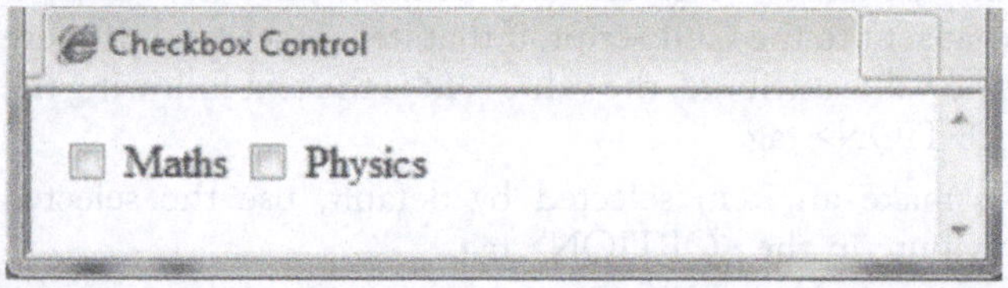

Radio Button

It provides a radio button on the form. Only one radio button of a group can be selected at one time. When a form is submitted, selected radio button's value (specified by the value attribute) is submitted to the destination.

The additional attribute is **checked** that indicates the radio button is selected, which can be deselected when another choice is made.

e.g.

```
<HTML>
<HEAD>
    <TITLE>Radio Box Control</TITLE>
</HEAD>
<BODY>
    <FORM>
        <INPUT type= "radio" name = "subject"
        value = "maths"> Maths
        <INPUT type = "radio" name= "subject"
        value = "physics"> Physics
    </FORM>
</BODY>
</HTML>
```

Output

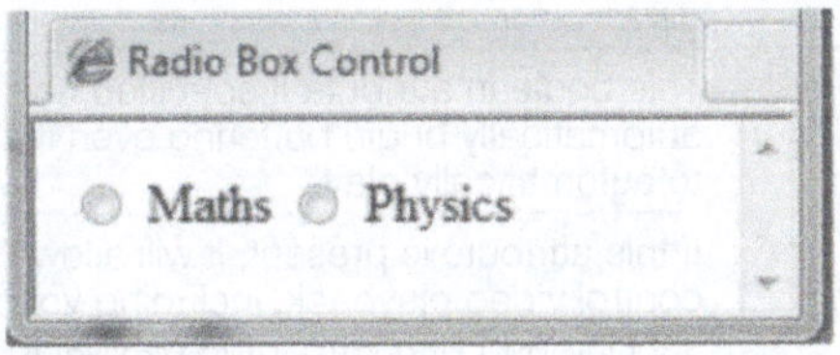

List Box

A list box is a graphical control element that allows the user to select one or more items from a list contained. The <SELECT> tag is used to create a drop-down list. The <OPTION> tag inside the <SELECT> tag define the available options in the list. By default, the first item in the drop-down list is selected.

As multiple attribute value is specified as "multiple" so, it gives ability to select more than one item from the box by holding Ctrl key.

e.g.

```
<HTML>
    <HEAD>
        <TITLE>List Box</TITLE>
    </HEAD>
    <BODY>
        <FORM>
            <SELECT name = "drop1" id = "select1"
            size = "4" multiple = "multiple">
        <OPTION value = "1">item 1</OPTION>
        <OPTION value = "2"> item 2</OPTION>
        <OPTION value = "3"> item 3</OPTION>
        <OPTION value = "4"> item 4</OPTION>
        <OPTION value = "0"> All</OPTION>
        </SELECT>
    </FORM>
</BODY>
</HTML>
```

Output

Combo Box

Combo Box in HTML is used to display a drop-down list of some options from which one can be selected. <SELECT> tag is supported in all the web browsers. <OPTION> tag is used inside the <SELECT> tag that displays the options in the list. It occupies less space but shows only one value for visibility. In this, multiple selection of items are not possible.

e.g.

```
<HTML>
    <HEAD>
        <TITLE> Combo Box</TITLE>
    </HEAD>
    <BODY>
        <FORM>
        <SELECT name = "dropdown">
        <OPTION value = "Maths" selected > Maths
        </OPTION>
        <OPTION> value = "physics" >Physics
        </OPTION>
        <OPTION> value = "Chemistry">Chemistry</OPTION>
        </SELECT>
        </FORM>
    </BODY>
</HTML>
```

Output

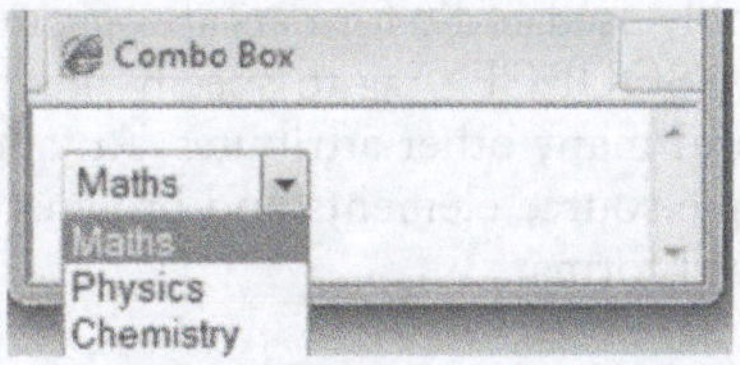

Embed Audio and Video in HTML Page

HTML allows us to create standards-based video and audio players that don't require the use of any plugins.

Embed Audio Element

The HTML <AUDIO> element is used to embed sound content in documents. It may contain one or more audio sources, represented using the src attribute. The <AUDIO> element defines an in-browser audio player. The audio player can provide a single piece of audio content. To specify the source file of the audio content, use one or more <SOURCE> elements inside the <AUDIO> element. All <SOURCE> files should contain the same audio content, but in different file formats. The browser will select the first file format that it is able to play. If you are not going to provide multiple source file formats, you may indicate the source file in the src attribute, instead of in a separate <SOURCE> element.

Attributes of <AUDIO> tag

Attribute	Description
autoplay	This boolean attribute if specified, the audio will automatically begin to play back as soon as it can do so without stopping to finish loading the data.
autobuffer	This boolean attribute if specified, the audio will automatically begin buffering even if it's not set to automatically play.
controls	If this attribute is present, it will allow the user to control audio playback, including volume, seeking and pause/resume playback.
loop	This boolean attribute if specified, will allow audio automatically see back to the start after reaching at the end.
src	This attribute specifies the location (URL) of the audio file. This is optional, you may instead use the <SOURCE> element within the audio block to specify the audio to embed.
type	This attribute specifies the audio file standard type.

Most commonly used audio formats are ogg, mp3 and wav. You can use <SOURCE> tag to specify media alongwith media type and many other attributes. An audio element allows multiple source elements and browser will use the first recognised format.

e.g.

```
<HTML>
  <BODY>
    <AUDIO controls autoplay>
      <SOURCE src = "/html/audio.ogg" type
      = "audio/ogg"/>
      <SOURCE src = "/html/audio.wav" type
                                = "audio/wav"/>
    Your browser does not support the <AUDIO>
    element.
    </AUDIO>
  </BODY>
</HTML>
```

Output

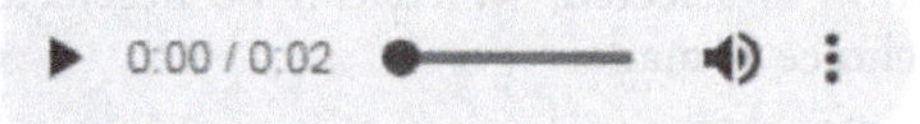

Embed Video Element

The <VIDEO> element allows us to embed video files into an HTML document, very similar to the way images are embedded. The HTML does not specify which video formats browser should support in the <VIDEO> tag, but most commonly used video formats are ogg, mpeg4.

Attributes of <VIDEO> tag

Attribute	Description
autoplay	This boolean attribute if specified, the video will automatically begin to play back as soon as it can do so without stopping to finish loading the data.
autobuffer	This boolean attribute if specified, the video automatically begin buffering even if it's not set to automatically play.
controls	If this attribute is present, it will allow the user to control video playback, including volume, seeking and pause/resume playback.
height	This attribute specifies the height of the video display area in pixels.
width	This attribute specifies the width of the video display area in pixels
src	The URL of the video to embed. This is optional, you may instead use the <SOURCE> element within the video block to specify the video to embed.
type	This attribute specifies the video file standard type.

e.g.

```
<HTML>
  <BODY>
    <VIDEO width = "300" height = "200" controls
                                  autoplay>
    <SOURCE src = "/html/foo.ogg" type
                              = "video/ogg"/>
    <SOURCE src = "/html/foo.mp4" type
                              = "video/mp4"/>
    Your browser does not support the <VIDEO>
    element.
    </VIDEO>
  </BODY>
</HTML>
```

Output

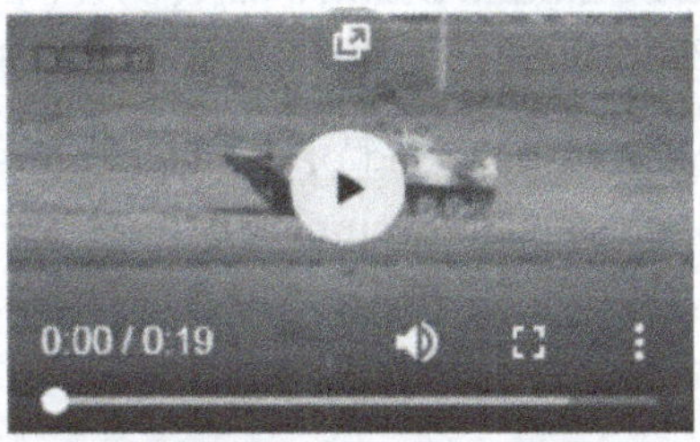

Check Point 01

1. Which tag is used to start the form?
2. Which of the following attribute specifies the fieldname of <INPUT> tag?
   (a) type (b) name (c) value (d) size
3. Write the names of two attribute of <SELECT> tag.
4. What is the use of combo box?
5. What is used to embed audio element in HTML?

Cascading Style Sheet (CSS)

It is a style sheet language used for describing the presentation of a document written in a markup language. CSS is designed primarily to enable the separation of document content from document presentation, including aspects such as the layout, colors and fonts. This separation can improve content accessibility, provide more flexibility and control in the specification of presentation characteristics, enable multiple HTML pages to share formatting by specifying the relevant CSS in a separate .css file, and reduce complexity and repetition in the structural content such as semantically insignificance tables that were widely used to format pages before consistent CSS rendering was available in all major browsers. CSS makes it possible to separate presentation instructions from the HTML content in a separate file or style section of the HTML file. For each matching HTML element, it provides a list of formatting instructions.

Syntax

A CSS rule-set consists of a selector and a declaration block.

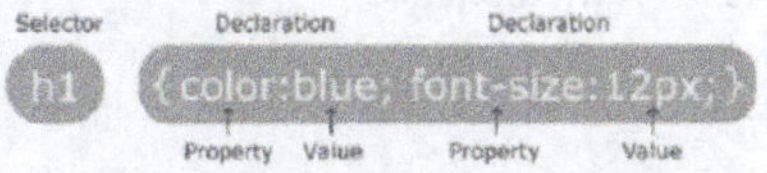

The selector points to the HTML element that you want to style.

The declaration block contains one or more declarations separated by semicolons.

Each declaration includes a CSS property name and a value that separated by a colon.

A CSS declaration always ends with a semicolon and declaration blocks are surrounded by curlybraces.

e.g.

```
P
{
   color : red;
   text-align: center;
}
```

Declaration of CSS in HTML is as follows:

```
P
{
   color:red;
   text-align: center;
}
BODY
{
   background-color:yellow;
}
H1
{
   font-size: 36pt;
}
H2
{
   color:blue;
}
P
{
   margin-left:50px;
}
```

Above code is Style-01.css file. CSS file declares as follows in which HTML document save as CSS-Example-01.html.

```
<HTML>
   <HEAD>
      <LINK rel= "stylesheet" type = "text/css" href
      = "Style-01.css"/>
   </HEAD>
   <BODY>
      <H1> This header is 36 pt</H1>
      <H2> This header is blue </H2>
      <P>This paragraph has a left margin of
      50 pixels </P>
   </BODY>
</HTML>
```

Output

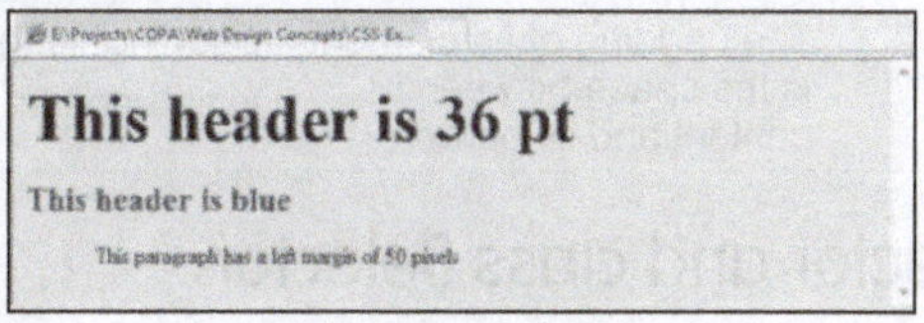

Property Value of CSS

Following table defines the property value of CSS.

Property	Description	Syntax
color	Sets the color of a text	color: color | initial | inherit;
background color	Sets the background color for HTML document.	background-color: color | transparent | initial | inherit;
border-style	This property sets the style of an element border. This property can have from one to four values.	border-style: none | hidden | dotted | dashed;
margin	The CSS margin properties are used to create space around elements, outside of any defined borders. CSS has properties for specifying the margin for each side of an element; margin-top, margin-right, margin-bottom, margin-left.	margin: length | auto | initial | inherit;
height	This property sets the height of an element.	height: auto | length | initial | inherit;
width	This property sets the width of an element.	width:auto | value | initial | inherit;
outline	An outline is a line that is drawn around elements, outside the borders, to make the element "stand out".	outline: outline-width | outline-style | outline-color;
font-family	It is used to set the font type of an HTML element.	font-family: family-name | generic-family | initial | inherit;
font-size	This property sets the size of a font.	font-size: font size value;
font-style	It is used to specify the font-style of an HTML element.	font-style: normal | italic | initial | inherit;
float	It is a CSS property written in CSS file or directly in the style of an element. The float property defines the flow of content.	float: none | left | right | initial | inherit;
text-align	The text-align property specifies the horizontal alignment of text in an element.	text-align: left | right | center | justify;
padding	The padding of an element is the space between its content and its border	padding: length | initial | inherit;

id Selector and class Selector

The id selector uses the id attribute of an HTML element of select a specific element.

An id should be unique within a page, so the id selector is used if you want to select a single and unique element. To select an element with a specific id, write a hash (#) character, followed by the id of the element.

Below code save as CSS-Example-02. html

```
<HTML>
    <HEAD>
        <STYLE type = "text/css">
        #para1
        {
            font-size : 36pt;
            text-align: center ;
            color : blue ;
        }
        </STYLE>
    </HEAD>
    <BODY>
        <P id="para1"> Hello World ! </P>
        <P> This paragraph is not affected
            by the style. </P>
    </BODY>
</HTML>
```

Output

In which, style rule will be applied to the HTML element with id= "para1".

The class selector selects elements with a specific class attribute.

To select elements with a specific class, write a period (.) character, all HTML elements with class = "center" will be red and center-aligned.

In below code, HTML document save CSS-Example-03. html.

```
<HTML>
    <HEAD>
        <STYLE type= "text/css">
        .center
        {
            text-align: center;
        }
        </STYLE>
    </HEAD>
    <BODY>
        <H1 class= "center">
            Arihant COMPUTER BOOKS </H1>
        <P class = "center"> Arihant Computer
                            Books for POLYTECHNIC</P>
    </BODY>
</HTML>
```

Output

As class, id should not be start from any number. Many browsers such as Internet Explorer, Mozilla Firefox do not support it.

Inserting CSS

In HTML, CSS can be inserted in various ways which are as follows:

(i) External Style Sheet

With an external style sheet, you can change the look of the entire Website by changing just one file.

Each page must include a reference to the external style sheet file inside the <LINK> element. The <LINK> element goes inside the <HEAD> section.

e.g.

```
<HEAD>
   <LINK rel = "stylesheet" type ="text/css"
   href = "mystyle.css">
</HEAD>
```

An external style sheet can be written in any text editor. The style sheet file must be saved with a .css extension.

```
HR
{ color : white; }
H1
{ font-size = 40;}
P
{ margin-left : 20px; }
BODY {background-image : url("E:\Projects\COPA\Web
Design Concepts\colorful.jpg");}
```

Above code is a file as Style-02.css.

e.g.

In HTML code, which is save as CSS-Example-o4.html.

```
<HTML>
   <HEAD>
      <LINK rel ="stylesheet" type = "text/css"
      href ="Style-02.css"/>
      <TITLE> Arihant BOOKS </TITLE>
   </HEAD>
   <BODY>
      <H1> Arihant Books </H1>
      <P>A wide range of books for school curricula,
      polytechinc, competitive and recruitment
      examinations are published by <B> Arihant
      publications India Ltd. </B> </P>
      <HR>
      For any query e-mail at info@arihantbooks.
      com and crm@arihantbooks.com
      or dial+91-11-40546380
   </BODY >
</HTML>
```

Output

(ii) Internal Style Sheet

An internal style sheet may be used if one single page has a unique style. Internal styles are defined within the <STYLE> element, inside the <HEAD> section of an HTML page.

e.g.

HTML code saves as CSS-Example-05.html.

```
<HTML>
   <HEAD>
      <STYLE type = "text/css">
      HR
      {color : white ;}
      H1
      {font-size = 40;}
      P
      {margin-left:20px;}
      BODY
      {background-image : url ("E :/Projects/COPA
      /Web Design Concepts/colorful.jpg")}
      </STYLE>
      <TITLE>Arihant BOOKS</TITLE>
   </HEAD>
   <BODY>
      <H1>Arihant Books </H1>
      <P> A wide range of books for school curricula,
      polytechnic, competitive and recruitment
      examinations are published by <B> Arihant
      Publications India Ltd. </B></P>
      <HR>
      For any query e-mail at info@arihantobooks.com
      and crm@arihantbnooks.com or dial
      +91-11-40546380
   </BODY>
</HTML>
```

Output

(iii) Inline Style

An inline style may be used to apply a unique style for a single element.

To use inline styles, add the style attribute to the relevant element. The style attribute can contain any CSS property.

e.g.

HTML code saves as CSS-Example-06.html.

```
<HTML>
   <HEAD>
      <STYLE type = "text/css">
         HR {color : white; }
         H1 {font-size = 40;}
         P {margin-left: 20px;}
      BODY
      {background-image: url ("E :\Projects\COPA\Web
      Design Concepts\colorful.jpg"); }
      </STYLE>
      <TITLE> Arihant BOOKS </TITLE>
   </HEAD>
   <BODY>
      <H1>Arihant Books </H1>
      <P> A wide range of books for shcool curricula,
      polytechnic, competitive and recruitment
      examinations are published by <B> Arihant
      Publications India Ltd. </B> </P>
      <HR style = "color: black"> For any query
      e-mail at info@arihantbooks.com and
      crm@arihantbooks.com or dial +91-11-40546380
   </BODY>
</HTML>
```

Output

(iv) Multiple Style Sheets

If some properties have been defined for the same selector (element) in different style sheets, the value from the last read style sheet will be used.

e.g. H3 selector for properties value of external style sheet in HTML document are as follows:

```
H3
{
color:red;text-align:left; font-size: 8pt;
}
```

H3 selector for internal style sheet are as follows:

```
H3
{
   text-align:right; font-size:20pt ;
}
```

If the internal style is defined after the link to the external style sheet, the H3 elements will be

```
color : red ; text-align: right; font-size : 20pt;
```

Check Point 02

1. What is the full form of CSS?
2. ______property sets the background color for HTML document.
3. Which of the following selector selects elements with a specific class attribute?
   (a) id (b) class
   (c) para (d) center
4. Which extension is used to save the CSS file?
5. Internal styles are defined within the <STYLE> element state.
   True or False

SUMMARY

- HTML form on a Web page allows a user to enter data that is sent to a server for processing.
- The <INPUT> tag specifies an input field where the user can enter data. These elements are used within a <FORM> element to declare input.
- <INPUT> elements of type password provide a way for the user to securely enter a password.
- Checkboxes are used when more than one option is required to be selected. They are also created using HTML <INPUT> tag but type attribute is set to a checkbox.
- Checkboxes allow multiple selections at a time and radio buttons allow only a single selection at a time, but both use the <INPUT> tag to create each box or button.
- <SELECT> tag is used to create drop-down list of options, which appears when clicking on form element and allows the user to choose one of the options.
- HTML <OPTION> tag is used within a form for defining options in the drop-down list.
- <TEXTAREA> tag is used within a form to declare a text area element-a control that allows the user to input text over multiple rows.
- HTML audio element is used to embed sound content in documents. The content inside the opening <AUDIO> and closing </AUDIO> tags.
- CSS (Cascading Style Sheets) is a style sheet language used for describing the presentation of a document written in a markup language.
- In the CSS, a class selector is a name preceded by a full stop (.) and an id selector is a name preceded by a hash character (#).
- The difference between an id and a class is that an id can be used to identity one element, whereas a class can be used to identify more than one.
- When a browser reads a style sheet , it will format the HTML document according to the information in the style sheet. Three ways of inserting a style sheet. i.e. external, internal and inline.

Exam Practice

Multiple Choice Questions

1 _____on a Web page allows a user to enter data.

(a) Form (b) Sever

(c) Client (d) None of these

Ans. (*a*) HTML form on a web page allows a user to enter data that is sent to a server for processing.

2 Which of the following tag specifies an input field?

(a) <INPUT> (b) <OUTPUT>

(c) <HEAD> (d) <TITLE>

Ans. (*a*) The <INPUT> tag specifies an input field where the user can enter data.

3 Which attribute of <INPUT> tag is used to resize the field?

(a) type (b) name

(c) value (d) size

Ans. (*d*) size attribute of <INPUT> tag is used to resize the field such as set the length of text box.

4 _____provides a single line text input field.

(a) Password (b) Text

(c) Checkbox (d) None of these

Ans. (*b*) Text provides a single line text input field where the user can enter text.

5 Which option provides a way for the user to securely enter a password?

(a) Text (b) Checkbox

(c) Password (d) All of these

Ans. (*c*) <INPUT> elements of type password provides a way for the user to securely enter a password.

6 ______allow only a single selection at a time.

(a) Checkbox

(b) Radio button

(c) Text

(d) None of the above

Ans. (*b*) Checkboxes allow multiple selections at a time and radio button allow only a single selection at a time.

7 Which of the following tag is used to create drop-down menus?

(a) <OPTION> (b) <SELECT>

(c) <INPUT> (d) <HEAD>

Ans. (*b*) Use the <SELECT> container tag to create drop-down menus.

8 Which of the following option allows the user to select one or more items from a list?

(a) Combo box (b) List box

(c) Option element (d) None of these

Ans. (*b*) A list box is a graphical control element that allows the user to select one or more items from a list.

9 What is the closing tag of <TEXTAREA> tag?

(a) <\TEXTAREA> (b) /TEXTAREA

(c) </TEXTAREA> (d) <TEXTAREA />

Ans. (*c*) <TEXTAREA> is a opening and </TEXTAREA> is a closing tag.

10 Which attribute of <AUDIO> element is used to give the URL of the audio to embed?

(a) controls (b) type (c) src (d) loop

Ans. (*c*) src attribute of <AUDIO> element is used to give the URL of the audio.

11 ______ is designed primarily to enable the separation of document content from document presentation.

(a) HTML (b) CSS

(c) CS (d) None of these

Ans. (*b*) CSS is designed primarily to enable the separation of document content from document separation, including aspects such as layout, colors and fonts.

12 Which property of CSS is used to set the font type of an HTML element?

(a) font-size (b) font-style

(c) font-family (d) float

Ans. (*c*) font-family property is used to set the font type of an HTML element.

13 In which of the following selector hash (#) character is used?

(a) id (b) class

(c) Both (a) and (b) (d) None of these

Ans. (*a*) To select an element with a specific id, write an hash (#) character followed by the id selector.

14 In _______, you can change the look of the entire Website.

(a) external style sheet (b) internal style Sheet

(c) inline style (d) None of these

Ans. (*a*) With an external style sheet, you can change the look of the entre website by changing just one file.

15 Consider the following form control in a HTML form:

○ Male ○ Female

Now, choose the correct line of code for the above, **CBSE SQP Term-I**

(a)
```
<INPUT type = "radio" name= "Gender" value= "male">Male<BR>
<INPUT type = "radio" name= "Gender" value= "female">Female<BR>
```
(b)
```
<INPUT type = "radiobutton" name= "Gender" value= "male">Male<BR>
<INPUT type = "radiobutton" name= "Gender" value= "female">Female<BR>
```
(c)
```
<INPUT type = "radio", name= "Gender">< value= "male">Male
<INPUT type = "radio", name= "Gender">< value= "female">Female
```
(d)
```
<INPUT type = "radio" name= "Gender" value= "male"><BR>
<INPUT type = "radio" name= "Gender" value= "female"><BR>
```
Ans. (*a*)
```
<INPUT type = "radio" name= "Gender" value= "male">Male<BR>
<INPUT type = "radio" name= "Gender" value= "female">Female<BR>
```

16 Tag to create password field in HTML document. **CBSE SQP Term-I**

(a) <PASSWORD> (b) <INPUT>
(c) <PWD> (d) <PWORD>

Ans. (*b*) <INPUT>

17 Which of the following tag is used to define options in a drop down selection list? **CBSE SQP Term-I**

(a) <SELECT> (b) <LIST>
(c) <DROPDOWN> (d) <OPTION>

Ans. (*d*) <OPTION>

18 Shambhavi is designing a HTML FORM to collect user's responses. Suggest her a suitable FORM element to take the entry of user's place of birth **CBSE 2021 Term-I**

(a) Check Box (b) Password field
(c) Radio button (d) Combo Box

Ans. (*d*) Combo Box

19 I am
- A square box
- Ticked when selected
- One or more options can be selected from the choices given by me

Who am I? **CBSE 2021 Term-I**

(a) Radio button (b) Text Box
(c) Check Box (d) Combo Box

Ans. (*c*) Check Box

Fill in the Blanks

1 Form starts with the ______ tag and ends with the ______ tag.

Ans. <FORM>, </FORM>

2 ______ method sends the form information in the HTTP environment.

Ans. POST

3 The additional attribute of checkbox is ______ that indicates the checkbox is to be displayed with a tick mark to show selection.

Ans. checked

4 ______ gives the ability to select only one item from the list.

Ans. Combo Box

5 Use the ______ container tag to create mutiline, scrollable, text entry boxes.

Ans. <TEXTAREA>

6 ______ attribute of <AUDIO> tag specifies the audio file standard type.

Ans. type

7 ______ is a style sheet language used for describing the presentation of a document written in a markup language.

Ans. CSS

8 ______ property of CSS sets the style of an element border.

Ans. border-style

9 ______ is the space between element content and its border.

Ans. padding

10 The id selector uses the ______ of an HTML element to select a specific element.

Ans. id attribute

11 Internal styles are defined within the ______, inside the ______ section of an HTML page.

Ans. <STYLE>, <HEAD>

12 ______ may be used to apply a unique style for a single element.

Ans. Inline style

True or False

1 The select element defines an object on the form, which can receive user input.

Ans. **False** <INPUT> tag defines an object on the form, which can receive user input.

2 Password provides a way for the user to securely enter a password.

Ans. **True** <INPUT> element of type password provide a way for the user to securely enter a password.

3 To make an item selected by default, use the selected attribute in the <SELECT> tag.

Ans. **False** To make an item selected by default, use the selected attribute in the <OPTION> tag.

4 Rows and cols attributes are used to identify the input field.

Ans. **False** name attribute is used to identify the input field.

5 The HTML <AUDIO> tag is used to embed sound content in documents.

Ans. **True** The HTML <AUDIO> tag is used to embed sound content in documents.

6 If controls attribute is present, it will allow the user to control video playback.

Ans. **True** controls attribute allow the user to control video playback, including volume, seeking and pause playback.

7 CSS document written in a Hypertext language.

Ans. **False** CSS document written in a markup language.

8 font-family is used to set the size of a font.

Ans. **False** font-family is used to set the font type of an HTML element.

9 class selector selects elements with a specific class attribute.

Ans. **True** class selector selects elements with a specific class attribute.

10 In inline style, some properties have been defined for the same selector in different style sheets.

Ans. **False** If some properties have been defined for the same selector, then multiple style sheets will be used.

Very Short Answer (VSA) Type Questions

1 Write the syntax of <INPUT> tag.

Ans. <INPUT type ="fieldtype" name ="fieldname" value = "fieldtext">

2 What do you mean by textbox?

Ans. Textbox provides a single line text input field where the user can enter the text.

3 What is the use of checkbox in HTML?

Ans. With checkboxes, we can give the users a list of items to choose from. The user can choose more than one items from the list.

4 Names the attributes of <SELECT> tag.

Ans. The attributes of <SELECT>tag are name, size and disabled.

5 Explain the use of selected attribute of <OPTION> tag.

Ans. Selected attribute defines the default option to be selected when page is loaded.

6 Write the difference between list box and combo box.

Ans. Listbox gives the ability to select more than one item from the box by holding Ctrl key but in combo box multiple selection of items are not possible.

7 Write the syntax of <TEXTAREA> tag.

Ans. <TEXTAREA name = "text">

8 Name the most commonly used audio formats.

Ans. Most commonly used audio formats are ogg, mp3 and wav.

9 Explain the CSS.

Ans. CSS (Cascading Style Sheet) is designed primarily to enable the separation of document content from document presentation, including aspects such as layout, colors and fonts.

10 In which tag, <LINK> element can be used?

Ans. The <LINK> element goes inside the <HEAD> section.

EXAM PRACTICE

Short Answer (SA) Type Questions

1 What is a form? Name the basic attributes for creating a form.

Ans. A Webform, or HTML form on a Web page allows a user to enter data that is sent to a server for processing. Forms can resemble paper or database forms because Web users fill out the forms using checkboxes, radio button, or text fields.

The HTML <FORM> tag is used for creating a form for user input. The HTML <FORM> tag also supports the following attributes.

(i) **name** This attribute defines a unique name for the form.

(ii) **action** This attribute specifies the URL of the program where to sent the form data when a form is submitted.

(iii) **method** This attribute specifies the HTTP method to use when sending form data.

2 Write HTML code to display a password.

Ans. HTML code to display a password

```
<HTML>
<BODY>
<FORM>
   Password:<input type = "password" name
   = "Password" value = "pass"/>
</FORM>
</BODY>
</HTML>
```

3 Differentiate between checkbox and radio button in HTML.

Ans. Differences between checkbox and radio button are as follows:

Checkbox	Radio button
In this, user can select any one option at a time. In HTML, the code for the checkbox is <input type = "checkbox">	It this, user can select one or more than one option at a time. In HTML, the code for the radio button is <input type = "radio>

4 Name the attributes of <SELECT> tag which are used to create drop-down menus.

Ans. Refer to text on Page No. 123

5 What is the combo box?

Ans. A select element presents a set of options to the user. If only a single entry can be selected and no visible size has been specified, the options are presented in a combo box (drop down menu). <SELECT> tag creates a combo box for selecting among choices. You specify each choice with an <OPTION> element enclosed between <SELECT> and </SELECT>.

6 What is the use of <AUDIO> element in HTML?

Ans. Refer to text on Page No. 126.

7 Explain the cascading style sheet.

Ans. Cascading Style Sheets (CSS) referred to as CSS, is a simple design language intended to simplify the process of making Web pages presentable. CSS handles the look and feel part of a Web page using CSS, you can control the color of the text, the style of fonts, the spacing between paragraphs, layout designs etc. CSS is easy to learn and understand but it provides powerful control over the presentation of an HTML document. Most commonly, CSS is combined with the markup languages HTML or XHTML.

8 Explain id selector in CSS.

Ans. Id selector is used to apply the style to an element based on the id of an element. e.g.

```
#elementid
{
color : #FFFFFF;
}
```

In the above code, all the elements having id. "elementid" will have the color white.

9 Write suitable HTML code to Embed audio and video in a webpage. **CBSE SQP Term-I**

Ans. The HTML <AUDIO> element is used to embed sound content in documents. It may contain one or more audio sources, represented using the src attribute.

```
<HTML>
<BODY>
<H2> Embedding an audio file</H2>
<AUDIO CONTROLS>
<SOURCE SRC="Audio.mp3" TYPE="audio/mp3">
File Format Not supported
</AUDIO>
</BODY>
</HTML>
```

The <VIDEO> element allows us to embed video files into an HTML document, very similar to the way images are embedded. The HTML does not specify which video formats browser should support in the <VIDEO> tag, but most commonly used video formats are ogg, mpeg4.

```
<HTML>
<BODY>
<H2> Embedding a video file</H2>
<VIDEO width="500" Height="400"controls
autoplay>
<SOURCE src="videoplayback.mp4"
TYPE="video/mp4">
</VIDEO>
</BODY>
</HTML>
```

Long Answer (LA) Type Questions

1 What is the use of <INPUT> tag. Explain its attributes.

Ans. Refer to text on Page No. 123.

2 Explain the checkbox with suitable example.

Ans. Refer to text on Page No. 124.

3 How to embed audio and video in a Web page?

Ans. Refer to text on Page No. 126-127.

4 Explain the different properties of the CSS.

Ans. Refer to text on Page No. 128.

5 What is the use of external style sheet. Explain its advantages and disadvantages.

Ans. With an external style sheet, you can change the look of the entire website by changing just one file. Each page must include a reference to the external style sheet, file inside the <LINK> element.

The <LINK> element goes inside the <HEAD> section. An external style sheet can be written in any text editor. The style sheet file must be saved with a .css extension.

Advantages

- With the help of external style sheets, the styles of numerous documents can be organised from one single file.
- In external style sheets, classes can be made for use on numerous HTML element types in many forms of the site.
- In complex contexts, methods like selector and grouping can be implemented to apply styles.

Disadvantages

- An extra download is essential to import style information for each file.
- The execution of the file may be delayed till the external style sheet is loaded.
- While implementing style sheets, we need to test Web pages with multiple browsers in order to check compatibility issues.

Application Oriented Questions

1 If you type the following code.

```
<HTML>
<HEAD>
   <STYLE type = "text/css">
   #para1
   {
   font-size: 10pt;
   text-align: center;
   color: blue;
   }
</STYLE>
</HEAD>
<BODY>
      <H2 id = "para1">Reaction of
      Magnesium with Hydrochloric Acid</H2>
      <B> The equation for the reaction
      is:</B><BR>
      Magnesium+Hydrochloric Acid =
      Magnesium
      Chloride + Hydrogen <BR>
      Mg(s)+2HCL(aq>=Mgcl<SUB>2</SUB>
      (ag)+H<SUB>2</SUB>(g)
   </BODY>
</HTML>
```

How the output will look like?

Ans.

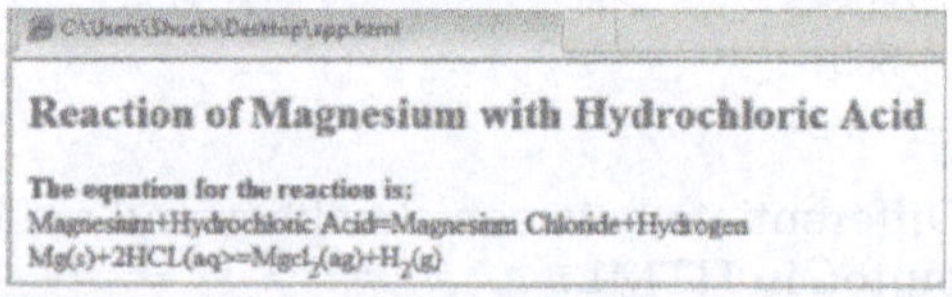

2 Consider the following HTML code given below:

```
<HTML>
<HEAD>
<TITLE>
   My first Web page
</TITLE>
</HEAD>
<BODY bgcolor = "red">
<H1> Form </H1>
<FORM action = "submission.html" method=
"GET">
<B> User Name </B>
<INPUT type = "text" name = "User Name"
value = "Enter your name" size = "30">
<INPUT type = "submit" value = "Submit">
</FORM>
</BODY>
</HTML>
```

EXAM PRACTICE

Now, answer the following questions.

(i) What will be displayed in the title bar of the browser?

(ii) Name the attributes of <FORM> tag which are being used in the above given code.

(iii) Name the tags that are used in the above code.

(iv) What will be the color of background?

Ans. (i) My first Web page.

(ii) action, method

(iii) <HTML>, <HEAD>, <TITLE>, <BODY>, <H1>, <FORM>, <INPUT>, <B>

(iv) red

3 Carefully observe the following screenshot **CBSE 2021 Term-I**

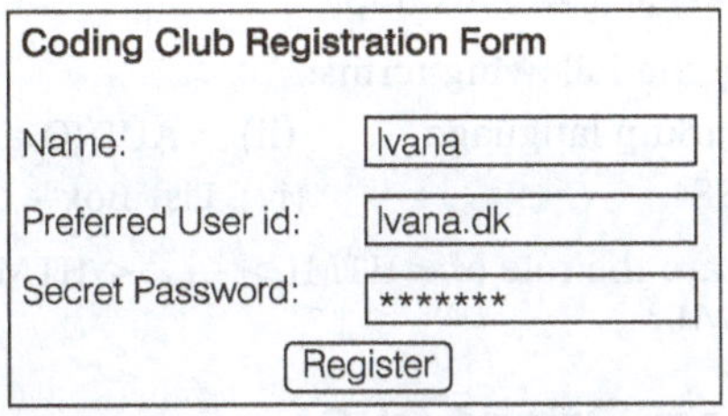

(i) An HTML ……… is used to collect user input.

(a) Frame (b) Table

(c) Box (d) Form

(ii) HTML element to create the box to accept the candidate's Name.

(a) <ACCEPT> (b) <INPUT>

(c) <NAME> (d) <BOX>

(iii) Correct attribute = "value" pair to create the box to accept the candidate's Name.

(a) type = "text"

(b) type = "name"

(c) accept = "text"

(d) accept = "name"

(iv) Choose the correct HTML control to create the text box having label as "Preferred User id".

(a) Id box

(b) Id field

(c) Text field

(d) Password field

(v) HTML element to create the box to accept the "Secret Password".

(a) <ACCEPT>

(b) <INPUT>

(c) <NAME>

(d) <BOX>

Ans. (i) (d) Form

(ii) (b) <INPUT>

(iii) (a) type = "text"

(iv) (c) Text field

(v) (b) <INPUT>

Unit Test 1

Multiple Choice Questions

1. To add a blue background to your Web page, which of the following would you use?
   (a) <BODY bgcolor = "blue">
   (b) <BODY color = "blue">
   (c) <BODY text = "blue">
   (d) None of the above

2. In a HTML form, which attribute method used to submit the form data?
   (a) name (b) method
   (c) action (d) get

3. .... uses the id attribute of an HTML element to select a specific element.
   (a) class selector (b) id selector
   (c) Both (a) and (b) (d) None of these

Fill in the Blanks

4. No two rows can contain same value in the .... field.
5. A .... field shows one dot for each character.
6. For linking to another Web page, its URL is specified with .... attribute of <A> tag.

True or False

7. CSS is a markup language used for describing the presentation of a document.
8. The valign attribute determines the placement of content in a cell.
9. A form enables user to enter or view data in the database easily.

Very Short Answer Type Questions

10. What is the use of <OPTION> tag?
11. Name the value in the rules attribute, in which no rules are drawn.
12. Explain the inline style.

Short Answer Type Questions

13. Explain the attribute, which is common to both <INPUT> and <OPTION> tags.
14. Identify the error(s) in the following HTML code. Also, write the correct code.
    <BODY bgcolor = "black" bgimage = "pic-jpg">
15. What is the need of setting relationship between tables?

Long Answer Type Questions

16. Write the syntax of height and width attributes. Explain each with example.
17. Define the following terms:
    (i) Markup language (ii) <AUDIO>
    (iii) CSS (iv) List Box
18. What are the role of <HTML> ......</HTML> tags in HTML?

Application Oriented Questions

19. Create a form for entry in your school as a annual function.
20. Write the HTML code to generate the following Web page :

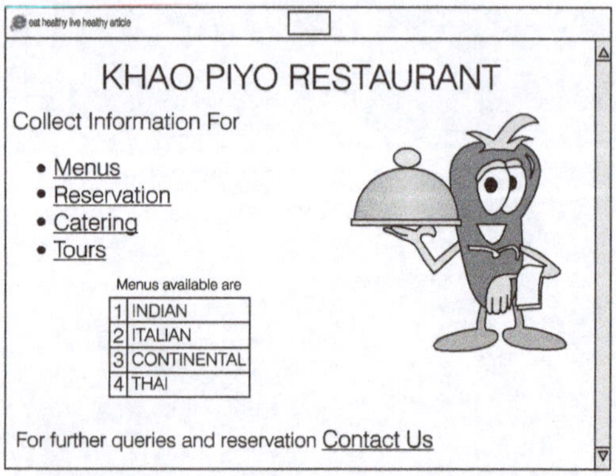

Note The following points while generating the Web page:

- Link color is green, active link color is blue and visited link color is red.
- Title of the page is "Eat healthy, live healthy".
- Image used is "Restaurant.jpg".
- Caption of table is blue.
- Table border is blue and size is 2.
- The links are one.html, two.html, three.html and four.html.
- The E-mail id for contact us is 'abc@xyz.com'.

Unit Test 2

Multiple Choice Questions

1. Symbol used in href for linking to the section in the same document.
   (a) # (b) @
   (c) ? (d) None of these
2. The float property of a CSS defines the
   (a) content (b) text
   (c) flow of content (d) None of these
3. <OPTION> tag inside the .... defines the available options in the list.
   (a) <SELECT>
   (b) <HEAD>
   (c) <TITLE>
   (d) None of the above

Fill in the Blanks

4. .... is the space between element content and its border.
5. When a form is submitted, ... radio button's value is submitted to the destination.
6. The textual content that appears in the HTML document, but is ignored by the browser is called ....

True or False

7. <DT> tag is an opening clause that defines the start of the definition list.
8. Video element is used to apply CSS to the document.
9. The closing tag of <SELECT> is </SELECT>

Very Short Answer Type Questions

10. Define the term CSS.
11. Write the syntax of </SELECT> tag.
12. How would you make the word flower appear whenever the actual flower.jpg image could not be displayed by a Web browser?

Short Answer Type Questions

13. What will happen, if you used bgcolor attribute with <TABLE> and <TR> tags separately?
14. Explain the role of external style sheet in the CSS.
15. What are the name of languages, which define new markup languages?

Long Answer Type Questions

16. Differentiate between checkbox and radio button.
17. What is wrong with following code?

```
<HTML><BODY>
<UL type = "bullet">
<LI> Apple
<LI> Mango
<LI> Orange </UL></BODY></HTML>
```

18. What is the use of <INPUT> tag? Explain its attributes.

Application Oriented Questions

19. Observe the following code and give the output

```
<HTML>
  <HEAD>
     <STYLE type = "text/CSS">
     #para1
     {
       font-size : 36 pt;
       text-align : center;
       color : blue;
     }
     </STYLE>
   </HEAD>
<BODY>
  <P id = "para1"> Hello world ! </P>
  <P> This paragraph is not affected by the style </P>
</BODY>
</HTML>
```

20 Observe the following Web page and write the HTML code to generate it.

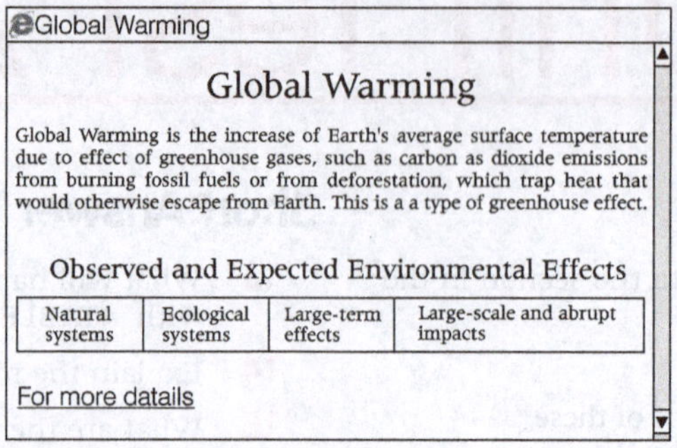

Note The following points while generating the Web page

- Title of the page is "Global Warming"
- Heading of the page is blue
- Table border is 1 px, cellspacing is 0 and border color is black
- E-mail id for bottom message is abc@xyz.com

Unit Test 3

Multiple Choice Questions

1 Which tag of HTML is used to create multiline, scrollable, text entry boxes?

(a) <SELECT>
(b) <TEXTAREA>
(c) <FORM>
(d) <OPTION>

2 Which is the correct order to use <DL> and its child tags?

(a) <DT><DL><DD>
(b) <DD><DL><DT>
(c) <DD><DT><DL>
(d) <DL><DT><DD>

3 ……… property of CSS specifies the horizontal alignment of text in an element.

(a) float (b) width
(c) text-align (d) padding

Fill in the Blanks

4 In ……… only one option can be selected at one time.

5 ……… attribute of audio element allows the user to control audio playback.

6 To display the text in bold form ……… tag is used and to display in the underlined form ……… tag is used.

True or False

7 HTML is about displaying information while CSS is about describing the presentation.

8 cellspacing attribute is used with <BODY> tag.

9 The name attribute is used to create the actual section within the current HTML document.

Very Short Answer Type Questions

10 Which attribute of <A> facilities internal and external linking?

11 Which document is used to define the style of a document?

12 What is the use of audio element?

Short Answer Type Questions

13 Explain the combo box with an example.

14 What is the use of cellspacing and cellpadding attributes in <TABLE> tag?

15 Explain the different attributes of <OPTION> tag with the syntax.

Long Answer Type Questions

16 Explain the superscript and subscript tags. Also, state the use of both tags.

17 How to embed audio and video in a document?

18 Define CSS. How to create a CSS file?

Application Oriented Questions

19 Create a Web page which contains the following elements in the given sequence:

(i) The background color of the page is Sky blue.
(ii) Title of the page is Web Page.
(iii) Heading of the page is My First Web Page where font face is Algerian. It is also center aligned.
(iv) A horizontal row.
(v) Insert an image that is right aligned, with height is 200 pixels and width is 250 pixels.
(vi) Write some text related to an image whose font face is Verdana and size is 4.
(vii) Create a hyperlink for More Details as Det.html.

20 If you type

```
<HTML>
   <BODY>
      <FORM>
         <SELECT name = "dropdown">
         <OPTION value = "Green" selected> Green
         </OPTION>
         <OPTION value = "Red"> Red </OPTION>
         <OPTION value = "Blue"> Blue </OPTION>
         </SELECT>
      </FORM>
   </BODY>
</HTML>
```

How the output will look like?

CHAPTER

Unit III

07 Cyber Ethics

Chapter Checklist

- Issues Related to Cyber Ethics
- Open Source Software Movement
- Freedom of Information
- Digital Divide
- E-Commerce
- Secure Data Transmission System

The word cyber ethics refers to a code of safe and responsible behaviour for the Internet community. Practicing good cyber ethics involves understanding the risks of harmful and illegal behaviour online and learn how to protect ourselves, and other Internet users from such behaviour.

It is the study of ethics pertaining to computers, encompassing user behaviour and what computers are programmed to, and how this affects individuals and society. Cyber ethics is the moral, legal and social issues relating to cyber technology. It examines the impact that cyber technology has for social, legal and moral systems. It also evaluates the social policies and laws that have been framed in reply to issues generated by the development and use of cyber technology.

Issues Related to Cyber Ethics

There are many advantages of living in an IT world but on contrary, there are many problems which our society is facing today. The crimes like abduction, fraud etc., have increased leaps and bounds. Hence, there are so many ethical issues as far as IT is concerned. Some of them are as follows:

1. Plagiarism

The word 'plagiarism' has emerged from a latin word *plagiarius*, which means **kidnapping.** Plagiarism is an act of copying another person's idea, words or work and pretend that they are our own. The intentions behind plagiarism could be malicious or it could be done accidently like copying data from other's computer without his/her permission and redistributing further. If we talk about the reasons behind plagiarism, then following could be the major factors:

(*i*) Fear of failure
(*ii*) Not having enough knowledge
(*iii*) Being lazy
(*iv*) Lack of enforcement
(*v*) Competition
(*vi*) Lack of management skills

Follow the below given guidelines to avoid plagiarism:

(i) To avoid plagiarism, instead of copying the language of the book as it is, try to put it in your own language/words.

(ii) One should have a clear understanding of plagiarism and its consequences, so that no one can perform it unintentionally.

(iii) If copying someone else's work in our task, word for word, then do not forget enclosing it in quotes and also mention its source.

(iv) Another way is to credit the author has write which was useful for your task and not taking credit for it yourself.

2. Intellectual Property Rights (IPR)

Any kind of information which a person puts his effort and time to create invention, literary and artistic work, design, symbols, names and image used in commerce is called the intellectual property of that person. Intellectual property rights reserves all the rights of the owner to the information to decide, how much information is to be exchanged, shared or distributed. The owner can decide the price for doing so.

The protection of intellectual property right of individuals lead to following features :

(i) It encourages people to create new softwares as well as helps them to improve the existing applications.

(ii) An environment is provided for the innovative thoughts and technologies.

(iii) Provides the assurity of good returns, people and businesses invest in the national economy.

Violation of IPR

Following are the violation of Intellectual Property Rights (IPR):

(i) If a third party were to assume ownership, copy or sell someone's previously copywritten work, that would legally be considered as copyright infringement.

(ii) Copyright law can still be enforced if others try to create simple material from the original source material.

(iii) If a court finds that patent infringement has occurred, the judge will award damages appropriate to compensate for the infringement.

Following are the controls of intellectual property rights:

- Avoid joint ownership.
- Get exact match domains
- Safeguard with strong access control.

3. Netiquettes

The word netiquette is a combination of net (from Internet) and etiquette. It means respecting other users' views and displaying common etiquette when posting your views to online discussion groups. The need of netiquette arises mostly when sending or distributing E-mail posting on usenet groups or chatting.

It is short for " Internet etiquette" . Etiquette is a code of polite behaviour in society, netiquette is a code of good behaviour on the Internet. This includes several aspects of the Internet, such as E-mail, social media, online chat, web forums, website comments, and other types of online communication. Below are the rules to follow for good netiquette.

(i) Avoid posting inframmatory or offensive comments online.

(ii) Respect other's privacy by not sharing personal information, photos or videos that another person may not want published online.

(iii) Never spam others by sending large amounts of unsolicited E-mail.

(iv) Don't troll people in web forums or website comments by repeatedly nagging or annoying them.

(v) Don't use offensive language.

(vi) Do not trust other when you are new.

(vii) Avoid replying to negative comments with more negative comments.

(viii) Stick to the topic when posting in online forums or when commenting on photos or videos, such as YouTube or Facebook comments.

4. Hacking

Hacking means stealing of required information by seeking and exploiting weakness in a computer or a computer network. For gathering required information, a hacker appears with malicious intention and breaks into the owner's system and steals the information illegally.

To prevent hacking, following points are to be used:

(i) Create complex passwords.

(ii) Don't give your password to anyone.

(iii) Log out of accounts when you are done with them.

(iv) Make sure you are on an official website when entering password.

5. Piracy

Software piracy means copying of data or computer software without the owner's permission. However, most peoples are aware about piracy and know that it is illegal, yet the piracy is uncontrollable. This is simply the violation of intellectual property rights and right to privacy.

The following are forms of software piracy:

(*i*) **Software counterfeiting** This type of software piracy that occurs when fake copies of software are produced in such a way that they appear to be authentic.

(*ii*) **Softlifting** Purchasing only one licensed copy of a software and distributing and loading it onto multiple systems is called softlifting.

(*iii*) **Renting** Selling of a software illegally for temporary use as on rent basis is called renting.

(*iv*) **Hard disk loading** Installing an illegal copy of software on the hard disk of a personal computer is called hard disk loading.

(*v*) **Uploading and downloading** Creating duplicate copies of the licensed software or uploading and downloading it from the Internet.

In order to stop software piracy, three types of laws are formulated as follows:

(*i*) **Copyright** is an exclusive right of the developer or author, to protect their works which is granted by law.

(*ii*) **Patent** is the special power of monopoly granted by the law. The work cannot be used or reproduced without obtaining a license from patent holder.

(*iii*) **Trademark** is the registered word or text/logo depicting the identity of a product, work or company.

6. Digital Property Rights

Digital property includes data, Internet accounts, and other rights in the digital world, including contractual rights and intellectual property rights. Data are the files and information stored and used by computers (such as E-mails, Word processing documents, spreadsheets, pictures, audio files and movies). This data may be stored locally on a computer's hard drive or on removable media or data may be stored remotely and accessed over the Internet.

Digital property rights disputes arise when some form of counterfeiting or piracy occurs between companies.

Following are the some digital property rights:

(i) Domain Name

First, make sure an outside company doesn't own your domain name. Then register your domain name under your business entity-not an individual. Individuals can leave your organisation, the business entity can be controlled by an employee. Protect your domain registrar password at all costs. No one but you will need direct access to this.

(ii) Content Management System

This is the back end of your website. Check who has access to this section of your website, and make sure they don't have unrestricted access to the site.

(iii) Site Hosting

If you don't have the capacity to host your websites in-house, you will likely need to use an outside hosting service. Make sure you know who is hosting your website, and keep a backup copy of your website's files.

(iv) Social Media Pages

Facebook, Twitter, Instagram, YouTube, etc. make sure there are multiple administrators on these accounts in case one person leaves the organisation. Also, report any duplicate profiles you find and make sure you know your passwords.

7. Software License

A software license is a license agreement that gives an individual, company or organisation permission to use a software program. It typically provide end users with the right to one or more copies of the software without violating copyrights.

The license also defines the responsibilities of the parties entering into the license agreement and may impose restrictions on how the software can be used.

Types of Software License

Software licenses typically are the either proprietary, free and open source, the distinguishing feature being the terms under which users may redistribute, or copy the software for future development or use.

(i) Proprietary Software License

The hallmark of proprietary software licenses is that the software publisher grants the use of one or more copies of software under the End-User License Agreement (EULA), but ownership of those copies remains with the software publisher. This feature of proprietary software licenses means that certain rights regarding the software are reserved by the software publisher.

In other words, without acceptance of the license, the end user may not use the software at all. One example of such a proprietary software license is the license for Microsoft Windows.

Sometimes one can choose between perpetual (permanent) and annual license. For perpetual licenses, one year of maintenance is often required, but maintenance renewals are discounted. For annual licenses, there is no renewal, a new license must be purchased after expiration.

(ii) Free and Open Source Software License

This license generally fall under two categories: those with the aim to have minimal requirements about how the software can be redistributed (permissive licenses) and those that aim to preserve the freedom that is given to the users by ensuring that all subsequent users receives those rights (copyleft licenses).

An example of a copyleft free software license is the GNU General Pubic License (GPL). This license is aimed at giving all user unlimited freedom to use, study and privately modify the software, and if the user adheres to the terms and conditions of GPL, freedom to redistribute the software or any modifications to it.

Examples of permissive free software licenses are the BSD license and the MIT license, which give unlimited permission to use, study, and privately modify the software, and includes only minimal requirements on redistribution.

Open Source Software Movement

The open source software movement is a movement that supports the use of open source licenses for some software. The open source movement was started to spread the concept of open source software.

The term open source refers to something that can be modified and shared as its designed is publicly accessible. Thus, open source software is a software whose source code is available for modification or enhancement by anyone. Examples of open source software are Linux, Unix, MySQL, etc. To be considered as open source software by the software development industry, certain criteria must be met as follows:

(*i*) Software must be available free or at a low cost.

(*ii*) Source code must be included.

(*iii*) Anyone must be allowed to modify the source code.

(*iv*) Modified versions can be redistributed.

Programmers develop the open source movement contribute to the open source community by writing and exchanging programming code for software development. The term open source requires that no one can discriminate against a group is not sharing the edited code from already edited. This approach for software development allows anyone to obtain and modify open source code of software modifications are distributed back to the developers within the open source community, who are working with the software.

The open source movement is branched from the free software movement which began in the late 80's with the launching of the GNU project by Richard Stallman.

Stallman is regarded within the open source community as sharing a key role in the conceptualisation of freely shared source code for software development.

Open source software gets stronger with every release and has less problems because the people using it are the ones who are developing it.

Check Point 01

1 Give the guidelines to avoid plagiarism.

2 Netiquette is a combination of …… .

3 Copyright is an exclusive right of the developer to protect their work. State, true or false.

4 A …… is a license agreement that gives an individual, company permission to use a software program.

Freedom of Information (FOI)

FOI or Right to Information (RTI) refers to a citizen's right to access information that is held by the state. In many countries, this freedom is supported as a constitutional right.

Freedom of information was established for transparency, government accountability, education and general public protection against mismanagement and corruption.

More than 70 countries with government representation approved the original freedom of information legislation.

Freedom of Information Act (FOIA)

FOIA is a federal law that generally provides that any person has a right to obtain access to federal agency records.

FOIA is intended to increase transparency. It does not provide access to all government documents.

The FOI Act provides that every person has the following legal rights:

(*i*) The right to access official records held by government departments as defined by the act.

(*ii*) The right to be given reasons for decisions taken by government that affect them.

(iii) The right to have personal information held on them corrected or updated.

Advantages of FOI or RTI

(i) **Control Corruption** When a person asks for the service, then it is necessary that the respective officer gives the response of the person's request within the time limit. So, there will be chances to control the corruption.

(ii) **Empowerment of Common People** With the RTI act, common people can ask questions regarding the work status of their complaints. They have the right to know the information which is related to them.

Disadvantages of FOI or RTI

Apart from the some advantages of RTI, some major disadvantages are also present. These are as follows:

(i) **Time Consuming** There are number of different departments established which work on various services. So, it is very time consuming task.

(ii) **Extra Burden on the Government Authority** In high populated nation, some people create disturbance and unnecessary request which is useless. So, it puts an extra burden on government authorities.

Digital Divide

Digital divide is a term that describes the uneven distribution of Information and Communication Technologies (ICTs) in society.

The digital divide appears in a number of different context, including:

- Differences between rural and urban Internet access.
- Socioeconomic differences between people of different races, income and education that affects their ability to access the Internet.
- Differences between developed, developing and emerging nations in terms of the availability of Internet.

Effects of Digital Divide

There are various effects of digital divide as given below:

(i) **Economic Inequality** Digital divide create economic inequality, because those who have access to modern technology can easily collect valuable economical information.

(ii) **Effect on Education** It has an impact on education. Because student who have Internet access and computer, can acquire more valuable knowledge from Internet.

(iii) **Economic Growth** It is effected by digital divide because productivity improvements tend to be associated with the use of information technologies and companies.

(iv) **Democracy** The use of the Internet can lead to a healthier democracy, increased public participation in elections and decision-making processes.

(v) **Social Mobility** Computers and computer networks are playing and increasingly important role in people's learning, professional work and career development.

Factors that Contribute to the Digital Divide

There are several factors that contribute to the digital divide. There are following some of the factors which contribute to this divide:

(i) **Relevant Content** One of the reasons why some people do not use Internet technologies because the content is not relevant and interesting to them.

(ii) **Age** It seems to be that young people feel more comfortable with the new technology and are able to benefit from it more than older people. Older people are less likely to have a computer and are less likely to be interested in using the Internet.

(iii) **Lack of ICT Skills and Support** People in many disadvantaged groups do not have proper skills about new modern technology.

(iv) **Attitudinal Factors** This derived from cultural and behavioural attitudes towards technology. Many people thought that new technologies are harmful for young generation.

(v) **Gender** It is stated that in some countries and organisations, females have less access to the Internet than males.

Challenges and Barriers to the Digital Divide

There are various challenges and barriers to the digital divide:

(i) **High Cost** Due to higher cost of Internet connection and modern technology, most of the people of developing country unable to use computer and Internet connection.

(ii) **Language Barriers** Today a large percentage of information content on the Internet is in English, which is a barrier for the people whose primary language is not English.

(iii) **Technology Barrier** People who live in village cannot get the touch of modern technology. So it also a barrier of the digital divide.

(iv) **Internet Connectivity Barrier** The high cost of Internet connection and lack of their connectivity also a barrier to the digital divide.

Check Point 02

1 Freedom of information is also known as …… .
2 Give any two effects of digital divide.
3 How to age contribute to the digital divide?

E-Commerce

E-Commerce (Electronic Commerce or EC) is the buying and selling of goods and services on the Internet. E-Commerce draws on technologies such as mobile commerce, electronic funds transfer, supply chain management, Internet marketing, online transaction processing, electronic data interchange, inventory management systems and automated data collection systems. There is no special software to install other than a Web browser and many banks do not charge for this service. Some banks even lower costs for online transactions versus real life banking transactions.

Many people think that E-Commerce is the same as E-Business, but as defined here it is only a subset. This may be true for many end customers who only deal with companies when buying goods. E-Commerce was one of the first business types to become digitally available, but the Internet offers more than just buying and selling products and services.

Types of E-Commerce

E-Commerce business models can generally be categorised into the following categories:

Business-to-Business (B2B)

It applies to businesses buying from and selling to each other over the Internet. Online access of data, including expected shipping date, delivery date and shipping status, provided either by the seller or a third party provider is widely supported by B2B models. It describes truncations between businesses, such as a business between a manufacturer and a wholesaler, or between a wholesaler and a retailer.

Business-to Consumer (B2C)

It describes activities of business serving and consumers with products and services. Common B2C E-Business models include E-Ships and E-mails. An example of a B2C transaction would be a person buying a pair or shoes from a retailer. The transactions that led to the shoes being available for purchase, which is the purchase of the leather, laces, rubber, etc. However, the sale of the shoes from the shoemaker to the retailer would be considered a (B2B) transaction.

Consumer-to-Business (C2B)

It applies to any consumer that sells a product or service to a business over the Internet. One example of this E-Business model is Priceline.com where bidders (or customers) set their prices for items such as airline tickets or hotel rooms and a sellers decide whether to supply them. The demand for C2B E-Business will increase over the next few years due to customer's desire for greater convenience and lower price.

Consumer-to-Consumer (C2C)

It involves the electronically facilitated transactions between consumers through third party. A common example is the online auction, in which a consumer posts an item for a sell and other consumer bid to purchase it a third party generally charges a commission. E-Bay is the most successful C2C online auction website.

Business-to-Government (B2G)

B2G model is a variant of B2B model. Such websites are used by governments to trade and exchange information with various business organisations. Such websites are accredited by the government and provide a medium to businesses to submit application forms to the government.

Privacy in E-Commerce

The privacy in E-Commerce means the protection of privacy of the parties involved in trading through E-Commerce. While doing trading in E-Commerce people are disclosing their personal information and those information are being generated and reaching to the hand of other parties and thereby increasing concern about privacy.

Trading in the online shop accessed through Internet between Business-to-Business (B2B), Business-to-Consumer (B2C), and Consumer-to Consumer (C2C) is the main purpose of E-Commerce. Parties involved in this kind of trading exchange information including private information like addresses, credit card number etc, to complete a transaction.

E-Commerce is considered as a powerful tool to collect consumer's private information. The same tool and their use in business also interfere on the privacy of individuals.

Existing Technologies, Policies and Privacy Seal Program to Protect Privacy

The E-Commerce community, respective government agencies and technology firms have been working to formulate policies and develop privacy protocols and tools to safeguard the privacy.

Many policies are already in effect and many technology firms' tools are in place. They are updated regularly depending on the changing scenarios.

Below are some of the technology firms and their field of service:

(*i*) **TRUSTe** It has launched "Trusted Download Beta Program", to certify that consumer software is not spyware.

(*ii*) **BBB Online** The Better Business Bureau (BBB) has with the help of nationally recognised security and privacy experts has created toolkit to help small business owners manage security and privacy challenge, named as "Security & Privacy-Made Simpler".

(*iii*) **PrivacyBot.com** PrivacyBot is a privacy seal program for websites created by Invisible Hand Software. It is much easier and affordable to create a privacy policy.

(*iv*) **CPA WebTrust** They provide services titled "WebTrust" and "SysTrust". It promises an audit of technology, security and business practices.

Frauds in E-Commerce

E-Commerce fraud shows no signs of slowing down. Online businesses are quickly becoming easy targets for cybercriminals as fraud in E-Commerce continues to rise. They also target phones, tablets , computers and even gift cards. Here are some methods of fraud that are used to target E-Commerce as:

(*i*) **Refund Fraud** In this case, fraudster using a stolen credit card makes an overpayment on purpose. He will ask to refund of the excess amount, claiming his credit card is closed so they need to send the money using an alternative method. That means that the original charge of the credit card is not refunded.

(*ii*) **Merchant Fraud** It is another method, which must be mentioned. It is very simple; goods are offered as cheap prices, but are never shipped of course, the payments are kept. This method of fraud also exists in wholesale.

(*iii*) **Fraud *via* Identity Theft** In this case, the fraudsters assumes another person's identity, creates credit cards in the victim's name and goes on a shopping. This type of fraud is increasing rapidly as the number and scope of data breaches increase. It is also the most difficult to identity as the fraudsters behind identity theft are quite sophisticated.

(*iv*) **Friendly Fraud** It is nearly identical to chargeback fraud, except that it is done without malicious intent. In the case of friendly fraud, the transaction was placed by a true customer, and the chargeback is initiated for something innocent like believing their package to be stolen or not recognising the merchant's name on their credit card statement.

Secure Data Transmission System

Security is an essential part of any transaction that takes place over the Internet. Customers will lose his/her faith in E-Commerce if its security is compromised.

Following are the essential requirements for safe E-Payments/transactions:

(*i*) **Confidentiality** Information should not be accessible to an unauthorised person. It should not be intercepted during the transmission.

(*ii*) **Integrity** Information should not be altered during its transmission over the network.

(*iii*) **Availability** Information should be available wherever and whenever required within a time limit specified.

(*iv*) **Authenticity** There should be a mechanism to authenticate a user before giving him/her an access to the required information.

(*v*) **Non-Repudiability** It is the protection against the denial of order or denial of payment. Once a sender sends a message, the sender should not be able to deny sending the message. Similarly, the recipient of message should not be able to deny the receipt.

(*vi*) **Encryption** Information should be encrypted and decrypted only by an authorised user.

(*vii*) **Auditability** Data should be recorded in such a way that it can be audited for integrity requirements.

Security Protocols in Internet

We will discuss here some of the popular protocols use over the data transmission to ensure secured online transactions.

1. Secure Sockets Layer (SSL)

SSL is a security protocol protects communications between any SSL-enabled client and server software running on a network that uses TCP/IP, Gopher, FTP, Telnet, etc. SSL approach is to add a layer on top of the existing network transport protocol and below the application. Data flowing between the client and the server on that connection is encrypted before transmission and decrypted before it can be used by the receiving system.

Advantages of SSL

(i) SSL provides security at the session layer, its presence is completely invisible either to the merchant's web shop software or the customer.

(ii) SSL is already built into commonly used web browsers and there is no need to install any additional software.

Disadvantages of SSL

(i) SSL protects the communication link between the merchants and customers. The merchant is allowed to see the payment information. But SSL can neither guarantee that the merchant will not misuse this information.

(ii) SSL cannot provide assurance of non-repudiation without a third party server.

2. Secure Electronic Transaction (SET)

SET is a system for ensuring the security of financial transactions on the Internet. It was supported initially by Mastercard, Visa, Microsoft, Netscape and others. SET is not some system that enables payment but it is a security protocol applied on those payments. It uses different encryption and hashing techniques to secure payments over Internet done through credit cards.

Advantages of SET

(i) SET prevents merchants from seeing the customer payment information.

(ii) To ensure merchant privacy, SET prevents the payment gateway from seeing the order information.

Disadvantages of SET

(i) The customer must install additional software, which can handle SET transactions.

(ii) Implementing SET is more costly than SSL for merchants as well.

(iii) Users must have credit card.

Check Point 03

1 B2B applies to businesses buying from and selling to each other over the Internet. State, True or False

2 Which services are provided by CPA WebTrust in E-Commerce?

3 Write the full form of SET protocol.

SUMMARY

- The cyber ethics refers to a code of safe and responsible behaviour for the Internet community.
- Plagiarism is an act of copying another person's idea, words or work and pretend that they are our own.
- Intellectual property rights are the legal rights that cover the privileges given to individuals who are the owners and inventors of a work, and have created something with their intellectual creativity.
- Netiquette is a code of good behaviour on the Internet.
- Hacking is the act of intruding into someone else's computer or network.
- Software piracy is the illegal copying, distribution or use of software.
- A software license is a license agreement that gives an individuals, organisation permission to use a software program.
- Open source software movement is a movement that supports the use of open source license for some software.
- Freedom of information was established for transparency, government accountability, education and general public protection against mismanagement and corruption.
- Digital divide is a term that describes the uneven distribution of information and communication technology.
- E-Commerce, also known as electronic commerce or Internet commerce, refers to the buying and selling of goods or services using the Internet.
- Privacy is the state of being free from public scrutiny or from having your secrets or personal information shared.
- E-Commerce fraud is an illegal transaction made in a webshop.
- Secure Sockets Layer (SSL) is a security protocol for establishing encrypted links between a web server and a browser in an online communication.
- Secure Electronic Transaction (SET) is a system for ensuring the security of financial transactions on the Internet.

Exam Practice

Multiple Choice Questions

1 The ...... refers to a code of safe and responsible behaviour for the Internet community.

(a) cyber law (b) cyber ethics
(c) Both (a) and (b) (d) None of these

Ans. (*b*) The word cyber ethics refers to a code of safe and responsible behaviour for the Internet community.

2 Intellectual property is a

(a) industrial property (b) copyright property
(c) Both (a) and (b) (d) None of these

Ans. (*c*) Intellectual property are of two types:
(i) Industrial property (ii) Copyright property

3 Netiquette is short for

(a) Etiquette (b) Internet etiquette
(c) Social etiquette (d) None of these

Ans. (*b*) Netiquette is short for Internet etiquette. Etiquette is a code of polite behaviour in society, Netiquette is a code of good behaviour on the Internet.

4 Making illegal copies of copyrighted software is called

(a) Software piracy (b) Browsing
(c) Collaboration (d) Electronic distribution

Ans. (*a*) Software piracy refers to making illegal copies of copyrighted software.

5 ...... is a license agreement that gives an organisation permission.

(a) Software (b) Software license
(c) Both (a) and (b) (d) None of these

Ans. (*b*) Software license is a license agreement that gives an individual or organisation permission to use a software program.

6 Which of the following is the example of open source software license?

(a) GPL (b) BSD
(c) MIT (d) All of these

Ans. (*d*) GPL (General Public License), BSD license and MIT license are the examples of free and open source software license.

7 ...... refers to a citizen right to access information is held by the state.

(a) Software license
(b) Freedom of information
(c) Digital divide
(d) None of the above

Ans. (*b*) Freedom of Information (FOI) refers to a citizen's right to access information that is need by the state.

8 Which of the following is the part for E-Commerce?

(a) B2B (b) B2C
(c) C2B (d) All of these

Ans. (*d*) Business-to-Business (B2B), Business-to-Consumer (B2C), Consumer-to-Business (C2B), Consumer-to-Consumer (C2C) and Business-to-Government (B2G), are the main types for E-Commerce.

9 The ...... in E-Commerce means the protection of privacy of the parties involved in trading.

(a) fraud (b) privacy
(c) security (d) None of these

Ans. (*b*) The privacy in E-Commerce means the protection of privacy of the parties involved in trading through E-Commerce.

10 In which of the following fraud, fraudster using a stolen credit card?

(a) Merchant fraud (b) Identity theft
(c) Refund fraud (d) Friendly fraud

Ans. (c) In refund fraud, fraudster using a stolen credit card makes an overpayment on purpose.

11 Which of the following security protocol, protects communications between client and server?

(a) SSL (b) SET
(c) Both (a) and (b) (d) None of these

Ans. (*a*) Secure Sockets Layer (SSL) is a security protocol protects communications between any SSL enabled client and server software running on a network.

12 Which one of the following software comes under open source software category? **CBSE SQP Term-I**

(a) Photoshop (b) MS-Paint
(c) Linux (d) Windows

Ans. (*c*) Linux

13 Preeti needs to send a very confidential message to her colleague in office over a secure channel. She uses a technique wherein an actual message (which is in readable form) can be converted into an unreadable message. This concept is known as............... . **CBSE SQP Term-I**

(a) encryption (b) decryption
(c) plagiarism (d) data security

Ans. (*a*) encryption

14 Arun clicks on a link received in a message on his phone which promises him a complimentary trip to a destination of his choice. He forwarded this message to his friend, Panshul and asked him to do the same. But Panshul refuses and tells Arun that his personal and private information, such as online account names, login information and passwords can be stolen and he should be careful of such .... attacks. **CBSE SQP Term-I**

(a) phishing (b) spamming
(c) scamming (d) plagiarism

Ans. (*a*) phishing

15 Identify the correct statement regarding OSS. **CBSE 2021 Term-I**

(a) It is available for nominal or zero licensing and usage charges.
(b) It can be shared with others freely.
(c) It is modifiable.
(d) All of the above

Ans. (*d*) All of the above

16
- This kind of software is "freely distributed to users on a trial basis".
- There's a time limitation inherent in the software and would be deactivated when the time period is finished.
- One has to pay for the software to use it after the time limit.

Identify the type of software. **CBSE 2021 Term-I**

(a) OSS (b) Proprietary
(c) Freeware (d) Shareware

Ans. (*d*) Shareware

17 A unique symbol or word used to represent a business or its products is known as **CBSE 2021 Term-I**

(a) patent (b) trademark
(c) copyright (d) None of these

Ans. (*b*) trademark

18 Manish has copied the information from the resources available on the Internet for his article without acknowledging the original source or taking the permission from the original creator. This unethical act is termed as **CBSE 2021 Term-I**

(a) phishing
(b) plagiarism
(c) spying
(d) identity theft

Ans. (*b*) plagiarism

19 Encryption is one of the most prominent technique used for **CBSE 2021 Term-I**

(a) fast data transmission
(b) secure data transmission
(c) far away data transmission
(d) free data transmission

Ans. (*b*) secure data transmission

20 **Statement I** FOSS is more user friendly as compared to proprietary software.

Statement II Proprietary software allows developers across the globe to participate in the ongoing development of the software. **CBSE 2021 Term-I**

Select the best option from the list given below to understand the correctness of both the statements.

(a) Both statements are correct.
(b) Statement I correct and statement II incorrect.
(c) Statement I incorrect and statement II correct.
(d) Statement I incorrect and statement II incorrect.

Ans. (*b*) Statement I correct and statement II incorrect.

21 Which of the following is privacy threats to e-Commerce? **CBSE 2021 Term-I**

(a) Password theft (b) Identity theft
(c) Phishing (d) All of these

Ans. (*d*) All of these

22 R in IPR stands for **CBSE 2021 Term-I**

(a) Role (b) Rights
(c) Range (d) RAM

Ans. (*b*) Rights

Fill in the Blanks

1 Directly copying text, word is called …… .

Ans. plagiarism

2 Plagiarism occurs due to lack of …… .

Ans. knowledge

3 The world netiquette is a combination of …… and …… .

Ans. net, etiquette

4 …… refers to attempts to gain information from undisclosed areas.

Ans. Hacking

5 …… refers to the unauthorised duplication of computer software.

Ans. Software piracy.

6 …… arise when piracy occurs between companies.

Ans. Digital property rights.

7 The hallmark of …… grants the use of one or more copies of software.

Ans. proprietary software license

8 The open source software movement was started to spread the concept of …… .

Ans. open source software.

9 Freedom of Information is also known as …… .

Ans. Right to Information.

10 Digital divide is a term that describes the uneven distribution of …… .

Ans. Information and Communication Technologies (ICTs)

11 …… is the buying and selling of goods and services on the Internet.

Ans. E-Commerce

12 TRUSTe technology has launched ……, to certify that consumer software is not spyware.

Ans. Trusted Download Beta Program

True or False

1 Lack of enforcement is called a plagiarism.

Ans. **True** Lack of planning, time is called a plagiarism.

2 Trademark is an intellectual property.

Ans. **True** Copyright, patents and trademarks are the intellectual property.

3 The need of netiquette arises mostly when stolen the password.

Ans. **False** The need of netiquette arises mostly when sending E-mail, posting on usenet groups or chatting.

4 Software piracy is the act of illegally copying software.

Ans. **True** Software piracy refers to the unauthorised duplication of computer software.

5 License defines the process of sending and receiving the E-mail.

Ans. **False** Licenses also defines the responsibilities of the parties entering into the license agreement.

6 Linux is an example of open source software.

Ans. **True** Examples of open source software are Linux, Unix, MySQL, etc.

7 Freedom of Information Act is a copyright law to protect their works.

Ans. **False** Freedom of Information Act (FOIA) is a federal law that generally provides any person has a right to obtain access to federal agency records.

8 C2B applies to any consumer that sells a product to a business over the Internet.

Ans. **True** Consumer-to-Business (C2B) E-Commerce applies to any consumer that sells a product or service to a business over the Internet.

9 E-Commerce is not considered as a powerful tool to collect consumer's public information.

Ans. **False** E-Commerce is considered as a powerful tool to collect consumer's private information.

10 In encryption, information should be encrypted and decrypted only by an unauthorised user.

Ans. **False** In encryption, information should be encrypted and decrypted only by an authorised user.

Very Short Answer (VSA) Type Questions

1 Define the term cyber ethics.

Ans. Cyber ethics refers to a code of safe and responsible behaviour for the Internet community.

2 What do you mean by plagiarism?

Ans. Stealing someone else's ideas or information and presenting them as your own is called plagiarism.

3 Define the only one rule for good netiquette.

Ans. Respect others' privacy by not sharing personal information, photos or videos that another person may not want published online.

4 Name three types of law that can help restrict software piracy.

Ans. The following are the three types of law that can help to restrict software piracy:
(i) Copyright (ii) Patent (iii) Trademark

5 Define the content management system of digital property right.

Ans. Content management system is the backend of your website. Check who has access to this section of your website, and make sure they don't have unrestricted access to the site.

6 Explain the Freedom of Information Act.

Ans. Freedom of Information Act (FOIA) is intended to increase transparency. It does not provide access to all government documents.

7 How to age contribute to the digital divide?

Ans. Age seems to be that young people feel more comfortable with the new technology and are able to benefit from it more than older people.

8 Define the example of Consumer-to-Consumer E-Commerce.

Ans. E-Bay is the most successful C2C (Consumer-to-Consumer) online auction website.

9 What do you means by fraud in E-Commerce?

Ans. E-Commerce fraud shows no signs of slowing down online businesses are quickly becoming easy targets for cybercriminals as fraud in E-Commerce continues to rise.

10 Write the full form of SET protocol.

Ans. SET (Secure Electronic Transaction) is a system for ensuring the security of financial transactions on the Internet.

Short Answer (SA) Type Questions

1 List the guidelines to avoid plagiarism.

Ans. Refer to text an page No. 143

2 Intellectual property right means that the person who produces the information is the only one who can use that information. Now, explain the need of protecting intellectual property right.

Ans. The intellectual property rights must be protected because of protecting them:

(i) encourages individuals and business to create new software and new software applications, as well as improving existing applications.

(ii) ensures new ideas and technologies are widely distributed.

(iii) promotes investment in the national economy.

3 Which three laws are formulated in order to stop software piracy?

Ans. Refer to text on Page. No. 144

4 Using copyright, software piracy can be stopped. How?

Ans. The copyright in the work of authorship immediately becomes the property of the author, who created the work. Only the author or those deriving their rights through the author, can rightfully claim copyright.

5 What is digital property rights? Explain the some digital property rights.

Ans. Refer to text on page No. 144.

6 What do you means by privacy in E-Commerce?

Ans. The privacy in E-Commerce means the protection of privacy of the parties involved in trading through E-Commerce.

Trading in the online shop accessed through Internet between Business-to-Business (B2B), Business-to-Consumer (B2C) and Consumer-to-Consumer (C2C) is the main purpose of E-Commerce. Parties involved in this kind of trading exchange information including private information like address, credit card number, etc, to complete a transaction.

Long Answer (LA) Type Questions

1 What is the use of netiquettes? Explain the different rules to follow for good netiquette.

Ans. Refer to text on page No. 143.

2 Explain the software license with its types.

Ans. A software license is a document that provides legally binding guidelines for the use and distribution of software. Software licenses typically provide end users with the right to one or more copies of the software without violating copyrights. The license also defines the responsibilities of the parties entering into the license agreement and may impose restrictions on how the software can be used.

Software licenses typically are either proprietary, free and open source.

(i) **Proprietary Software License** This means that certain rights regarding the software are reserved by the software publisher. Therefore, it typical of end-user license agreement to include terms which define the uses of the software, such as the number of installations allowed or the terms of distribution. In other words, without acceptance of the license, the end user may not use the software at all. One example of such a proprietary software license is the license for Microsoft windows.

(ii) **Free and Open Source Software License** There are several organisation in the Free and Open Source Software (FOSS) license domain who give out guidelines and definitions regarding software licenses. Free and open source licenses are commonly classified into two categories: permissive and copyleft licenses.

A permissive license is simple and is the most basic type of open source license. It allows you to do whatever you want with the software. This license provide the software with no warranties. Copyleft license is aimed at giving and protecting all users unlimited freedom to use, study and privately modify the software.

3 What is the use of Freedom of Information (FOI)? Explain its advantages and disadvantages.

Ans. Refer to text on Page No. 145-146.

4 What do you mean by digital divide? Explain the factors that contribute to the digital divide.

Ans. Refer to text on Page No. 146.

5 Define the Secure Data Transmission systems. Explain the security protocols to ensure secure online transactions.

Ans. Refer to text on Page No. 148-149.

Application Oriented Questions

1 It is an act of copying another person's idea, words or work and pretend that they are our own. The intentions behind this could be malicious or it could be done accidently like copying data from other's computer without his/her permission and redistributing further. What is it?

(i) Piracy (ii) Plagiarism
(iii) Hacking (iv) Intellectual Property Right

Ans. (ii) Plagiarism

2 Complete the blank spaces using words from the list. You should use each word only once. Plagiarism, rights, illegally, cyber ethics, hacker.

(i) ______ is the moral, legal and social issues relating to cyber technology. Intellectual property rights reserves all the (ii) ______ of the owner to the information. For gathering required information, a (iii) ______ appears with malicious intention and breaks into the owner's system and steals the information (iv) ______.

Ans. (i) Cyber ethics (ii) rights (iii) hacker (iv) illegally

3. Geetika has recently created her social accounts. She is very excited as she waited so long to go online. She has recently also got admission in a prestigious high school and does not know many students.

When she logs into her social media a few days later, she finds that someone is posting negative, demeaning comments on her social media profile. She is also getting repeated mails from unknown people. Whenever she goes online, she is trolled by multiple unknown people. **CBSE SQP Term-I**

EXAM PRACTICE

Based on the given information, answer the questions (i) to (iv).

(i) Which of the following is the most appropriate action she should take?
   (a) She should stop going online and delete her social media accounts.
   (b) She should not share this with anyone as she might face more of such kind of behaviour.
   (c) She should file a complaint at the nearest police station.
   (d) She should inform her parents and bring to the notice of school authorities.

(ii) After hearing her ordeal, the school decides to publish a set of moral principles that determines the appropriate behaviour of students while using the Internet. The school is referring to ....
   (a) intellectual property rights
   (b) internet privacy
   (c) computer ethics
   (d) cyber ethics

(iii) Geetika is advised by her best friend, Seerat to protect her personal information from intentional or unintentional attacks by others. This is also known as ....
   (a) digital right
   (b) copyright
   (c) data privacy
   (d) intellectual property

(iv) The computer teacher of Geetika's class decides to take an online session on the topic Netiquettes, which generally includes
   (a) safeguarding one's passwords and sensitive online information
   (b) logging out of social media accounts after the session
   (c) not bullying or trolling anyone by disrespecting them or passing inappropriate remarks
   (d) All of the above

Ans. (i) (d), (ii) (d), (iii) (c), (iv) (d)

4 Now-a-days, we spend more time in the cyber world. Anyone who uses digital technology along with the Internet is a digital citizen or a netizen. Being a good netizen means practicing safe, ethical and legal use of digital technology. A responsible netizen must abide by net etiquettes, communication etiquettes and social media etiquettes.

We follow certain etiquettes during our social interactions. Similarly, we need to exhibit proper manners and etiquettes while being online. One should be ethical, respectful and responsible while surfing the Internet. We should not use copyrighted materials without the permission of the creator or owner. In a group or public forum, we should respect the diversity of the people in terms of knowledge, experience, culture and other aspects.

CBSE 2021 Term-I

Based on the given paragraph, answer the questions (i) to (v).

(i) Identify the net etiquette which every netizen should follow.
   (a) One should be responsible
   (b) One should be ethical
   (c) One should be respectful
   (d) All of the above

(ii) Being ethical in the cyber world means
   (a) we should share information in the cyber world
   (b) we should not use copyrighted materials without the permission of the creator or owner
   (c) we should further forward the information without checking its reliability at our own end
   (d) All of the above

(iii) Being respectful in the cyber world means
   (a) we should respect different opinion of others
   (b) we should use respectful language
   (c) we should respect others privacy
   (d) All of the above

(iv) A netizen will be considered very irresponsible in nature if he or she
   (a) feed the troll
   (b) avoid cyber bullying
   (c) checks the details before befriending on social media
   (d) All of the above

(v) Person who spends more time in the cyber world may be termed as
   (a) Netizen (b) C-Citizen
   (c) D-Citizen (d) All of these

Ans. (i) (d), (ii) (b), (iii) (d), (iv), (a), (v) (a)

Unit Test

Multiple Choice Questions

1 The need of ...... arises mostly when sending E-mail.
(a) etiquette
(b) netiquette
(c) plagiarism
(d) None of the above

2 ...... is an exclusive right of the developer to protect their works.
(a) Patent
(b) Trademark
(c) Copyright
(d) None of the above

3 Freedom of Information is also called
(a) Right of Information
(b) Right to Information
(c) Finance of Information
(d) None of the above

Fill in the Blanks

4 ...... refers to attempts to gain information from undisclosed areas.

5 ...... applies to any consumer that sells a product to a business over the Internet.

6 PrivacyBot is a privacy seal program for websites created by ....

True or False

7 Intellectual property rights reserves all the rights of the owner to the information.

8 The open source software movement is a movement that supports the use of proprietary software license.

9 Digital divide describe the uneven distribution of E-mail message.

Very Short Answer Type Questions

10 How to gender contribute to the digital divide?

11 Give any two factors of plagiarism.

12 Give the examples of open source software license.

Short Answer Type Questions

13 What do you mean by cyber ethics?

14 Explain the violation of intellectual property right.

15 Describe the effects of digital divide.

Long Answer Type Questions

16 What is software license? Explain its types.

17 What do you mean by secure data transmission systems in E-Commerce? Explain different security protocols in Internet.

18 What is Freedom of Information? Explain its advantages and disadvantages.

Application Oriented Questions

19 It reserves all the rights of the owner to the information to decide, how much information is to be exchanged, shared or distributed. The owner can decide the price for doing so. What is it?

20 The following paragraph describes, the term E-Commerce.

E-Commerce is the buying and selling of goods and services on the (i) .... E-Commerce draws on technologies such as (ii) ...., electronic funds transfer, online transaction processing, Internet marketing and automated data collection systems. There is no special software to install other than a (iii) .... It was one of the first business types to become (iv) .... available.

Fill in the blanks with words from the list below:
E-Commerce, digitally, Internet, mobile commerce, inventory management, web browser.

All in One

COMPLETE STUDY | COMPLETE PRACTICE | COMPLETE ASSESSMENT

Computer Applications

Project Report

Abbreviation and Glossary

PROJECT REPORT

A project report is a written document of what the *analyser* analyses in his/her project work. The project report needs to be prepared with great care and consideration.

ELEMENTS OF THE PROJECT

Try to ensure that your report contains the following elements

Title Page

This should include the project title, name of the company/product on which you are conducting your research and name of the student. You can also list the name of your school, class and subject teacher.

Acknowledgment

It is usual to thank those individuals, who have provided particularly useful assistance, technical or otherwise, during your project through acknowledgment.

Content Page

This should list the main sections and sub-sections of your report. Choose self-explanatory titles with their respective pages and use double spacing for clarity. Content should be impressive and explanatory, so that the reader would clearly understand the purpose of the project.

Introduction

This is one of the most important component of the project report. It should begin with a clear statement of what the project is about, so that the nature and scope of the project can be understood by the reader. It should summarise everything which you set out to achieve and provide a clear summary of the project's background, relevance and main contributions. The introduction should set the context for the project and should provide the reader with a summary of the key things to look out for, in the remainder of the report. It is useful in stating the main objectives of the project as part of the introduction.

Background

The background section of the report should set the project into action. It specifies the problem, what remedial actions are taken, what are its effects etc. It proposes the layout of the whole project.

Body of Report

The central part of the report usually consists of three or four sections detailing the technical work undertaken during the project. The structure of these sections is highly project dependent. They can reflect the chronological development of the project. It includes the detailed description regarding the matter of the project.

Evaluation

This might involve quantitative and qualitative evaluation such as expressibility, functionality, ease-of-use, etc of a product. At some point, you should also evaluate the strengths and weaknesses of what you have done. It includes certain questionnaires, sampling test, etc. which help in evaluating the result on the basis of truths and facts.

Conclusion

The conclusion should list the things, which have been learnt as a result of the work you have done. It shows the ultimate response of the project undertaken by a student. It should be expressive and impressive, so that a reader would clearly evaluate the result and rate you on the basis of your presentation.

ACKNOWLEDGEMENT

I would like to express my special thanks & gratitude to my teacher________ as well as our Principal ________ who gave me the golden opportunity to do this wonderful project.

This project helped me a lot in gaining adequate knowledge about the topic. I have completed this project after proper analysis and research and I came to know about so many new things.

I am really thankful to all of my friends, partners and guide, who have devoted their precious time in completing my project. Secondly, I would also like to thank my parents or guardians who helped me a lot in finishing this project within the prescribed time.

I am making this project not only for marks but also to increase my knowledge and intellect development.

Thanks again to all who helped me.

CERTIFICATE

This is to Certify that these projects are the bonafide work of .... (Name of the student) who carried out the work under my supervision

....

Name and Signature of Teacher/Supervisor).

CONTENTS

PROJECT REPORT

HTML PROJECTS

HTML is a markup language, which is used to define the layout and attributes of a World Wide Web (www) document as well as to create links between Web pages. It allows images and other objects to be embedded that can be used to create interactive forms. HTML documents are described through HTML tags or elements.

Project 1 Creating a Web Page for Paradise Company in HTML.

Procedure

- **Source code of company.html file:**

```
<HTML>
<HEAD>
<TITLE>Company</TITLE>
</HEAD>
<BODY>
<H1><FONT color="green" face =" lucida handwriting">Paradise Wheels CO.
<IMG src ="par.jpg" height = "120" width = "200" align = "left"></FONT></H1>
<CENTER><H2><FONT color = "magenta">Because You're Worth It </FONT></H2></CENTER>
<TABLE align = "right" cellpadding = "5"> <TR><TH>Home</TH><TH>About Us</TH>
<TH>Services</TH><TH>Products</TH> <TH>Contact US</TH></TR> </TABLE><BR><BR> <HR>
<TABLE align = "right" width = "200" ><CAPTION><FONT face      = "lucida
handwriting" size = "4" color = "maroon">Our Services</FONT></CAPTION>
<TR><TD><IMG src = "web.jpg" height = "80" width = "120"><BR> <A href=
"web.html">Web Design</A></TD></TR> <TR><TD align = "right"><IMG src =
"prog.jpg" height ="80" width ="120"><BR>
<A href="programming.html">Programming</A></TD></TR> <TR><TD>
<IMG src ="ani.png"  height ="80"  width ="120"><BR>
<A href="animation.html">Animation</A></TD></TR>
</TABLE>
<H3><FONT face ="verdana" size ="4">Features of This Company </FONT></H3>
<FONT face ="cambria" size ="3" color ="purple">
<UL>
<LI>Good businesses need good plans.</LI>
<LI> To be successful, a company must be motivated by something beyond financial success.
</LI>
<LI>To make their businesses successful, business owners need good attitudes. </LI>
<LI>To be successful, businesses need to commit resources and time to training their
employees, <BR>
as well any independent contractors with whom they work. </LI>
<LI>Creating, enhancing, and celebrating teamwork is at the heart of every successful
   company culture.</LI>
<LI>Effective communication patterns within successful organizations have three main
   characteristics:
```

```
<BR> clarity, courtesy, and proactivity. </LI>
<OL type="i">
<LI>Clarity is a vital element in effective communication, because it's important for messages and information to be transferred in a transparent, clear, and concise manner.</LI><LI>Courtesy is another important aspect of communication, as it allows for messages to be transmitted within an atmosphere of safety and respect.</LI><LI>Proactivity is a yet another crucial aspect of an effective communication pattern, because the only way to conduct a productive discussion is to conduct a proactive one.</LI></OL>
</UL>
</FONT>
</BODY>
</HTML>
```

The output of company.html file is shown below.

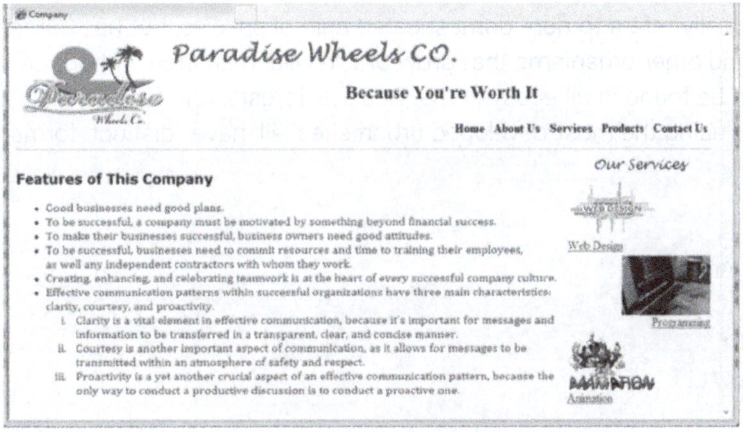

Project 2 Creating a Home Page Named Wildlife in HTML.

Procedure

- **Home.html**

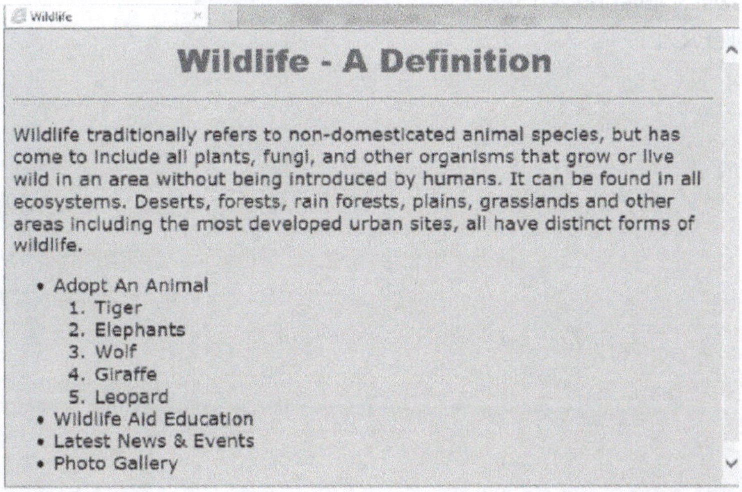

- **Source code for Home.html**

```
<HTML>
<HEAD>
<TITLE>Wildlife</TITLE>
</HEAD>
<BODY bgcolor="pink">
<H1 align="center">
<FONT face="arial" color="red">
<B>Wildlife-A Definition</B>
<HR>
</FONT>
</H1>
<FONT face="verdana" size="4" color= "black"><P>
Wildlife traditionally refers to non- domesticated animal species, but has come to include all
plants, fungi, and other organisms that grow or live wild in an area without being introduced by
humans. It can be found in all ecosystems. Deserts, forests, rain forests, plains, grasslands and
other areas including the most developed urban sites, all have distinct forms of wildlife.
<BR>
</P>
<UL>
<LI>Adopt An Animal</LI>
<OL>
<LI>Tiger</LI>
<LI>Elephants</LI>
<LI>Wolf</LI>
<LI>Giraffe</LI>
<LI>Leopard</LI>
</OL>
<LI>Wildlife Aid Education</LI>
<LI>Latest News & Events</LI>
<LI>Photo Gallery</LI>
</UL>
</FONT>
</BODY>
</HTML>
```

Project 3 Creating a Web Page for My School in HTML.

Procedure

- MySchool.html

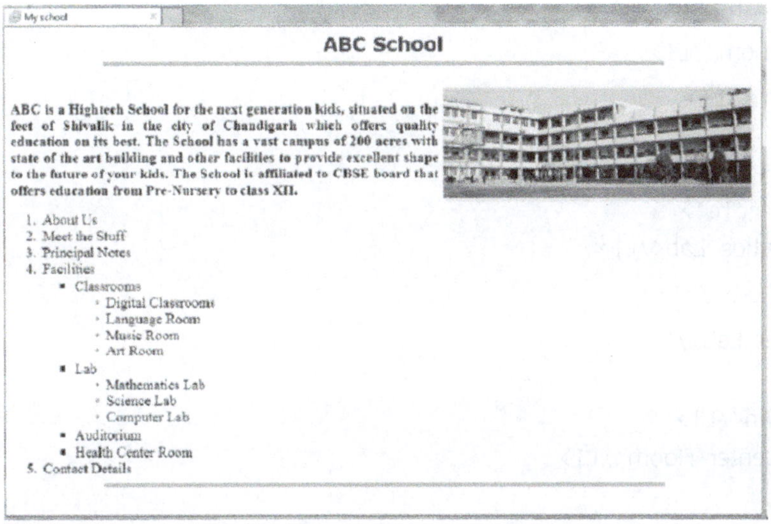

- Source code for MySchool.html

```
<HTML>
<HEAD>
<TITLE>My school</TITLE>
</HEAD>
<BODY text="black">
<CENTER>
<FONT face="verdana" color="maroon" size="5">
<B>ABC School</B>
</FONT>
</CENTER>
<HR  size="4" width="75%" noshade><BR>
<IMG src="School.jpg" height="150" width="400" align="right">
<FONT size="4">
<P align="justify"><B>
ABC is a Hightech School for the next generation kids, situated on the feet of Shivalik in the city
of Chandigarh which offers quality education on its best. The School has a vast campus of 200
acres with state of the art building and other facilities to provide excellent shape to the future of
your kids. The School is affiliated to CBSE board that offers education from Pre-Nursery to class
XII</B></P>
<OL>
<LI>About  Us</LI>
<LI>Meet  the  Stuff</LI>
<LI>Principal  Notes</LI>
<LI>Facilities</LI>
```

```
<UL type="square">
<LI>Classrooms</LI>
<UL type="circle">
<LI>Digital Classrooms</LI>
<LI>Language Room</LI>
<LI>Music Room</LI>
<LI>Art Room</LI>
</UL>
<LI>Lab</LI>
<UL type="circle">
<LI>Mathematics Lab</LI>
<LI>Science Lab</LI>
<LI>Computer Lab</LI>
</UL>
<LI>Auditorium</LI>
<LI>Health Center Room</LI>
</UL>
<LI>Contact Details </LI>
</OL>
</FONT>
<HR size="4" width="75%" noshade>
</BODY>
</HTML>
```

Project 4 Creating a Web Page for My Family in HTML.

Procedure

- Myfamily.html

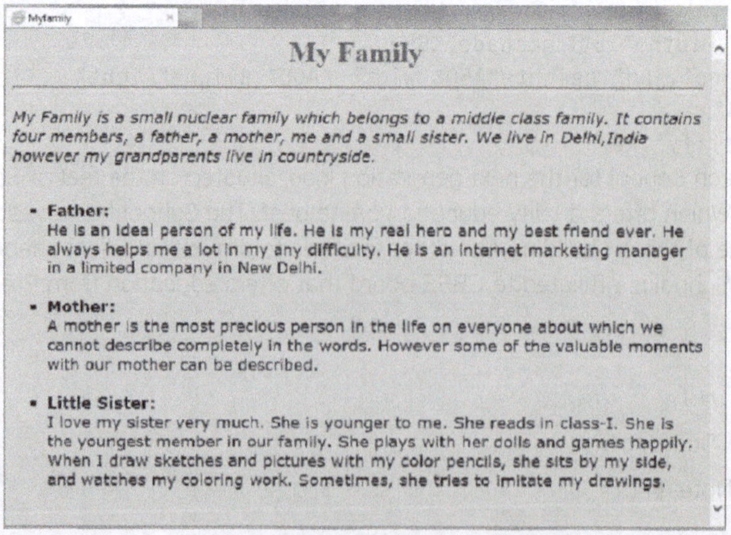

- **Source code for Myfamily.html**

```
<HTML>
<HEAD>
<TITLE>Myfamily</TITLE>
</HEAD>
<BODY  bgcolor="pink">
<CENTER>
<H1><FONT color="red">My Family</FONT>
</H1>
</CENTER>
<HR size="4">
<FONT face="verdana" size="4" color="black">
<P><I> My Family is a small nuclear family which belongs to a middle class family. It contains four
members, a father, a mother, me and a small sister. We live in Delhi,India however my grandparents
live in countryside.  </I><BR><BR>
<UL  type="square">
<B><LI>Father:</LI></B>
He is an ideal person of my life. He is my real hero and my best friend ever. He always helps me a
lot in my any difficulty. He is an Internet marketing manager in  a  limited  company
in  New  Delhi.<BR><BR>
<B><LI>Mother:</LI></B>
A mother is the most precious person in the life on everyone about which we cannot describe
completely in the words. However some of the valuable moments with our mother can be
described.<BR><BR>
<B><LI>Little Sister:</LI></B>
I love my sister very much. She is younger to me. She reads in class-I. She is the youngest
member in our family. She plays with her dolls and games happily. When I draw sketches and
pictures with my color pencils, she sits by my side, and watches my coloring work. Sometimes,
she tries to imitate my drawings.
</UL></P>
</FONT>
</BODY>
</HTML>
```

Project 5 Creating a Web Page for Personal Blog in HTML.

Procedure

- blog.html

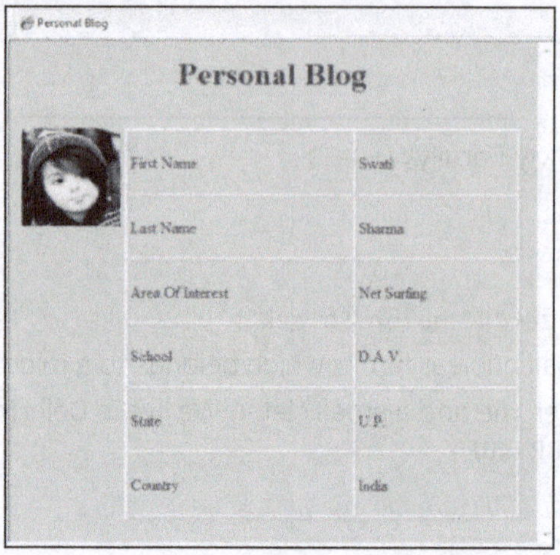

- Source code for blog.html

```
<HTML>
<HEAD>
<TITLE>Personal Blog</TITLE>
</HEAD>
<BODY bgcolor="darkseagreen" text="darkslategrey">
<CENTER><H1>Personal Blog</H1></CENTER>
<HR noshade>
<TABLE height="80%" width="80%">
<TR>
<TD rowspan ="6" valign="top">
<IMG src="pic.jpg" height="100" width="100"></TD>
<TD>
<TABLE border="2" height="400" width="400" align="center">
<TR>
<TD>First Name</TD>
<TD>Swati</TD>
</TR>
<TR>
<TD>Last Name</TD>
<TD>Sharma</TD>
</TR><TR>
<TD>Area Of Interest</TD>
<TD>Net Surfing</TD>
</TR>
<TR>
<TD>School</TD>
<TD>D.A.V.</TD>
```

```
</TR>
<TR>
<TD>State</TD>
<TD>U.P.</TD>
</TR>
<TR>
<TD>Country</TD>
<TD>India</TD>
</TR>
</TABLE>
</TD></TR>
</TABLE>
</BODY>
</HTML>
```

Project 6 Create a Website on Travel and Tourism.

Procedure

- **For creating a Website on travel and tourism, follow the below mentioned steps:**

Step 1 Source code of travel.html file:

```
<HTML>
<HEAD>
<TITLE>Travel and Tourism</TITLE>
</HEAD>
<BODY>
<H1><FONT color="red" face="magenta"><I><CENTER>Travel and Tourism
</CENTER></I>
</FONT></H1>
<HR noshade size="4" color="green">
<P><FONT size="4">
<IMG src="travel-tourism.jpg" align="right" height="150" width="400">
Travel refers to taking a trip or a journey to another place, and tourism refers to the act
of traveling as well as to the business side of the travel industry. Travel can also be used
to describe the act of moving from one place to the other.<BR> Additionally, it is used in
basketball to describe what happens if someone takes more than two steps without
dribbling the ball. </FONT></P><BR>
<FONT size="4"> <UL type="square">
<LI><A href="northsouth.html">North and South Tourism</A></LI><BR><BR>
<LI><A href="westeast.html">West and East Tourism</A></LI>
</UL></FONT>
</BODY>
</HTML>
```

PROJECT REPORT

The output of this file is shown below:

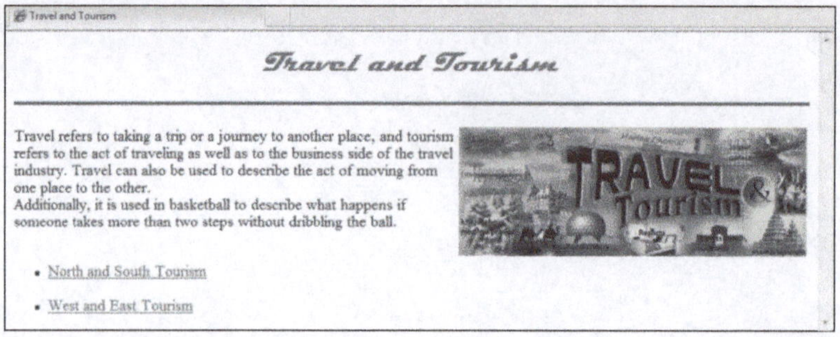

Step 2 Source code of northsouth.html file:

```
<HTML>
<HEAD>
<TITLE>North and South Tourism</TITLE>
</HEAD>
<BODY>
<H1><FONT color="green"><CENTER>North and South Tourism </CENTER></FONT>
</H1>
<HR color="blue" size="2"><BR>
<CENTER><IMG src="north.jpg" height="150" width="400">
<IMG src="south.jpg" height="150" width="250"></CENTER>
<P><FONT size="4" face="arial" color="red">
The preferred destinations include- Shimla, Kinnaur, Lahaul and districts of Spiti, Chamba, Kangra, Mandi Nainital, Kullu, Manali, Massourie, Dalhousie, Kufri, Kashmir valley in winters with snowfall being the main attraction. Rajasthan, as always, will remain a favourite and places like Udaipur, Jaipur, Jodhpur, Bikaner, etc will see a mix of domestic and foreign tourists.
Besides, the top destinations in south would include Ooty, Mysore, Pondicherry, Rameshwaram and Goa, Mahabaleshwar in west, according to just concluded survey conducted by the Associated Chambers of Commerce and Industry of India (ASSOCHAM).</FONT></P>
</BODY>
</HTML>
```

The output of this file is shown below:

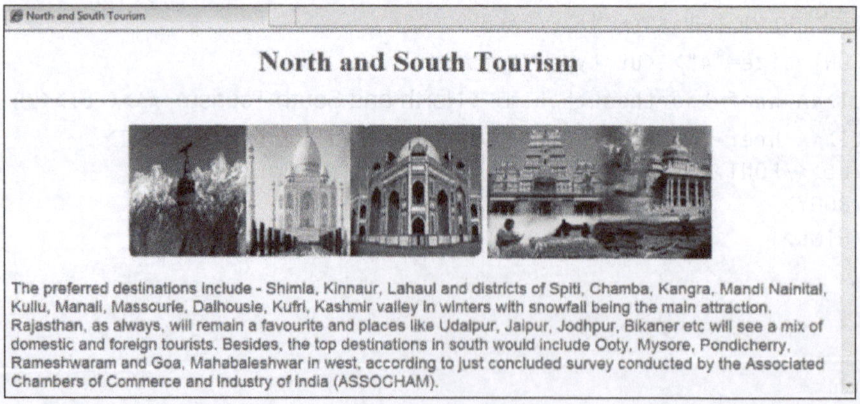

Step 3 Source code of westeast.html file:

```
<HTML>
<HEAD><TITLE>West and East Tourism</TITLE></HEAD>
<BODY><H1><FONT color="green"><CENTER>West and East Tourism</CENTER></FONT></H1>
<HR color="blue" size="2">
<CENTER><IMG src="west.jpg" height="150" width="400">
<IMG src="east.jpg" height="150" width="350"></CENTER><BR>
<FONT size="4" face="arial" color="red"><P>East India offers you an interesting
combination of rich cultural traditions and a wide variety of tourist attractions such as beaches, hill
stations and pilgrimage centers. East India also offers you plenty of scope for adventure sports such
as trekking. It is an ideal honeymoon destination as well.</P>
<P>West India is a region in the western part of India. It includes the states Gujarat, Maharashtra,
Rajasthan and Goa. It also houses the Union Territory Dadra and Nagar Haveli, and Daman and Diu.
This region is highly industrialized, with a large urban population. Regional languages like marathi,
rajasthani, gujarati are widely spoken here.</P></FONT>
</BODY>
</HTML>
```

The output of this file is shown below:

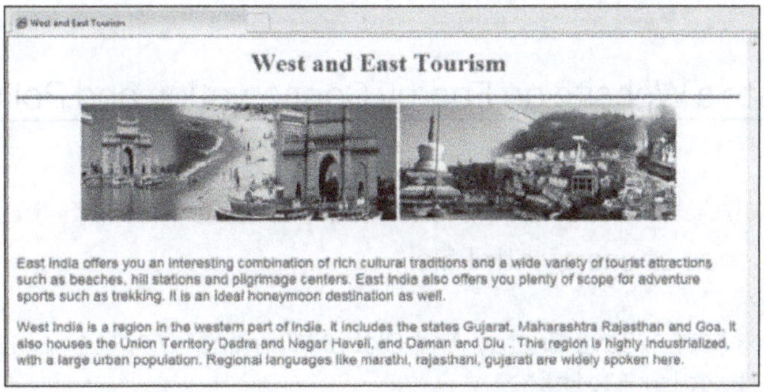

Project 7 Create a Website on Indian Institute of Technology, Delhi

Procedure

Source code of Delhi.html file

```
<HTML>
<HEAD>
<TITLE>IIT Delhi</TITLE>
</HEAD>
<BODY>
<A href ="web1.html"><B> Home </B></A>
<H2><FONT color ="green"><CENTER> India Institute of Technology, Delhi
</CENTER></FONT></H2><HR color = "blue" size ="2"><BR>
<CENTER><IMG src ="delhi.jpeg" height ="150" width ="400"></CENTER>
<P><FONT size ="4" face ="arial" color ="red"> The Indian Institute of
Technology Delhi (abbreviated IIT Delhi or IITD ) is a public engineering institution located in
Hauz Khas, Delhi, India. Established in 1961, with a vision to contribute to India and the world
through excellence in scientific and technical education and research, to serve as a valuable
resource for industry and society and to remain a source of pride for all Indians was formally
inaugurated August 1961 by Prof. Humayun Kabir, Minister of Scientific Research & Cultural
Affairs. First admissions were made in 1961.<BR>
```

```
The Institute was later decreed in Institutes of National Importance under the Institutes of Technology Amendment Act, 1963 and accorded the status of a Deemed University with powers to decide its own academic policy to conduct its own examinations, and to award its own degrees.
</FONT></P>
</BODY>
</HTML>
```

The output of the above file is shown below:

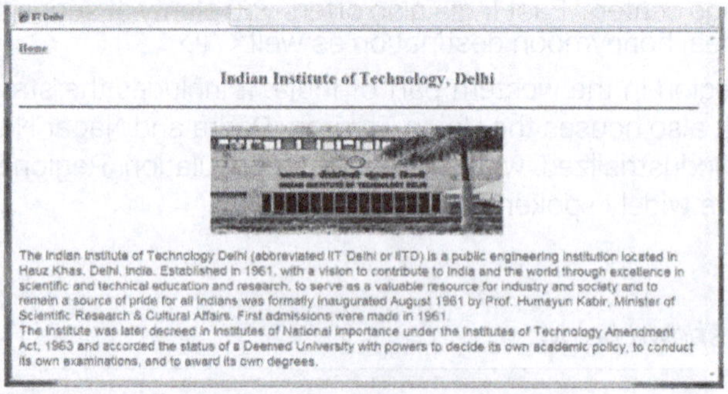

Project 8 Create a Website on Energy Conservation and Pollution using HTML.

Procedure

- **For creating a Website on energy conservation and pollution, follow the below mentioned steps:**

Step 1 Source code of energy.html file:

```
<HTML>
<HEAD><TITLE>Save Energy And Global Warming </TITLE></HEAD>
<BODY bgcolor="pink">
<CENTER><FONT color="green" size="6"><B>Save Energy And Global Warming</B>
</FONT></CENTER><BR>
<CENTER><IMG src="bulb.jpg" width="480" height="100">
<IMG src="a.jpg" width="480" height="100"></CENTER>
<TABLE border="2">
<TR><TD width="250" height="100"><FONT size="4"> The rapidly growing population and economic development are leading to the environmental degradation in India through the uncontrolled growth of urbanization and industrialization, expansion and massive intensification of agriculture and the destruction of forests.<BR>
<BR><UL><LI><A href="energy1.html">Energy Conservation</A></LI>
<LI><A href="warming.html">Global Warming</A></LI>
<LI><A href="poll.html">Pollution</A></LI></FONT></TD>
<TD width="1000" height="100"><FONT size="6" color="teal"><CENTER>Live Green. Save Green.</CENTER></FONT><BR>
<P><FONT size="3" face="cambria"> The atmosphere is something that is around us everyday. Everyday gases are released into the air by all living material. The gases in the air are used for many important things. For example, hydrogen is released by volcanoes, which can give energy to the cell; photosynthesis has evolved to take the gas carbon dioxide and create food and release oxygen; nitrogen is a gas used in our air, oceans, and solid earth, as
```

PROJECT REPORT

```
an essential part of living things. <BR> Carbon dioxide is also involved in processes where it is stored as limestone and marble, as gas and oil and coal, and is in organic material in the soil. Not only do these gases make up our atmosphere, but they also keep the temperature of the earth stable. Carbon dioxide absorbs the radiation that would otherwise escape the earth. By adding oxygen and taking away carbon dioxide this causes the earth to be cooler than it would otherwise be.
<BR>These are just two of the many gases that make up the atmosphere we live in today. The temperature in our earth is directly determined by these five gases. Even though the causes of global warming are known, the exact effects it will have on us in the future are yet to be determined.
</FONT></P></TD></TR>
</TABLE>
</BODY>
</HTML>
```

The output of this file is shown below:

Step 2 Source code of energy1.html file:

```
<HTML>
<HEAD><TITLE>Energy Conservation</TITLE></HEAD>
<BODY background="b.jpg"><H2><A href="energy.html">Back</A></H2>
<H1 align="CENTER">
<FONT face="algerian" color="maroon">ENERGY CONSERVATION</FONT></H1><BR>
<P><FONT size="5" face="andalus">Energy conservation refers to reducing energy consumption throu gh using less of an energy service. Energy conservation differs from efficient energy use, which refers to using less energy for a constant service. For example, driving less is an example of energy conservation. Driving the same amount with a higher mileage vehicle is an example of energy efficiency. <BR> Energy conservation and efficiency are both energy reduction techniques. Even though energy conservation reduces energy services, it can result in increased, environmental quality, national security, and personal financial security. It is at the top of the sustainable energy hierarchy.</FONT></P></BODY>
</HTML>
```

PROJECT REPORT

The output of this file is shown below:

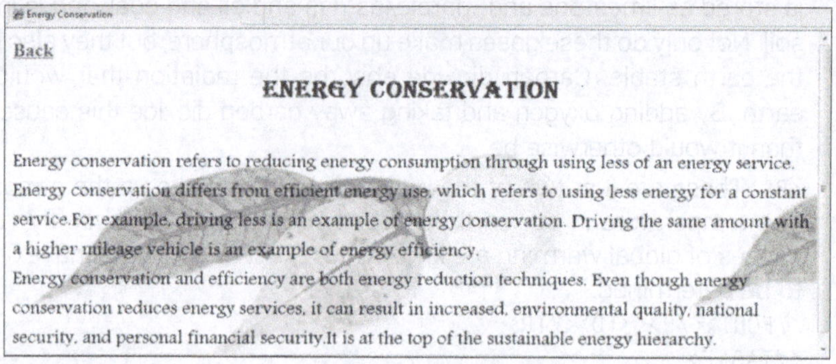

Step 3 Source code of warming.html file:

```
<HTML>
<HEAD><TITLE>Global Warming</TITLE></HEAD>
<BODY background="Global_2.jpg">
<H2><A href="energy.html">Back</A></H2>
<H1 align="center"><FONT face="arial" color="maroon">
<U>Global Warming</U></FONT></H1>
<IMG src="greenhouse.jpg" aign="right" height="200" width="250"><BR>
<P><FONT size="4"> Global Warming is the increase of Earth's average surface temperature
due to effect of greenhouse gases, such as carbon dioxide emissions from burning fossil fuels
or from deforestation, which trap heat that would otherwise escape from Earth. This is a type of
greenhouse effect.
<BR><BR>Earth's climate is mostly influenced by the first 6 miles or so of the atmosphere
which contains most of the matter making up the atmosphere. This is really a very thin layer if
you think about it. In the book The End of Nature, author Bill McKibbin tells of walking three
miles to from his cabin in the Adirondack's to buy food. Afterwards, he realized that on this
short journey he had traveled a distance equal to that of the layer of the atmosphere where
almost all the action of our clilmate is contained.<BR> <BR> In fact, if you were to view Earth
from space, the principle part of the atmosphere would only be about as thick as the skin on
an onion! Realizing this makes it more plausible to suppose that human beings can change
the climate.</FONT></P>
</BODY>
</HTML>
```

The output of this file is shown below:

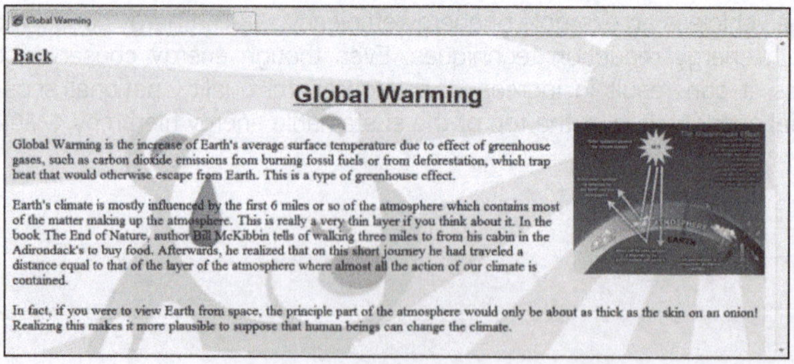

Step 4 Source code of poll.html file:

```
<HTML>
<HEAD><TITLE>Pollution</TITLE></HEAD>
<BODY bgcolor="pink"><H2><A href="energy.html">Back</A></H2>
<H1 align="center"><FONT face="georgia" color="maroon">Pollution</FONT></H1>
<P><FONT size="4" face="cambria"> <BR>
<IMG src="poster.jpg" align="right" height="250" width="200">
Pollution is the introduction of contaminants into the natural environment that cause adverse change. Pollution can take the form of chemical substances or energy, such as noise, heat or light. Pollutants, the components of pollution, can be either foreign substances/energies or naturally occurring contaminants. <BR>
<BR> Pollution is often classed as point source or nonpoint source pollution. Pollution is when something is added to the environment that is harmful or poisonous to living things. <BR>
<BR> Smoke in the air from factories is a type of pollution as it is bad for the lungs when breathed in sewage in drinking water is another type of pollution, as it can make people ill because it contains germs and viruses. People living next to a building site where there is too much noise can become sick as they cannot sleep or relax. This is called noise pollution.</FONT></P>
</BODY>
</HTML>
```

The output of this file is shown below:

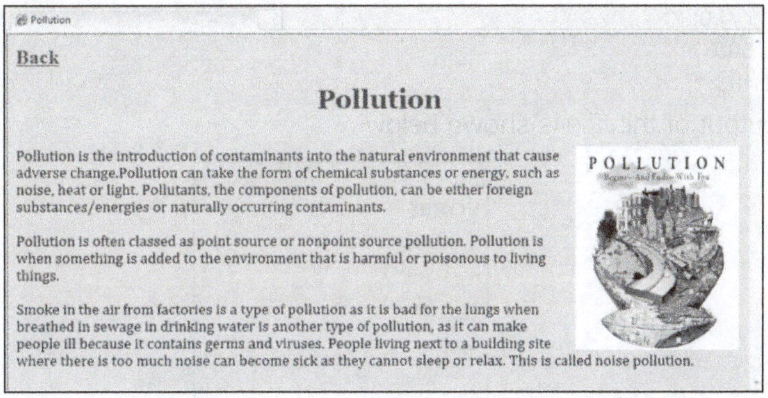

Project 9 Create a Web Page for User Registration Form in HTML.

Procecdure

- **Source code for Form.html**

```
<HTML>
  <HEAD><TITLE>FORM</TITLE></HEAD>
  <BODY>
    <H1>FORM</H1>
    <FORM action="submission.html"method="GET">
      <B>User Name</B>
        <INPUT type="text"name="User Name"value="Enter your Name"
        size="30" height="15" width="80"><BR><BR>
```

```
<B>Password</B>
  <INPUT type ="password" name="Password" value="Pass"size="30"
  height="15" width="80"><BR><BR>
<B>Address</B>
<TEXTAREA rows="2" cols="30" name="Address">Enter your Address
</TEXTAREA><BR><BR>
<B>Country</B>
<SELECT name="s1" size="1" >
  <OPTION label="America">America</OPTION>
  <OPTION value="US">US</OPTION>
  <OPTION value="India" selected>India</OPTION>
  <OPTION value="Japan" >Japan</OPTION>
</SELECT><BR><BR>
<B>Gender</B>
  <INPUT type="radio" name="Radio Button"> Male
  <INPUT type="radio" name="Radio Button">Female<BR><BR>
<B>Hobbies</B>
  <INPUT type="checkbox" name="CheckBox">Drawing
  <INPUT type="checkbox"name="CheckBox">Story Writing<BR><BR>
<INPUT type="submit" value="Submit">
<INPUT type="reset" value="Reset">
<INPUT type="button" value="Cancel">
</FORM>
</BODY>
</HTML>
```

The output of this file is shown below

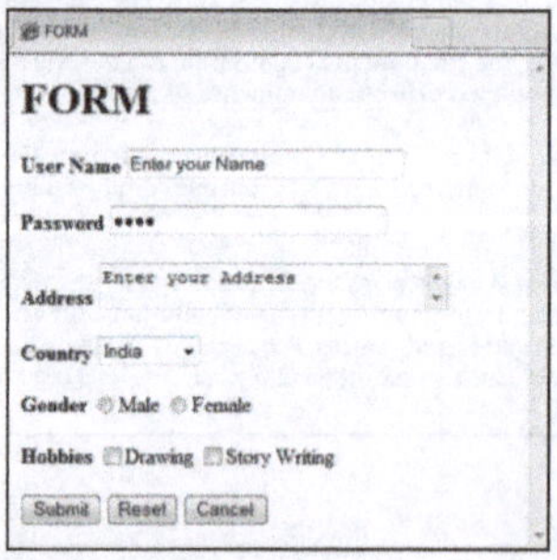

Project 10 Create a Web Page for Arihant Books Using Cascading Style Sheets in HTML.

Procedure

- **Source code for CSS-Example-06.html file**

```
<HTML>
  <HEAD>
    <STYLE type="text/css">
    HR {color:white;}
    H1 {font-size=40}
    P {margin-left:20px;}
```

PROJECT REPORT

```
BODY
  {background-image:url("E:\Projects\COPA\Web Design Concepts\colorful.jpg")}
  </STYLE>
  <TITLE>Arihant BOOKS</TITLE>
</HEAD>
<BODY>
  <H1>Arihant Books</H1>
  <P>A wide range of books for school curricula, polytechnic, competitive and
  recruitment examinations are published by <B>Arihant Publications India
  Ltd.</B></P>
  <HR Style = "color:black">For any query e-mail at info@arihantbooks.com and
  crm@arihantbooks.com or dial +91-11-40546380
</BODY>
</HTML>
```

The output of this file is shown below

VIVA VOCE

1. *What is tag?*

Ans. A tag is defined as the building block of codes in an HTML document.

2. *Define the purpose of the <BODY>tag.*

Ans. The <BODY>tag contains all tags and information that you want to view in a Web page.

3. *Give the name attributes of the <FONT> tag.*

Ans. size, color and face

4. *What is the difference between the <UL> and <OL> tags?*

Ans. The <UL>tag is used to define items in an unordered format and the <OL> tag is used to create an ordered list.

5. *Which tag is used to insert heading of third level on a Web page?*

Ans. <H3> tag

6. *What is the method of viewing the source code of the current page in the Web browser?*

Ans. Right click on the Web page and then select view source from the context menu.

7. *Name two common graphic files formats that most browser recognise.*

Ans. .gif and .jpg

8. *Explain the following statement:*

<HR size ="5" align =" right" width ="60">

Ans. The given HTML code produces a horizontal rule with size 5, aligning right on page and of width 60.

9. *Which HTML tag is used to insert an image in a page?*

Ans. <IMG> tag

10. *What do you mean by src ?*

Ans. The src is an attribute of <IMG> tag that gives the URL of the image document.

11. *In HTML, how linking can be done?*

Ans. Linking can be done by using anchor <A> tag followed by href attribute.

12. *Define cellspacing.*

Ans. The cellspacing is used to create space between different cells in a table.

13. *Which tag is used for giving heading to the columns?*

Ans. <TH>

14. *What is the use of align attribute in <TABLE> tag?*

Ans. The align attribute defines the center, right or left alignment of the <TABLE> tag.

15. *Which tag is used to add columns to tables ?*

Ans. <TD>

16. *What is the closing tag of HTML?*

Ans. </HTML>

17. *What is the difference between container elements and empty elements?*

Ans. Container elements have opening and closing tags and empty elements has only one tag that is opening.

18. *What is the use of size attribute of <HR> tag?*

Ans. The size attribute specifies the height of the rule in pixels.

19. *Write the extension of HTML code file.*

Ans. .html or .htm.

20. *What is the use of <SUP> tag in HTML?*

Ans. The <SUP> tag defines superscript text, which appears half a character above the normal line.

21. *What do you mean by hypertext?*

Ans. Hypertext acts as a link on which you click to navigate to the desired location.

22. *Which attribute is used to set an image in the background of the table?*

Ans. background

23. *Define rowspan attribute.*

Ans. rowspan attribute is used to span multiple rows.

24. *What is the difference between <THEAD> and <TFOOT> tags?*

Ans. The <THEAD> tag is used to add a header in a table while <TFOOT> tag is used to add a footer in a table.

25. *How is a password text box different from ordinary text box?*

Ans. In password text box, the text entered is shown as asterisk (*) whereas in ordinary text box, the text is simply shown in as it is.

26. *Name different control types supported by HTML form.*

Ans. HTML supports various control types, these are : checkbox, radio button, text box, password, listbox and combo box.

27. *Which method of HTML form is used to send the information to the server?*

Ans. GET

28. *Write the syntax of <INPUT> tag in HTML.*

Ans. <INPUT type = "fieldtype" name = "fieldname" value = "fieldtext">

29. *Give the attributes of the <SELECT> tag.*

Ans. name, size and disabled

30. *Which selector use the hash (#) character in CSS?*

Ans. id selector

31. *What is the difference between check box and radio button?*

Ans. Checkbox allow multiple selections at a time and radio buttons allow only a single selection at a time.

32. ***Elaborate the term CSS.***

Ans. Cascading Style Sheets

33. ***What do you mean by margin property in CSS?***

Ans. The CSS margin properties are used to create space around elements, outside of any defined borders.

34. ***How can you use a picture as a link?***

Ans. We can put an <IMG> tag between <A> and </A> tags, so the user can click on the picture to follow the link.

35. ***How is spacing in cells of table controlled?***

Ans. Cellspacing can be controlled by cellspacing and cellpadding attributes of table.

Abbreviation and Glossary

Abbreviation

ADSL	Asymmetric Digital Subscriber Line
AMV	Animated Music Video
ARPANET	Advanced Research Projects Agency NETwork
ASCII	American Standard Code for Information Interchange
ATM	Automated Teller Machine
B2B	Business to Business
B2C	Business to Consumer
Bcc	Blind carbon copy
B2G	Business to Government
BPL	Broadband over Power Lines
BWA	Broadband Wireless Access
C2B	Consumer to Business
CBI	Computer-Based Instruction
CBT	Computer-Based Training
C2C	Consumer to Consumer
Cc	Carbon copy
CGI	Common Gateway Interface
CPU	Central Processing Unit
CSS	Cascading Style Sheets
DNS	Domain Name System
DSL	Digital Subscriber Line
E-Banking	Electronic Banking
E-Commerce	Electronic Commerce
E-Governance	Electronic Governance
E-Groups	Electronic Groups
E-Learning	Electronic Learning
E-mail	Electronic Mail
E-Reservation	Electronic Reservation
E-Shopping	Electronic Shopping
EULA	End User License Agreement
FAQ	Frequently Asked Questions
FOI	Freedom of Information
FTP	File Transfer Protocol
GBPS	Gigabits Per Second
GPL	General Public License
GUI	Graphical User Interface
HDSL	High-bit-rate Digital Subscriber Line
HTML	HyperText Markup Language
HTTP	HyperText Transfer Protocol
IAB	Internet Architecture Board
IBT	Internet-Based Training
ICT	Information and Communication Technology
IE	Internet Explorer
IETF	Internet Engineering Task Force
IIS	Internet Information Server
IMAP	Internet Message Access Protocol
InterNIC	Internet Network Information Center
IP	Internet Protocol
IPR	Intellectual Property Rights
IPS	Internet Protocol Suite
IRTF	Internet Research Task Force
ISBN	International Standard Book Number
ISOC	Internet Society
ISDN	Integrated Services Digital Network
IT	Information Technology
ISP	Internet Service Provider
Kbps	Kilobits per second
Mbps	Megabits per second
NNTP	Network News Transfer Protocol
NSFnet	National Science Foundation Network
OOS	Open Source Software
PC	Personal Computer
PDA	Personal Digital Assistant
PHP	Personal Home Page/Hypertext Preprocessor
POP	Post Office Protocol
PSTN	Public Switched Telephone Network
RTI	Right to Information
SDSL	Symmetric Digital Subscriber Line
SET	Secure Electronic Transaction
SMTP	Simple Mail Transfer Protocol
SSL	Secure Sockets Layer
TCP	Transmission Control Protocol
URL	Uniform Resource Locator
VHDSL	Very High-bit-rate Digital Subscriber Line
VoIP	Voice over Internet Protocol
WBT	Web-Based Training
Wi-Fi	Wireless Fidelity
WiMAX	Worldwide Interoperability for Microwave Access
WWW	World Wide Web
W3C or **WWWC**	World Wide Web Consortium

Glossary

A

Anchor tag Mark the text as hyperlink.

Animation project It is a project that generally consists of a sequence of images of the motion of objects to create a video.

Application programmer An individual who writes application programs in a user organisation.

ARPANET First operational packet switching network.

Ask Block This block allows users to input any text they want it is widely used when a user must communicate with the project.

Asymmetric Digital Subscriber Line Technology that enables faster data transmission over copper telephone line.

Attributes Provide additional information about the tag in HTML.

B

Backup Copy of file or other item of data made in case the original is lost or damaged.

Blog Discussion or informational site consisting of discrete entities displayed in reverse chronological order.

Blogger A person who writes a blog.

Blogging Act of posting content on a blog.

Broadband connection It is a high speed Internet connection.

Broadband over Power Line It is a method of power line communication that allows relatively high speed digital data transmission over the public electric power distribution wiring.

Bulletin board system Computer or an application dedicated to the sharing of messages on a network.

C

Cascading Style Sheets It is a style sheet language used for describing the presentation of a document written in a markup language like HTML.

Chat Real time informal communication between two users *via* Internet.

Chat rooms Area on Internet that allows users to communicate with each other through instant messaging.

Client Application run on a personal computer.

Colspan This attribute defines the number of columns a table cell should span.

Combo Box It is used to display a drop-down list of some options from which one can be selected.

Communication Activity of exchanging information.

Computer program Sequence of instructions written to perform a specified task with a computer.

Container tag Tag that requires a starting as well as ending tag.

Copyright It is a legal right created by the law of a country that grants the creator of an original work exclusive rights to its use and distribution, usually for a limited time.

Cyber fraud Crime involving the use of Internet to obtain money.

Cyber ethics It refers to a code of safe and responsible behaviour for the Internet community.

D

Data sharing It is the ability to share the same data resource with multiple applications or users.

Definition list It is a list of terms and corresponding definitions. These are typically formatted with the term on the left with the definition following on the right or on the next line.

Dial-up connection Uses a standard phone line and modem to access the Internet at data transfer rates of upto 56 kbps.

Digital Subscriber Line It is a family of technologies that are used to provide Internet access by transmitting digital data over telephone lines.

Domain name Unique name that identifies an Internet resource.

Domain Name System Hierarchical distributed naming system for any resource connected to the Internet.

Download Copy from server computer to client computer over the Internet.

Draft folder Contains messages you started to write but not sent.

E

E-Banking Method of banking in which the customer conducts transactions electronically *via* Internet.

E-Commerce Buying and selling products and services over the Internet.

E-Governance Governing of a Country/State using Information and Communication Technology.

E-Group Group of persons who come together for a specific purpose over the Internet.

E-Learning Use of electronic educational technology in learning and teaching.

E-Mail Electronic method of sending and receiving messages.

E-Mail Address It identifies an E-mail box to which E-mail messages are delivered.

Emoticons Metacommunicative pictorial representation of a facial expression.

Empty tag Element that only has a starting tag but not ending tag.

End User It is the person that a software program or hardware device is designed for.

E-Reservation Reservation *via* Internet.

E-Shopping Form of electronic commerce which allows consumers to directly buy goods or services from a seller over the Internet.

F

File processing system Collection of files and programs that access/modify these files.

Freedom of Information It refers to a citizen's right to access information that is held by the state.

FTP Protocol used to transfer files between server and client.

H

Hacking It is the gaining of access to a computer and viewing, copying or creating data without the intention of destroying data or maliciously harming the computer.

Hardware Physical components that make up a computer system.

High-bit-rate Digital Subscriber Line One of the earliest form of DSL, it is used for wideband digital transmission within a corporate site and between the telephone company and a customer.

Home page First or main page of the Website.

HTML It is used for creating and visually representing a Web page.

HTTP It is the underlying protocol used by the WWW.

Hyperlink It is a word, phrase or image that you can click onto jump to a new document or a new section within the current document.

HyperText Text that links to other information.

I

Identifier It is a name used to identify a variable, function, class, module or other object.

IMAP It is a protocol for E-mail retrieval and storage.

Inbox folder Contains incoming E-mails.

Information Facts provided or learned about something or someone.

Information and Communication Technology It refers to technologies that provide access to information through telecommunications.

Intellectual Property Rights It refers to a general term for the assignment of property rights through patents, copyrights and trademarks.

Internet Global system of interconnected computer networks.

Internet backbone It refers to one of the principle data routes between large, strategically interconnected networks and care routers on the Internet.

Intranet Network that uses IP technology to share information or service within an organisation.

IP address Numerical address assigned to each device participating in a computer network.

ISP It is a company that provides Internet services.

Iteration It means repetition of a set of statements, depending upon a test condition.

K

Keywords These are reserved words that cannot be used as ordinary identifiers.

M

Markup language Way of writing layout information within documents.

Message It is a discrete unit of communication intended by the source for consumption by some recipient or group of recipients.

N

Nested list A list item that can contain another entire list.

Netiquettes It is a code of good behaviour on the Internet.

Net surfing Exploration of WWW.

Newsgroup Internet based discussion about a particular topic.

O

Operators These are special symbols in program that carry out arithmetic or logical computation.

Ordered list A number list of items.

Outbox folder Contains outgoing E-mails or text messages.

P

Packet It is the unit of data that is routed between an origin and destination on the Internet.

Packet Switched Telephone Network It is the aggregate of the world's circuit-switched telephone networks that are operated by national, regional or local telephony operators providing infrastructure and services for public telecommunication.

Plagiarism It is the act of copying or stealing someone else's ideas or information and presenting them as your own.

Piracy It refers to the unauthorised duplication of copyrighted content that is them sold at substantially lower prices in the market.

Pixel It is one of the small units that make up an image on a computer or television screen.

POP It is a protocol used by local E-mail clients to retrieve E-mail from a remote server.

Post Entries of blog.

Privacy It is the state of being free from public scrutiny or from having your secrets or personal information shared.

Programmer A person who writes computer programs.

Protocol Set of rules for data exchange within or between computers.

Python It is an interpreted high-level programming language for general purpose programming.

R

Radio button A radio button or option button is a graphical control element that allows the user to choose only one of a predefined set of mutually exclusive options.

Repeat ( ) block It is a control block and a C block. Blocks held inside this block will loop a given amount of times, before allowing the script to continue.

Rowspan This attribute specifies the number of rows a cell should span.

S

Satellite Artificial object which has been intentionally place into orbit.

Scratch It is a free programming environment that runs in your web browser.

Search engine Software system that is designed to search for information on the WWW.

Search engine algorithm Algorithm applied to Web pages in the search engine idea to determine what are the more relevant pages.

Sent mail folder Contains sent mails or messages.

Server Computer or computer program which manages access to a centralised resource or service in a network.

SMTP It is an Internet standard for E-mail transmission.

Social networking sites Online platform that allows users to create a public profile and interact with other users on the Website.

Software Set of instructions.

Software License It is a license agreement that gives an individual, company or organisation permission to use a software program.

Spam folder Contains junk E-mails or unsolicited E-mails.

Sprite In Scratch, it performs functions controlled by scripts.

Symmetric Digital Subscriber Line It is a type of DSL, which is used for transferring data over copper telephone lines.

T

Table Set of data elements using a model of vertical columns and horizontal rows, the cell being the unit where a row and a column intersect.

Tag Refers to a string enclosed within angular brackets (<and>).

TCP/IP It is the suit of communications protocols that is used to connect hosts on the Internet.

Telnet It is a network protocol that is used on the Internet or LAN to provide a bi-directional interactive text-oriented communication facility using a virtual terminal connection.

Template Complete tracking application.

Token It is the smallest element in a Python program that is meaningful to the compiler. It represents a sequence of characters that can be treated as a single logical unit.

Tempo In a project, it controls how fast or slow the instrumental blocks in Scratch play notes and drum beats.

Trash folder Contains deleted E-mails.

U

Unordered list A bulleted list of items.

Upload Copy from client computer to server over the Internet.

URL It is the global address of documents and other resources on the WWW.

User A person who uses a computer or network service.

User friendly Easy to use, operate and understand.

V

Variable It is a reserved memory location to store values.

Very High-bit-rate Digital Subscriber Line It is a DSL technology that providing data transmission faster than ADSL over a single flat untwisted or twisted pair of copper wires and on co-axial cable.

VoIP It is a technology that allows you to make voice call using a broadband connection.

W

Web address Internet address of a Website, file or document. It is also known as URL.

Web browser Software for retrieving, presenting and traversing information resources on the WWW.

Web crawler Program that visits Websites and reads their pages and other information in order to create entries for a search engine index.

Web Form A web form or HTML form on a Web page allows a user to enter data that is sent to a server for processing.

Web page Web document that is suitable for the WWW and Web browser.

Web portal Website that offers a broad array of resources and services, such as E-mail forums etc.

Web server Computer system that processes request *via* HTTP.

Website Set of related Web pages typically served from a single Web domain.

while loop This statement repeatedly executes a target statement as long as a given condition is true.

Wi-Fi It is a local area wireless technology that allows an electronic device to exchange data or connect to the Internet using radio waves.

WiMAX Technology supporting long distance wireless broadband.

Wired connection Connection establish using cables.

Wireless connection Connection establish using wireless technology.

WWW It is a system of interlinked hypertext document.

Full Form of HTML Tags/Attributes

A	Anchor	**I**	Italic
ALIGN	Alignment	**IMG**	Image
ALINK	Active Link	**LI**	List Item
B	Bold	**OL**	Ordered List
BGCOLOR	Background Color	**P**	Paragraph
BR	Line Break	**SRC**	Source
DD	Definition Description	**TT**	TeleType
DL	Definition List	**U**	Underline
DT	Definition Term	**UL**	Unordered List
HR	Horizontal Rule	**VLINK**	Visited Link

Assertion & Reason Questions

CHAPTER – 1

Directions *In the following questions, A statement of Assertion (A) is followed by a statement of Reason (R). Mark the correct choice as*

(a) Both A and R are true and R is the correct explanation of A.
(b) Both A and R are true but R is not the correct explanation of A.
(c) A is true but R is false.
(d) A is false and R is true.

1. **Assertion** (A) WWW is a subset of the Internet that contains a large set of documents, pictures, videos, links, etc.

Reason (R) WWW is cross-platform dependent.

Ans. (b) Both A and R are true but R is not the correct explanation of A.

2. **Assertion** (A) Web server is a system that delivers the content to an end user over the Internet. Every web server has an IP address and a domain name.

Reason (R) Web client is an application that communicates with a web server using an HTTP protocol.

Ans. (b) Both A and R are true but R is not the correct explanation of A.

3. **Assertion** (A) The content in web site are easily accessible to everybody.

Reason (R) As, it does not require any login credentials.

Ans. (a) Both A and R are true and R is the correct explanation of A.

4. **Assertion** (A) Web portal is the first page which appears when you open a web site.

Reason (R) Social media web sites are platforms which allow the sharing of images or ideas.

Ans. (d) Web portal is an idea of a website or service that offers a broad range of services such as email, games, etc. Only portal member can access the content. It requires login credentials. Social media is a platforms through which you can share your ideas, experience, thoughts or you can upload, download images, audio, video, etc. Facebook, Instagram are some of the popular social media platforms. Hence, A is false and R is true.

5. **Assertion** (A) Static web page is called flat or stationary web page.

Reason (R) The static web page is a page whose changes are not automated.

Ans. (a) Both A and R are true and R is the correct explanation of A.

CHAPTER – 2

Directions *In the following questions, A statement of Assertion (A) is followed by a statement of Reason (R). Mark the correct choice as*

(a) Both A and R are true and R is the correct explanation of A.
(b) Both A and R are true but R is not the correct explanation of A.
(c) A is true but R is false.
(d) A is false and R is true.

1. **Assertion** (A) People may use the ATM cards for withdrawing the cash amount from their accounts.

Reason (R) People can also transfer money online from one bank to another bank.

Ans. (b) Both A and R are true but R is not the correct explanation of A.

2. **Assertion** (A) E-learning refers to the use of the network and communication technology in teaching and learning. The letter "E" in E-learning stands for the word electronic. You can use the information from the internet in your work.

Reason(R) It is not easy for students to access the study material any time and at any place.

Ans. (c) E-learning or "electronic learning" describes education using electronic devices and digital media. It increases your knowledge and skills. E-learning has now been used by various companies, organisations and schools to educate and upgrade the abilities of their employees and students. The term E-learning is used also in further and higher education to describe the use of the web and other Internet technologies to enhance the teaching and learning experience. Hence, A is true but R is false.

3. **Assertion** (A) E-banking saves time of the customer for doing bank transactions.

Reason(R) E-banking allows you to access your accounts on the Internet from anywhere in the world at any time. It provides secure transaction on the Internet.

Ans. (b) Both A and R are true but R is not the correct explanation of A.

4. **Assertion** (A) One can do video conferencing anytime anywhere according to his/her convenience unless the device is connected to the internet.

Reason(R) All video conferences must have these three basic elements, however simple or complex. The conference can always be synthesised into environment, equipment and network.

Ans. (b) Both A and R are true but R is not the correct explanation of A.

5. **Assertion** (A) E-commerce saves time as with just a couple of clicks of the mouse, you can purchase your shopping orders and instantly move to other important things, which can save time.

Reason(R) Going through market requires a lot of time and efforts. And, also there is not guarantee whether the things will be best suited or not.

Ans. (b) Both A and R are true but R is not the correct explanation of A.

CHAPTER – 3

Directions *In the following questions, A statement of Assertion (A) is followed by a statement of Reason (R). Mark the correct choice as*

(a) Both A and R are true and R is the correct explanation of A.
(b) Both A and R are true but R is not the correct explanation of A.
(c) A is true but R is false.
(d) A is false and R is true.

1. **Assertion** (A) The source code to create a web page are to be written in text editors.

Reason(R) Text editors are used by the users who have complete knowledge of HTML.

Ans. (b) Both A and R are true but R is not the correct explanation of A.

2. **Assertion** (A) The <!DOCTYPE> declaration is not an HTML tag.

Reason(R) The <!DOCTYPE> is an instruction to the web browser about what version of HTML the page is written in.

Ans. (b) Both A and R are true but R is not the correct explanation of A.

3. **Assertion** (A) With HTML, you can develop and publish documents and data with headings, text, tables, lists, hyperlinks, photos, etc., in static form.

Reason(R) You can create forms for managing transactions, for use in searching the information, making reservations, ordering products, etc.

Ans. (b) Both A and R are true but R is not the correct explanation of A.

4. **Assertion** (A) HTML is a platform independent language.

Reason(R) As the same HTML program works on any operating system without any modification.

Ans. (a) Both A and R are true and R is the correct explanation of A.

5. **Assertion** (A) In HTML, the tag <HTML>is same as <html>.

Reason(R) HTML is not a case sensitive language.

Ans. (a) Both A and R are true and R is the correct explanation of A.

6. Assertion (A) Attributes provides additional information about HTML elements used to create a web page.
   Reason(R) Attributes are always mentioned in the end tag.

Ans. (c) Attributes gives some additional information about the tag. All HTML elements can have their own attributes. Attributes are always mentioned in the start tag. Hence, A is true but R is false.

CHAPTER – 4

Directions *In the following questions, A statement of Assertion (A) is followed by a statement of Reason (R). Mark the correct choice as*

(a) Both A and R are true and R is the correct explanation of A.
(b) Both A and R are true but R is not the correct explanation of A.
(c) A is true but R is false.
(d) A is false and R is true.

1. Assertion (A) External links which link your pages to another web page. i.e. linking between two different documents.
   Reason (R) In order to create an external link to another website, you need to know the other website's URL with Full path.

Ans. (b) Both A and R are true but R is not the correct explanation of A.

2. Assertion (A) The full form of href is higher text reference.
   Reason(R) The value of the href attribute is the location (URL) of the external resource.

Ans. (d) The full form of href is hyper text reference. Hence, A is false and R is true.

3. Assertion (A) The mailto link is a type of HTML link that activates the default mail client on the computer for sending an e-mail.
   Reason (R) The web browser requires a default e-mail client software installed on his computer in order to activate the e-mail client.

Ans. (b) Both A and R are true but R is not the correct explanation of A.

CHAPTER – 5

Directions *In the following questions, A statement of Assertion (A) is followed by a statement of Reason (R). Mark the correct choice as*

(a) Both A and R are true and R is the correct explanation of A.
(b) Both A and R are true but R is not the correct explanation of A.
(c) A is true but R is false.
(d) A is false and R is true.

1. Assertion (A) Cell spacing in a table is used to put more space around each cell. It defines the space between cells.
   Reason (R) By default, cell spacing width is 2 pixels.

Ans. (b) Both A and R are true but R is not the correct explanation of A.

2. Assertion (A) You can have rows with different columns.
   Reason (R) The colspan attribute of <TABLE> tag is used to merge two or more columns in one.

Ans. (a) Both A and R are true and R is the correct explanation of A.

3. Assertion (A) When data is arranged in a table, it gives a more flexible and attractive way to represent information.
   Reason (R) A table is used to arrange data in the form of rows and columns.

Ans. (a) Both A and R are true and R is the correct explanation of A.

4. **Assertion** (A) The border attribute in <TABLE>is used to specify the border of the table.

Reason (R) If the border attribute is not specified then the table will appear without any border.

Ans. (a) Both A and R are true and R is the correct explanation of A.

5. **Assertion** (A) The valign attribute specifies the alignment of the cell contents vertically.

Reason (R) The value of the valign attribute can be Top, Middle or Bottom.

Ans. (b) Both A and Rare true but R is not the correct explanation of A.

6. **Assertion** (A) The width attribute specifies the height of a table.

Reason (R) The width attribute of <TABLE> is not supported in HTML5.

Ans. (d) width attribute specifies the width of the cells in the table. Hence, A is false and R is true.

CHAPTER – 6

Directions *In the following questions, A statement of Assertion (A) is followed by a statement of Reason (R). Mark the correct choice as*

(a) Both A and R are true and R is the correct explanation of A.
(b) Both A and R are true but R is not the correct explanation of A.
(c) A is true but R is false.
(d) A is false and R is true.

1. **Assertion** (A) It is not possible to have a form inside a form.

Reason (R) A form cannot be nested.

Ans. (a) Both A and R are true and R is the correct explanation of A.

2. **Assertion** (A) The <FORM NAME="Form Name"> specifies the name of the form.

Reason (R) The form name is always displayed on the form.

Ans. (c) The name of the form is not displayed on the form. As the user can have more than one <FORM> tags in an HTML document, so to differentiate one Form from another, a name is required to be given. Name attribute is optional if only one <FORM> tag is used. Hence, A is true and R is false.

3. **Assertion** (A) The <INPUT> tag is required when the user has to give some input/data.

Reason (R) The <INPUT> tag is not a compulsory tag used within the <FORM> tag.

Ans. (c) The <INPUT> tag is required when the user has to give some input/data. This tag is always used within the <FORM> tag. Hence, A is true but R is false.

4. **Assertion** (A) The controls attribute of < VIDEO > tag takes Boolean value (True or False).

Reason (R) The user had to give the value as True or False to controls attribute.

Ans. (a) Both A and R are true and R is the correct explanation of A.

CHAPTER – 7

Directions *In the following questions, A statement of Assertion (A) is followed by a statement of Reason (R). Mark the correct choice as*

(a) Both A and R are true and R is the correct explanation of A.
(b) Both A and R are true but R is not the correct explanation of A.
(c) A is true but R is false.
(d) A is false and R is true.

1. **Assertion** (A) Digital rights are the process of relationship between copyrighted digital works and user permissions and rights related to computers, networks and electronic devices.

Reason (R) Certain digital right/digital rights management (DRM) sub categories are of growing concern such as information/Internet privacy and freedom of information.

Ans. (b) Both A and R are true but R is not the correct explanation of A.

2. **Assertion** (A) Digital divide includes the imbalance both in physical access to technology and the resources and skills needed to effectively participate as a digital citizen.

Reason (R) The term global digital divide refers to similarities in access between countries in regards to the Internet and its means of information flow.

Ans. (c) Digital divide refers to the gap between individuals, households, businesses and geographic areas at different socio-economic levels with regard both to their opportunities to access Information and Communications Technologies (ICT's) and to their use of the Internet for a wide variety of activities. Hence, A is true but R is false.

3. **Assertion** (A) E-commerce security is defined as a set of protocols that safely guide ecommerce transactions.

Reason (R) Security is an important part of any transaction that takes place over the internet.

Ans. (a) Both A and R are true and R is the correct explanation of A.

4. **Assertion** (A) Credit card details can be safely sent with SSL (Secure Socket Layer), but then also it is not saved.

Reason (R) Once the details are stored on the server, they are vulnerable to outsiders hacking into the server and accompanying network.

Ans. (a) Both A and Rare true and R is the correct explanation of A.

CBSE
EXAMINATION PAPERS 2023-25

CBSE

EXAMINATION PAPER 2023

COMPUTER APPLICATIONS

Instructions

1. This questions paper has 5 Sections A-E.
2. All questions are compulsory. However, an internal choice of approximately 30% is provided.
3. Section A has 12 questions carrying 1 mark each.
4. Section B has 7 Very Short Answer (VSA) type questions carrying 2 marks each.
5. Section C has 4 Short Answer (SA) type questions carrying 3 marks each.
6. Section D has 1 Long Answer (LA) type question carrying 4 marks.
7. Section E has 2 Source-based/Case-based/Passage-based questions carrying 4 marks each.

Time : 2 hours ***Max. Marks : 50***

FULLY SOLVED

Section A

(12 × 1 = 12)

1. Suhani asks her colleague for her project work and then copies the entire work and submits it to her team leader claiming it to be her own work. The act performed by Suhani is known as ....

(a) Phishing (b) Plagiarism (c) Spamming (d) Virus

2. Which of the following is the correct expansion of SMS?

(a) Small Message Service (b) Small Multimedia Service

(c) Short Multimedia Service (d) Short Message Service

3. Which of the following is an E-Shopping portal?

(a) Diksha (b) Swayam (c) Flipkart (d) NPTEL

4. Which of the following is not an E-Governance portal?

(a) e-Aadhaar (b) DigiLocker (c) Sarathi (d) Zomato

5. The protocol that is used to send e-mails is ....

(a) HTTP (b) POP (c) SMTP (d) FTP

6. SFTP is used for

(a) sending files over the Internet in a secure manner

(b) sending mail over the Internet in a secure manner

(c) video conferencing

(d) secure chat service

7. Which of the following is not an attribute of <IMG> tag in HTML?

(a) source (b) width (c) alt (d) color

8. HTML provides us with .... levels of headings that can be inserted in a web page.

(a) 5 (b) 6 (c) 7 (d) 8

9. Which of the following options is an invalid attribute of <FONT> tag in HTML?

(a) face (b) width (c) size (d) color

10. The default starting value for an ordered list in HTML is ....

(a) i (b) 1 (c) a (d) .

Directions *Q.Nos. 11 and 12 are Assertion and Reason types. Each question consists of two statements, namely, Assertion (A) and Reason (R). Select the most suitable option considering the Assertion and Reason.*

11. **Assertion** (A) MOOC helps geographically dispersed students to pursue any online course.

Reason (R) MOOC is a free web-based distance learning program.

(a) Both Assertion (A) and Reason (R) are true and Reason (R) is the correct explanation of Assertion (A).
(b) Both Assertion (A) and Reason (R) are true and Reason (R) is not the correct explanation of Assertion (A).
(c) Assertion (A) is true but Reason (R) is false.
(d) Assertion (A) is false and Reason (R) is true.

12. **Assertion** (A)
 is a container tag.

Reason (R) HTML elements that have both opening and closing tags are considered container tags.

(a) Both Assertion (A) and Reason (R) are true and Reason (R) is the correct explanation of Assertion (A).
(b) Both Assertion (A) and Reason (R) are true and Reason (R) is not the correct explanation of Assertion (A).
(c) Assertion (A) is true and Reason (R) is false.
(d) Assertion (A) is false and Reason (R) is true.

Section B

(7 × 2 = 14)

13. Write one difference between chat and E–mail service.

14. (a) What is E–Governance? Write the names of any two services that can be provided using E–Governance.

Or

(b) What is Internet? How can we retrieve information from the Internet?

15. How can we embed audio in an HTML document? Give an example to support your answer.

16. (a) Define licensed software. Write names of any two licensed software.

Or

(b) How can we reduce digital divide? Give any two points.

17. How is CSS beneficial for web page development? Give any two points.

18. (a) Illustrate the use of the radio button input type on an HTML form with an appropriate code and the corresponding output.

Or

(b) Write the difference between <OL> and <UL> tags in HTML. Also write suitable examples of each to illustrate the difference.

19. What is the difference between <BR> tag and <P> tag in context of HTML? Illustrate using suitable examples.

Section C

(4 × 3 = 12)

20. How do Intellectual Property Rights provide protection to digital work? Write any two ways to avoid plagiarism.

21. Consider the following URLs

https://www.practicepayment.com____ URL1.

http://www.practicepayment.com____URL2.

(a) What is the difference between URL1 and URL2?

(b) Which of the two URLs will you prefer to use and why?

(c) Expand www.

FULLY SOLVED

22. (a) Write the equivalent CSS code to set the following styles for a web page

(i) Entire page background color should be yellow

(ii) Second level Heading properties should be as follows:

- Text color should be Red
- Left margin should be 25 px.

Or

(b) (i) Write a CSS code to display the first level heading text as "My School" in Green color and center-aligned.

(ii) Write the CSS code to display the following paragraph below the above mentioned heading:

This is my School

I study in class 12

The properties of the paragraph content should be as follows:

- Text color should be yellow
- Font size should be 25 px
- Font style should be bold.

23. Write the full form of the following protocols

(a) HTTPs (b) TCP (c) SSH

Section D

(4)

24. (a) Write the HTML code to design the web page as shown below, considering the specifications that follow. You can write the code for any four specifications out of the given six specifications.

Home Services

We are happy to provide you all help at your residence.

Special discount offers from (1st May, 2022 to 30th June, 2022).

Please contact us for the following services:

- Maid/Servant (Cleaning)
- Maid/Servant (Cooking)
- Driver

Queries:help@homeservices.com

Specifications:

- The background color of the page should be yellow and the text for the page should be in blue color.
- Heading 'Home Services' should be the first level of heading.
- The image named 'service.png' should be placed on the web page.
- Font size for the paragraph and the list of services should be 4 and Font face should be Verdana. Superscript tags should be used wherever required.

- The services (as shown in the above web page) should be written with the help of the unordered list.
- The bottom-most line of 'Queries: help@homeservices.com' should be a link to open the user's default mail client to send queries to the mentioned email id.

Or

(b)

> **Events**
> The following events are scheduled to be held on 1st April, 2023.
> The timings are as follows:
> 1. 9.00 AM–10.00 AM Flag Hoisting
> 2. 10.00 AM–11.00 AM Painting Competition
> 3. 11.00 AM–12.30 PM Dance Competition
> 4. 12.30 PM–1.30 PM Song Competition
> 5. 1.30 PM–2.00 PM Closing Ceremony
>
> For any queries contact queries@event.com
> Phone : 9999999999

Write the HTML code to design the above shown web page titled 'Events', considering the specifications as given below. You can write the code for any four specifications out of the given six specifications.

Specifications:

- The background color of the page should be cyan, the font face for the page should be Arial.
- Heading 'Events' should be the first level of heading.
- Font size for the paragraph and the list of products should be 5.
- The schedule (as shown in the above web page) should be written with the help of the numbered list. Superscript tags should be used wherever required.
- The bottom-most lines of 'For any queries...' and 'Phone : ...... ' should be in bold.
- The contact email queries@event.com should be a link to open the user's default mail client to send queries to the mentioned email id.

Section E

(2 × 4 = 8)

(Case Study)

25. Arif works in a school as a web designer. He has been assigned the task of uploading the calendar of holidays for the month of March. He was supposed to design an HTML table for the same.

Help him to complete the table with the right statements in the blanks. Observe the table and attempt any four questions (out of five) given after the table.

MARCH 2023							
DAYS	Mon	Tue	Wed	Thu	Fri	Sat	Sun
DATES	6	7	8	9	10	11	12
		14					

```
<HTML>
<HEAD>
   <TITLE> </TITLE>
</ HEAD>
```

```
<BODY>
<TABLE>
  <TR>
    <TD colspan =..........> MARCH 2023 </TD>            Statement-1
  </TR>
...............                                        Statement-2
    <TH> DAYS </TH>
    <TH> Mon </TH>
    <TH> Tue </TH>
    <TH> Wed </TH>
    <TH> Thu </TH>
    <TH> Fri </TH>
    <TH> Sat </TH>
    <TH> Sun </TH>
    ...............                                    Statement-3
  <TR>
    <TD ............ = 2 > DATES </TD>                 Statement-4
    <TD> 6 </TD>
    <TD> 7 </TD>
    <TD> 8 </TD>
    <TD> 9 </TD>
    <TD> 10 </TD>
    <TD> 11 </TD>
    <TD> 12 </TD>
  </TR>
  <TR>
    <TD> </TD>
    <TD>..........</TD>                                Statement-5
  </TR>
</TABLE>
</BODY>
</HTML>
```

(a) Write the attribute value to complete Statement-1 to achieve the output as given in the above table.
(b) Write the tag to complete Statement-2 to achieve the output as given in the above table.
(c) Write the attribute value to complete Statement-3 to achieve the output as given in the above table.
(d) Write the attribute name to complete Statement-4 to achieve the output as given in the above table.
(e) Write the appropriate answer for the blank given in Statement-5 to achieve the output as given in the above table.

26. Rashmi is a student of ABC School. She has been provided with an email id from the school to use for all academic correspondences. She generally receives all her school's correspondences on this email.

One day she was working in the computer lab, and after her work was over, she forgot to logout of her email account. When she left the computer lab, her classmate, Prabhnoor sends objectionable emails from the same email id, to her teachers, so as to malign Rashmi.

Based on the given situation, attempt any four (out of five) fill-ups/questions given below:

(a) Prabhnoor has invaded _______ of Rashmi.

FULLY SOLVED

(b) Rashmi informs her class teacher about the incident. The teacher calls Prabhnoor and makes him aware of_______, which is following ethical principles while working online.

(c) The teacher also advises all students never to share their _____ with anyone.

(d) Rashmi has learnt that she should always ______ of her email account once her work is complete.

(e) Prabhnoor is now aware of ethical practices to be followed while working over the Internet and decides to guide his friends and relatives about the same. Write any two points that Prabhnoor should advise them to do while working online.

Answers

1. (*b*) The act performed by Suhani is known as plagiarism.
2. (*d*) Short Message Service is the correct expansion of SMS.
3. (*c*) Flipkart is an e-Shopping portal.
4. (*d*) Zomato is not an e-Governance portal.
5. (*c*) SMTP is a protocol that is used to send e-mails.
6. (*a*) SFTP is used for sending files over the Internet in a secure manner.
7. (*d*) color is not an attribute of <IMG> tag in HTML.
8. (*c*) HTML provides us with 6 levels of headings that can be inserted in a web page.
9. (*b*) width is an invalid attribute of <FONT> tag in HTML.
10. (*b*) The default starting value for an ordered list in HTML is 1.
11. (*a*) Both Assertion (A) and Reason (R) are true and Reason (R) is the correct explanation of Assertion (A).
12. (*d*) HTML elements with no content are called empty elements.
 is an empty element without a closing tag (the <BR> tag defines a line break). So <BR> tag is not a container tag. Hence, Assertion (A) is false and Reason (R) is true.
13. The difference between chat and E-mail service chat needs the permission of both parties while Email does not require. Chat is generally software-reliant while Email is not. Chat requires accounts on the same provider while Email does not. Chat is able to convey voice and audio while Email cannot.
14. (a) E-Governance refers to the use of electronic means and technology to facilitate and enhance the delivery of government services and information to citizens, businesses, and other stakeholders. It involves the use of various digital technologies such as the internet, computers, mobile devices, and other electronic media to provide information and services to the public.

    Two examples of services that can be provided using E-Governance are Online Tax Filing, E-Passports.

    Or

    (b) Internet is a global system of interconnected computer networks that allows communication and sharing of information among users worldwide.

    We can retrieve information from the Internet in various ways, including:

    (i) Search Engines
    (ii) Websites
    (iii) Social Media
    (iv) Online Libraries
    (v) Online Forums
    (vi) Online Videos
15. Refer to text on page no. 126.
16. (a) Refer to Q.No. 2 on page 154.

    Or

    (b) To reduce digital divide, we can consider two points as given below

    (i) **Increasing accessibility** The first step towards reducing the digital divide is to increase accessibility. Governments and NGOs can provide access to digital technologies and the Internet in remote, rural and underserved areas. This can be done by setting up community centers, providing low-cost or subsidized devices and data plans, and training people on how to use them.

(ii) **Improving digital literacy** It's not enough to just provide access to digital technologies, people also need to be empowered with the skills to use them effectively. Digital literacy programs can be conducted in schools and communities to help people learn basic computer skills, digital communication, online safety and security, and more. This will enable them to access the benefits of the digital world and participate in the digital economy.

17. CSS beneficial for web page development, we can consider two points as given below

(i) CSS helps to separate the presentation of a web page from its structure and content. This makes it easier to update and maintain a site, as changes to the design can be made quickly and easily without affecting the underlying HTML code.

(ii) CSS allows web designers to create a consistent and cohesive look and feel across multiple pages of a site. By defining styles and formatting rules in a single stylesheet, designers can ensure that all pages on a site have a unified appearance and are easy to navigate. This can help to improve user experience and increase engagement with the site.

18. (a) Refer to text on page no 125.

Or

(b) Here is a table summarizing the differences between <OL> and <UL> tags in HTML:

	<UL> (unordered list)	**<OL> (ordered list)**
Display	Displays list items with bullet points.	Displays list items with numbers or letters.
Order	Does not follow a specific order or sequence.	Follows a specific order or sequence.
Default Style	Default bullet point style can be customized using CSS.	Default numbering or lettering style can be customized using CSS.
e.g.	<UL><LI>Item 1</LI><LI>Item 2</LI><LI>Item 3</LI></UL>	<OL><LI>First item</LI><LI>Second item</LI><LI>Third item</LI></OL>
Output	• Item 1 • Item 2 • Item 3	1. First item 2. Second item 3. Third item

19. Refer to Q.No. 6 on page 68.

20. Intellectual Property Rights (IPR) provide protection to digital work by granting exclusive rights to the creators of digital works, such as software, music, movies, and books. These rights allow the creators to control the distribution, reproduction, and use of their works, and prevent others from using them without permission. The two main forms of IPR that provide protection to digital works are:

Copyright Copyright is a legal right that grants the creator of an original work exclusive rights to its use and distribution. In the digital realm, copyright protects digital works such as software, music, movies, and books from being copied, distributed, or used without permission.

Patents Patents are legal rights that protect inventions, including digital ones such as software and hardware. A patent gives the inventor the exclusive right to use and license their invention, preventing others from copying or using it without permission.

Two ways to avoid plagiarism are:

Cite your sources Whenever you use someone else's work, whether it's a direct quote, paraphrase, or summary, you should always give credit to the original source. This can be done by including a citation in your text, such as a footnote or in-text citation, and by including a bibliography or works cited page at the end of your document.

Use plagiarism detection tools There are many tools available that can help you check your work for plagiarism. These tools compare your text to a vast database of existing content to identify any similarities and can help you identify areas where you may need to revise your work to avoid plagiarism. Examples of such tools include Turnitin, Grammarly, and Copyscape.

21. (a) The difference between URLI and URL2 is that URL1 uses HTTPs while URL2 uses HTTP. HTTPs stands for HyperText Transfer Protocol secure, which means that the website is using a more secure connection, encrypted with SSL/TLS. This is important for protecting sensitive information, such as payment information, that is being transmitted through the website. HTTP stands for HyperText Transfer Protocol. It is a protocol using which hypertext is transferred over the Web. Due to its simplicity, http has been the most widely used protocol for data transfer over the Web but the data (i.e. hypertext) exchanged using http isn't as secure.

(b) I would prefer to use URL1 (https://www.practicepayment.com) because it uses a more secure connection, which is important for protecting any payment information that I may enter on the website.

FULLY SOLVED

(c) www stands for World Wide Web. It is the prefix used to identify the host or website on the internet.

22. (a) (i)
```
body
        background-color: yellow;
        }
```
(ii)
```
h2 {
        color: red;
        margin-left: 25px;
        }
```
Or (b) (i) Here's the CSS code to achieve that:
```
h1 {
    color: green;
    text-align: center;
    }
```
This will select all the first level headings (<h1> tags) on your page and apply the specified styles to them. The color property sets the text color to green, while the text-align property centers the text within the heading element.

(ii)
```
<h1>This is the heading</h1>
<p>This is my School<br>
I study in class 12</p>
```
Make sure to place this code in the '<style>' tag or in an external CSS file and link it to your HTML document. And then, wrap the paragraph text in a <p> tag:
```
p {
        color: yellow;
        font-size: 25px;
        font-weight: bold;
        }
```
This will display the paragraph with yellow text, bold font, and a font size of 25 pixels.

23. (a) HTTPs stands for HyperText Transfer Protocol secure.

(b) TCP stands for Transmission Control Protocol.

(c) SSH stands for Secure Shell.

24. (a) Here is the HTML code to design the home services web page with the given specifications
```
<HTML>
<HEAD>
  <TITLE>Home Services</TITLE>
  <STYLE type = "text/css">
    body
    {
      background-color: yellow;
      color: blue;
      font-family: Verdana, sans-serif;
      font-size: 4em;
    }
  </STYLE>
</HEAD>
<BODY>
  <H1>Home Services</H1>
  <IMG src="service.png" alt="Service Image">
  <P>We are happy to provide you all help at your residence. </P>
  <P>Special discount offers from (1 <SUP>st</SUP>May, 2022 to 30<SUP>th</SUP> June, 2022). </P>
  <P>Please contact us for the following services:</P>
```

FULLY SOLVED

```
  <UL>
     <LI>Maid/Servant (Cleaning)</LI>
     <LI>Maid/Servant (Cooking)</LI>
     <LI>Driver</li>
  </UL>
  <P>Queries:<A href="mailto:help@homeservices.com">help@homeservices.com</A></P>
</BODY>
</HTML>
```

Or

(b) Here is the HTML code to design the Events web page with the given specifications:

```
<HTML>
<HEAD>
  <TITLE>Events</TITLE>
  <STYLE>
     body
     {
        background-color: cyan;
        font-family: Arial;
        font-size: 5em;
     }
     H1
     {
        font-size: 1.5em;
     }
     .bold
     {
        font-weight: bold;
     }
  </STYLE>
</HEAD>
<BODY>
  <H1>Events</H1>
  <P>
     The following events are scheduled to be held on 1<SUP>st</SUP> April, 2023.
  </P>
  <OL>
     <LI>
        9.00 AM -10.00 AM Flag Hoisting
     </LI>
     <LI>
        10.00 AM - 11.00 AM Painting Competition
     </LI>
     <LI>
        11.00 AM - 12.30 PM Dance Competition
     </LI>
     <LI>
        12.30 PM - 1.30 PM Song competition
     </LI>
     <LI>
        1.30 PM - 2.00 PM Closing Ceremony
     </LI>
```

FULLY SOLVED

```
    </OL>
    <P class="bold">
      For any queries contact <A href="mailto:queries@event.com">queries@event.com</A>
    </P>
    <P class="bold">
      Phone : 9999999999
    </P>
  </BODY>
  </HTML>
```

25. (a) 8

(b) <TR>

(c) </TR>

(d) rowspan

(e) 14

26. (a) Prabhnoor has invaded the privacy of Rashmi.

(b) Rashmi informs her class teacher about the incident. The teacher calls Prabhnoor and makes him aware of the importance of cyber security, which is following ethical principles while working online.

(c) The teacher also advises all students never to share their login credentials with anyone.

(d) Rashmi has learnt that she should always log out of her email account once her work is complete.

(e) Prabhnoor is now aware of ethical practices to be followed while working over the Internet and decides to guide his friends and relatives about the same. Two points that Prabhnoor should advise them to do while working online are:

(i) Use strong passwords and enable two-factor authentication: Prabhnoor should advise his friends and relatives to use strong passwords that are difficult to guess and enable two-factor authentication whenever possible. This will help prevent unauthorized access to their accounts and keep their personal information secure.

(ii) Be cautious when clicking on links or downloading attachments: Prabhnoor should advise his friends and relatives to be cautious when clicking on links or downloading attachments from unknown sources. They should verify the source and check for any signs of suspicious activity before clicking on any links or downloading any attachments. This will help prevent malware infections and phishing attacks.

CBSE
EXAMINATION PAPER 2024
COMPUTER APPLICATIONS

FULLY SOLVED

Instructions

1. This question paper has 5 Sections A, B, C, D, E.
2. All questions are compulsory. However, an internal choice of approximately 30% is provided.
3. Section A has 12 questions carrying 1 mark each.
4. Section B has 7 Very Short Answer (VSA) type questions carrying 2 marks each.
5. Section C has 4 Short Answer (SA) type questions carrying 3 marks each.
6. Section D has 1 Long Answer (LA) type question carrying 4 marks.
7. Section E has 2 Source-based/Case-based/Passage-based questions carrying 4 marks each.

Time : 2 hours ***Max. Marks : 50***

Section A

(12 × 1 = 12)

1. The letter S in the abbreviation HTTPS in context of Networking protocols, stands for
(a) Single (b) Static (c) Secure (d) Sensitive

2. Which of the following in not a web service?
(a) Using Diksha learning portal (b) Sending and receiving email
(c) File transfer over bluetooth (d) Using a banking portal for online transaction

3. In 3G and 4G mobile technologies, the character 'G' stands for
(a) Generation (b) GPRS (c) Grid (d) Google

4. A website or online platform where individuals or groups regularly publish written content, typically in a reverse chronological order is known as
(a) News Group (b) Blog (c) Chat Group (d) Social Networking

5. Which of the following is not an attribute of the <font> tag?
(a) face (b) height (c) size (d) color

6. In HTML, we start a comment using
(a) <!-- (b) !--> (c) --!> (d) <--!

7. Which of the following elements have both the opening and the closing tags in HTML?
(a)
 (b) <h1> (c) <hr> (d) <img>

8. The default colour of vlink is ......
(a) Green (b) Purple (c) Blue (d) Yellow

9. Which of the following tags in not used while creating a description list?
(a) <dt> (b) <dl> (c) <td> (d) <dd>

10. Which of the following is not an example of an Open Source Software?
(a) Linux (b) Android (c) Photoshop (d) OpenOffice

Direction *Questions No. 11 and 12 are Assertion and Reason type questions. Each question consists of two statements, namely, Assertion (A) and Reason (R). Select the most suitable option considering the Assertion and Reason.*

11. **Assertion** (A) When you enter a query into a search engine, it retrieves and presents a list of web pages, documents, images, videos, or other types of content that are relevant to your search.
Reason (R) The goal of information retrieval is to effectively and efficiently find and present information that matches the user's search criteria.
(a) Both Assertion (A) and Reason (R) are true and Reason (R) is the correct explanation of Assertion (A).
(b) Both Assertion (A) and Reason (R) are true but Reason (R) is the not the correct explanation of Assertion (A).
(c) Assertion (A) is true, but Reason (R) is false.
(d) Assertion (A) is false, but Reason (R) is true.

12. **Assertion** (A) It becomes difficult to update and maintain a website's design using CSS.
Reason (R) CSS allows web developers to separate the presentation layer (styles and layout) from the content layer (HTML).
(a) Both Assertion (A) and Reason (R) are true and Reason (R) is the correct explanation of Assertion (A).
(b) Both Assertion (A) and Reason (R) are true but Reason (R) is not the correct explanation of Assertion (A).
(c) Assertion (A) is true, but Reason (R) is false.
(d) Assertion (A) is false, but Reason (R) is true.

FULLY SOLVED

Section B

($7 \times 2 = 14$)

13. Write any two points of comparison between Chat and Email in context web services.

14. (a) Write in brief about any two advantages of e-Banking.

Or

(b) Write in brief one advantage and one limitation of e-Reservation.

15. Write any one point of difference between a webpage and a website.

16. (a) Explain in brief about any two factors that are responsible for the digital divide.

Or

(b) What are software licenses ? Give one example each of a free license and a proprietary software.

17. Write any two significances of using links in an HTML webpage.

18. (a) Match the tag with their corresponding correct attribute.

Tag	Attribute
<table>	start
<input>	rowspan
<ol>	type
<td>	border

Or

(b) Differentiate between bgcolor and background attributes of <body> tag. Write one HTML statement explaining the use of each attribute.

19. Write suitable html statements to display the following text on a webpage in appropriate subscript and superscript form
(a) H_2O
(b) $E = MC^2$

Section C

(4 × 3 = 12)

20. A school wants to create a webpage for the announcement of orientation programme of its Cultural Club as shown below

> **ABC International School**
> Cultural Club
> Orientation programme on 15th March 2024

The school wants all the 3 lines to appear a Headings and Subheadings

- The first line containing its name to have the boldest possible appearance as a heading in Blue color.
- The second line containing the Club name should appear as a heading but its size should be smaller than the first line in green color.
- The third line containing the Programme details should appear as a heading and its size should be smaller than the previous two lines in Cyan color.

Suggest the html code to get the desired appearance of the lines in the webpage.

21. Ayesha has shot some videos. She wants to create a webpage so as to share her creations with her followers across the world. Help Ayesha to embed her video file in the web page with the following specifications

- The name of video file in Ayeshahits .mp4
- The video should play in a window of width 350 pixels and height 250 pixels.
- The video controls such as Play, Pause and and Volume should be visible.

22. (a) Online Gadgets is an electronic products company.The company wishes to sell its products online for which they want to launch its website. The homepage of the website should contain the images of its products which are saved as PHONE .JPG and TV. JPG. The company wishes to open the webpage named ALLPHONES. HTML when the image PHONE. JPG is clicked.Similarly, on clicking the image TV. JPG a different webpage named as ALLTVS. HTML should open. Ensure that both the image should get displayed with a width of 200 pixels and a height of 150 pixels.
Write the code to achieve the desired result.
Note : Assume that the image and both the webpages are stored in the same folder.

Or

(b) Write the HTML code to design the content of the webpage in the form of lists as shown below.

> Here is a shopping list with categories and items
> 1. Vegetables
>   - Carrots
>   - Broccoli
>   - Spinach
> 2. Fruits
>   - Apples
>   - Oranges
>   - Bananas

23. Explain the term "Plagiarism". Write in brief any two examples to illustrate acts of Plagiarism.

Section D

(4)

24. (a) Write the HTML code to design a Student's Data input form as shown below

Student Data Input Form

Name : [   ]

Subscribe for Newsletter : ☐

Gender :

Male ○ Female ○ Other ○

Country

[USA ∨]

The following input elements should be included in the form

- A textbox to enter student's name.
- A checkbox to allow the student to subscribe to a newsletter.
- Radio buttons to select the gender. The buttons should be grouped with individual values as Male, Female, Other.
- A list box (select dropdown) to choose the country. The available options are USA, Canada, UK and Australia.

Or

(b) Observe the screenshot of the following content in a webpage and write the HTML code to generate the desired output

	ACTIVITY	MEMBER NAME	AGE	EMAIL
DETAILS	Chess Club	John Doe	28	john.doe@example.com
	Photography Club	Jane Smith	24	jane.smith@example.com
	Football Club	Michael Johnson	31	michael.johnson@example.com

Note : The table border size should be 1.

Section E

(Case Study)

$(2 \times 4 = 8)$

25. Suraj is a novice in digital communication. He has recently joined a company, where most communications happen over the Internet. On multiple occasions Suraj faces problems while working over the Internet. Help him by answering the following questions

(a) Suraj is asked to send an email to his supervisor. He types in the content and provides the email address of the recipient as **www.gmail.com**. How is the address typed by Suraj different from the email address of the recipient?

(b) Suraj has been asked to create a video conferencing link and share the link with all co-workers who are working from home. Suggest any two softwares which he can use for the purpose.

(c) Suraj has been asked to upload a file containing transaction details and send it to his colleagues in the office. Which Internet protocol will be used by him and by his colleagues in the office to upload and download the file over the Internet? Write the abbreviation as well as the full form of the protocol to be used.

(d) Suraj has been asked to use a social networking site to promote sales of the company's products. Suggest him two commonly used social networking sites, where he can post about the product and promote the company's sales.

26. Raghu is a painter and blogger. He regularly updates his paintings on his blog. Recently he saw one of his paintings being used in a presentation by his friend, Nityananda, without acknowledging Raghu as the creator.

(a) What crime (if any) has been committed by Nityananda?

(b) Raghu appraised Nityananda about IPR and its associated violations. Expand the term IPR.

(c) Raghu wants to use e-Commerce to sell his paintings online. Write any two precautions that he should take while using e-Commerce.

(d) Mention any two netiquettes which Raghu should follow while being online.

Answers

1. (c) The letter S in the abbreviation HTTPS in context of Networking protocols, stands for Secure.
2. (c) File transfer over Bluetooth is not done through web services; it's a direct wireless connection method.
3. (a) In 3G and 4G mobile technologies, the character 'G' stands for Generation.
4. (b) A website or online platform where individuals or groups regularly publish written content, typically in a reverse chronological order is known as blog.
5. (b) height is not an attribute of the <font> tag.
6. (a) In HTML, we start the comment using <!- -
7. (b) <h1> element have both the opening and the closing tags in HTML.
8. (b) The default color of vlink is purple.
9. (c) <td> tag is not used while creating a description list. It is used for table data cell.
10. (c) Photoshop is not an example of an Open Source Software.
11. (a) Both Assertion (A) and Reason (R) are true, and Reason (R) is the correct explanation for Assertion (A).
12. (b) Both Assertion (A) and Reason (R) are true, but Reason (R) is not the correct explanation for Assertion (A).
13.

Chat	Email
Chat offers immediate communication, where users can exchange messages instantly.	Email can be access later through mail box, where responses may not be immediate.
Chatting is used for quick, informal conversations with a more conversational tone	It is generally considered more formal, suitable for professional or longer-form communication.

14. (a) (*i*) If the fund transfer has to be made outstation, where the bank does not have a branch, the bank would demand outstation charges, whereas with the help of online banking, it will be absolutely free for you.

(*ii*) Internet banking deploys the Internet as a medium for financial transaction.

Or

(b) Advantage of e-Reservation

e-Reservations allow you to book appointments or reservations at any time, from anywhere with an internet connection. This eliminates the need to call during business hours or wait in line.

Limitation of e-Reservation

e-Reservations can limit your ability to interact with a person and ask questions or get personalised recommendations.

15.

Website	Webpage
Website is a collection of web pages displayed on the web with a client-like browser.	It is part of website that includes information and content and is displayed on the browser to user or visitor.

16. (a) There are various effects of digital divide as given below:

(*i*) **Economic Inequality** Digital divide create economic inequality, because those who have access to modern technology can easily collect valuable economical information.

(*ii*) **Effect on Education** It has an impact on education. Because student who have Internet access and computer, can acquire more valuable knowledge from Internet.

Or

(b) A software license is a license agreement that gives an individual, company or organisation permission to use a software program. It typically provide end users with the right to one or more copies of the software without violating copyrights.

Free software license : GNU (General Public License)

Proprietary software license : Microsoft Windows

17. There are two simple significances of using links in HTML webpages:

1. **Navigation** Links help users move around your webpage and other webpages on the internet. When you click on a link, it takes you to another page or a different section of the same page.
2. **Connectivity** Links connect different parts of the internet together. They allow you to share resources, such as articles, videos, or pictures, with others.

18. (a)

Tag	Attribute
<table>	border
<input>	type
<ol>	start
<td>	rowspan

Or

(b)

bgcolor attribute	background attribute
This attribute sets the background color of the webpage.	This attribute sets a background image for the webpage.
e.g. <body bgcolor="lightblue">	**e.g.** <body background="image.jpg">

19. (a) H₂O

(b) E = MC²

20.

```
<!DOCTYPE html>
<html lang="en">
<head>
<meta charset="UTF-8">
<meta name="viewport" content="width=device-width, initial-scale=1.0">
<title>Orientation Programme</title>
</head>
<body>
<table style= " border: 1px solid black;border-collapse: collapse;"> <!-- Added border attribute
-->
<tr>
<td colspan="3" style="text-align: center;">
<h1 style="color: blue; font-weight: bold;">ABC International School</h1>
<h2 style="color: green;">Cultural Club</h2>
<h3 style="color: cyan;">Orientation Programme on 15th March 2024</h3>
</td>
</tr>
</table>
</body>
</html>
```

21.
```
<!DOCTYPE html>
<html lang="en">
<head>
<meta charset="UTF-8">
<meta name="viewport" content="width=device-width, initial-scale=1.0">
</head>
<body>
<video width="350" height="250" controls>
<source src="Ayeshahits.mp4" type="video/mp4">
Your browser does not support the video tag.
</video>
</body>
</html>
```

22. (a)
```
<!DOCTYPE html>
<html lang="en">
<head>
<meta charset="UTF-8">
<meta name="viewport" content="width=device-width, initial-scale=1.0">
<title>Online Gadgets</title>
</head>
<body>
<!-- Clickable Image for Phones -->
<a href="ALLPHONES.HTML"><img src="PHONE.jpg" alt="Phones" width="200" height="150"></a>
<!-- Clickable Image for TVs -->
<a href="ALLTVS.HTML"><img src="TV.jpg" alt="TVs" width="200" height="150"></a>
</body>
</html>
```

Or

(b)
```
<!DOCTYPE html>
<html lang="en">
<head>
<title>Shopping List</title>
</head>
<body> Here is a shopping list with categories and items
<ol>
<li>
<strong>Vegetables</strong>
<ul>
<li>Carrots</li>
<li>Broccoli</li>
<li>Spinach</li>
</ul>
</li>
<li>
<strong>Fruits</strong>
<ul>
<li>Apples</li>
<li>Oranges</li>
<li>Bananas</li>
</ul>
</li>
```

FULLY SOLVED

```
</ol>
</body>
</html>
```

23. The word 'plagiarism' has emerged from a latin word plagiarius, which means kidnapping. Plagiarism is an act of copying another person's idea, words or work and pretend that they are our own. The intentions behind plagiarism could be malicious or it could be done accidently.
Two simple examples:

1. **Copying from a book without citing it** Let's say you have to write a report about pandas. Instead of doing your own research or writing your own words, you copy a paragraph directly from a book about pandas without mentioning where you found it.
2. **Copying a friend's essay** Imagine your friend writes a really good essay for class. Instead of writing your own, you ask your friend if you can copy theirs and hand it in as your own work. This is also plagiarism because you're passing off someone else's work as your own.

24. (a)
```
<!DOCTYPE html>
<html lang="en">
<head>
<title>Student Data Input Form</title>
</head>
<body><h2> Student Data Input Form </h2>
<form action="#" method="post">
Name: <input type="text" id="name" name="name" required><br>
Subscribe for Newsletter: <input type="checkbox" id="newsletter" name="newsletter"><br>
Gender:<br>
<input type="radio" id="male" name="gender" value="male"> <label for="male">Male</label>
<input type="radio" id="female" name="gender" value="female"> <label for="female">Female</label>
<input type="radio" id="other" name="gender" value="other"> <label for="other">Other</label><br>
Country:
<select id="country" name="country">
<option value="USA">USA</option>
<option value="Canada">Canada</option>
<option value="UK">UK</option>
<option value="Australia">Australia</option>
</select>
</form>
</body>
</html>
```

Or

(b)
```
<!DOCTYPE html>
<html lang="en">
<head>
<meta charset="UTF-8">
<meta name="viewport" content="width=device-width, initial-scale=1.0">
<title>Activity Details</title>
</head>
<body>
<table border="1">
<tr>
<th rowspan="5" style="text-align:center;">DETAILS</th>
</tr>
<tr>
<th>ACTIVITY</th>
```

FULLY SOLVED

```
<th>MEMBER NAME</th>
<th>AGE</th>
<th>EMAIL</th>
</tr>
<tr>
<td>Chess Club</td>
<td>John Doe</td>
<td>28</td>
<td>john.doe@example.com</td>
</tr>
<tr>
<td>Photography Club</td>
<td>Jane Smith</td>
<td>24</td>
<td>jane.smith@example.com</td>
</tr>
<tr>
<td>Football Club</td>
<td>Michael Johnson</td>
<td>31</td>
<td>michael.johnson@example.com</td>
</tr>
</table>
</body>
</html>
```

25. (a) The address Suraj typed, www.gmail.com is a web address (URL) for accessing Gmail's website, not an email address. An email address typically consists of a username followed by the "@" symbol and the domain name of the email service provider, such as "example@gmail.com".

(b) Suraj can use Zoom or Microsoft Teams for video conferencing.

(c) Suraj and his colleagues will use the FTP to upload and download the file. FTP stands for File Transfer Protocol.

(d) Suraj can use Facebook or Instagram to promote the company's products on social media.

26. (a) Nityananda may have committed copyright infringement by using Raghu's painting without permission or acknowledgment.

(b) IPR stands for Intellectual Property Rights.

(c) (i) Raghu should ensure secure payment gateways to protect customer data.

(ii) He should use watermarks or low resolution images to prevent unauthorised use or copying of his paintings.

(d) Two netiquettes which Raghu should follow while being online.

(i) Never spam others by sending large amounts of unsolicited E-mails.

(ii) Stick to the topic when posting in online forums or when commenting on photos or video's, such as YouTube or Facebook comments.

FULLY SOLVED

CBSE

EXAMINATION PAPER 2025

COMPUTER APPLICATIONS

Instructions

Please read the instructions carefully.

1. This question paper has 5 Sections A, B, C, D, E.
2. All questions are compulsory. However, internal choices have been provided in some of the questions.
3. Section A has 12 questions carrying 1 mark each.
4. Section B has 7 Very Short Answer (VSA) type questions carrying 2 marks each.
5. Section C has 4 Short Answer (SA) type questions carrying 3 marks each.
6. Section D has 1 Long Answer (LA) type question carrying 4 marks.
7. Section E has 2 Source-based/Case-based/Passage-based questions carrying 4 marks each.

Time : 2 hours ***Max. Marks : 50***

Section A

(All questions are compulsory) (12 × 1 = 12)

1. Arun is sending an e-mail to his office. Which protocol out of the following options will be used for the purpose?
(a) FTP (b) HTTP (c) SMTP (d) SCP

2. Which of the following is not an e-Reservation portal in India ?
(a) https://www.amazon.in (b) https://www.yatra.com
(c) https://www.makemytrip.com (d) https://www.irctc.co.in

3. Which of the following attributes is not a valid attribute of the <font> tag in HTML?
(a) face (b) type (c) size (d) color

4. What is the full form of FTP?
(a) File Transfer Protocol (b) File Transmission Protocol
(c) Fast Transfer Protocol (d) Fast Transmission Protocol

5. Which of the following attributes is not a valid attribute of the <body> tag in HTML?
(a) text (b) background (c) bgcolor (d) width

6. Select the correct option to fill in the blank:
A .... is an online platform or website where individuals or businesses regularly publish articles/journals, known as posts, on various topics.
(a) Browser (b) Blog (c) News Group (d) Web Server

7. The default value for the type attribute of an unordered list in HTML is:
(a) circle (b) disc (c) square (d) triangle

8. Which of the following is not a search engine available over the Internet?
(a) Google (b) Bing (c) Diksha (d) Yahoo

9. Which of the following options is a network protocol that enables secure and encrypted file transfers between a client and a server?

(a) SFTP (b) Telnet (c) SCP (d) HTTP

10. Which of the following options will set the font family of all paragraphs to 'Arial'?

(a) `<style> p { font-family: Arial;} </style>`
(b) `<style> p { fontfamily: Arial; } </style>`
(c) `<style> p { font: Arial; } </style>`
(d) `<style> p {font-type: Arial; } </style>`

Direction *Questions No. 11 and 12 are Assertion and Reason type questions. Each question consists of two statements, namely, Assertion (A) and Reason (R). Select the most suitable option considering the Assertion and Reason.*

(a) Both Assertion (A) and Reason (R) are true and Reason (R) is the correct explanation of Assertion (A).
(b) Both Assertion (A) and Reason (R) are true but Reason (R) is not the correct explanation of Assertion (A).
(c) Assertion (A) is true, but Reason (R) is false.
(d) Assertion (A) is false, but Reason (R) is true.

11. **Assertion** (A) FTP is a networking protocol used for transferring files.
Reason (R) FTP is used when we want to view some data from a website.

12. **Assertion** (A) SMS is an acronym for Smart Message Service.
Reason (R) SMS is the most common technology for delivering short, concise and important messages quickly.

Section B

(7 × 2 = 14)

13. What is a Digital Property? Write any two examples of digital property.

14. (a) What is e-Shopping? Write names of any two commonly used e-Shopping portals.

Or

(b) What is a Social Network? Write names of any two popular social networking sites on the Internet.

15. State whether the following statements are True or False:

(i) <h1> is the highest level of heading and <h4> is the lowest level of heading in HTML.
(ii) A visited link is purple coloured by default in HTML.
(iii) The character '#' is used to start a comment text in HTML.
(iv) <b> is an empty tag in HTML as it does not need to be closed.

16. (a) Write the HTML code to create a link to the web page having URL as:
www.festivals.com/india/diwali.html
The mentioned web page should get opened in a new window/tab on clicking the text, 'FESTIVALS'.

Or

(b) (i) Write HTML code to display the following line of text in bold and italics:
Happiness is not by chance, but by choice.
(ii) Write the HTML code to set the background color of the web page as blue.

17. Write the purpose of the following HTML tags:

(i)
 (ii) <DL>

18. (a) An incomplete CSS code within <head> . . . . </head> is given below. Complete this code by filling in the blanks as per the specifications that follow:

```
<head>
<style>
```

FULLY SOLVED

```
body {.......... : .......... ;}        <!--Line 1 -->
P {
.......... : .......... ;               <!--Line 2 -->
.......... : .......... ;               <!--Line 3 -->
}
...........                             <!--Line 4 -->
{
Color : Blue;
}
</style>
</head>
```

(i) Line 1: Page background color should be Yellow.

(ii) Line 2: Color of the paragraph text should be Red.

(iii) Line 3: Font family of the paragraph text should be Arial.

(iv) Line 4: The second biggest heading should be Blue in color.

Or

(b) The following HTML code is expected to create an ordered list for a web page:

```
<html>
<body.......... :yellow>                <!-- Line 1 -->
<p>
<font .......... = Helvetica>           <!-- Line 2 -->
FESTIVALS OF INDIA
</p>
<..........>                            <!-- Line 3 -->
  <..........>HOLI <.......... >        <!-- Line 4 -->
  <..........>DIWALI <..........>       <!-- Line 5 -->
< ..........>                           <!-- Line 6 -->
```

Complete this code by filling in the blanks as per the specifications that follow:

(i) Line 1: Background color of the web page should be Yellow.

(ii) Line 2: Font for the paragraph should be Helvetica.

(iii) Line 3 and Line 6: An ordered list should start and end.

(iv) Line 4 and Line 5: Listing of the ordered list items.

19. Write any two differences between Web Server and Web Client.

Section C

(4 × 3 = 12)

20. The following HTML statements are not written properly. Re-write the correct statements with underlined corrections. The desired purpose of each statement is mentioned under it.

(i) `<BODY image="background.jpg">`

`<!--Page background should display the image named background.jpg-->`

(ii) `<FONT height=5>`

`<!--Font should be 5 in size-->`

(iii) `<img src="img.jpg" text="An Image">`

`<!-Image source should be img.jpg and its alternate text should be "An Image">`

21. (a) Give the full form of the following:

(i) TCP/IP (ii) SSH

Or

(b) Consider the given URL:

http://www.mypage.com/

Is it a secure website ? Justify your answer.

22. (a) Explain how to insert an audio on a web page using <audio> tag. Give example to support your answer.

Or

(b) Akhil, an entrepreneur, has made some videos for marketing purposes. He wants to create a web page and share these videos to increase his customers on the online platform. Help Akhil to do the same with the given instructions:

(i) Use HTML to put a video "products.mp4" in the web page.

(ii) The video should autoplay in the width of 400 pixels and height 300 pixels in the browser window.

(iii) The video controls buttons-Play, Pause and Volume should be visible.

23. (a) Write suitable HTML statements to display the following text on a web page:

(i) $Ca(OH)_2$

(ii) $2(A^2 + B^2)$

(b) Give any one advantage of CSS.

Section D

(4)

24. (a) Write the HTML code to design the web page as shown below:

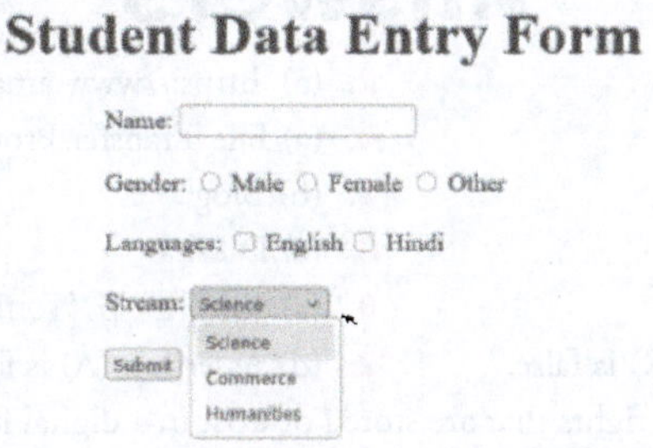

Note

- *The title of the page should be 'Student Data Entry Form'.*
- *The heading 'Student Data Entry Form' on the web page should be of largest possible size.*

Or

(b) Write the HTML code to design the web page as shown below (Table border should be 1, height = 150 and width = 350 with cellpadding = 15):

JANUARY 2025	
NAME	**ATTENDANCE**
Abha	Present
Alok	Absent
Teacher: Ms. Anju	

Section E

(Case Study) (2 × 4 = 8)

25. Sujata is a class 10 student and has to submit her project work to her teacher. She uses the Internet to find out content related to her project work and prepares her document by copying the contents into her submission.

With respect to the given case study, answer the following questions:

(i) What is the name of the act that Sujata has committed by copying contents from Internet to her projects?

(ii) The content available over the Internet which Sujata is copying could be another person's .... property. (Digital/Physical)

(iii) To copy someone else's content from the Internet is not considered as good behaviour. What is the term used for good behaviour that should be followed on the Internet?

(iv) Sujata is violating IPR of the original content creator. Expand the term IPR.

26. Jessica runs a small graphic design company called ABC Vision. To save money, she decided to use a pirated version of a popular design software instead of buying a licensed software. Her legal advisor told her to go for open source software instead of pirated software.

Answer the questions based on the above case study:

(a) What is open source software?

(b) Give any two examples of open source software.

(c) Mention any two advantages of open source software.

(d) Define the term "Software License".

FULLY SOLVED

Answers

1. (c) SMTP

2. (a) https://www.amazon.in

3. (b) type

4. (a) File Transfer Protocol

5. (d) width

6. (b) Blog

7. (b) disc

8. (c) Diksha

9. (a) SFTP

10. (a) `<style> p {font-family: Arial;} </style>`

11. (c) Assertion (A) is true, but Reason (R) is false.

12. (d) Assertion (A) is false, but Reason (R) is true.

13. Digital Property refers to any assets or rights that are stored or exist in a digital format.

Example

1. A domain name (e.g., www.example.com).
2. Copyrighted digital content (e.g., e-books, music, software).

14. (a) Refer to text on page no. 26 (e-shopping).

Two commonly used e-Shopping portals are: Amazon, eBay.

Or

(b) Refer to text on page no. 27 (Social networking).

Two popular social networking sites are:

1. Facebook 2. Instagram

15. (i) False (ii) True (iii) False (iv) False

16. (a) `<a href= "http://www.festivals.com/india/diwali.html"target= "_blank"> FESTIVALS</a>`

- **href** attribute is used to define the link's destination.
- **target= "_blank"** ensures that the link opens in a new tab or window.

Or

(b) (i)
```
<html>
<head>
    <title>Text Styling</title>
```

```
</head>
<body>
    <p><b><i>Happiness is not by chance, but by choice.</i></b></p>
</body>
</html>
```

(ii)
```
<html>
<head>
    <title>Background Color</title>
    <style>
        body { background-color: blue;}
    </style>
</head>
<body>
    <p>This page has a blue background.</p>
</body>
</html>
```

17. (i) **
 (Line Break Tag)** It is used to insert a line break in the text. It forces the content to move to the next line.

(ii) **<DL> (Definition List Tag)** It is used to create a list of definitions or description lists, where items have a term and a description.

18. (a)
```
<head>
<style>
        body {background-color: Yellow;}
        p {
            color: Red;
            font-family: Arial;
        }
        h2
        {
            color: Blue;
        }
    </style>
</head>
```

Or

(b)
```
<html>
<body bgcolor="yellow">
<p>
<font face="Helvetica">
FESTIVALS OF INDIA
</p>
<ol>
    <li>HOLI</li>
    <li>DIWALI</li>
</ol>
```

19. Two differences between a Web Server and a Web Client:

Web Server	Web Client
It is a computer system or software that provides resources or services to clients over the internet.	It is a device that requests information from a web server.
Processes incoming requests from clients, retrieves requested resources, and sends them back to the clients.	Sends requests to the web server and displays the received data to the user.

FULLY SOLVED

20. The corrected HTML code with underlined corrections:

(i) <BODY background="background.jpg">

Correction Use background instead of image.

(ii) <FONT size="5">

Correction Use size instead of height.

(iii) <img src="img.jpg" alt="An Image">

Correction Use alt instead of text.

21. (a) (i) **TCP/IP** Transmission Control Protocol / Internet Protocol.

(ii) **SSH** Secure Shell.

Or (b) No, it is not a secure website.

The URL starts with "http://" instead of "https://". The absence of 's' in HTTPS means that data is not encrypted during transmission, making it vulnerable to interception by attackers.

22. (a) The <audio> tag in HTML is used to embed audio files into a webpage.

Example

```
<html>
<head>
    <title>Audio Example</title>
</head>
<body>
    <h2>Listen to the Audio:</h2>
    <audio controls>
        <source src="song.mp3" type="audio/mpeg">
    Your browser does not support the audio element.
            </audio>
</body>
</html>
```

Explanation

- **controls** Adds play, pause, and volume controls.
- **<source>** Specifies the path to the audio file and its type.
- The fallback text ("Your browser does not support the audio element.") is displayed if the browser does not support the <audio> tag.

Or (b) Here's the HTML code to help Akhil embed his video on a webpage:

```
<!DOCTYPE html>
<html>
<head>
    <title>Product Video</title>
</head>
<body>
    <h2>Watch Our Product Video</h2>
    <video src="products.mp4" width="400" height="300" controls autoplay></video>
</body>
</html>
```

Explanation

- **<video>** Embeds the video file.
- **src** Specifies the video file name (products.mp4).
- **width & height** Sets the video display size to 400 × 300 pixels.
- **controls** Adds playback controls (Play, Pause, Volume).
- **autoplay** Automatically starts playing the video when the page loads.

FULLY SOLVED

23. (a) HTML Statements to display the following text:

(i) Ca $(OH)_2$

Ca (OH)₂

(ii) 2 $(A^2 + B^2)$

2 (A² + B²)

(b) One Advantage of CSS is that, CSS allows the separation of content (HTML) from presentation (design), making webpages easier to style and maintain.

24. (a)

```
<!DOCTYPE html>
<html>
<head>
    <title>Student Data Entry Form</title>
    <style>
        h1 {
            font-size: 2.5em;
            text-align: center;
        }
        form {
            margin: auto;
            width: 300px;
            font-size: 1.1em;
        }
    </style>
</head>
<body>
    <h1>Student Data Entry Form</h1>
    <form>
        <label>Name: </label>
        <input type="text" name="name"><br><br>
        <label>Gender: </label>
        <input type="radio" name="gender" value="Male"> Male
        <input type="radio" name="gender" value="Female"> Female
        <input type="radio" name="gender" value="Other"> Other
        <br><br>
        <label>Languages: </label>
        <input type="checkbox" name="language" value="English"> English
        <input type="checkbox" name="language" value="Hindi"> Hindi
        <br><br>
        <label>Stream: </label>
        <select name="stream">
            <option value="Science">Science</option>
            <option value="Commerce">Commerce</option>
            <option value="Humanities">Humanities</option>
        </select>
        <br><br>
        <input type="submit" value="Submit">
    </form>
</body>
</html>
```

Or

(b)

```
<!DOCTYPE html>
<html>
```

```
<head>
    <title>Attendance Table</title>
</head>
<body>
    <table border="1" width="350" height="150" cellpadding="15">
        <tr>
            <th colspan="2">JANUARY 2025</th>
        </tr>
        <tr>
            <th>NAME</th>
            <th>ATTENDANCE</th>
        </tr>
        <tr>
            <td>Abha</td>
            <td>Present</td>
        </tr>
        <tr>
            <td>Alok</td>
            <td>Absent</td>
        </tr>
        <tr>
            <td colspan="2">Teacher: Ms. Anju</td>
        </tr>
    </table>
</body>
</html>
```

FULLY SOLVED

25. (i) Copyright Infringement (ii) Digital property
(iii) Netiquette (iv) Intellectual Property Rights

26. (a) Open source software is software whose source code is freely available for anyone to view, modify, and distribute.

(b) (i) Linux (ii) GIMP

(c) Two advantages of Open Source Software are:

- **Cost-effective** Generally free to use.
- **Customizable** Users can modify the source code according to their needs.

(d) A software license is a legal agreement that specifies the terms and conditions under which software can be used, modified, and distributed.

Sample
Question Papers (1-3)

SAMPLE QUESTION PAPER 1

A Sample Question Paper for CBSE Class 10th

Computer Applications

FULLY SOLVED

Instructions

Please read the instructions carefully.

1. This question paper has 5 Sections A, B, C, D, E.
2. All questions are compulsory. However, internal choices have been provided in some of the questions.
3. Section A has 12 questions carrying 1 mark each.
4. Section B has 7 Very Short Answer (VSA) type questions carrying 2 marks each.
5. Section C has 4 Short Answer (SA) type questions carrying 3 marks each.
6. Section D has 1 Long Answer (LA) type question carrying 4 marks.
7. Section E has 2 Source-based/Case-based/Passage-based questions carrying 4 marks each.

Time : 2 hours ***Max. Marks : 50***

Section A

$(12 \times 1 = 12)$

1. Netiquette is short for
(a) Etiquette (b) Internet etiquette (c) Social etiquette (d) None of these

2. A search engine is a program to search ....
(a) for information (b) Web pages
(c) Web pages for specified index terms (d) Web pages for information using specified search terms.

3. When you copy a Web page or a file from a server to your local computer, this process is called
(a) conferencing (b) downloading (c) uploading (d) None of these

4. E-reservation is a process of making reservations of
(a) tickets (b) hotel rooms (c) tourists packages (d) All of these

5. Identify the software that helps you in sending and receiving an E-mail.
(a) MS-Office (b) Internet Explorer (c) Gmail (d) None of these

6. An organisation responsibles for providing Internet services to customer is commonly known as ....
(a) government (b) ISP (c) TCP/IP (d) HTTP

7. The correct HTML code for inserting an image is ....
(a) <IMG href="image.gif"> (b) <IMG> image.gif</gif>
(c) <IMG src = "image.gif"> (d) <IMAGE src = "image.gif">

8. Which type of tags used by HTML?
(a) tags only for image (b) user defined tags
(c) tags only for linking (d) fixed tags defined by the language

9. Which of the following will give smallest size of the text?
(a) <H3> (b) <H6> (c) <H2> (d) <H4>

10. In a Web page, you can place ....
(a) 2 levels of headings (b) 6 levels of headings (c) 4 levels of headings (d) 7 levels of headings

Directions *Q.Nos. 11 and 12 are Assertion and Reason Types. Each question consists of two statements, namely Assertion (A) and Reason (R). Select the must suitable option considering the Assertion and Reason.*

11. **Assertion** (A) People may use the ATM cards for withdrawing the cash amount from their accounts.
Reason(R) People can also transfer money online from one bank to another bank.
(a) Both A and R are true and R is the correct explanation of A.
(b) Both A and R are true but R is not the correct explanation of A.
(c) A is true but R is false.
(d) A is false and R is true.

12. **Assertion** (A) The source code to create a web page are to be written in text editors.
Reason(R) Text editors are used by the users who have complete knowledge of HTML.
(a) Both A and R are true and R is the correct explanation of A.
(b) Both A and R are true but R is not the correct explanation of A.
(c) A is true but R is false.
(d) A is false and R is true.

Section B

(7 × 2 = 14)

13. Give the name of any two Websites which are used to send E-mail.

14. (a) What do you understand by uploading a file on Internet? Name software used for it.
Or (b) Can we use URL to access a Web page? How?

15. State whether the given statements are True or False:
(a) The <br> tag is used to create a horizontal line on a webpage.
(b) Every HTML document must always begin with the <html> tag.
(c) The <a> tag is used to create hyperlinks in HTML document.
(d) By using <ul> tag in HTML document, we can create an ordered list.

16. (a) Name three types of law that can help restrict software piracy.
Or (b) What do you means by fraud in e-commerce?

17. Write the difference between list box and combo box.

18. (A) An incomplete css code is given below. Complete this code by filing in the blanks as per the specifications that follow:

```
<head>
<style>
body {
....... : Arial;              <!-- line 1-->
...... : #F4F4F4;               <!--line 2 -->
........ : #333;              <!-- line 3-->
}
</style>
</head>
```

line 1: Font style of the paragraph text should be arial.
line 2: Page background color should be "# F4F4F4".
line 3: Color of the text should be "#333".

Or (B) Ruchi is writing an HTML code to create a table for a webpage as follow:

```
<html>
<body>
<h1> student marks <_____>                <!--line 1-->
<table border = "1" ______=blue>          <!--line 2-->
<tr>
```

```
<th> Student Name <______>              <!--line 3-->
<th> Marks </th>
<_____>                                 <!--line 4-->
<tr>
<td> Jhon </td>
<td> 90 </td>
</tr>
<______>                                <!--line 5-->
</body>
</html>
```

Based on the above code fill in the blanks given in line 1, line 2, lin 3, line 4 and line 5 so that Ruchi's webpage displays correct output?

19. How would you display text in the title bar of a browser?

Section C

(4 × 3 = 12)

20. Answer the following questions regards networking protocols.

I. Which protocol ensures reliable data transmission by establishing a connection before sending data?

II. Which protocol is used to automatically assign IP addresses to devices on a network?

III. Which protocol is used to convert IP address into domain name and vice-versa?

21. Write the Web extensions (top level domain names) given to a Websites of the following types of organisations.

(i) educational (ii) government

Or What do you understand by the term URL? How is it different from an email address?

22. (a) Write suitable HTML code to Embed audio and video in a webpage.

Or (b) Differentiate between checkbox and radio button in HTML.

23. Write suitable HTML statements to display the following chemical equations on a webpage:

(I) H_2O (II) NaCl (III) $(X+Y)^2$

Section D

(4)

24. (a) Write an HTML code to produce the following:

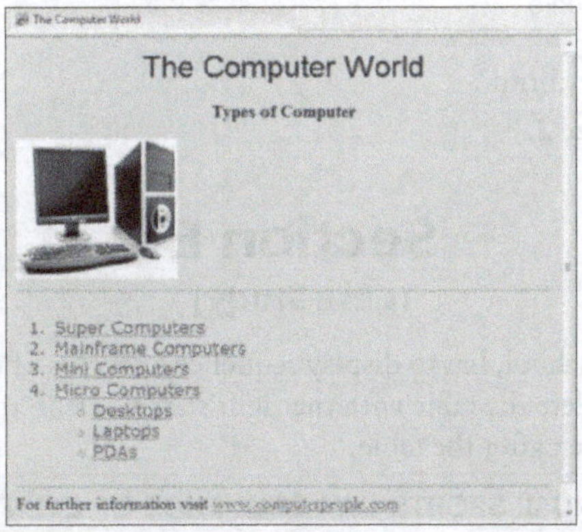

Consider the following points while writing the code:

(i) Title of the page is "The Computer World".

(ii) Background color of the page is "Yellow".

(iii) Active link color is Green and Visiting link color is Red.

(iv) All font face in the page is Verdana but heading is in Arial and Black.

FULLY SOLVED

(v) Image is from the file "computer.jpg"
(vi) Use horizontal rule wherever required.
(vii) Use ordered and unordered lists wherever required.
(viii) Pages linked with

Super Computers	:Super.html
Mainframe Computers	:Main.html
Mini Computers	:Mini.html
Micro Computers	:Micro.html
Desktops	:Desk.html
Laptops	:Laptop.html
PDAs	:PDA.html

Note You can use any other attributes that are not mentioned above to produce a similar output.

Or

(b) Observe following output and write HTML code to generate it.

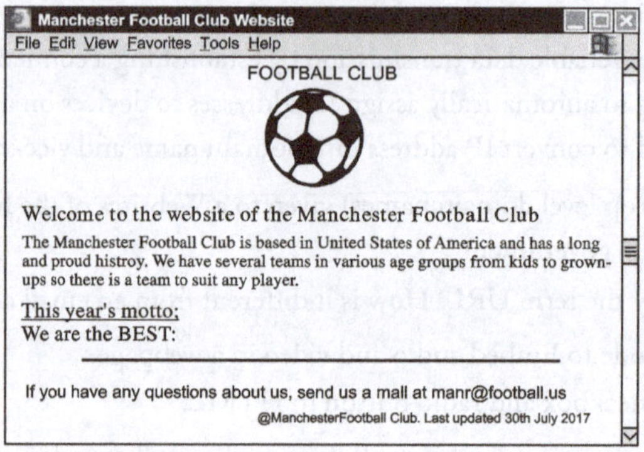

Consider the following points while generating the Web page
(i) The title of the page is "FOOTBALL CLUB"
(ii) The heading is blue color
(iii) Font of entire document is arial
(iv) Image used is "football.jpeg"
(v) The page is linked to:
Proud history to "history.html"
(vi) Bottom message is of size 2.

Section E

(2 × 4 = 8)

(Case Study)

25. Mr. Ayush, Sports Captain of the school, has to display sequence of events of the upcoming Annual Sports Day on the school website. Help him to complete the table with the right statements in the blanks. Observe the table and attempt any four questions (out of five) given after the table.

ANNUAL SPORTS DAY–SEQUENCE OF EVENTS		
8:00 AM–9:00 AM	9:00 AM–1:00 PM	1:00 PM–2:00 PM
CULTURAL EVENTS	TRACK EVENTS	PRIZE DISTRIBUTION

```
<HTML>
    <BODY>
```

```
<TABLE .......... = "1">                                          Statement-1
  <........>                                                      Statement-2
     <TH colspan ="3" align ="center" ANNUAL
                                    SPORTS DAY-SEQUENCE OF EVENTS</TH>
  </TR>
  <TR .......... ="center">                                       Statement-3
  <TD>8:00 AM-9:00 AM</TD>
  <TD>9:00 AM-1:00 PM</TD>
  <TD>1:00 PM-2:00 PM</TD>
  <........>                                                      Statement-4
  <TR align ="center">
     <TD>CULTURAL EVENTS</TD>
     <TD>TRACK EVENTS</TD>
     <TD>.............</TD>                                       Statement-5
  </TR>
  </TABLE>
  </BODY>
  </HTML>
```

(i) Write the attribute value to complete Statement-1 to achieve the output as given in the above table.
(ii) Write the tag to complete Statement-2 to achieve the output as given in the above table.
(iii) Write the attribute value to complete Statement-3 to achieve the output as given in the above table.
(iv) Write the tag to complete Statement-4 to achieve the output as given in the above table.
(v) Write the appropriate answer for the blank given in Statement-5 to achieve the output as given in the above table.

26. Based on the following case study, answer the questions that follow:

Aryan is working on a class project that involves using open-source software. However, instead of reading the license agreement, he modifies the code and presents it as his own in the project.

I. What ethical violation has Aryan committed by presenting the modified code as his own?
II. How does this incident highlight the importance of understanding software licenses?
III. Mention one difference between proprietary software and open-source software.
IV. What netiquette should Aryan follow while using and sharing open-source resources?

Answers

1. (b) Netiquette is short for Internet etiquette. Etiquette is a code of polite behaviour in society, Netiquette is a code of good behaviour on the Internet.
2. (d) A search engine is a software system that is designed to search for information on the Web pages.
3. (b) The process of copying files from a remote server to a local drive is as known as downloading.
4. (d) E-reservation is a process of making reservation of tickets, hotel rooms, tourists package etc.
5. (c) Gmail is preferred E-mail client which is used for sending or receiving an E-mail.
6. (b) An ISP is a company that provides individuals and organisations access to the Internet and other related services.
7. (c) <IMG src="image.gif">
8. (d) HTML provides predefined and fixed tags.
9. (b) From the given options, <H6> tag displays the smallest size of heading text.
10. (b) Web page provides six levels of headings.
11. (b) Both A and R are true but R is not the correct explanation of A.
12. (c) A is true but R is false.

FULLY SOLVED

13. www.gmail.com and www.rediffmail.com
14. (a) To transfer a file from your computer to a server is called uploading a file on Internet. FileZilla is the software which is used for it.

Or

(b) Yes, as a location on a Web server, which is called a Website and each Website has a unique address known as URL. So, URL can be used to access a Web page.
15. (a) False (b) True (c) True (d) False
16. (a) The following are the three types of law that can help to restrict software piracy
(i) Copyright (ii) Patent (iii) Trademark

Or

(b) Fraud in e-commerce refers to deceptive activities like online scams, identity theft, or unauthorized transactions that result in financial loss. It involves illegal practices aimed at tricking buyers or sellers.
17. List box gives the ability to select more than one item from the box by holding Ctrl key but in combo box multiple selection of items are not possible.
18. (A) line 1 : font-family
line 2 : background-color
line 3 : color

Or (B) line 1: /h1
line 2 : bordercolor
line 3 : /th
line 4 : /tr
line 5 : /table
19. To display text in a title bar of a browser, use the <TITLE> tag inside the <HEAD> tag in the HTML document.
e.g.

```
<HTML>
   <HEAD>
     <TITLE> HTML document </TITLE>
  </HEAD>
</HTML>
```

20. I. TCP (Transmission Control Protocol)
II. DHCP (Dynamic Host Configuration Protocol)
III. DNS (Domain Name System)
21. (i) .edu (ii) .gov

Or

Uniform Resource Locator (URL) refers to the address or the location of a web page or the website on the Internet. Each website on the Internet has a unique address. For example, http://www.google.com is a URL.
The difference between URL and email address are

URL	Email Address
URL is the address of the website.	An email address is an account on a mail server.
A URL never had an '@' sign in it.	An email address contains an '@' sign.
URL starts with www.	An email address does not start with www.

22. (a) The HTML <AUDIO> element is used to embed sound content in documents. It may contain one or more audio sources, represented using the src attribute.

```
<HTML>
<BODY>
<H2> Embedding an audio file</H2>
<AUDIO CONTROLS>
<SOURCE SRC="Audio.mp3" TYPE="audio/mp3">
File Format Not supported
</AUDIO>
```

```
</BODY>
</HTML>
```

The <VIDEO> element allows us to embed video files into an HTML document, very similar to the way images are embedded. The HTML does not specify which video formats browser should support in the <VIDEO> tag, but most commonly used video formats are ogg, mpeg4.

```
<HTML>
<BODY>
<H2> Embedding a video file</H2>
<VIDEO width="500" Height="400"controls
autoplay>
<SOURCE src="videoplayback.mp4" TYPE="video/mp4">
</VIDEO>
</BODY>
</HTML>
```

Or

(b) Differences between checkbox and radio button are as follows:

Checkbox	Radio button
In this, user can select any one option at a time.	It this, user can select one or more than one option at a time.
In HTML, the code for the checkbox is <input type = "checkbox">	In HTML, the code for the radio button is <input type = "radio>

23. (I)
```
<p>H<sub>2</sub>O</p>
```
(II)
```
<p>NaCl</p>
```
(III)
```
<p>(X+Y)<sup>2</sup</p>
```

24. (a) The HTML code is

```
<HTML>
  <HEAD>
    <TITLE>The Computer World</TITLE> </HEAD>
  <BODY bgcolor="yellow" alink ="green" vlink="red">
   <FONT face="arial"color="black">
   <H1>
   <CENTER>The Computer World</CENTER>
   </H1>
   </FONT>
   <BASEFONT face="verdana">
    <P align="center"><B>
    Types of Computer
    </B></P>
    <IMG src="computer.jpg">
    <HR>
    <OL type="1">
    <LI><A href="Super.html">
    Super Computers </A></LI>
    <LI><A href="Main.html">
      Mainframe Computers</A></LI>
    <LI><A href="Mini.html">
      Mini Computers</A></LI>
```

FULLY SOLVED

```
<LI><A href="Micro.html">
 Micro Computers</A></LI>
<UL>
<LI><A href="Desk.html">Desktops
</A></LI>
<LI><A href="Laptop.html">Laptops
</A></LI>
<LI><A href="PDA.html">PDAs
</A></LI>
</UL> </OL> <HR>
<FONT size="4">
For further information visit
<A href="www.computerpeople.com">
www.computerpeople.com</A>
</FONT>
</BODY>
</HTML>
```

Or

(b) The code is

```
<HTML>
<HEAD><TITLE>FOOTBALL CLUB</TITLE></HEAD>
<BODY>
<FONT face="arial" size="3">
<H1 align="center"><FONT color="blue">FOOTBALL CLUB</FONT></H1>
<CENTER><IMG src="football.jpg" height="150" width="150"></CENTER>
<H3>Welcome to the website of the Manchester Football Club</H3>
<P>The Manchester Football Club is based in United States of America and has a long <BR>
and <A href="history.html">proud history</A>. We have several teams in various age
groups from kids to grown-<BR>ups so there is a team to suit any player. <BR><BR>
<U>This year's motto:</U><BR>
We are the BEST:<BR>
<HR size="3" noshade size ="75%">
<FONT size="2"><B>If  you have any questions about us, send us a mail at
manr@football.us</B></FONT><BR>
<H5 align="right">
<IMG src="copy.jpg" height="20" width="30">Manchester Football Club. Last updated
30<SUP>th</SUP>July 2017</H5>
</FONT>
</BODY>
</HTML>
```

25. (i) border (ii) TR (iii) align (iv) /TR (v) PRIZE DISTRIBUTION

26. I. Copyright infringement

II. It emphasizes the importance of respecting intellectual property rights

III. Open-source software is freely accessible and modifiable, whereas proprietary software is not

IV. Always credit the original creator or source

FULLY SOLVED

SAMPLE QUESTION PAPER 2

A Sample Question Paper for CBSE Class 10th

Computer Applications

Instructions See Sample Question Paper 1.

Time : 2 hours ***Max. Marks : 50***

FULLY SOLVED

Section A

$(12 \times 1 = 12)$

1. The ...... refers to a code of safe and responsible behaviour for the Internet community.
(a) cyber law
(b) cyber ethics
(c) Both (a) and (b)
(d) None of these

2. Which mobile technology system provides mobile ultra-broadband Internet access?
(a) 3G
(b) 4G
(c) SMS
(d) MMS

3. Which part of TCP/IP is responsible for dividing a file or message into very small parts, at the source computer?
(a) TCP
(b) IP
(c) Both (a) and (b)
(d) None of these

4. A software that searches through a database of Web pages for particular information is known as ....
(a) domain
(b) E-mail client
(c) modem
(d) search engine

5. Nick connects to the Internet at home using a laptop computer with a wireless connection. Nick is going to change to a desktop computer using a 1 Gbps ethernet cable connection.
Which of these should be the result of making the changes?
(a) Increased portability and decreased speed.
(b) Decreased portability and increased speed.
(c) Increased portability and increased speed.
(d) Decreased portability and decreased speed.

6. Which communication protocol is used by Internet?
(a) TCP/IP
(b) WWW
(c) HTML
(d) W3C

7. src attribute used with <IMG> tag stands for ....
(a) screen
(b) screen resolution count
(c) source
(d) structure

8. Which of the following is the correct code of HTML page?

(a)
```
<HTML>
<TITLE> Hello
</TITLE>
</HTML>
```

(b)
```
<HTML>
<HEAD>
<TITLE> Hello
</TITLE>
</HEAD>
</HTML>
```

(c)
```
<HTML>
<BODY> Hello
</HTML>
```

(d)
```
<HTML>
<HEAD> Hello
<BODY>
</HTML>
```

9. An example of HTML editor is
(a) Notepad
(b) Dreamweaver
(c) Microsoft frontpage
(d) All of these

10. HTML tags are enclosed in
(a) curly brackets
(b) square brackets
(c) double quotes
(d) angular brackets

Directions *Q.Nos. 11 and 12 are Assertion and Reason Types. Each question consists of two statements, namely Assertion (A) and Reason (R). Select the must suitable option considering the Assertion and Reason.*

11. **Assertion** (A) E-learning refers to the use of the network and communication technology in teaching and learning. The letter "E" in E-learning stands for the word electronic. You can use the information from the internet in your work.

Reason(R) It is not easy for students to access the study material any time and at any place.
(a) Both A and R are true and R is the correct explanation of A.
(b) Both A and R are true but R is not the correct explanation of A.
(c) A is true but R is false.
(d) A is false and R is true.

12. **Assertion** (A) The <!DOCTYPE> declaration is not an HTML tag.

Reason(R) The <!DOCTYPE> is an instruction to the web browser about what version of HTML the page is written in.
(a) Both A and R are true and R is the correct explanation of A.
(b) Both A and R are true but R is not the correct explanation of A.
(c) A is true but R is false.
(d) A is false and R is true.

Section B

(7 × 2 = 14)

13. How multiple E-mail addresses are defined in To, Cc, Bcc field?

14. (a) What are e-groups?

Or

(b) Name any two Internet protocols used by Web.

15. State whether the given statements are True or False:
I. The <style> tag in HTML is used to define CSS styles.
II. CSS can be used to change the font color of the text in an HTML document.
III. Inline CSS is written within the <head> section of an HTML document.
IV. The background-color property in CSS is used to set the color of text.

16. (a) What do you mean by plagiarism?

Or

(b) How to age contribute to the digital divide?

17. What do you mean by textbox?

18. (A) An incomplete CSS code is given below. Complete this code by filling in the blanks as per the specifications that follow:

```
<head>
<style>
{h1
________: red;                    <!--line 1-->
```

FULLY SOLVED

```
________: 3em;                      <!--line 2-->
________: underline;                <!--line 3-->
}
</style>
</head>
```

line 1: Color of the heading should be red.

line 2: Font size should be 3em.

line 3: Text direction should be underline.

Or (B) Rahul is writing HTML code for creating a html form as follows:

```
<html>
<head>
  <title>Form in HTML<______>              <!--line 1-->
<______>                                   <!--line 2-->
<body>
  <form>
        Enter your address:<br>
  <______ rows="2" cols="20"></textarea>   <!--line 3-->
  </form>
</body>
</html>
```

Based on the above code fill in the blanks given in line 1, line 2, and line 3 so that his webpage displays output correctly?

19. Write the extension of HTML code file.

Section C

(4 × 3 = 12)

20. Consider the below given statement and answer the following questions:

"You need to configure a network with 50 devices and ensure they all have a unique IP address."

I. What type of IP addressing scheme would you use?

II. How would you assign IP addresses automatically to these devices?

III. What is the purpose of a subnet mask in IP addressing?

21. Write Web extensions given to sites of the following types of organisations.

(i) network organisation (ii) government agencies

Or Write three disadvantages of using Internet.

22. (a) What is a form? Name the basic attributes for creating a form.

Or

(b) Name the attributes of <SELECT> tag which are used to create drop-down menus.

23. Write suitable HTML statements to display the following text formulas on a webpage:

(i) $C_6H_{12}O_6$

(ii) $A^2 + B^2 = C^2$

(iii) $(P+Q)^3$

FULLY SOLVED

Section D

(4)

24. (a) Write the code to generate the following web page :

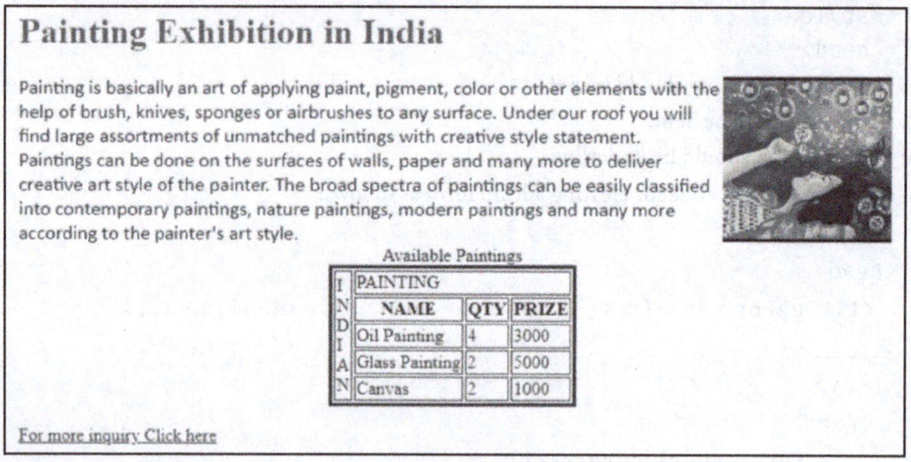

Note The following points while generating the web page

(i) Title of the page is "Painting Exhibition in India".
(ii) The heading text color should be red.
(iii) Font style for the page is "calibri".
(iv) vlink color should be red and alink color should be orange.
(v) Table border is 3px and border color is blue.
(vi) Image used in the page is paint1.jpg.
(vii) E-mail id as inquiry@abc.com for bottom message as "For more inquiry Click here".

Or

(b) Write an HTML code to produce the following:

Consider the following points while writing the code:

(i) Title of the page is "Save the Earth"
(ii) The background color of the page is Silver.
(iii) The font used for heading is "Arial", size is 6 and color is Black.
(iv) The sub heading is in "Verdana" font, font size is 4 and color is Brown.
(v) Rest of the text is in "Verdana" font, font size 4 and black color.
(vi) Image used is from file "Main.jpg"
(vii) The links are provided in an unordered list with ordered list used in between.

FULLY SOLVED

(viii) The pages are linked as follows

Home	Home.html
Faqs	Faq.html
Pollution	Poll.html
Deforestation	Defores.html
Poaching	Poach.html
Forests	Forest.html
Endangered Species	Specie.html

(ix) The categories 'Controlling' and 'Saving' in the unordered list are not linked to any page.

(x) The width and height of horizontal line is 820 and 80, respectively.

Note You can use any other attributes that are not mentioned above to produce a similar output.

Section E

(2 × 4 = 8)

(Case Study)

25. Help to complete the table with the right statements in the blanks. Observe the table and attempt any four questions (out of five given after the table.

Shopping Mall			
Floor	No. of Toy Shops	No. of Food Shops	No. of Sports Shops

```
<HTML><BODY>
  <TABLE ............ ="1">                         Statement-1
    <..........>                                    Statement-2
      <TH ............ ="4" align="center">         Statement-3
      Shopping Mall</TH>
    <..........>                                    Statement-4
    <TR align = "center">
      <TD>Floor</TD>
      <TD>No. of Toy<BR>Shops</TD>
      <TD>No. of Food<BR>Shops</TD>
      <TD>............<BR>Shops</TD>                Statement-5
    </TR>
  </TABLE>
  </BODY>
</HTML>
```

(i) Write the attribute value to complete Statement-1 to achieve the output as given in the above table.

(ii) Write the tag to complete Statement-2 to achieve the output as given in the above table.

(iii) Write the attribute value to complete Statement-3 to achieve the output as given in the above table.

(iv) Write the tag to complete Statement-4 to achieve the output as given in the above table.

(v) Write the appropriate answer for the blank given in Statement-5 to achieve the output as given in the above table.

26. Based on the following case study, answer the questions that follow:

Kavya is part of an e-commerce website development team. During her research, she saves user data insecurely, which could lead to privacy issues if accessed by unauthorized users.

I. What cyber ethics concern is Kavya violating in this case?

II. How can e-commerce platforms ensure the secure transmission of user data?

III. Why is privacy critical in e-commerce transactions?

IV. Suggest two netiquettes that customers should follow while using e-commerce platforms.

FULLY SOLVED

Answers

1. (*b*) The word cyber ethics refers to a code of safe and responsible behaviour for the Internet community.
2. (*b*) 4G stands for Fourth Generation. It provides mobile ultra broadband Internet access.
3. (*a*) TCP part breaks the message into smaller packets that are transmitted over the Internet.
4. (*d*) Search engine searches a software through a database of Web pages for particular information.
5. (*b*) Decreased portability and increased speed will be the result.
6. (*a*) TCP/IP is a communication protocol used by Internet which manages the transmission of data/file document on the Internet.
7. (*c*) src (source) attribute takes URL of an image file.
8. (*b*) Because <TITLE> tag must close inside the <HEAD> tag.
9. (*d*) HTML provides various text editors like Notepad, Microsoft frontpage, Dreamweaver etc.
10. (*d*) HTML tags are enclosed within angular brackets (< and >).
11. (*c*) A is true but R is false.
12. (*b*) Both A and R are true but R is not the correct explanation of A.
13. By using comma between E-mail addresses.
14. (a) An e-groups is a group of persons who come together over the Internet for a specific or common purpose using the best Internet communication tools to share ideas, different opinions, experiences and to learn from each other.

    Or

    (b) HTTP and FTP.
15. I.True II. True III. False IV. False
16. (a) Stealing someone else's ideas or information and presenting them as your own is called plagiarism.

    Or

    (b) Age seems to be that young people feel more comfortable with the new technology and are able to benefit from it more than older people.
17. Textbox provides a single line text input field where the user can enter the text.
18. (A) line 1 : color
    line 2 : font-size
    line 3 : text-direction

Or (B) line 1 : /title
    line 2 : /head
    line 3 : textarea

19. .html or .htm
20. I. Use a private IP address range with a subnet mask that accommodates all 50 devices.
    II. Implement a DHCP server.
    III. A subnet mask defines the range of IP addresses within a subnet.
21. (i) .net (ii) .gov

Or The three disadvantages of using Internet are as follows:
    (i) Cyber frauds (ii) Information misuse (iii) Computer virus circulation

22. (a) A Webform, or HTML form on a Web page allows a user to enter data that is sent to a server for processing. Forms can resemble paper or database forms because Web users fill out the forms using checkboxes, radio button, or text fields.
    The HTML <FORM> tag is used for creating a form for user input. The HTML <FORM> tag also supports the following attributes.
    (i) **name** This attribute defines a unique name for the form.
    (ii) **action** This attribute specifies the URL of the program where to sent the form data when a form is submitted.
    (iii) **method** This attribute specifies the HTTP method to use when sending form data.

Or

(b) Refer to text on Page No. 123

23. (i) <p>C₆H₁₂O₆</p>

(ii) <p>A²+ B²= C<sup<2</sup></p>

(iii) <p>(P+Q)³</p>

24. (a) Following is the HTML code to generate the given web page:

```
<HTML>
   <HEAD><TITLE> Painting Exhibition in India </TITLE></HEAD>
   <BODY alink="orange" vlink="red">
      <FONT face="times new roman"  color="red">
         <H1 align="left"> Painting Exhibition in India </H1>
      </FONT>
      <IMG src="paint1.jpg" align="right" width="150" height="150">
      <FONT size="4" face="calibri">
      Painting is basically an art of applying paint, pigment, color or other
      elements with the help of brush, knives, sponges or airbrushes to any
      surface. Under our roof you will find large assortments of unmatched
      paintings with creative style statement. <BR>
      Paintings can be done on the surfaces of walls, paper and many more to
      deliver creative art style of the painter. The broad spectra of paintings
      can be easily classified into contemporary paintings, nature paintings,
      modern paintings and many more according to the painter's art style.
      </FONT>
      <TABLE border="3" align="center" bordercolor="blue">
         <CAPTION color="red"> Available Paintings </CAPTION>
         <TR>
            <TD rowspan="5"> I <BR> N <BR> D <BR> I <BR> A <BR> N </TD>
            <TD colspan="3"> PAINTING </TD>
         </TR>
         <TR>
            <TH> NAME </TH>
            <TH> QTY </TH>
            <TH> PRIZE </TH>
         </TR>
         <TR>
            <TD> Oil Painting </TD>
            <TD> 4 </TD>
            <TD> 3000 </TD>
         </TR>
         <TR>
            <TD> Glass Painting </TD>
            <TD> 2 </TD>
            <TD> 5000 </TD>
         </TR>
         <TR>
            <TD> Canvas </TD>
            <TD> 2 </TD>
            <TD> 1000 </TD>
         </TR>
      </TABLE><BR>
      <A href="inquiry@abc.com"> For more inquiry Click here </A>
```

```
    </BODY>
</HTML>
```

Or

(b) The HTML code is

```
<HTML>
    <HEAD> <TITLE> Save the Earth </TITLE> </HEAD>
    <BODY bgcolor ="silver">
        <H1>
        <FONT face="arial" color="black"
        size="6">
        <CENTER>Save the Earth!! </CENTER>
        </FONT>
        </H1>
        <FONT face="verdana" color="brown"
         size="4">
        <P align="center">NGo Group dedicated
        to Saving the Earth's Natural Environment</P>
        </FONT>
        <FONT face ="verdana" color="black"
        size="4">
        <CENTER>
        <IMG src ="Main.jpg">
        </CENTER>
        <UL type = "disc">
        <LI>
        <A href="Home.html">Home</A>
        </LI>
        <LI>
        <A href="Faq.html">Faqs</A>
        </LI>
        <LI>
        <B> Controlling </B>
        </LI>
        <OL type="1">
        <LI>
        <A href="Poll.html">
    Pollution</A>
        </LI>
        <LI>
        <A href="Defores.html">
    Deforestation</A>
        </LI>
        <LI>
        <A href="Poach.html">
    Poaching</A>
        </LI>
        </OL>
```

```
        <LI>
        <B> Saving </B>
        </LI>
        <OL type="1">
        <LI>
        <A href="Forest.html">
      Forests</A>
        </LI>
        <LI>
        <A href="Specie.html">
      Endangered Species</A>
        </LI>
        </OL>
        </UL>
        </FONT>
        <HR noshade width="820"
       height="80" size="2">
        <B><FONT size="4">Do visit:
       www.saveearth.com</FONT></B>
     </BODY>
  </HTML>
```

25. (i) border (ii) TR (iii) colspan (iv) /TR (v) No. of Sports

26. I. Data privacy

II. Use encryption technologies for data transmission

III. To protect sensitive information from unauthorized access

IV. 1. Avoid sharing personal information publicly

2. Use strong passwords and two-factor authentication

FULLY SOLVED

SAMPLE QUESTION PAPER 3

A Sample Question Paper for CBSE Class 10th

Computer Applications

Instructions See Sample Question Paper 1.

Time : 2 hours ***Max. Marks : 50***

Section A

(12 × 1 = 12)

1. ...... is a license agreement that gives an organisation permission.
(a) Software (b) Software license
(c) Both (a) and (b) (d) None of these

2. A two way video conversation among multiple participants is called
(a) video chatting (b) video talking
(c) video conferencing (d) video watching

3. Digital information is converted into analog information by the modem at
(a) destination computer (b) source computer
(c) Both (a) and (b) (d) Neither (a) nor (b)

4. Image files uploaded and downloaded over the Internet can be processed with a compression application. Why are image files compressed before transmitted over Internet?
(a) to increase security (b) to make them easier to open
(c) to reduce transmission time (d) to improve the quality of images.

5. The first network was
(a) ARPANET (b) Internet
(c) NSFnet (d) NET

6. What can you do with the Internet?
(a) Exchange information with friends and colleagues
(b) Access pictures, sounds, video clips and other media elements
(c) Find diverse perspective on issues from a global audience
(d) Exchange information, access pictures, find diverse perspective on issue from a global audience.

7. Consider the following code:

```
<IMG src="Computers.jpg" width=" ________ " height="________">
```

Fill in the blanks to set the image size to be 250 pixels wide and 400 pixels tall.
(a) 250, 400 (b)400, 250
(c) <250><400> (d) <400><250>

8. Which of the following is not a container element?
(a) P (b) B
(c) OL (d) HR

9. A Web page normally consists of
(a) head and body
(b) top and bottom
(c) body and font
(d) body and title

10. M in HTML stands for
(a) MANAGEMENT
(b) MARKUP
(c) MODIFIED
(d) MACHINE

Directions *Q.Nos. 11 and 12 are Assertion and Reason Types. Each question consists of two statements, namely Assertion (A) and Reason (R). Select the must suitable option considering the Assertion and Reason.*

11. **Assertion** (A) E-banking saves time of the customer for doing bank transactions.
Reason(R) E-banking allows you to access your accounts on the Internet from anywhere in the world at any time. It provides secure transaction on the Internet.
(a) Both A and R are true and R is the correct explanation of A.
(b) Both A and R are true but R is not the correct explanation of A.
(c) A is true but R is false.
(d) A is false and R is true.

12. **Assertion** (A) With HTML, you can develop and publish documents and data with headings, text, tables, lists, hyperlinks, photos, etc., in static form.
Reason(R) You can create forms for managing transactions, for use in searching the information, making reservations, ordering products, etc.
(a) Both A and R are true and R is the correct explanation of A.
(b) Both A and R are true but R is not the correct explanation of A.
(c) A is true but R is false.
(d) A is false and R is true.

UNSOLVED

Section B

(7 × 2 = 14)

13. How is newsgroup different from E-mail messages?

14. (a) Write the purpose of search engine.

Or

(b) Name any two major services provided by Internet.

15. Answer the following questions.
(i) Which attributes of <TABLE> tag are used for specifying its dimensions in a web page?
(ii) Name the attribute of <TABLE> tag which is used for specifying the alignment of text in table.
(iii) Name the attribute for changing text color.
(iv) Write the name of attribute for giving alternate text for image.

16. (a) Define the content management system of digital property right.

Or

(b) Define the only one rule for good netiquette.

17. Write the syntax of <TEXTAREA> tag.

18. (A) An incomplete CSS code is given below. Complete this code by filling in the blanks as per the specifications that follow:

```
<head>
<style>
body{
```

```
________: yellow;          <!--line 1-->
________: center;          <!--line 2-->
________: bold;            <!--line 3-->
________: pink;            <!--line 4-->
}
</style>
</head>
```

line 1 : Page background color should be yellow.
line 2 : Alignment of the text should be center.
line 3 : Text style should be bold.
line 4 : Text color should be pink.

Or

(B) Aashi is writing a HTML code to create a food item list as follows:

```
<html>
<______>                                   <!--line 1-->
<ul type= "disc"> <b> food mood <___>     <!--line 2-->
<li><b> Appetizers </b>
<ol type="1">
<li>Spring rolls<______>                   <!--line 3-->
<li> honey chilly</li>
<______>                                   <!--line 4-->
</ul>
</body>
</html>
```

Based on the above code fill in the blanks given in line 1, line 2, line 3 and line 4 so that her webpage displays the correct output?

19. What is the purpose of using the tags <h1>...<h6>?

UNSOLVED

Section C

$(4 \times 3 = 12)$

20. Consider the below given statement and answer the following questions:
"You need to configure a network with 50 devices and ensure they all have a unique IP address."
I. What type of IP addressing scheme would you use?
II. How would you assign IP addresses automatically to these devices?
III. What is the purpose of a subnet mask in IP addressing?

21. Expand the following Web extensions using with Web addresses.
(i) .org (ii) .in

Or How do you differentiate between a Web address and an E-mail address?

22. (a) Write HTML code to display a password.

Or

(b) What is the combo box?

23. Write suitable HTML statements to display the following mathematical expressions on a webpage:
(I) $E = mc^2$ (II) $(X-Y)^3$
(III) $(a+b)^2$

Section D

24. (a) Write HTML code for the following output: (4)

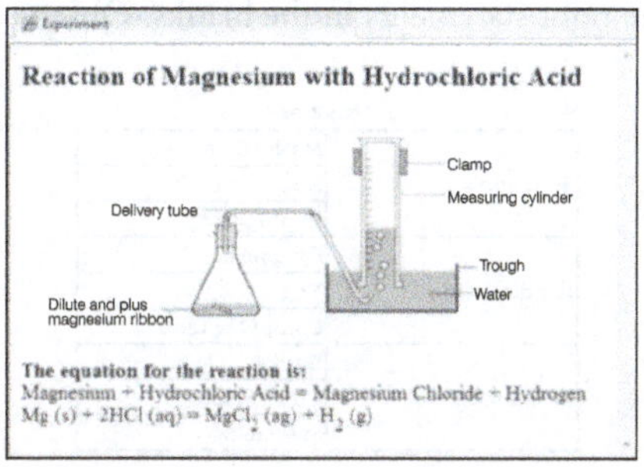

Note Consider the following points while generating output:

(i) Title of the page should be Experiment.

(ii) In whole Web page font face is "Times New Roman" and size is "4".

(iii) The second heading text "Reaction of Magnesium with Hydrochloric Acid".

(iv) The image used in the page is reaction.jpg with alternate text is "magnesium with hydrochloric acid", width is 500 pixels and height is 200 pixels.

Or

(b) Write the code to generate the following web page:

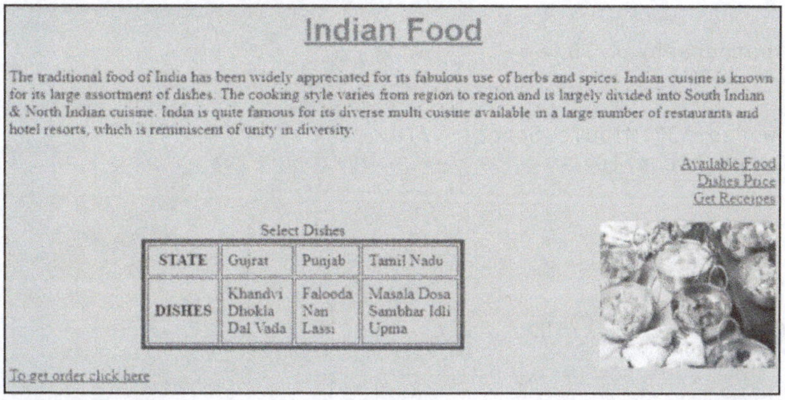

Note The following points while generating the web page:

(i) Title of the page is "Indian Food".

(ii) Link color is blue, vlink color is brown and alink color is pink.

(iii) Font face of heading is "arial".

(iv) The color of the heading of the page is green.

(v) Image used as food1.jpg.

(vi) Table border is 4px and border color is maroon.

(vii) Use link as: For Available Food as F1.html
For Dishes Price as F2.html
For Get Recipes as F3.html

(viii) E-mail id for bottom message "To get order click here" as inquiry@abc.com.

Section E

(Case Study)

(2 × 4 = 8)

25. Help to complete the table with the right statements in the blanks. Observe the table and attempt any four questions (out of five) given after the table.

Activities

Sr School	Maths Club
	Robotics Club
	Photography
Middle School	Gymnastic
	Yoga
	Computer Club
Primary School	Dance
	Vocal Music
	Swimming

```
<HTML>
  <BODY><BASEFONT face="cambria">
  <TABLE border="1"  ........ ="black"   cellspacing="0" width="320">   Statement-1
  <.............> Activities </CAPTION>                                 Statement-2
   <TR>
     <TD ............="3"> Sr School </TD>                              Statement-3
      <TD> Maths Club </TD>
   </TR>
   <TR>
      <TD> Robotics Club </TD>
   </TR>
   <TR>
      <TD> Photography </TD>
   </TR>
   <TR>
     <TD rowspan="3">Middle School </TD>
      <TD> Gymnastic </TD>
   </TR>
   <TR>
      <........> Yoga </TD>                                             Statement-4
   </TR>
   <TR>
      <TD> Computer Club </TD>
   </TR>
   <TR>
   <TD rowspan="3"> Primary School </TD>
      <TD> Dance </TD>
   </TR>
   <TR>
      <TD> .......... </TD>                                             Statement-5
   </TR>
   <TR>
      <TD> Swimming </TD>
   </TR>
  </TABLE>
  </BODY>
</HTML>
```

(i) Write the attribute value to complete Statement-1 to achieve the output as given in the above table.

(ii) Write the tag to complete Statement-2 to achieve the output as given in the above table.

(iii) Write the attribute value to complete Statement-3 to achieve the output as given in the above table.

UNSOLVED

(iv) Write the tag to complete Statement-4 to achieve the output as given in the above table.

(v) Write the appropriate answer for the blank given in Statement-5 to achieve the output as given in the above table.

26. Based on the following case study, answer the questions that follow:

Riya is a budding photographer and loves sharing her work on social media platforms. Recently, she noticed that one of her photographs was used by a blog without giving her credit or seeking her permission.

(i) Identify the ethical issue highlighted in this case study.

(ii) Explain how this incident relates to Intellectual Property Rights (IPR).

(iii) Suggest a way for Riya to protect her work in the future.

(iv) Why is it important to respect intellectual property online?

Answers

1. (b) **2.** (c) **3.** (b) **4.** (c) **5.** (a) **6.** (d) **7.** (a) **8.** (d)

9. (a) **10.** (b) **11.** (b) **12.** (b)

25. (i) border-color (ii) CAPTION (iii) rowspan (iv) TD (v) Vocal Music

26. (i) Plagiarism (ii) Intellectual Property Rights (iii) Use a watermark or digital rights management (DRM)

(iv) To protect the original creator's work and respect copyright laws

CBSE

LATEST SAMPLE PAPER

COMPUTER APPLICATIONS

Instructions

1. This question paper has 5 Sections A-E.
2. All questions are compulsory. However, internal choices have been provided in some of the questions.
3. Section A has 12 questions carrying 1 mark each.
4. Section B has 7 Short Answer (SA-I) type questions carrying 2 marks each.
5. Section C has 4 Short Answer (SA-II) type questions carrying 3 marks each.
6. Section D has 1 Long Answer (LA) type question carrying 4 marks.
7. Section E has 2 Source-based/Case-based/Passage-based questions carrying 4 marks each.

Time : 2 hours — ***Max. Marks : 50***

Section A

(12 × 1 = 12)

1. Shreya wants to securely copy files between two Servers or two connected machines over the Internet. Which Protocol should she prefer for getting her task completed?
(a) FTP (b) HTTP (c) SCP (d) Telnet

2. Which of the following is not an e-governance project in India?
(a) www.drdo.nic. in (b) www.passport.gov.in
(c) www.incometaxindia. gov.in (d) www.flipkart.com

3. Which tag besides <B> can be used to make the text bold in HTML?
(a) <strong> (b) <dark> (c) <fat> (d) <I>

4. What is the full form of SMTP?
(a) Simple Message Transfer Protocol (b) Secure Message Transmission Protocol
(c) Simple Mail Transfer Protocol (d) Secure Mail Transmit Protocol

5. Which protocol is used for video conferencing among multiple participants?
(a) Telnet (b) HTTP (c) VoIP (d) SFTP

6. Select the correct option to fill in the blank:
A website may consist of ______
(a) Static Webpages (b) Dynamic Webpages (c) Both (a) and (b) (d) Domain

7. Aman, a student of Class X, wants to create numbered list in HTML, which of the following tag should he use?
(a) <UL> (b) <OL> (c) <DL> (d) <list>

8. Making a copy of your webpage on the computer is known as ....?
(a) Uploading (b) Browsing (c) Downloading (d) None of these

9. Himani, a class X student, wants to remotely access a computer system far from her house. Which protocol, out of the following, should she prefer to access or log in it remotely?
(a) FTP (b) SFTP (c) TCP/IP (d) TELNET

10. Anshu, a class X student, is writing CSS code for making all <span> elements bold.
Choose the correct code for getting the desired output from the following options:
(a) span{text-size:bold}
(b) span {font-weight:bold}
(c) <span style="font-size:bold">
(d) <span style="text-size:bold">

Directions (Q. Nos. 11 and 12) *are Assertion and Reason types. Each question consists of two statements, namely. Assertion (A) and Reason (R). Select the most suitable option considering the Assertion & Reason.*
(a) Both Assertion (A) and Reason (R) are true and Reason (R) is a correct explanation of Assertion (A).
(b) Both Assertion (A) and Reason (R) are true but Reason (R) is not a correct explanation of Assertion (A).
(c) Assertion (A) is true and Reason (R) is false.
(d) Assertion (A) is false and Reason (R) is true.

11. **Assertion (A)** A set of rules, used over the networks, is called a Protocol.
Reason (R) HTML is an example of a Protocol.

12. **Assertion (A)** Chat and e-mail are live/real time conversation between people/machines.
Reason (R) We have to be online in both.

Section B

(7 × 2 = 14)

13. Mishika, a class X student, wants to use a software but does not want to pay for it.
Which type of software can she use? Write one example of this type of software.

14. (A) Write any two differences between e-Banking and e-Commerce.

Or

(B) What is e-learning? Name any one e-learning platform.

15. State whether the following statements are True or False:
I. HTML file extension is .tml.
II. Rowspan attribute is used to make a cell span multiple rows.
III. Unordered list type creates a bulleted list.
IV. HREF Stands for hyper reference.

16. (A) Your best friend emails you and tells you that he/she has created a webpage on an internet site having URL as: www.children.com/india/~abc. html
Now you want to create a link to this web page from your web page. Write the HTML code to do this.

Or

(B) I. Write HTML code to display Horizontal line of red colour.
II. Write HTML Code to create a paragraph whose text colour is blue.

17. What is the purpose of HTML forms? Write HTML Code to create a Textbox in an HTML form.

18. (A) An incomplete CSS code within <head> . . . </head> is given below. Complete this code by filling in the blanks as per the specifications that follow:

```
<head>
<style>
body {_______ : blue;  }      <!--line 1 -->
p {
 _______: green;              <!--line 2 -->
 _______: Dotum;              <!--line 3 -->
}
_____                         <!--line 4 -->
{
```

FULLY SOLVED

```
Color : black;
}
</style>
</head>
```

Line 1: Page background colour should be Blue.
Line 2: Colour of the Paragraph text should be green.
Line 3: Font family of the Paragraph text should be Dotum.
Line 4: The biggest heading should be black in colour.

Or

(B) Hemant, a class X Student, is writing HTML code to create ordered and unordered lists for a webpage as follows:

```
<html>
<body bgcolor="yellow">
<h1>My First Heading <_____>  <!-- line 1 -->
<p>
<font color="red" size="5"
      _____="Times New Roman">  <!-- line 2 -->
SOME STATES IN INDIA
</p>
<ul>
<li>DELHI: <_____>         <!-- line 3 -->
<li>MUMBAI    </li>
<_____>              <!-- line 4 -->
```

Based on the above code fill in the blanks given in line 1, line 2, line 3, and line 4 so that Hemant's webpage displays output correctly?

19. Write any two differences between SMS and MMS.

FULLY SOLVED

Section C

(4×3 = 12)

20. The following HTML statements are not written properly. Re-write the correct statements with underlined corrections. The desired purpose of each statement is mentioned under it.

I. <BODY color="red">
<!--Page background color should be red-->

II. <FONT type="arial">
<!--Type of Font should be Arial-->

III. <img source="img_girl.jpg" size="500" height="600">
<!--Image source should be img_girl.jpg, width and height both should be 500-->

21. Consider the URL: https://www.cbse.gov.in and answer the following questions:

I. Which component identifies the protocol?
II. What is the significance of "s" in https?
III. Expand the terms URL and WWW?

22. (A) Write any two ways to add an audio file in a web page using HTML? Explain with sample code.

Or (B) Write any two ways to add a video file in a web page using HTML? Explain with sample code.

23. Write suitable HTML statements to display the following text on a webpage:

(I) NH_3 (II) X^3 (III) $(A + B)^3$

Section D

(4)

24. (A) Write the HTML code to design the web page as shown below:

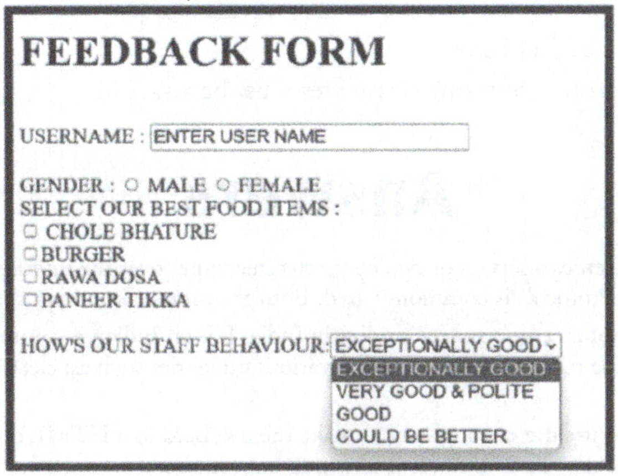

Or

(B) Write the HTML code to design the web page as shown below (Table border should be 2, height=100 and width=300 with cellpadding =20): -

EMPLOYEE TABLE		
EMPLOYEE ID	EMPLOYEE NAME	DEPARTMENT
1	ANKIT	SALES
2	HEMA	HR
3	MANISH	FINANCE

Section E

(2 × 4 = 8)

25. Mr. Anek comes from a village, which recently started seeing the digital revolution, and now the people of his village have access to the internet. They can shop online, make payments online, sell online and so on. Anek is also excited with these new changes. He ordered some items online and entered his bank card details on the webpage to make the payment.

But still after passing of the promised due date, he has not received his ordered items. There is no way to contact the company as phones are unreachable and emails are not being responded. He also noticed after some days that someone is sending emails on his behalf, using his personal data.

Based on the above information answer the following question: -

I. Mr. Anek is a victim of _____________.

II. Mr. Anek finds that his personal details are now leaked. This means his _______ is compromised.

III. While filling out details online, Mr. Anek should have checked _____ in the URL.

IV. This type of incident will be recognized as a case of _________ (Specify the type of crime)

26. Based on the following information, answer the questions which follows:

Shresth was a bright student who excelled in academics and extracurricular activities.

He intent to take some quotes and literature from internet to write an Article for Newspaper.

I. Identify the type of ethical issue he will face, in case he copies the work as discussed in the above case study.

II. Does the above incident described above can be considered as example of IPR (Intellectual Property Rights) Violation?

III. How can he avoid this ethical issue?

IV. Suggest two netiquettes that Shresth's classmates must be aware of.

Answers

1. (c) To securely copy files between two servers or two connected machines over the internet, the SCP (Secure Copy Protocol) or SFTP (Secure File Transfer Protocol) is commonly used. Both the protocols encrypt the file transfer to ensure security.

2. (d) The www.flipkart.com is not an e-governance project in India. It is an Indian e-commerce website which is used for online shopping. It offers a wide range of products across various categories such as: electronics, fashion, home and kitchen appliances, furniture etc.

3. (a) Besides <B> tag we can also use the <strong> tag to make the text bold in a HTML document. The <strong> tag in HTML is used to indicate that the text it encloses is of strong importance.

4. (c) SMTP stands for Simple Mail Transfer Protocol. It is a protocol used for sending email messages over the internet from one server to another. It is designed specifically for transmission of email messages.

5. (c) VoIP (Voice Over Internet Protocol) protocol is used for video conferencing among multiple participants. It play a crucial role in video conferencing among people by enabling the transmission of both voice and video data over IP networks, such as internet.

6. (c) A website may consist of both static and dynamic webpages. A static webpage is a type of web page that displays fixed content, while content of a dynamic webpage keeps changing, it displays different content based on user interactions.

7. (b) The HTML <OL> tag is used to create ordered or numbered list, where the list items are numbered or alphabetically ordered. Each item within the list tag is represented by the <li> (list item) tag.

8. (c) Making a copy of a webpage on your computer is known as downloading a webpage. Downloading refers to the process of transferring data from a remote server to a local computer. This process involves copying files or data from an online source to your device so that you can access or use them offline.

9. (d) The Telnet (Teletype Network) protocol allows users to connect to remote systems and execute commands as if they were sitting directly in front of the remote system's terminal.

10. (b) To make all <span> elements bold using CSS, we can use the code: span {font-weight:bold}.

11. (c) Assertion (A) is true and Reason (R) is false because HTML is not a protocol it is a hypertext markup language used to design webpages.

12. (d) Assertion is false because chat is a real-time conversation but e-mail is not a real-time conversation. While Reason is true because online is necessary for both.

13. Mishika can use the free and open source software if she doesn't want to pay. Open source software is freely available for public use. **Example** Open Office.

14. (A) Differences between e-Banking and e-Commerce

e-Banking	e-Commerce
E-banking focuses on providing financial services, such as checking balances, transferring funds or paying bills, through electronic platforms.	E-Commerce refers to the buying and selling of goods and services through the internet. It involves online shopping, digital marketing etc.
It is primarily used by banking customers to manage their financial activities online.	It involves buyers and sellers, including businesses and consumers.

Or (B) E-learning refers to the use of electronic technologies to deliver educational content, or learning experiences over the internet. It allows learners to access courses, tutorials, and resources anytime from anywhere.

Example Udemy

15. I. False II. True III. True IV. False

16. (A)
```
<!DOCTYPE html>
<html lang="en">
<head>
    <title>My Web Page</title>
</head>
<body>
    <h1>Welcome to My Web Page</h1>
    <p>Check out my friend's web page :</p>
    <a href="http://www.children.com/india/~abc.html" target="_blank">Visit my friend's page</a>
</body>
</html>
```

Or (B) I.
```
<!DOCTYPE html>
<html lang="en">
<head>
    <title>Horizontal Line Example</title>
</head>
<body>
    <h1>Example of a Horizontal Line</h1>
    <hr style="border: 2px solid red;">
</body>
</html>
```

II.
```
<!DOCTYPE html>
<html lang="en">
<head>
    <title>Blue Text Paragraph</title>
</head>
<body>
    <h1>Example of a Blue Text Paragraph</h1>
    <p style="color: blue;">This is a paragraph with blue text color.</p>
</body>
</html>
```

17. HTML forms are used to collect user input and send it to a server for processing.
```
<!DOCTYPE html>
<html lang="en">
<head>
    <title>Text Box Example</title>
</head>
<body>
    <h1>Text Box Example</h1>
    <form>
        <label for="textInput">Enter text:</label>
        <input type="text" id="textInput" name="textInput">
    </form>
</body>
</html>
```

18. (A)
```
<head>
<style>
body {background-color : blue;}
p {
        color : green;
```

```
            font-family : Dotum;
        }
        <h1>
        {
          Color: black;
        }
         </style>
        </head>
```

Or (B)
```
<html>
        <body bgcolor= "yellow">
        <h1> My First Heading </h1>
      <p>
<font color= "red" size= "5" face= "Times New Roman">
SOME STATES IN INDIA
</p>
<ul>
<li> DELHI: </li>
<li> MUMBAI </li>
</ul>
```

19. (i) SMS (Short Message Service) is used for sending plain text messages while MMS (Multimedia Messaging Service) is used for sending multimedia messages such as audio, video, images etc.

(ii) SMS does not require an internet connection to send messages while MMS requires data or an internet connection to send multimedia files.

20. I. <BODY <u>bgcolor</u>= "red">

II. <FONT <u>face</u>= "arial">

III. <img <u>src</u>= "img_girl.jpg" <u>width</u>= "500" height= "<u>500</u>">

21. I. https

II. In https the "s" stands for Secure, it signifies that the connection between the user's browser and the website is secure or encrypted.

III. URL- Uniform Resource Locater

WWW- World Wide Web

22. (A) There are two common ways to add an audio file to a webpage using HTML:

1. Using the <audio> element:

```
<!DOCTYPE html>
<html lang="en">
<head>
    <title>Audio Example</title>
</head>
<body>
    <h1>Embed Audio using the audio element</h1>
        <audio controls>
        <source src="audio-file.mp3" type="audio/mpeg">
Your browser does not support the audio element.
    </audio>
</body>
</html>
```

2. Using the <embed> element:

```
<!DOCTYPE html>
<html lang="en">
<head>
    <title>Embed Audio using embed element</title>
</head>
```

FULLY SOLVED

```
<body>
    <h1>Embed Audio using the embed element</h1>
    <embed src="audio-file.mp3" type="audio/mpeg" width="300" height="50">
</body>
</html>
```

Or (B) Similar to audio file we can also add video file in a webpage in two common ways:

1. Using <video element>

```
<!DOCTYPE html>
<html lang="en">
<head>
    <title>Video Example</title>
</head>
<body>
    <h1>Video Example using video element</h1>
    <video width="640" height="360" controls>
        <source src="video-file.mp4" type="video/mp4">
        Your browser does not support the video file.
    </video>
</body>
</html>
```

2. Using <embed> element

```
<!DOCTYPE html>
<html lang="en">
<head>
    <title>Video Example</title>
</head>
<body>
    <h1>Video Example using embed</h1>
    <embed src="video-file.mp4" type="video/mp4" width="640" height="360">
</body>
</html>
```

23. (I)

```
<!DOCTYPE html>
<html lang="en">
<head>
    <title>Subscript Example</title>
</head>
<body>
        <p>This is the example of subscript:  NH<sub>3</sub></p>
</body>
</html>
```

(II)

```
<!DOCTYPE html>
<html lang="en">
<head>
    <title>Superscript Example</title>
</head>
<body>
    <p> This is the example of superscript: X<sup>3</sup></p>
</body>
</html>
```

(III)

```
<!DOCTYPE html>
<html lang="en">
<head>
```

FULLY SOLVED

```
    <title>Superscripted text</title>
</head>
<body>
    <p> (A+B)<sup>3</sup></p>
</body>
</html>
```

24. (A) HTML code to design form:

```
<html>
<head>
<title> FEEDBACK FORM </title>
</head>
<body>
<form>
<H1 >FEEDBACK FORM</H1> <BR>
USERNAME: <input type="TEXT" NAME="ENAME1"
SIZE="30" VALUE="ENTER USER NAME "> <BR>
<BR>
GENDER: <input type="Radio" NAME="GENDER">
MALE
<input type="Radio" NAME="GENDER"
VALUE="FEMALE"> FEMALE
<BR>
SELECT OUR BEST FOOD ITEMS :<BR>
<INPUT TYPE="CHECKBOX" NAME="FOOD"
VALUE="CHOLE BHATURE" > CHOLE BHATURE<BR>
<INPUT TYPE="CHECKBOX" NAME="FOOD"
VALUE="BURGER" >BURGER <BR>
<INPUT TYPE="CHECKBOX" NAME="FOOD"
VALUE="RAWA DOSA">RAWA DOSA <BR>
<INPUT TYPE="CHECKBOX" NAME="FOOD"
VALUE="PANEER TIKKA">PANEER TIKKA<BR>
<BR>
HOW'S OUR STAFF BEHAVIOUR :<SELECT NAME="LIST NAME">
<OPTION>EXCEPTIONALLY GOOD
<OPTION>VERY GOOD & POLITE
<OPTION>GOOD
<OPTION>COULD BE BETTER
</SELECT>
<BR>
<BR>
</form>
</body>
</html>
```

Or (B)

```
<HTML >
    <BODY> <BASEFONT face= "cambria">
<TABLE border = "2" bordercolor= "black" cellspacing = "0" height = "100" width= "300">
<TR>
<TD rowspan= "3"> EMPLOYEE TABLE</TD>
<TR>
<TD> EMPLOYEE ID </TD>
<TD> EMPLOYEE NAME</TD>
<TD> DEPARTMENT</TD>
```

FULLY SOLVED

```
</TR>
<TR>
<TD> 1</TD>
<TD> ANKIT</TD>
<TD> SALES</TD>
</TR>
<TR>
<TD> 2 </TD>
<TD> HEMA</TD>
<TD> HR</TD>
</TR>
<TR>
<TD>3 </TD>
<TD> MANISH </TD>
<TD> FINANCE</TD>
</TR>
</TABLE>
</BODY>
</HTML>
```

25. I. Mr. Anek is a victim of online fraud or scamming.

II. Mr. Anek finds that his present details are now leaked. This means his data privacy is compromised.

III. While filling out details online, Mr. Anek should have checked https in the URL.

IV. This type of incident will be recognized as a case of identity theft (specify the type of crime)

26. I. If Shresth copies someone else's work from the internet without proper attribution, he will face the ethical issue of plagiarism.

II. Yes, the incident described above can indeed be considered an Intellectual Property Rights (IPR) violation.

III. Shresth can avoid the ethical issue by providing proper citation and attribution and by using plagiarism detection tools.

IV. Two essential netiquettes (internet etiquette) that Shresth's classmates should be aware of when interacting online are:

1. Proper Use of Digital Resources
2. Respectful Communication